THE IRISH TIMES

BOOK

of the

YEAR

2008

EDITED BY
PETER MURTAGH

Gill & Macmillan

Gill & Macmillan Ltd
Hume Avenue
Park West
Dublin 12
with associated companies throughout the world
www.gillmacmillan.ie

© 2008 *The Irish Times*
978 0 7171 4286 6
Design by Identikit Design Consultants, Dublin
Print origination by Carole Lynch
Index compiled by Helen Litton
Printed by Butler Tanner & Dennis, Somerset

*The paper used in this book is made from the wood pulp
of managed forests. For every tree felled, at least one tree
is planted, thereby renewing natural resources.*

A catalogue record is available for this book
from the British Library.

1 3 5 4 2

Contents

Introduction

The past year has been one of unprecedented editorial development at *The Irish Times* – unprecedented in my memory, at any rate. In one fell swoop, two new supplements – *Go*, a travel section with Saturday's newspaper, and *Gallery*, an image supplement with Monday's paper – were launched. Two other supplements – *HEALTHplus* and *Motors* – were reformatted, with the former broadening its content beyond pure medical and personal health matters to include material on parenting. A new sports section was added on Wednesdays. The Opinion and Analysis daily offering was doubled from one to two pages, allowing us to introduce to readers a more diverse range of writers and analysts.

On top of that, the entire newspaper was redesigned.

All of this happened in the last week in February 2008, with *Go* launched on Saturday, 1 March. In July, the newspaper's subscription-based website, formerly ireland.com, was transformed into irishtimes.com, with the content made available free online. *Irish Times* journalists now routinely write reports, as events unfold, for the website's breaking news service, which is updated throughout the day, and also compile audio reports of background information, which are also broadcast on the website. The newspaper continues to be the main focus of attention, however, but both it and the website will develop further as we seek to provide our readers with all the material they require to inform themselves about national and international affairs, accessed by a means of their choosing.

The past 12 months have thrown up the usual motley collection of events at home and abroad which *Irish Times* journalists have reported for our readers, while attempting also to analyse them and set them in context. But three events dominate: the electorate's rejection of the Lisbon Treaty and the consequences of that decision for the country as a whole; the changing of the guard at the White House (and by the time this volume is on the shelves, we will know whether January 2009 will see the inauguration as president of Barack Obama or John McCain); and finally, and perhaps most importantly for most people, the economic downturn at home, perhaps gradually turning to recession, and the related global financial crisis.

The three have one thing in common – they all relate to Ireland's engagement with the wider world (and it with us).

Navigating a way through the consequences of the Lisbon Treaty rejection will consume many column inches in the newspaper, and many web pages, before we will know what is to be the relationship between Ireland and the rest of the European Union. How the financial crisis plays out (in Ireland and the world), and how the new US president performs in his first year in office will take up many pages in next year's *Book of the Year*.

During 2009, the Irish Times will also mark its founding, 150 years ago, by the 23-year-old Lawrence Knox.

For now, however, my thanks are due again this year to those who have helped in the compilation of this, the ninth consecutive *Irish Times Book of the Year*. Those to thank include Michael Ruane and his colleagues Mark McGrath, Paul Hayden, Angelo McGrath, Paul Scott and Denis Crawley in the Imaging Department for gathering together all the photographs I requested; Peter Thursfield and Shay Kenny on the Picture Desk; Lynda O'Keeffe and Emma Allen in the Editor's Office; and my *Irish Times* colleagues for their memorable writing and wonderful photographs and illustrations without which there would be no book and an infinitely less satisfying newspaper. And finally thanks also to Sarah Liddy and Aoife O'Kelly at Gill & Macmillan who put up with me.

Peter Murtagh
Managing Editor
25 September 2008

Journalists and Photographers

David Adams is based in Northern Ireland and writes a bi-weekly column for the Opinion and Analysis pages.

Paddy Agnew is Rome Correspondent.

Eileen Battersby is Literary Correspondent.

Arthur Beesley is Senior Business Correspondent.

Brian Boyd is an *Irish Times* journalist writing mainly about music and comedy.

Adam Brophy is a stay-at-home father who writes a weekly column, A Dad's Life, in the HEALTHplus supplement.

Lt Paddy Bury, from Co. Wicklow, is a soldier in the British Army Royal Irish Regiment. He wrote A Soldier's Diary while on duty in Afghanistan.

Elaine Byrne writes a weekly column for the Opinion and Analysis pages.

Simon Carswell is a business journalist with *The Irish Times*.

John Cassidy works in the *Irish Times* studio.

Donald Clarke is a freelance film critic and a feature writer.

Stephen Collins is Political Editor.

Clifford Coonan is Beijing Correspondent.

Peter Crawley is Theatre Critic.

Rob Crilly is based in Nairobi, Kenya, and reports on east African affairs.

Kevin Cullen is a journalist with *The Boston Globe* newspaper. He writes occasionally for *The Irish Times* on Irish-American matters.

Paul Cullen is Consumer Affairs Correspondent and has reported in detail on the planning tribunal.

Deaglán de Bréadún is a political correspondent and colour writer.

Eithne Donnellan is Health Correspondent.

Kilian Doyle writes Emissions, a column loosely pegged to cars and driving, which appears in the Motors supplement on Wednesdays.

Keith Duggan is a sports writer.

Michael Dwyer is *Irish Times* Film Critic.

Newton Emerson is a political satirist from Northern Ireland. He writes a weekly column on the Opinion and Analysis pages.

Hilary Fannin is *Irish Times* TV Critic.

Mary Fitzgerald is Foreign Affairs Correspondent.

Quentin Fottrell is *Irish Times* Radio Critic and a contributor to the Opinion and Analysis pages.

Paul Gillespie is Foreign Affairs Editor and writes World View, a column on the Opinion and Analysis pages each Saturday.

Richard Gillis is an *Irish Times* sports journalist.

Ciarán Hancock is a business journalist.

Michael Harding is a writer who lives in Mullingar from where he describes his life's ups and downs.

Kate Holmquist is a feature writer and editor of Go, the travel supplement published with Saturday's newspaper.

Ann Marie Hourihane is an *Irish Times* columnist.

Tom Humphries is chief sports feature writer and writes a weekly column, LockerRoom, for Monday's sports supplement.

Róisín Ingle is a columnist and feature writer. Her column appears weekly in the *Irish Times* Magazine.

Sara Keating is a freelance writer and theatre critic.

Lorna Kernan is TV Editor.

Miriam Lord is an *Irish Times* journalist specialising in political colour writing.

Ferdia Mac Anna is a writer and broadcast producer.

Ruadhán Mac Cormaic is Migration Correspondent.

Fiona McCann is an *Irish Times* features writer.

Ronan McGreevy is an *Irish Times* reporter.

Susan McKay is a freelance author and journalist specialising in Northern Ireland affairs.

John McManus is Business Editor. He writes a Business Opinion column each Monday.

Frank McNally writes An Irishman's Diary.

Brendan McWilliams wrote the daily column Weather Eye, until his death in October 2007. A collection of his columns has been published by Gill & Macmillan.

Lara Marlowe is Paris Correspondent and specialises also in Middle Eastern and Turkish affairs.

Seán Moran is GAA correspondent.

Bryan Mukandi was born in Zimbabwe and now lives in Galway. He writes an occasional column for the Opinion and Analysis pages and a blog for the *Irish Times* website, irishtimes.com, called Outside in.

Breda O'Brien is an *Irish Times* columnist.

Carl O'Brien is Social Affairs Correspondent.

Danny O'Brien is a technology journalist and writes Wired, a column in Friday's Business This Week supplement.

Robert O'Byrne is a freelance journalist.

Ross O'Carroll-Kelly is the alter ego of writer and satirist Paul Howard.

Claire O'Connell is a freelance journalist.

Olivia O'Leary is a broadcaster and writer.

Fintan O'Toole is an *Irish Times* columnist and commentator. He contributes to the Opinion and Analysis pages and also writes Culture Shock in the Weekend Review supplement.

Peter Preston was Editor of The Guardian newspaper from 1975 to 1995. He continues to write for the newspaper.

Philip Reid is Golf Correspondent.

William Reville is professor of biochemistry at University College, Cork, and writes a weekly column on the Science Today page of *The Irish Times*.

Derek Scally is Berlin Correspondent.

Kathy Sheridan is a feature writer.

Lorna Siggins is Marine Correspondent and Western Correspondent.

Jamie Smyth is Europe Correspondent.

Denis Staunton is Washington Correspondent.

Gerry Thornley is Rugby Correspondent.

Orla Tinsley is a student. Her campaigning and writing in *The Irish Times* about cystic fibrosis saw her given a People of the Year award in 2008.

Michael Viney is a naturalist and artist. He writes a weekly column, Another Life, from his home in west Mayo, which he also illustrates.

Michael Walker is a freelance journalist who specialises in soccer, writing mainly about the English Premier League.

John Waters is an *Irish Times* columnist.

Noel Whelan is a barrister, political analyst and columnist in Saturday's *Irish Times*.

Photographers and illustrators whose work features in this year's edition include *Irish*

Times photographers Cyril Byrne, Alan Betson, Dara Mac Dónaill, Brenda Fitzsimons, Eric Luke, Frank Miller, Matt Kavanagh, Bryan O'Brien, David Sleator, Martyn Turner, Peter Hanan and Michael Viney. Kate Geraghty was on secondment to *The Irish Times* from the *Sydney Morning Herald*, where her place was taken by Bryan O'Brien.

The Irish Times Book of the Year 2008 also features the work of freelance photographers, illustrators or photographers attached to Irish and international photo agencies, including: Carlos Barrira/Reuters, Julien Behal/PA Wire, Patrick Browne jnr, Liam Burke/Press 22, Alan Clarke, Niall Carson/Press Association, China Photos/Getty Images, Collins Photos, James Connolly/PicSell8, Courtpix, Aidan Crawley, James Crombie/Inpho, Whitney Curtis/Getty Images, Matt Dunham/AP Photo, Paul Faith/Press Association, Eamonn Farrell/Photocall Ireland, Simon Fergusson/Getty Images, Brian Gavin/ Press 22, Michael Kelly, Eamonn Keogh/

MacMonagle, Ross Kinnaird/Getty Images, Mac Innes Photography, Michael Mac Sweeney/Provision, David Moir/Reuters, Brendan Moran/Sportsfile, Kenneth O'Halloran, Joe O'Shaughnessy, Lorraine O'Sullivan/Inpho, Valerie O'Sullivan, John Power, Crispin Rodwell/Bloomberg News, Jewel Samad/AFP, Mickey Smith, Mario Tama/ Getty Images, Gilles Toucas, Morgan Treacy/Inpho, Dylan Vaughan, Domnick Walsh/Eye Focus, Haydn West, John Moore/Getty Images, David Cannon/Getty Images, Garry O'Neill, Melinda Sue Gordon, NUTAN, Michael Brophy, Alex Wong/Getty Images, Ronald Zak/AP, Qilai Shen Photographs, Kyran O'Brien, Garrett White/Collins, Mark H. Milstein/Northfoto, Sergei Grits/AP, David Cheskinpa, Matthew Staver/Bloomberg, Charles Dharapak/AP, Win McNamee/Getty Images, Karl Gehring/The Denver Post, Ryan Anson/Bloomberg News, Robyn Beck/AFP/Getty Images, Seth Wenig/AP Photo.

MONDAY, I OCTOBER 2007

'I Ask Myself if Europeans Really Know Us'

Lara Marlowe, in Istanbul

Fermude Tuarhan sits on a cushion on the pavement outside her home in the poor suburb of Bagcilar, a few hundred metres from the motorway to Istanbul airport. It's a hot day, but the 63-year-old woman wears heavy wool socks and black plastic sandals, a long skirt, jumper and flowered headscarf.

When I ask if I can talk to her, she squints at the sun: 'But I have no education.' The widow Tuarhan's grandsons look smart as they set off in their school uniforms. 'It's a 40-minute walk,' she explains. 'There's a bus, but it costs 80 lire (€47) a month. I don't have enough to pay. I have heart problems and I live with my son Ersin, who works in a plastics factory. He has respiratory problems. The doctor gave him an inhaler. I wish he could find another job.'

Mrs Tuarhan's son earns 500 Turkish lire (€294) per month. Her daughter-in-law Asiye is a seamstress in one of Bagcilar's sweatshops, for 640 lire (€376) per month. Asiye worked from 9 a.m. until 11 p.m. the previous day to fill a big foreign order. At least her present boss pays overtime, Mrs Tuarhan sighs. The previous one went bankrupt, and didn't pay his employees.

The Tuarhan family are typical of the Anatolian peasants who have tripled the size of this city in recent decades to 12 million. Officially, unemployment runs close to 10 per cent, though experts suggest the real rate is much higher.

Mrs Tuarhan was in her early 20s when she moved here from the Black Sea town of Samsun, with Hamit. 'It was his blue eyes I fell for,' she recalls, smiling, but with tears in her eyes. 'My parents were against it; so was his stepmother. So we ran away and came here. That was my happiest time, when I was a young bride.'

Hamit worked in a factory, and died seven months ago. 'He had diabetes,' Mrs Tuarhan explains. 'I asked the municipality to help us take his body to Samsun for burial, but they said no. We barely have enough to eat, let alone buy a car. We had to take him in a goods lorry. His brothers paid for the funeral.'

Mrs Tuarhan's sister Fatima has retired in Munich. 'Her husband worked in an eyeglass factory, and Fatima was a cleaning lady. It would have been better for us in Germany, but my sister knows how to read and write; I don't.

'On television, they say Turkey is going to enter the European Union, or it's not; I'm not sure which,' Mrs Tuarhan continues, summing up uncertainty about the long accession negotiations. 'If Turkey joins Europe, it could be good for us. When Europeans go to the market, they buy what they want to. They live better than us. The only time I eat meat is during the Eid. It's been years since I could buy a sheep to share with the neighbours for [the upcoming Muslim feast of] Bayram.'

A half-hour taxi ride and a world away, Istiklal Caddesi is Istanbul's Grafton Street, always packed with shoppers. A balcony festooned with European and Turkish flags and a banner saying 'Istanbul 2010' catches my eye. (In 2000, the EU decided to include cities outside the Union in its European Capital of Culture programme.) On the second floor of the magnificent 19th-century building, I find Ahmet Cakaloz, a banker with an American accent and the project manager for Istanbul 2010. 'This palace was built in the mid-19th century by a banker,' he tells me. 'Imagine! The Sultan Abdul Mecit had 40 wives in his harem, but he still came here to meet his mistress. Look at the French and Italian frescoes.'

Like many educated Istanbulites, Mr Cakaloz believes the process of Turkey's EU application may have become more important than the end result. 'It's a matter of democratisation, of more rights for women and children, of fairer distribution of income. Things like that bring you closer to the EU. Personally, I don't think Turkey will become a member. It's too big a country; I don't think it will be acceptable for the EU in the foreseeable future. They can always find more excuses. Becoming more European is something we have to do for ourselves.'

Every day, thousands of Istanbulites cross the narrow body of water that divides the European, Thracian part of their country from infinitely vaster Anatolia, in Asia. Although the geographic symbolism of the journey rarely occurs to passengers on the ferry across the Bosphorus, most have clear ideas about Europe. Turkey can live without Europe, Hasan Iscan, a retired security guard, boasts proudly. 'But they can't live without us. My mother was veiled, but my daughter dresses like you.'

Arif Iseri, a building foreman sitting near Mr Iscan, begins to argue. 'You have to admit that human rights and freedoms are better in Europe!' he tells the retired security guard. Another man, a Bosnian Muslim and naturalised Turk, rises from the seats behind us to interrupt angrily, because he mistakes me and my French-speaking interpreter for French journalists. 'How dare you come here and ask us questions, after what Nicolas Sarkozy has said!' The French president opposes Turkish membership of the EU.

On the return journey, from Asia back to Europe, Sevtap Atasever, a middle-aged advertising production assistant, tells me she feels 'very, very' European. 'I feel modern, attentive, sensitive, and I am filled with good will,' she adds. 'These are European values. For example, I never throw rubbish in the street. Turkey may not join Europe in my lifetime, but it's important to be on that path, for our country to change, for better building standards, the treatment of animals, the environment.'

Ms Atasever says her country can offer Europe 'spectacular countryside, a huge labour pool, a strategic location, and intelligent, flexible people.' She feels hurt that many Europeans are reluctant to accept Turkey. 'I ask myself whether they really know us.'

WEDNESDAY, 3 OCTOBER 2007

October Marks a Turning of the Year

WeatherEye, by Brendan McWilliams

With the arrival of October, the year has entered the youth of its old age. It marks a turning of the year, being colder, wetter, darker and windier than its predecessors, and there is less sun than in September if for no other reason than that the days are significantly shorter; the average September day has some four or five hours of sunshine, while the October average is only three.

The temperature on an average October day rises to a mere 13°C or 14°C, three or four degrees less than the September norm. Only very rarely does the temperature exceed 20°C, while at the other end of the scale ground frost occurs on five or six of October's 31 days. Very occasionally the air temperature even falls below zero – an occurrence almost unheard of in September.

The waters around our coasts are also becoming colder; the usual sea temperature is about 12°C or 13°C, compared with the August peak of 15°C or 16°C. And about every 10 years or so, a little snow may fall in October, but it tends to melt as soon as it touches ground and rarely causes trouble. But if October is a reminder to us of the rigours of returning winter, the month sometimes has a gentler side: Jack Frost has begun dabbing with his paint brush.

Here and there, against the background of the surviving summer foliage, the first of the autumn leaves are hanging, as the poet Andrew Marvell put it, 'like golden lamps in a green night'.

It must be said, however, that Ireland's autumnal splurge, even in areas blessed with an abundance of deciduous trees, can never quite match the razzle-dazzle of Vermont, or of the Black Forest or the Odenwald in Germany. The colours displayed by the individual trees in autumn are not, *per se*, more splendid or intense in New England or continental Europe than they are in Co. Wicklow. But the precise trigger for the yearly colour change varies with the different species, being a combination of declining day-length and the falling temperature.

Here in Ireland the autumnal cooling process is gradual and sporadic; some trees that of their nature react early to the falling temperatures will have shed their leaves entirely before other slow-starting species have begun to even think of changing colour.

In places like New England, however, the transition from one season to another is more sudden. The sharp autumnal fall in temperature takes place quickly over a short interval, and catches not just a few trees at a time, but all the trees planning to change their colour. All the leaves are simultaneously transformed, and the whole process from green foliage to bare trees may take little more than two weeks. In between is a short, shrill, spectacular extravaganza of very brilliant colour.

Brendan McWilliams died on 22 October 2007. This WeatherEye column was his final one for the newspaper. His death prompted many expressions of sadness and appreciation from readers who held him in high esteem.

SATURDAY, 6 OCTOBER 2007

Busby, Backhanders, Brio and Barbs

Michael Walker

There were reasons to think otherwise – around the corner Bertie Ahern was squeaking his way through the Mahon mangle, while the Garda shot on North Strand was said to be stable. But up on St Stephen's Green, where the sun-dappled tranquillity was

Brendan McWilliams.

beguiling, it was possible to see why Dublin charms still. Even the resident dissident said so.

'I still love living here,' said Eamon Dunphy. 'I love the temper of the people, the calmness of an average day like this.'

Taking a different stance is nothing new to Dunphy. Some would argue, even himself sometimes, that it could be his job description. But it's not often that Dunphy would plump for the cosier aspect. Maybe sitting in a corner of the Shelbourne hotel contributed, Magda pouring tea for two, but Dunphy sounded sincere.

'I still love the people, the atmosphere, the ambience of Ireland. On the whole, the people are very nice, gentle; there is decency here that endures. There is some of the vulgarity, brashness and coarseness that the new wealth has inspired, that's there if you go to certain places, and certainly people are consumed by materialism in a way that they weren't.

'Irish values have been infected by materialism, but that has to be put in some perspective – we had nothing for so long, now we're diving on it. But the vast majority of Irish people have a soul. The country has its own culture.'

Measured and warm, this is a Dunphy many will not recognise. To a chunk of Ireland he is loud and bitter, a man revelling in controversy. This is Dunphy the soccer pundit, sitting in judgment alongside John Giles and Liam Brady and telling it like it is, or isn't – depending on your perspective.

But you do not require the insight of the Buddha to see a man can have more than one dimension, and Dunphy does. The reason for drinking tea together is to discuss *A Strange Kind of Glory*, the story of Matt Busby and Manchester United, a book Dunphy wrote 16 years ago, which has been reissued as the 50th anniversary of the Munich air crash approaches.

It is a fantastic piece of work, seminal, as they say; 'the one thing I'm really proud of,' according to the author. You can understand why. This is some read as we are taken inside Old Trafford by someone who was there for five years from 1960. We are given the guts as well as glory.

In language Dunphy described as 'deliberately understated', Busby is shown to be romantic, cruel,

Eamon Dunphy. Photograph: Brenda Fitzsimons.

pure, corrupt, loyal, devious, a creator. The detail is striking, though Dunphy said: 'I didn't want the book to end up being serialised in the *News of the World*. I didn't want the story to be obscured by anecdotes that were sensational.

'Busby was an awesome man. He was huge, very graceful, almost feline for a big man. Very clever. You'd never see him lose the head. He had a vision of what a football club should be, what values it should have, how the game should be played. It was uncompromising – you should attack; skill was everything.'

Busby came from the mines of west Scotland to Manchester City as a player, then to Liverpool, and, as a manager, to United in 1945. He never did leave Old Trafford and, crucially, Busby allowed Dunphy back in. Dunphy's contention is that Busby is 20th-century English football's true visionary, and in a week of Champions League football you can hear the argument.

'The other thing was Busby's vision of the English game and its place in the world. In the 1950s there was always this mystique about the Hungarians who came to Wembley and hammered England, and about Real Madrid.

'England didn't enter the World Cup for ages. The English game was insular. They felt there was nothing to prove to these continentals. Busby realised this would enrich English football and he was prepared to defy the Football League. Chelsea, who had won the league the previous year, had not been prepared to defy them and had given in. Busby did defy them – he was a serious rebel – and ultimately this, of course, leads to the Munich air crash.

'He was into floodlights and creating these great European nights. He was the visionary who saw this. No one else in England saw it. He opened up vistas. He put Duncan Edwards in the team when he was 16.

'The closest to him now is Wenger, as a purist. To be fair to Alex Ferguson, him as well. He has been faithful to the values of Manchester United when others might have been tempted otherwise,

because this is the high-risk way to go. But there isn't anybody like Busby. He loved the game as a spectacle. He would not be interested in the functionality of a Mourinho.'

A gentle Dunphy barb. The book has a few. There is a line about Maurice Setters 'lacking the coherence of real conviction'. It's quite a put-down, but then the professional dressing-room does not breed compassion. That is a theme.

'It's a bloody tough game,' Dunphy said. 'You couldn't survive without being tough. Busby was a miner during the General Strike, 1926. It was hell on earth to be a miner. In the General Strike they were starved. They were out for six months. It was a formative experience in the lives of everyone there. The ruling class, led by Winston Churchill, were brutal.

'But Busby was a statesman. He was the first football man to be knighted. He should have had a knighthood the day he was born because he was a natural aristocrat. He had a bearing that made him extraordinary.

'He played on that and yet his story is rendered tragic by the Munich air crash. He was never the same man after that, but he went on to build another great team that won the European Cup. But a bit of the life went out of him.'

Munich, Manchester and the early days of professional football are portrayed with care. Two years after Munich, on his 15th birthday, on an aeroplane for the first time, Dunphy went to Manchester on trial. 'It was 35 minutes and Busby watched. That was it, in Chorlton, a cricket facility. Just amazing.'

Dunphy had done enough. He was to be part of a new United. 'Munich was one of those JFK moments. I was 13 and in a barber's shop in Drumcondra when I heard. The pall of despair in this city is unforgettable because Billy Whelan was in the team and United had played here six months earlier. They beat Shamrock Rovers 6-0 at Dalymount Park and I was there. It was in the early rounds of the European Cup, September '57. The whole city was "Wow". It was like Elvis or the

Beatles coming. Magical. When they died it was "Oh". They were loved in this city.

'I remember that evening going out, just to find somebody. Because you didn't have television, you were going to find out what's the story. Busby's life was in danger for 48 hours before we knew he'd be okay. It was terrible.'

Soon, Dunphy would be in his company, and that of Charlton, Law and Best. He was able to return to them for the book. It was not straightforward. Busby was secretive and, from 1945, had generally got things his way. But Dunphy was a United old boy. His foot was in the door. In return, he showed respect.

'The book's understated. There was stuff I could have put in about Busby. It's there, but you have to look closely. He took backhanders – and I know because he took one for me. There was a match-fixing thing. Well, they were betting on games and they did throw a game. God love him, Shay Brennan, a friend of mind, was in the middle of that. Busby used to come here, to Dublin. He was a gambler, big gambler. He had gambling problems. There's a reference to that, but no more than that.

'There's a methodology now to biography where the publisher would almost demand that you blow that stuff up and they can serialise it, be sensational. So you could have written the book another way, especially as most of the protagonists were dead and you can write what you want. But I wasn't into that. The Manchester United story, the Busby story, is the great football tale. I thought it spoke for itself.'

Some would say this is a strange kind of Dunphy. From his columnist days on the *Sunday Independent* to RTÉ punditry, he has been outspoken, sensational. From John Hume to Cristiano Ronaldo, Dunphy has had his say, sometimes revising, occasionally reversing, along the way.

'I was going to write a memoir, which I will, and I was thinking of calling it Wrong About Everything. But the thing about journalism is that you have to write what you think on the day; you can't be second-guessing history.'

It was Mary Holland who helped him break into journalism. Having left for United in 1960, Dunphy did not return to Dublin until 1977. He was with Giles at Shamrock Rovers, 'on this grand project to make Shamrock Rovers the Celtic of Ireland. John had this vision. I shared it. Ray Treacy, Paddy Mulligan, we all came home. I was coach as well as playing. We won the cup, but after one year I realised it was a non-runner and I left. Financially, and because the other clubs pulled you down to their level, you couldn't do it. There wasn't the base.

'So I quit and went on the dole for one year while I tried to get a union card to be a journalist. That was tough in those days. You couldn't get a freelance card unless you had a portfolio and you couldn't get a portfolio unless you had a freelance card. Mary Holland was wonderful. She became chair of the freelance branch and she reformed that and allowed a lot of us to get in. That was a big break in my life.'

Dunphy is 62, seemingly simultaneously mocked and cherished. He is conscious of what he does for RTÉ and how he does it, but said that does not make it false.

'I suppose the question is: "Why engage in hyperbole?" The answer is no. What I try to do on television, what we all try to do on RTÉ, is forget the cameras are there and talk about the game as if you were with a group of friends. The only governing principle is that you cannot break the laws of libel, but just go for it.

'By saying what I think I can at least encourage a viewer to have another look. So you're challenging the prevailing orthodoxy. I don't think there's anything wrong with that. You don't even have to be right all the time, though you have to be right often enough to be credible. But it's genuine. It's only 9.30 a.m. and I'm wound up. I know they say it's manufactured and I understand why people say that, but it happens not to be true. So therefore, what's the problem with me?

'What I do on TV has to be seen against this backdrop – soccer people of my generation, Giles, we've lived with the FAI's ineptitude all our lives. As players, as fans, as journalists, mistake after mistake after mistake. Therefore you are forced into a position where you appear to be cynical, appear to be just controversial, saying the unsayable.

'I mean, John Giles said to me the other day that Jack was the worst of Staunton, Kerr, McCarthy because he had the greatest squad of players. Now that's a "controversial" thing to say, but it's actually a point of view. You could argue that Jack took us to places we'd never been before – and he did – and he did give the country a great time, and he wasn't a bad man.

'But how far could that team have gone? Lawrenson, Brady, Moran, Packie Bonner, Frank Stapleton, Aldridge, Houghton . . . Ronnie Whelan! Paul McGrath! All these great players, he either threw them out of the squad or played them in the wrong position.

'I just feel the basic position should be that if you have these deep convictions and you want to express them then don't expect to be loved. And I don't think I'm the story. John Delaney is a good pal of mine, but the FAI's ineptitude is the story. Those of us on the soccer beat have had the misfortune to cover what I call yellow-pack managers. Now that's tough language, but I think managing the Irish soccer team is a privilege.

'I've had plenty of stick too, but I don't want to be loved. It doesn't bother me. I know that the soccer-going public here are fine with me. On the Staunton question, for example, I think the public's opinion is accurate, that he is not up to the job and he doesn't have the qualifications to do it.'

The Staunton question. A week today and Germany are the visitors to Dublin. Dunphy does not expect to be won over. He said he named three alternatives at the time of Staunton's appointment – Paul Jewell, Iain Dowie and Leo Beenhakker, who has taken Poland to the top of their group. 'This', he added, 'is not rocket science. As Staunton himself said in Prague, he's been on an 18-month learning curve. I just don't think when managing a national team that you should be on a learning curve.

'Now, of course, when you're saying he should be sacked, you are asking for a man to lose his job. He's on €400,000 or €500,000 a year. I had a television show here on TV3 to take on *The Late, Late Show*. After 15 weeks it was pulled. I was sacked. The press were saying, "Sack him, Pat Kenny's the man." Now I didn't take it personally or start whinging. I thought, "You're getting paid a fortune to do this and you're not doing it very well." It wasn't the press's fault.'

'Part of the thing on television is that you can crystallise the doubts of others. "Am I seeing?" Like, with Irish rugby I haven't a clue what's happened, but I want one of the pundits to tell me. I see it as, "Look, this is how I see it," and it's an informed view of someone who has been in the game all their life.

'The same with John and Liam and they're not headbangers. You can say I'm a headbanger. I don't think I am, but you could argue it.'

SATURDAY, 6 OCTOBER 2007

An Irishman with Global Vision

Ciarán Hancock

Irish aviation owes a large debt to Dr Tony Ryan, who passed away earlier this week, but it could all have been so, so different, according to Ryanair chief executive Michael O'Leary. In 1954 Ryan took a job with Aer Lingus in Shannon, having previously worked with the local sugar factory in Thurles on leaving school.

'In the space of a month or two, he went to the personnel department and said that he'd had an offer of a job as a teacher in London. Because he was a traffic officer [with Aer Lingus], he had skills that they couldn't replace easily and he eventually negotiated a full-time contract there.'

Ryan had no university education and no offer of a job as a teacher. It was the first of many gambles he would take as he made his way through life. 'He was just bluffing,' says O'Leary. 'If that personnel manager in Aer Lingus in Shannon had said: "Well, bugger off to London," the history of Irish and European aviation would have been entirely different.'

O'Leary first met Ryan in the mid-1980s as a young accountant working with Stokes Kennedy Crowley (now KPMG). At the time, he would attend meetings with Ryan in his then home at Killboy in Co. Tipperary. 'I was brought along as the gofer. I was very impressed by him because he was rich, successful and was running a company that had terrific mystique. Nobody knew what the hell aircraft leasing was.'

He was particularly taken by Ryan's global vision. 'He was the first businessman I'd met who had this global ambition. Everybody else was worried about the cost of women's knickers and the cost of this, that and the other.

'He had maps of the world looking at where he could lease aircraft. It was revolutionary in the mid-1980s because Ireland back then was very insular. He was one of only a few businessmen putting an Irish stamp on the world.'

O'Leary decided to grab the bull by the horns and made contact with the Tipperary-born entrepreneur with an interesting proposition. 'I called him up at the weekend,' O'Leary recalls. 'I said: "I think if you did this, this and this you could save some money – but don't tell the [SKC] partners that I told you." That's when I first made an impression on him.'

O'Leary left KPMG in 1986, at which point Ryan offered him a job. 'I said no. I'd bought a shop in Walkinstown and wanted to go and do my own thing for a year or two.

'At that stage GPA was a big organisation. Every six months he'd give me a call and ask how I was getting on and ask if I wanted to go and work for him.

'After a couple of years I'd done quite well and said: "Look, I'd love to work for you for a year. I don't want to work for GPA, but I'll work for you personally. The deal was, I'd work for nothing but I'd get 5 per cent of the action.'

O'Leary recalls how every year he'd have to threaten to 'resign' in order to get his 5 per cent but the money would always come through in the end. 'It would be a negotiation, but that's where you learn and it's why he was so good and why he was so tough.'

O'Leary was parachuted into Ryanair in 1988 at a time when it was making heavy losses. The airline required a €25 million cash injection from Ryan in the early 1990s to keep the aircraft in the air. O'Leary saw only one solution to its difficulties. 'I was begging him, shut it down, close it down, it will never make money. It was doomed.

'Tony was the only person who said no, partly because his name was on the side of it but also partly, I think, because he didn't like being beaten. He wasn't going to be beaten by the Government and the State monopoly. He had great balls.'

O'Leary subsequently tried to sell the airline to Aer Lingus for €25 million and, after some years, to British Airways for about €130 million, but both attempts came to naught.

'Bernie Cahill [the former Aer Lingus chairman] wouldn't or couldn't do the deal. I don't know why. It would've been a steal. I think he thought we were just a bunch of jumped-up pups. We were never sure that BA was serious.'

Ryan decided that a change of tack was required, and dispatched O'Leary to the US to meet Herb Kelleher of Southwest Airlines and learn all he could to put in place a low-cost model for Ryanair. 'We followed the Southwest model, but we have taken it way beyond Southwest. Much of that was down to Tony.

'We were the first to take the food off the planes and the first to charge for drinks. This was

Tony Ryan. Photograph: David Sleator.

revolutionary stuff and every time Tony said: "Go for it, providing you reduce air fares."'

Ryanair began to turn a corner and was operating in the black. The airline made its stock exchange debut in 1997, after which Ryan's role became less hands-on. It is now the biggest low-cost carrier in Europe by a large margin.

O'Leary also observed Ryan's lowest moment, when the flotation of GPA was pulled at the last moment in 1992. 'At a stroke he lost practically everything. GPA was worthless. He took ferocious abuse in the press, from the financial community. They must have been dark days for him.

'He was remarkable in the way he fought on through that, restructured the company and eventually sold it off. And he kept GPA in Shannon.'

The pair didn't always agree on everything. A proposal by Ryan in the mid-1990s to launch a second airport for Dublin in Baldonnel was not supported by his protégé. 'I never thought it would work from a Ryanair point of view, only because we were so big at Dublin Airport and you couldn't just move to Baldonnel.

'There's no doubt that he was absolutely right about a second competing airport for Dublin, but the timing was just wrong.'

O'Leary says he was a regular visitor to Ryan's Lyons Estate in Celbridge. 'Every week, or maybe twice a month, I'd pop down to Lyons for a cup of tea. We'd have a chat, talk about strategy, what's happening, problems and so on.'

He recalls fondly how Ryan loved puffing on a big cigar and having a few jars and a bit of craic down the pub. He recalls, too, how Ryan loved picking up knick-knacks from around the world.

'He was in Mexico one year and bought an old antique door and shipped it back to Killboy. He thought, "What the hell am I going to do with this thing?", so he built a chapel in Killboy to fit the door.

'He was a great man for buying a statue that no one could use and building a garden around it.'

Last Monday evening, O'Leary saw Ryan for the last time. 'I went down for a cup of tea at half past six and left at about a quarter to 11,' he says.

'He was in great form, talking about the past, talking about the future, wanting to know what the five-year strategy was with Ryanair, what would we do when we got to 2012, where would we go next. Should we export Ryanair to a different part of the world. Maybe do it to Latin America or some other part of the world. He was full of ideas.'

And will any be adopted?

'Yes is the answer. You are fortunate to come across geniuses like that. You would be stupid to ignore their advice. You may not agree with it all the time, but you'd be stupid to ignore it.'

O'Leary believes Ryan's legacy will be long and lasting. His patronage of the arts and education; his love for restoring old properties to their former glory; his support of the bloodstock industry.

In the final analysis, however, he believes Ryanair will be his lasting memorial. 'He has changed the lives of millions of people. Ryanair started the low-fares revolution in Europe. I think and hope that Ryanair would be the lasting and enduring legacy.'

'He was a genius. Most people are good at one thing in their lives but Tony had so much going on.

'I don't think I'd be capable of setting up Ryanair. I'm not sure I'd be capable of doing any other job you gave me to do, either.

'Tony was smart. Art, sport, education, there were so many aspects to his life. He was an incredible man.'

SATURDAY, 13 OCTOBER 2007

Who Was the Man in the Skip?

Ruadhán Mac Cormaic, in Derby, England

May Fitzpatrick knew. So strong was the feeling that, on opening the door that Wednesday morning to find two police officers standing awkwardly before her, it was she who spoke first. 'Is it Kevin?'

Seven years after the third of her six children last crossed the threshold of the family home in Derby and set off in search of a new start in Ireland, the policemen brought news of a man they believed was 36-year-old Kevin Fitzpatrick. He had been found dead in a warehouse in Limerick, they explained. Only later did they call back to tell her there was more bad news.

'It's just so awful for her. She's been in a daze for weeks,' says Kevin's sister, Maria, of her mother. 'She can't bear the thought. In life you have loss, don't you? You lose your parents as you get older. But not your child – and in such tragic circumstances.'

Over the next few days the Fitzpatricks would learn that Kevin had been crushed to death when the commercial rubbish bin in which he was sleeping was emptied into a collection lorry. His body was discovered by workers at the Mr Binman waste recycling centre in Grange, Co. Limerick, when they were sorting rubbish that Monday morning.

The family would be told that local gardaí thought he had come to Limerick from Cork the day before, for reasons unknown. Instead of making contact with groups helping the destitute in Limerick, he had taken shelter in the bin when temperatures dropped on Sunday night. He was asleep when it was loaded on to the lorry.

Last Wednesday, three weeks to the day since they heard of his lonely death, Kevin Fitzpatrick was buried at Derby's Nottingham Road Cemetery, in a quiet, elevated part of the graveyard that gives an expansive panorama of the city below. He rests beside his late father, Joe – a Dubliner who died almost two years ago – at the end of a small path yellowed with freshly fallen leaves.

Earlier that day a large funeral Mass took place across town at St Joseph's Church, in the parish where Kevin had served as an altar boy, not far from the house where he and his siblings were raised in the Irish satellite district of Normanton. In a congregation of people mostly with Irish accents, the pews were tight with friends and neighbours who hadn't seen him in almost a decade.

This was Kevin Fitzpatrick's milieu. At school in St Joseph's his would have been a classroom filled with the children of Irish emigrants who settled in the area in the 1950s and 1960s, and at home, too, the Fitzpatrick children were ensconced in their Irishness. Like many of Derby's émigrés, holidays were spent 'at home' in Ireland and ears were tuned devotedly to Irish sport and politics. 'These are my Irish children,' Joe would say when introducing his kids to strangers.

The third Fitzpatrick child – he came after Martin and Maria and was an older brother to Joseph, Jeanette and Philip – is recalled by his teachers as a clever and thoughtful pupil who came from a good family. 'He was a very bright lad,' says Sr Raphael Lynch, a family friend who taught Kevin at primary school. 'Academically, he had no problem. Right from the age of seven he played chess in school, and he was the number one player we had.'

With the hope of eventual return, Kevin's father, Joe, had left Dublin in the mid-1960s to join his brothers in Derby and find work on the building sites of Britain's east midlands. He met his future wife, May – who was in Derby for a visit, but ended up staying for life – in 1967, at a time when buses could be filled with the Irish who were arriving every month. Manageably sized and close to regional centres such as Nottingham and Leicester, this was an industrial town on the rise. The large power stations were then being built along the River Trent and the two totemic employers – British Rail and Rolls Royce – offered a regular wage to tens of thousands of men and women.

Fr Tim O'Sullivan, a Kerryman and parish priest at St Mary's across town, believes that whereas that first generation found comfort in each other's company, and by following events at home as though they had never left, their children – though ostensibly better equipped to integrate – did not have the same cohesive comforts available to them. Many found themselves straddling an uneasy divide: Irish in England, English in Ireland.

'This next generation – Kevin's generation – I often have sympathy for them because they were caught. They were English, they were Derby – they supported Derby County – but at home it was always about being Irish,' he says wearily.

'Then you had the stuff in the North, where they were pulled in several directions. First of all they abhorred the violence and the bombing. Then they had to cope with the fact that they were being blamed for it, and some of them abused because of it.

'They had a problem with identity. And I have often wondered, since it happened, why did Kevin go to Ireland? Why did he want to stay there? He would have found it difficult enough in Dublin with a Derby accent, and maybe more so in Cork.'

When he finished school in the mid-1980s, Kevin spent a few years drifting in and out of factory jobs in the town. He lived in a couple of council flats but, like his brothers and sisters, never strayed far from the family home in Normanton. In recent weeks the family have scoured their memories for explanations, for turning points, for the telling anecdote that might shine light on the seven-year-old question.

'He stayed at school, and then he had jobs here,' says Maria. 'But I think by that time he had

Launching Arthritis Ireland's national arthritis campaign is Frankie Scott (20) who was diagnosed when she was four, Robert Courtney who was diagnosed with juvenile arthritis when he was 16 months, and Leigh Arnold who plays Dr Clodagh Delaney in RTÉ's The Clinic. *The photograph features large 'faces of arthritis', people who have arthritis; however, they are not the faces that many people would typically expect of arthritis sufferers. The campaign aims to raise public awareness of arthritis and draw particular attention to the occurrence of the disease among people of all ages.*

got in with a wrong crowd and he'd started to drink . . . and he was easily led.'

A major – and difficult – part of his life in these years was the collapse of a long-term relationship with a local girl. The couple had three children, but after a few years together they parted and the children – all close in age – were given up for adoption. By then Kevin had lost contact with many of his old school friends.

At the time, nobody was too concerned when Kevin told his family he was going to Ireland. He'd be back before long, they presumed. But in retrospect the family think he wanted to start afresh and

felt removing himself from Derby was the only sure way of going about it.

Dublin was his first stop, and to his family's knowledge he never found a job there or anywhere else in Ireland. He fell into a routine of sleeping rough, first in Dublin, then in Cork – and was known to charitable groups in both cities. Some who crossed his path in city hostels recall a quiet man who kept largely to himself. But throughout his time in Ireland he kept in touch with his family, calling home on family birthdays and often writing good-humoured letters. His mother last heard from him on her birthday last

July, when he said for the first time that he'd be home for Christmas.

Sitting in her living room in Derby's Alvaston area, amid a thicket of Mass cards and letters, Maria recalls her conversations with Kevin being studded with laughs and jokes. She remarks that, whatever his private turmoil, he never complained about his lot. During a call last year he told her he had fallen for a local girl. 'He said she was the love of his life. I said, "Where are you stopping tonight?" And he said, "We've got our sleeping bags – we're stopping underneath the bridge." He wasn't with her the next week,' she remembers.

Over the years Joe and May came to visit their son many times, bringing him warm clothes and pleading with him to return. Their last meeting was around Christmas almost two years ago, when they got word that he was in St James's Hospital with a broken hip. His father was to die a month after the visit, aged 61. 'They told him his home was there waiting for him, but what can you do with a 30-year-old lad if he doesn't want to come back?' says Sr Raphael Lynch.

May Fitzpatrick's children – teachers, businessmen, accountants and nurses – have done well for themselves, and Maria wonders whether the favourite child – for that he was, she says – was intimidated by his siblings' achievements. Did he perhaps feel he had let his parents down, and did this keep him from returning? 'There was no reason why he had to feel like that, because he was clever – he could have been anything he wanted to be.'

When Joe Fitzpatrick died, the family had trouble finding Kevin and didn't track him down until the day before the funeral – but without a passport or any photo ID, he couldn't travel. 'He was sobbing on the phone – it was really bad,' says Maria. 'And mum was saying, "Kevin, just come home and it will be all right." But I think he didn't want to face it. Afterwards he said he had gone into church and lit candles, so he was mourning as well, but it must have been difficult.'

She laughs at the recollection of his knowing joke to his mother at the time: 'Don't be ringing me with any more bad news, Mum.'

Losing her husband and her son in such a short time has taken a toll on May Fitzpatrick, a warm-hearted woman whose strong Lurgan accent mocks a 40-year remove. 'If he had died in bed or something like that, I think she could have accepted it,' says Maria. 'Deep down, as the years went on, I think she knew one day something would happen to him. Living like that, in that wild way, eventually it will catch up with you.

'But he was 36. He had a life in front of him. It's a waste, isn't it? A complete and utter waste. To go like that. She can't get her head around it.'

As Fr Bill Naylor brought Wednesday's funeral mass to a close, the small church fell silent and, taking their cue from the first bars of Sinatra's 'My Way', the pall-bearers prepared to hoist the coffin. Then May Fitzpatrick rose suddenly and moved quickly towards the coffin before wrapping her arms tightly around it and dropping her head to its hard surface. 'Kevin,' she sobbed. 'Kevin.'

In his eulogy, Martin Fitzpatrick – May's eldest – spoke of the special bond between his mother and her third child. Kevin's was never a conformist mind, he said. He lived a short, unconventional life, but the family's memories of him are alight with warmth, with colour. 'Kevin was my mum's hat trick, and like a footballer who gets to keep the match ball when he scores a hat trick, Kevin remained mum's match ball – one that she will keep for her life.'

It could have been yesterday, Martin said, that he was standing on the same altar at St Joseph's, bidding farewell to his father. On that day he quoted from 'The Broken Chain', a poem of unknown authorship whose last verse likens death to a breaking of the family chain. But with God's will, the poet has it, that chain may one day be restored. 'This afternoon, when Kevin is laid to rest, that will be the first link, and some day the whole chain will be put back together again.'

SATURDAY, 20 OCTOBER 2007

A Fighter Against Her Illness and the Health System

Obituary

Susie Long, who has died aged 41, came to public attention when she exposed the cruel inadequacies in the public health system that, she believed, led to her premature death. Battling against bowel cancer, she highlighted her plight under the pseudonym 'Rosie' on RTÉ radio last January, appearing on the media on several subsequent occasions under her real name.

She was prompted to contact the media by a public health advertisement on television that urged viewers to lose no time in getting tested for bowel cancer if they had any cause for concern. The advertisement implied that patients at risk would receive immediate attention, but this was not her experience.

In an email to *Liveline* presenter Joe Duffy, she outlined how she had waited seven months for her cancer to be diagnosed, because she was a public patient. By contrast, she knew of a private patient who had been treated within three days, although she expressed relief that he had received the necessary treatment.

Notwithstanding the fact that she and her husband were in employment, they could not afford private health insurance. 'But even if we could have, we wouldn't have gotten it because we believed . . . that all people should get good care despite their incomes.' She was convinced that her cancer would have been diagnosed sooner and treated successfully if she had private insurance.

She was in no doubt as to where blame lay. 'It is government policy that put me on a seven-month waiting list for a colonoscopy. The blame for the failure to diagnose me in time to save my life lies squarely with the Minister for Health, Mary Harney, and the Taoiseach, Bertie Ahern.' Likewise, she was critical of those who voted for Fianna Fáil and the PDs 'because they thought they'd get a few more shillings in their pockets'. However, she had nothing but admiration for health service workers, who were expected to do a good job in conditions where underfunding prevailed and services were poorly organised.

At the funeral service this week, family friend Malcolm Noonan said: 'She really mobilised a country into thinking about itself and thinking about ourselves, as to where we're going as a society.' Another friend Teresa Ryan said: 'Engaging with Susie was always uplifting, particularly in these last few months. One friend told me that she went in to see her, expecting it to be difficult, [but] she came out elated.'

Born in Orrville, a small town in Ohio, she grew up as Karen Sue Long. A tomboy as a teenager, she enjoyed motorcycling with her brother Mike Fejes, since deceased.

An interest in Irish history and a liking for the novels of Jennifer Johnston lay behind her decision to travel to Ireland. She arrived in Dublin, aged 18, in 1984 and supported herself by selling jewellery from a street stall and working as a waitress in a city-centre restaurant.

In 1986 she met Conor Mac Liam, a secondary school teacher, and they were married a year later. The couple moved to Higginstown, near Kilkenny city, in 1991 and quickly became involved in the local community. They were active in the Kilkenny School Project and Susie became school secretary. She also raised funds for Amber, Kilkenny's Women's Refuge, and later worked on a part-time basis for the refuge.

She inherited her activism and sense of social justice from her great-grandmother, Sis Coyle, a member of the Wobblies and supporter of Eugene V. Debs, a five-time socialist candidate for the US presidency. A member of Amnesty International, she was also a member of Earth Watch.

During her second pregnancy, she was involved in legal action to secure health board support for home births. However, she had to make her own arrangements as she had done in the case of her first child.

A question she put to Bono for a *New York Times* feature in September 2005 was selected for publication. 'Will there ever be just one too many broken promises that will make you join the great unwashed?' she asked the singer. 'Could you ever see yourself standing at the head of the march the way Martin Luther King did, demanding, instead of asking nicely?' Bono replied that he would have lunch with the devil if he thought it would make a difference and that he would be proud to march – 'at the front or at the back'.

She had a great sense of humour and loved music, particularly alternative country and the songs of Hank Williams and Johnny Cash. In recent years she enjoyed visiting Barcelona, Bordeaux, Paris and Berlin. She had hoped to visit Cuba, partly for the satisfaction of getting a Cuban stamp on her US passport, but it was not to be.

Invited in May to join the Ossory diocesan pilgrimage to Lourdes, she dutifully attended Mass at the basilica and then left the 'holy trail for the tourist trail'. Unfortunately she took ill and was hospitalised.

She acknowledged that her lack of religious belief made dying harder. 'I would love to have a belief in religion because it makes you feel safe but, unfortunately, I just don't . . . I was a very strong Catholic until I moved to Ireland.'

In 2004 the family settled in Callan. She spent her final months at Our Lady's Hospice, Harold's Cross. Elizabeth Coyle, the hospice's lay chaplain,

The helmet and uniform of firefighter Mark O'Shaughnessy are carried ahead of his coffin as it leaves the Church of Our Lady Queen of Peace in Bray, Co. Wicklow. Photograph: Eric Luke.

said Susie 'really made a difference, and that's what she wanted. She gave so much in the short time she had'. There are plans to commemorate her in a permanent way in the 24-bed day services unit to be built at St Luke's Hospital, Kilkenny.

She is survived by her husband Conor, daughter Áine, son Fergus and sister Linda Huntsbuerger.

Susie Long: born 24 February 1966; died 12 October 2007.
Irish Times *obituaries are unsigned.*

WEDNESDAY, 24 OCTOBER 2007

Read and Destroy – A Lesson Learned on Leaked Information

Peter Preston

There is a personal pain to writing about it even now, almost a quarter of a century later. In many ways the scars still bleed easily when you scratch at them. Don't think journalism is always a flip, cynical business. Sometimes the things you do – or don't do – live on as a permanent reproach.

So here I go again, one more time. It's a dark autumn evening in 1983 and the night news editor of the *Guardian*, John Hooper, rushes in to talk to the paper's editor (me). John has started his shift by leafing through the bumf in his tray – and look, look at this, a ministry of defence document from Michael Heseltine, marked 'secret', and just lying there, almost magically, amid the routine hand-outs. It tells you how and when the cruise missiles will come to Greenham Common, what Hezza will tell the House of Commons, how he'll deal with Greenham's vexatious women. There's no covering note, no clue where the document came from.

But it is, if genuine, a story. Not a massive story: the juice is in the dates and timings, which will surely be changed once they're public. But still a necessary yarn.

I call in my defence editor. He makes some calls, pronounces the document genuine, and we lead on it. Then nothing much happens. The turbulent cruise pool continues choppy, but the government doesn't react. Parliament talks of other things. Correspondents for the paper are asked to scan the text and hunt for a follow-up. Ronald Reagan invades Grenada. The focus shifts. It isn't until well over a week later – on a flat news Sunday – that we come back to the Greenham stuff.

I'm in Bristol on family business. The duty editor, after due consultation, thinks it might be interesting to run the document verbatim, just to show readers how it's couched. He puts it on page two. Again, nothing happens, until – 48 hours on – there's a sudden intervention: the treasury solicitor, all-purpose Whitehall legal enforcer, wants his paperwork back. Worse, at least on the rumour circuit, special branch may be around for an office search.

And there's the immediate rub. We'd copied the document for staff specialists to look at. So there are at least half a dozen copies in other hands, some of them kilometres away and not answering their phones. The natural instinct is to destroy: the practical conclusion is that this can't be done fast enough. I've been sloppy and distracted. We're in a mess. So we call our own solicitor. He's experienced and upright. Since we can't physically destroy the document, he offers the 1981 Contempt of Court Act instead, with its specific provisions allowing journalists to defend their sources. We stake our case for not handing over the document on that new law. The treasury solicitor agrees – providing, of course, that we solemnly agree to hand it over if we lose. I sign, on behalf of the paper, on the bottom line. Was there any inkling then that fate had already taken over? Not really.

We didn't know who the source was, or how he'd infiltrated John Hooper's tray. We didn't know who we were defending, or what steps he (or she) had taken to protect himself or herself. We hadn't, in that sense, been trusted. We thought we might be being merely quixotic. Weeks of waiting ticked by. Then, suddenly, we were in the law courts in the Strand, mounting our defence before Mr Justice (Richard) Scott . . . and losing on an agonisingly narrow property point. We appealed. Three judges were miraculously available that afternoon to deliver a similar but different verdict. It wasn't that the document was dangerous, or whose property it was. It was the fact that the 'disloyal civil servant' who'd leaked it might go on to leak something about 'national security'.

At which point, the jaws of the system snapped shut. There were other appeals that could be made (and were) but the government wanted its document back first, and invoked daily escalating fines against the *Guardian* to make sure it got it. I'd signed my name on behalf of the company, promising to hand over those copies. Did I resign, tear them up and face the consequences?

Heads or tails, everybody loses. But wasn't that double-dealing, too? So (after much debate) the document was handed over, in person and in misery. And, more weeks later, a 24-year-old foreign office clerk, Sarah Tisdall, was arrested, pleaded guilty and was sentenced to six months in prison.

She had used a foreign office photocopier that could be identified. She'd been horrified by what she saw as the government's ruthless parliamentary tactics over bringing the cruise missiles. She thought the public ought to know. The fact that – to me – the tactics Heseltine outlined were standard issue for any British government with a dodgy decision to implement made it all worse, rather than better.

Tisdall wasn't some hardened politician chucking a spanner in Thatcher's works. She was innocent in the purest sense of the word (and might, like Clive Ponting soon after, have been acquitted if she'd taken her case to a jury).

Are there lessons from all this that linger no matter how much you'd like to forget? Of course. They come winging back the moment any parallel case crops up. Judith Miller of *The New York Times* in prison? America's press demands 'shield laws', which come automatically to the aid of journalists protecting their sources. And we have certain shields, too – not just in the 1981's updated provisions but via the European Convention on Human Rights and the press complaints commission's code (which has some influence on British law).

But is there truly any shield a writer or his editor would be wise to rely on? Alas, I don't think so. Alas, I've seen what happens when the pincers of the state snap shut.

The plain fact, in three interlocking courts, is that the *Guardian* failed to protect its sources – but that, in each and every case, the reasons for our loss were different.

The plain fact is that some hugely distinguished judges – Lord Scarman for one – took our side, whilst others barely got to the starting line. The plain fact is that any shield is a potential mockery if 'national security', however vestigially involved, can be invoked. And in my mind, too, the plain fact is that an editor's duty to a source applies even when the source has deliberately kept himself anonymous.

Of course we'd have gone to any lengths to protect a known informant, but not knowing made matters altogether muddier. We didn't know who, or what, we were trying to defend. We blundered around in the dark. But the crux, it seemed to me later, was putting the material as supplied in print.

That was the moment a bargain with persons unknown was clinched. Unspoken, unsigned, but still a bargain. Publication was the defining deal. None of this seemed quite so clear at the time, of course. You wandered instead around a moral maze of speculation. But the results were clear enough.

Tisdall went to prison. She, and her wonderful parents, shouldered a great deal of responsibility and showed a great deal of understanding over what had gone wrong. I felt wretched, because I should have been wiser. The paper endured months of pretty facile name-calling and, much worse, a temporary news drought as its sources dried up.

One enduring lesson emerged. Occasionally, under some bit of law in some particular circumstance, a shield law can function. Both sides – politicians and journalists – know that protecting sources is vital, which is why they try to legislate in search of such protection. But when push comes to shove, any shield defence and its chances of success turns frail. Any developed legal system has plenty of ways around a problem. Shields can become flimsy in a trice. Then, because you've started down a legal route, you're stuck with its verdict.

So editors, if they want to be sure, have only one solid recourse if they want leaked information to flow in freedom. They can't dissemble or vacillate or brood. They have to put any potentially incriminating document out of harm's way. Perhaps – as in our case – that's not physically easy at a crunch. Perhaps, from fascination or for future reference, some paperwork is merely stowed away.

But the lesson of the Greenham leak, a lesson bitterly learned, puts all doubts to one side. Read and destroy. You do it, as I did many times after, because that is the only true way, a principle and course of action within your own control. And if protecting sources is as important as governments themselves say when they sign human rights conventions, who can argue with that?

Peter Preston was editor of The Guardian *newspaper from 1975 to 1995. He continues to write for it and its sister paper,* The Observer. *Sarah Tisdall served four months of her six-month sentence.*

An English bulldog models a lingerie item at the canine Ultimate Fashion Show which is part of Pet Expo 2007, a consumer pet exhibition that took place at the RDS. Photograph: Matt Kavanagh.

SATURDAY, 27 OCTOBER 2007

The Dream Turns Sour

Róisín Ingle

Avril Bailey cried last Saturday when she picked up her copy of this newspaper and read allegations concerning the Roebuck Counselling Centre in Dublin. 'After all this time the truth about that place was finally coming out. I cried all morning, tears of relief and vindication,' says Bailey, who in the early 1990s was a client at the centre, where she later trained as a psychotherapist.

Last Saturday's story detailed how large payments had been sought by a counsellor at the centre from a number of people, including Dubliner John Hanrahan. After paying €3,300 upfront for a diploma in psychotherapy, Hanrahan was asked for €100,000 for what counsellor Claire Hoban and her boss Bernie Purcell, director of the centre, said were 'life mentoring' services. Dozens of people have since contacted *The Irish Times* with negative stories about their experiences. One man, Des Martin, gave almost €250,000 over the course of a year. It was eventually refunded.

Over the past 17 years the centre has evolved from being purely a counselling provider to an organisation which also conducts financial deals with clients involving hundreds of thousands of euro.

Purcell, a former director of the Rape Crisis Centre, has always prided herself on introducing what she calls 'cutting edge' therapies. When she set up Roebuck Counselling Centre in 1990, first in Clonskeagh and then Rathgar, she introduced Grof or holotropic breath work, a method pioneered in Ireland by Prof. Ivor Browne at St Brendan's Hospital in Dublin. The work involved clients lying on mattresses while engaged in deep and rapid breathing patterns so they enter an altered state during which they uncovered repressed memories.

At Roebuck, Purcell offered such 'mattress therapy' sessions along with one-to-one counselling and a wide variety of group therapy work covering subjects such as sexuality and spirituality.

This week people have expressed concerns about their experiences of participating in the centre. One woman who doesn't wish to be named says she had moved to Dublin from a rural part of the country, escaping her dysfunctional family background. 'I was 21 and totally alone. For nine years Roebuck became my family. Bernie reminded me of my mother and I wanted to please her. I was spending around £75 a week there, while earning £12,000 a year,' she says.

Her average week involved one-to-one counselling with Purcell, along with participation in group therapy and Grof sessions whenever she could afford them. 'You kind of got addicted to Grof. We would come out of the session and then interpret the experience. It always seemed to centre around sexual abuse. I remember being in one group of around 15 people and everyone except myself and one other person had uncovered memories of having had babies in their teenage years. It didn't seem possible but I was so messed up at the time that I didn't trust my own judgment,' she says.

Sue Saunders and Avril Bailey attended the centre at the same time. It took years after leaving, they say, for them to recover. They maintain they were encouraged to break off ties with their families. *The Irish Times* has spoken to others who were encouraged to leave their jobs, becoming mired in debt and almost totally dependent on the centre. Saunders and Bailey say a culture of secrecy developed where they became afraid to question anything that went on in the centre.

'We had isolated ourselves so much from the outside world that the centre became the only place where we felt safe and understood,' says Bailey. Saunders claims some clients became 'fragmented'. She says it appeared Roebuck's philosophy was that, if clients broke down or left the centre, it was because they didn't have the courage to face their issues. 'A nervous breakdown was seen as some kind of cop-out,' she says.

Having built up a client base, Bernie Purcell had offered her inaugural Psychotherapy and Counselling Course in 1993. The first participants were all people who up to that point had come to her for therapy. Two of these, Claire Hoban and Ann Cahill, are now the main counsellors at the centre. Originally, Purcell was the only facilitator on the course and her husband, John Milton, was the only therapist available to participants at that time. 'There were no assessments and no external assessor. The woman who had been your therapist was now your teacher,' says Bailey.

Over this period Saunders and Bailey became increasingly uneasy. 'When I would tell John Milton these concerns, he was dismissive and turned the issues back on me. In my last session with him I said that the truth would come out about the place eventually and he said, well you know what happened to Jesus Christ when he told the truth,' says Bailey.

When the two women eventually plucked up the courage to leave Roebuck they found they needed medical support to cope with 'life outside'. 'I was shattered. My doctor at the time told me that I was displaying all the symptoms of someone who had just left a cult. I trusted nobody and had to leave the country to seek help,' Saunders says.

These days many people who attend Roebuck for counselling are offered a place on the psychotherapy training course, whether or not they are interested in becoming a counsellor. All fees are paid upfront to ensure, according to Purcell, that clients commit to the therapy. Over the past few days, *The Irish Times* understands, a number of former clients were at the centre requesting refunds.

In the past two years the centre has moved into the area of 'life mentoring' which includes a package where people pay €100,000 for two years' worth of unlimited counselling, business advice and life tutoring. If participants don't make one million within the two years, they will, according to Purcell, get their money back.

As the story unfolded this week, it emerged that over the years a number of complaints have been made concerning Roebuck to bodies such as the Irish Association of Counselling and Psychotherapy and the National Association of Pastoral Counselling and Psychotherapy (NAPCP) which currently accredits Roebuck's psychotherapy course. Nothing came of these complaints although John Farrelly of the NAPCP is now urging people to write to it, detailing their experiences.

Claire Hoban resigned from the centre's Life Mentoring programme, following an investigation by *The Irish Times*, although it is understood she is still employed at the centre. However, more than one former client of Roebuck has expressed the concern that Hoban is being made a scapegoat. 'I am particularly sad about Claire Hoban,' says one woman who does not want to be named. 'I trained with her and knew her quite well. The Claire being written about and spoken about on the radio this week is not the Claire I knew. The Claire I knew was wildly intelligent and creative. She was a vibrant woman with a kind and open heart. I don't know what has become of her and I only hope she does not become the fall guy for this whole debacle.'

In conversation, Purcell and Hoban both display an unwavering conviction in their work. Hoban speaks of 'motivation' and 'life choices' and 'helping people to achieve their dreams, whether that is moving to Barbados or buying a Ferrari'. Purcell is positive about the development whereby the centre is working more with 'well' people as distinct from those who are, as the Roebuck website states, 'lacking'. 'Psychotherapy began with everyone having problems,' Purcell told this reporter last week. 'This last five years we are working a lot in wellness. Claire engaged with them to keep them in wellness, increase their success and their capacities for relationships and communication. It's an expansive programme and Claire chose to speak to those people. One of them [John Hanrahan] had the real capacity to actually do this programme with her. He chose not to and that was it . . . I think he was disappointed. I wouldn't be surprised if he ended up at the centre in two years' time.'

The Irish Times attempted to contact Bernie Purcell for a response yesterday but was unsuccessful.

The Irish Times wishes to clarify there is another Bernie Purcell, living in Rathgar, Dublin, who has no connection with Roebuck Counselling Centre. She is a registered member of the Psychological Society of Ireland, a member of the Association of Psychoanalytic Psychotherapists in Ireland, and works as a senior psychologist in a state-run organisation.

SATURDAY, 27 OCTOBER 2007

Ocean Patterns Resistant to Global Warming

Another Life, by Michael Viney

A still October morning; an overnight raindrop pendant from every berry. Mooching out to measure what fell, a different sound catches my ear, a snatch of football rattle. A different bird flies up from the ruby platters of the guelder rose and perches on the wire: a big, long thrush bibbed with dark spots like a chest of medals; an upright, military bearing. One brief bugle of song, then it spots me and is gone.

A mistle thrush, as you knew. Plenty everywhere else, just not here at Thallabawn – our first, in fact. But we have berries and to spare: not only hawthorn and guelder rose, but firethorn brandishing wands across my window, bush roses smothered with hips, the apple trees bowed down. No mistletoe, of course, so stick with the mistle thrush's older name, the stormcock.

But that could lead us off to reveries quite disallowed by climate change: the stormcock perched on a bare branch in the bleak mid-winter etc, the first bird to sing in January, stuff borrowed from bards in the island next door. Will it still need to commandeer a loaded holly tree and bully all the other birds away? Without winter, what's a stormcock for? News of frost the other morning was marvellous: we haven't quite lost the seasons after all. I'm at an age to trot out talk of exquisite frost ferns on the inside of my bedroom window (I was 11) and frost still does beautiful things for hedgerows and trees. So long, of course, as we don't have to drive anywhere, and our water pipe from the hill stream doesn't freeze.

But I was also thinking of nature's own needs, for a spell of rest or even death: a cleansing interval. In Ireland's ecological scheme of things, plants and insects have been chosen over centuries to fit certain rhythms of senescence and growth, of seasonal extinction and renewal. Yes, our species will all 'move north', very slowly and sequentially, to make way for unguessable successions. But when change overtakes nature's pace of selection, the prospect is a sort of tumbling anarchy. Midges bearing bluetongue – who'd have thought? Even the cold was a bit odd, after all those weeks of pampering warmth.

In Monkstown, Co. Dublin, a butterfly-watcher spotted third-generation holly blues mating optimistically. Then brrr! and our first autumn logs in the stove. But this could, apparently, be that sort of winter – colder and drier than average – for the North Atlantic Oscillation (NAO) is in a weakly negative phase.

Given that the NAO is one of the oldest weather patterns on record, and that its influence seems, for the moment, well able to hold its own with the impact of global warming, it really is surprising how little we know about it.

What oscillates in the NAO is sea-level pressure of the atmospheric mass between Iceland and the Azores – islands on the same line of longitude, but with two very different climates. In winter, the mass swings between Iceland's low-pressure centre that generates so many Atlantic storms, and a high-

Autumn colours by Michael Viney.

pressure centre on warm, sub-tropical waters between the Azores and Iberia.

When there is a very large and consistent difference between barometer readings in the Azores and Iceland, the NAO is said to be 'positive', with 'a high seasonal index'. In this state, there are more and stronger winter storms travelling northeast across the Atlantic, bringing warm, wet air to Ireland but giving cold, dry winters to the Mediterranean.

In a 'negative' NAO winter, the difference in pressure is small. There are fewer and weaker storms, which bring warm, moist air to the Mediterranean and cold, dry, polar air from the north and east blowing into northern Europe.

Knowing that this happens is one thing:

predicting it, quite another. UK meteorologists plumped for a statistical method using the slow variations in Atlantic sea-surface temperature. Clinching evidence for a link with the winter NAO did not come until 1999. Even now, for all the ocean's supposed inertia, big changes in the NAO can happen from one winter to the next and even within the winter months.

The recent run of dry, sunny days and cool nights should reward us with brilliant autumn colours in the trees. It is just the weather to promote the annual death of chlorophyll, leaving other pigments − yellow carotenes, red and purple anthocyanins − to blaze out in a brief biochemical glory before the fall of leaves.

Our native trees are already yielding a little to climate change in the timing of spring budburst, but are slower, supposedly, to move their autumn rhythm. Nature watchers might like to track their progress by sending records of colour change and leaf fall to *www.biology.ie*.

Bread Pudding in the Land of Milk and Honeys

Displaced in Mullingar, by Michael Harding

There's a great line in Marina Carr's play, *Woman and Scarecrow*, about domestic appliances.

'Why didn't you have more sex?' Scarecrow asks the woman as she nears the end of her life. To which the woman replies, 'I was too busy hoovering.'

I thought of it last week, when I saw Gráinne outside Harvey Norman. She was carrying a Black and Decker vacuum cleaner.

Gráinne is what people used to call a tonic. Whenever I'm feeling a bit low I have a cappuccino with her. She's a mother of two, with a shiny black jeep, and sunglasses. I've often asked her about the sunglasses: they seem *de rigueur*, as jeepwear for the matrons of Mullingar.

We had lunch in the Courtyard Kitchen, a homely restaurant tucked away in a sidestreet below the cathedral. She had soup and I had quiche.

I said, 'It's getting cold in Mullingar. The windscreen of the jeep gets iced up these mornings. There was no ice on the windscreens in Leitrim.' She said, 'You're out early.' I said, 'I like to drive out the road and look at the big beech trees in the fog, before the sun breaks through.'

And even though the nights are freezing cold, my house seems unusually warm. It must be all the other houses huddled around in close proximity. I'm going through only half a bale of briquettes on the coldest of nights, whereas in Leitrim I was shovelling on a full bucket of Arigna coal every hour.

Gráinne asked me how I was getting on with the big telly. I told her that since I can now actually see *Fair City*, I find it a horrid poor excuse for drama. It didn't seem so awful on a small screen that was fuzzy and flecked with green lines. But now, watching it in 32-inch digital clarity, I am convinced that the moment is coming when the number of viewers will dwindle to a last solitary fan, still hanging on, like a watchman for daybreak. Maybe then the electricians will pull the plug.

Gráinne said, 'Too much telly is bad for a man.' I said, 'Too much hoovering is bad for a woman.' 'Do you know,' I said, 'I imagine I meet you everywhere. I keep seeing this black jeep, this woman with blonde hair and sunglasses, and I always think it's you.

'I was convinced I saw you on Saturday, in a Humvee, purring like a cat outside Super Valu: the woman driver had blonde hair, shades like yours, and she waved at me.

'The thing is that since Mullingar women discovered blonde hair and sunglasses, and sit behind the wheels of black jeeps, I have to look at the registration plates to figure out who it is. It wasn't you. Was it?'

Gráinne explained that women feel safer in jeeps. Her daughter is in UCG, where the students' union operates a 'walking bus'. When students are leaving the library, or going into town after dark, they can assemble at various points on the hour, so that they don't have to walk alone.

For dessert we had home-made bread pudding, and when the lady came over with it, she placed the dishes before us with a phrase as comforting as the gurgle of milk: 'Mind the plates,' she said. 'They're hot.' Half way through the bread pudding, Gráinne took off her sunglasses. It was as if she were suddenly naked. I delighted in her beautiful hazel eyes, at last unveiled.

Aisling McLaughlin views a Women's Aid installation of 137 tiles outside the Dáil yesterday that records the dates of 137 women murdered in Ireland since 1996. Ms McLaughlin's sister, Siobhán Kearney, was murdered on 28 February 2006. Photograph: Alan Betson.

She said, 'Do you see the woman over by the window?' I did. 'Well,' she said, 'Do you know who she is?' I didn't. She mentioned a famous gentleman on television. I said, 'It doesn't look at all like him!' 'No no,' she said, 'that's the Mammy!' On the street outside, she put her glasses back on. They made her look like a fly, or something out of a science fiction movie.

It's a beautiful mask, and truly enigmatic, because I haven't a clue whether her smiling lips mean boredom or desire, and the ambiguity is tantalising. And it makes me happy to know that she is a goddess, and that she is everywhere; that there are a thousand versions of her, cruising around the motorways, roundabouts and housing estates of Mullingar.

Mother Macree, after surviving the masculine claws of her tiger cubs, has re-emerged, not as the 'floury-faced ould wan in the kitchen', but as a yummy mummy, in clothes from Khan or Cocoon, and smothered in Christian Dior.

FRIDAY, 2 NOVEMBER 2007

An Irishman's Diary

Frank McNally

Sad news from the US, where Washoe the talking chimpanzee has died. She passed away peacefully on Tuesday, aged 42, in a facility at the Central Washington University, where she had spent her final years.

The website *friendsofwashoe.org* says a memorial service is planned later this month. Donations in lieu of flowers, please.

Washoe did not talk in the conventional sense, of course. Before she was born experiments had already concluded that chimps lacked the vocal apparatus to reproduce human sounds. Instead, her pioneering work was in the area of sign language.

At the height of her career, she was credited with a vocabulary of 250 words. She also had an ability to combine them in multiple short sentences; although, to the end, critics questioned whether any of this constituted language in the true sense.

Excitement peaked in the late 1960s when Washoe was the focus of a formal experiment in the Nevada county after which she was named. The idea was simple: to teach her American Sign Language (ASL), as used by deaf people in the US.

As a toddler, the chimp learned to request rewards – including tickles – by making the sign for 'more'. From there she made rapid progress. She could be truculent if pushed too hard: occasionally expressing frustration, as any student might, by biting the teacher. But her vocabulary soon extended even to swear-words: or at least to adding the adjective 'dirty' to the names of people she didn't like.

By the age of four, she knew 132 words. Not impressive compared with the 3,000 you can expect from a four-year-old human, but excellent for a chimp. She could also form at least 30 two- and three-word combinations. A high-point of the study occurred when, shown a swan and asked what it was, she made the sign for 'water bird'. One researcher described the excitement of the moment as 'like getting an SOS from outer space'.

But there were sceptics. A few years after the initial experiment, a Columbia University researcher conducted his own tests with a subject named – in a backhanded compliment to a certain famous linguist – Nim Chimpsky. He concluded that both Chimpsky and Washoe were engaging in mimicry rather than real conversation: that

essentially they had developed an elaborate way to beg for food.

The doubters were supported by the fact that Washoe had a poor grasp of grammar. Although she used some word combinations in the right order consistently – for example 'tickle me' rather than 'me tickle' – she was quite indifferent about other sequences.

One thing she was very particular about, however, was footwear. 'She always checked out your shoes, and if you had new ones she'd sign for you to show them to her,' a spokeswoman at CWU recalled this week. 'Then she might sign something about the colour. She was a real shoe lady in that way.'

Which suggests that perhaps researchers were barking up the wrong tree with the language thing. Washoe might have been the focus of an even more interesting project on the intense relationship that females of certain advanced mammal species have with footwear, especially the expensive kind. The urge involved is clearly very primal. But if we understood more about it, maybe scientists could work on a cure.

The demise of Washoe reminds me that while the primate world may not yet have cracked language, it has made great strides in other creative disciplines: modern art, for example, where admittedly the bar may be a bit lower. You might recall that only two years ago, a collection of posthumous paintings by a chimp called Congo fetched more than £12,000 sterling at Bonham's auction rooms in London. The price was a multiple of the pre-show estimate.

Dubbed the 'Cézanne of the ape world', Congo was born in 1954 and although based in London – an artistic backwater at that time – his career paralleled that of the abstract expressionists, with whom he attracted inevitable comparisons. Certainly his paintings were abstract. And as a chimp, he arguably had an edge over his human contemporaries in achieving the spontaneity that abstract expressionism so prized.

Most of Congo's output happened during a short but intensely creative period during the late 1950s. His supervisors were first impressed just by his confident handling of paintbrushes and pencils, and the fact that he made no attempt to eat them.

But soon they were struck by the care he took with his work. He always stayed within the boundaries of his canvas. And, unlike many painters, he always knew when he was finished: laying down his brush and never returning to a picture he'd done earlier.

As well as the expressionists, his oeuvre seemed to owe something to the Fauves (literally 'wild beasts'), another 20th-century art movement.

Unfortunately, he never gave any interviews – even in sign language – so we don't know what he was thinking.

Like many artists, Congo died young: struck down in his prime at the age of 10. Had he enjoyed a longer career, it is interesting to speculate whether he would have continued to insist on the primacy of paint as an expressive medium, or branched into the installation work so beloved of the 'Brit-art' movement. I like to think that, had he lived, the Turner Prize would not have been beyond him.

SATURDAY, 3 NOVEMBER 2007

Alone He Stands

Michael Dwyer

Now 71 and a grandfather since 1991, Robert Redford has aged gracefully. The lines crossing his features are more accentuated, but he looks remarkably fit in his denim shirt and jeans as he settles into a day of interviews in London. His new movie, *Lions for Lambs*, is his seventh as a director – he won the Oscar for his first, *Ordinary People* (1980) – and his most overtly political. The tagline in its advertising campaign is: 'If you don't stand for something, you might fall for anything.'

Taking place in real time in three locations, it introduces six characters faced with taking a stand. Redford plays an idealistic California college professor confronting one of his brightest students (Andrew Garfield) about his apathy. Two of his other students (Derek Luke and Michael Peña) are young working-class men who enlist and are sent to fight in Afghanistan. And in Washington, a confident, fast-rising Republican senator (Tom Cruise) is feeding his war strategies as a story to a cynical veteran journalist (Meryl Streep).

Redford has been producing politically themed movies since the 1970s, but 'that was a different time, and maybe it's gone,' he says. 'There's no Hollywood anymore, so let's just call it the mainstream. There's more investment capital available now and there are a lot more films out there, as you can see from this fall. The mainstream usually follows trends and seldom sets them.'

He believes it is much easier in the present political climate to make movies critical of the US administration. 'They have tanked in terms of popularity, whereas four or five years ago, you would be accused of being unpatriotic if you were negative about what the administration is doing. Now, with the exposure of the truth, it's easier, and there will be a lot of films about Iraq and about Afghanistan. I wasn't interested in making a film about the Iraq war because I knew that would be well covered by other films and documentaries, although the film contains the war as an element.'

One scene features the professor in a restaurant with the two students who go to war, and there is a striking contrast between the comfort of that environment and the fate that awaits them on the snowy mountains of Afghanistan. It makes one wonder why they would even dream of enlisting.

'These two young men have already been through far greater risks than other people, such as the student I'm trying to connect with in the film,' Redford says. 'Those guys grew up in neighbourhoods that are extremely risky, with drug wars and drive-by shootings, and they were lucky to survive that. They are in college on a part-time athletics scholarship, but they want to get an education and to get ahead.

'My character sees their potential, and his job is to inspire his students to aspire to greater things. What he didn't figure was they would make the choice to enlist, particularly as he had been in another war – Vietnam – that was a wrong one. Having told them not to sit on the sidelines, he is disappointed that they decide on the course of action that is to fight for their country.' We are living in a very complicated time with horrible results, he says.

'That's what I wanted to explore in the film – to look at the issues of where education is today, and the political administration and the media and the role of the citizen today. The film attempts to raise all these issues so that there is a debate going on and the audience can respond to it in their own way. The film provides questions rather than answers.'

Redford says that when he was growing up in Los Angeles, he couldn't have cared less about politics. 'Richard Nixon was my state senator and he was so boring. I thought that if that's what politics is – boring people in suits saying boring things – then I don't want any part of it.' His interests were in sport and in art and he decided to pursue his education by getting out into the world. He went to Paris when he was 18.

Nicole Hempenstall, from Ferns National School, Co. Wexford, with a water dragon from 'Dave's Jungle' presentation at Waterford Institute of Technology, as part of Science Week. Photograph: John Power.

'I didn't really think about politics until I came to Europe,' he says. 'I was asked to leave school because I was a very poor student, and anyhow, I wanted to experience other cultures and other histories. I had very little money and I stayed in a bohemian section of Paris with a lot of students from different backgrounds. We all lived in a communal way.

'I began to feel challenged politically because I didn't have a clue. That was in the late 1950s. The Algerian war was on at the time and was a hot issue in France. I felt humiliated that I didn't even know much about my own country's politics.

'That made me want to learn about it, which I did from European perspectives. When I did, I realised their point of view was very different from what I had been raised with. I was raised in California during the Second World War and into the 1950s, and everything was fine. The sun always shone. Everybody looked healthy, wore ties and smoked in restaurants, and there were cars for everybody.'

By the time Redford returned to the US after a year and a half away, he says he felt much more focused on his own country, politically and culturally.

As he became a successful actor, he took control over his career and began to produce his own films, expressing a critical outlook on his country in such politically themed films as *The Candidate*, *All the President's Men* and *Three Days of the Condor*.

In preparing *Lions for Lambs*, he says he was determined to avoid stereotyping, particularly in the case of the smooth Republican senator played by Cruise. I mention that the character resembles Democratic presidential contender John Edwards rather than a stock Republican caricature.

'I think they have the same hair stylist,' Redford jokes. 'But I don't believe in agit-propaganda. It would have been very easy just to talk about the present administration and the state of the country, but to me, that would have just been shallow. We all have some responsibility, all of us,

and we should look at it in a broader, deeper way.

'What could make the Cruise character dangerous is that he could be a better dressed-up version of what we have now. The idea was to present him as someone who was attractive and articulate and would be popular, tough-minded – and dangerous. To depict him as a moustache-twirling villain would have been pointless.'

Redford's stated intention was that each of the six main characters in the film would have a clear point of view. At one stage the senator asks the journalist what happens if the US leaves Afghanistan and the Taliban metastasises into something far worse than it is now. 'It is already far worse there since we started making the film in January,' Redford says. 'But the senator's main theme is winning. When he is asked why we invaded a country that did not attack us, he just dismisses it as the same old question people ask over and over, which is exactly what this administration says. I know that when this film is shown in the more conservative states, people will agree that the senator has a point and they will wonder why this lady is giving him a hard time in her interview.'

Given Redford's record as a supporter of the Democrats, conservative viewers surely will approach the film with caution, if they go at all. 'Considering where we are in this country and with all those right-wing bloggers out there, they're already condemning the film without even seeing it. They assume it is a left-wing film and I expected that. I've been an activist, but certainly not on the level of Michael Moore, for example. I haven't been out there slashing away.

'I've been focused more on the environment. I've very strong feelings about that, so I tend to stay in that area. I've been an activist on that since 1969, which was not an easy time. Those were the days when the oil and gas companies controlled the show in terms of propaganda. Anyone speaking about solar energy was dismissed as a radical or a tree-hugger or a granola-cruncher. I was out there feeling very often alone.'

The sunken fishing vessel Maggie B, *raised to the surface by a Dutch barge crane and re-floated off the Dunmore East coastline in Co. Waterford. Photograph: Eric Luke.*

The conversation turns to Al Gore receiving the Nobel Prize for his campaign on global warming. While Redford clearly welcomes the spotlight shone on the issue, he evidently is not an admirer of Gore.

'Al Gore is making a lot of money and he's having a belle époque, a heroic moment. He suffered enormously in the last election, partly through his own fault because he didn't run a good campaign. He presented himself as wooden and stiff, and Bush went in like a regular guy you could have a drink with, if that's what you want for your president. Our country is very focused on cosmetics. But I never believed that Bush won, or that it was a fair election. Anyhow, Gore has come back through speaking on the environment, and he got a lot of money behind him. The Clinton adminis-tration had a lot of money contacts, as you can see now with Hillary. They're capitalising on those contacts. Gore was able to call on that money to build himself a new campaign and pick an issue. And he picked an issue that just happened to arrive at its moment in time. Wall Street realised there was money to be made by going green, and the health issues finally came to roost.'

Having played a political contender in *The Candidate* and one of the journalists whose exposure of the Watergate scandal brought down Richard Nixon in *All the President's Men*, Redford insists that he has no interest whatsoever in pursuing a political career. 'No way,' he says. 'Right now the political system so restricts public office with compromise. First of all, I've no interest in compromise. And it's too constipated a system.'

Wesley Akinsehinde and Siobháin McCaffrey attract beams of light to their noses at yesterday's launch of Science Week 2007 in City Hall, Dublin. Photograph: Matt Kavanagh.

And who would Redford like to see in the White House in 2009? 'Well, just somebody different from what we've got, obviously, but I haven't found it out there yet. So far there's not anybody terribly inspiring.'

SATURDAY, 10 NOVEMBER 2007

Another One Down and A Few More to Get Across

Lorna Kernan

'Hello, my dear, Derek here.' It's John Derek Crozier, Mr Crosaire to *Irish Times* readers, on the other end of the telephone in Harare, Zimbabwe, last weekend. It's been a few years since we last spoke, but his rich, clipped tone has not changed.

Our distance is marked by that weird time delay which adds a double take. 'It's rather a fussy line. I can hear you more or less. Anyway, let's get down to it, what can I do for you?', and off we crackle about special numbers and the weaving of words.

The numbers are impressive: Derek Crozier celebrates his 90th birthday on Monday and has compiled the daily, cryptic, mind-bending Crosaire crossword for this newspaper for 65 years. 'When you come to think of it, I've made up the better part of 14,000 crosswords,' he says. For his 90th year, he has compiled a special crossword to accompany the weekly Saturday grid – he knows that its four-sided, 13-lettered edge is a particular favourite.

Crosaire was born in 1942 during a Christmas Eve party in the Palace Bar in Dublin's Fleet Street when, in a moment of bravado, Crozier announced that 'it's a sort of hobby of mine, making up crosswords' to *Irish Times* journalist Jack White. By the end of the night, after meeting legendary editor Bertie Smyllie and his deputy Alex Newman, the deal was done, and as Crozier has recounted, 'before you could say "word of six letters", I found myself committed to producing some samples in a few days.'

Crosaire has played a significant role for Crozier, and its support has come full circle. Nowadays, his retirement in troubled Zimbabwe is helped by compiling Crosaire. 'I try to do one Crosaire each day. The thing is, it takes about three to four hours and, there being eight working hours in the day, by the time I've completed one I'm like a wrung-out dishcloth and I really don't feel up to producing another. However, I do speed things up and try to do one-and-a-half a day if I fall behind. I can keep things going. That is if they are all right.' Of his early days on the land in the late 1940s, Crozier admits that 'whatever small importance the crosswords may have had for *Irish Times* readers, they certainly became of the greatest importance to us. They were our only, slender means of support while I was learning how to become a tobacco farmer.'

Currently, inflation is running at over 8,000 per cent and rising (€1 = 44,066 Zimbabwe dollars). 'Prices here have reached outlandish heights. Food can be scarce and Brian [his son] saw a leg of lamb for sale in a supermarket, but when he saw the price – $30 million – he thought again. Matches, the little things you use to light fires with, cost $1,000 each. That's not for a box of them, but for each match.'

Because of the problematic postal system in Zimbabwe, Crozier has had to entrust his precious brown packages to willing friends and friends of friends to bring to Ireland or the UK and post them on. One such reliable and willing friend of both Crozier and *The Irish Times* is Mona Watters from Inchicore in Dublin.

Mona, a few years behind Crozier at 84, is also a committed cruciverbalist, completing Simplex before doing the Crosaire every day. Mona has visited her sister Rita and family, near the Crozier family in Harare, every Christmas for many years. 'One day, my nephew's wife's grandmother,

Granny Pat, who used to look after Derek's wife Marjorie, God be good to her, said something and Crozier made a smart remark back to her. "Oh, be God", I said to him, "that was a right belt of a crozier." Pat didn't get it, of course, because as Derek said: "You're not Irish".'

Unfortunately, Mona won't be making the trip this year, and Christmas for Rita's family and the Croziers will be much poorer in her absence, not only for her brimming enthusiasm for life and her sense of humour, but for the many essential treats and goodies that she brought to make the season special.

Crozier explains how he manages the safe passage of his bundles of crosswords. 'You people send me Saturday's *Irish Times* and I pass that on to someone and, in return, he has a friend who often goes to Ireland with the crosswords. Are they not getting through?' They are indeed. 'Oh, I am glad they are.' Not only the post, electricity and essential services are turbulent. The family computer has been out of action for a while. 'A quack, if you would like to put it that way, who didn't know what he was doing, made a pig's ear of it and my other son, Brian's twin, is arriving tomorrow from New Zealand and he was hoping to bring something that would make things an awful lot better. I hope so, anyway.'

Crosaire's fans are numerous. Sheila Smith, who won the Crosaire competition last Christmas, says, 'I love doing it. I'm doing it 10 years. If you get to know the conventions it's kind of easy and it does exercise the mind.' Sarsfield Donovan, the 2005 Crosaire winner who has been doing it every day for 20 years and acknowledges that it is in the detail that Crosaire flourishes, says, 'Recently, within the clue he had the words "Blue" and "Malone". I thought it was a jazz trumpeter or something. I was wrong. The answer was "The last rose of summer", which blooms alone. It's a convoluted clue but they're the type I like.'

Michael Booth, who won a number of crossword competitions, is also a fan and friend: 'He's only a few years older than me; we went to the same school in Castle Park in Dalkey. I still do Crosaire every day. I couldn't live without it. I do it in very small letters because I have a friend who takes my paper and does the same crossword the very next day. She turns the crossword upside down, crosses out my letters, turns it back the right way and does it herself.'

Alan Dukes, who has been doing it every day for 20 years, acknowledges he enjoys 'second-guessing the way he does the clues. 'It's a mind-game. The day doesn't feel right if I haven't done the crossword.' Ruth Buchanan, who compiles and presents RTÉ Radio 1's *Playback* on Saturday mornings, has also been a Crosaire fan for years, and appeared with, among others, Sen. Feargal Quinn, on *The Late Late Show* in 1993, when Crozier was in Dublin for Crosaire's 50th anniversary.

Her Crosaire tale is generational. 'My father, who died in 1978, did Crosaire, and long before that I was always interested in words and word games. I used to do Simplex and sneak a look at Crosaire, but I just could never work it out for ages. In the end, my father said to me, "look, wait until I've finished it and then you can look at the answers and then at the clues." Of course, he would never give it to me anyway because there was only one *Irish Times* in the house.'

Speaking about his health, Crozier maintains he is 'feeling not a day over 90, but then again I'm not 90 yet, you see', while offering a message to his fans: 'I am eternally grateful to them because, for so many elderly people I know, time hangs heavily on their hands. I always have something to do and while it sounds very pompous, to feel I will still be of some use at 90 is just wonderful.'

Having put together a special birthday celebration crossword and sent on a recent photograph from Zimbabwe, and drawn breath at the kind words from fans and admirers, there is something very poignant in Crozier's concluding observation: 'I reckon that's all that poor old Crosaire deserves.'

Frankie Gavin plays 'Goldsmith's Lament' at the dedication of a seat in memory of Dr Noel and Phyllis Browne at Clochmór graveyard in Co. Galway. Photograph: Joe O'Shaughnessy.

MONDAY, 12 NOVEMBER 2007

Bench Marks Memory of Brownes

Lorna Siggins

'It is over now. His hands no longer reach out to mine as they did when, sitting by the turf fire in the evenings, we would listen to our favourite music. His goodnight smile and kiss upon my head are but memories.

'Yet I hear his gentle voice still, talk with him still. I feel his presence, but there is no consolation. It would probably surprise some people to know that Noel had a most loving, romantic side to his character.'

The words of the late Phyllis Browne, as read by Labour Party president Michael D. Higgins at the weekend, when a cut-stone bench in memory of her and her late husband, Dr Noel Browne, was unveiled at Clochmór graveyard, south Connemara.

'If a cemetery can be a beautiful place, Clochmór is one. It is such a fitting tribute that this is something that everyone can use and share,' Susan Browne, daughter of the couple, said, as she paid tribute to the friends involved in the project. Accompanying her at the memorial was her son Ruairí and daughter-in-law, Áine.

After the death of the former health minister in May 1997, his widow called almost every day to her neighbours, Garda Pat O'Connor and his wife, Annette, at Indreabhán until her death a year ago at the age of 86. 'They were wonderful to my parents, to my mother after my father's death, and now they have initiated this,' Ms Browne said.

Garda O'Connor, now retired, said, 'Well, Phyllis would go back to Noel's grave, and she would spend time there but she had nowhere to sit. So Annette and some friends decided this would be a good idea. And I think Noel would like the fact that this bench is already full of history, because the limestone came from a former Lady Gregory home at Roxborough house,' he noted.

Designed by Denis Goggin and Reamonn Ó Flaithearta, the bench of limestone and inscribed Connemara marble overlooks the Aran islands and the Atlantic. 'Those who sit here and reflect will be making a testament that an ethical view, or a radical dream of equality, does not end with one's physical passing,' Mr Higgins said.

The bench was funded by private contributions, and was blessed in bright sunshine at Clochmór cemetery by retired archdeacon Anthony Previte. The occasion was celebrated with music, including 'Goldsmith's Lament', played by fiddler Frankie Gavin and a box set by Kitty Noonan.

MONDAY, 12 NOVEMBER 2007

An Irishwoman's Diary

Eileen Battersby

It was late. The all-night car park had in fact closed at 1 a.m. and our station wagon was locked in. We had to wait. It was nearly 4 a.m. before that happy reunion took place.

In an attempt to salvage the night, I decided to post my credit card payment in Donnybrook, as the traffic was bound to be lighter than during working hours. Not since the days when I used to live in Dublin and always travelled by bike had I had such a pleasant few minutes gliding through the dry city streets.

All those bright lights. You forget about them in the country. Bright lights and that cold neon glow. The car was clean. I felt organised and was enjoying the fluency of driving without the usual city bumper-to-bumper crawl. But the fun lasted only about three minutes.

A riot appeared to be going on in Leeson Street. What political demonstration could possibly be taking place in the middle of the night? But no, there was no 'cause' at stake – it was not about race or religion; it was only the crowds vacating the night clubs.

People falling against each other, screaming, making vulgar gestures, four 20-something males, pants down, were busy seeing who could urinate the farthest. The watching girls added their comments, desperate not to be left out of something apparently as cultural as a urinating contest.

The car in front of us screeched to a halt as a youth threw himself in front of it. We slowed down; it would have been too easy to hit one of the drunken, flaying figures. Then, a couple of young men jumped on to the bonnet of my car while their pals slapped their hands against the windows and made grabbing gestures. My view was filled with smirking faces, teeth, fingers and hands.

Suddenly a jeering voice shouted at me. I turned around as a lanky character in a pink shirt screamed obscenities at me, lifted the tail gate and proceeded to climb into the back of my station wagon. I'd had enough and wasn't scared, just furious.

I stopped the car and pushed open the door, forcing another fellow who had been pounding on my window, busy calling me a 'fat old cow', to jump back out of my way. He seemed surprised and backed off.

Absolute rage is a strange sensation. It is as if your mind splits into two; one half was telling me to stay in the car and lock the door – the guy was already in the boot space – the other half was saying: 'Use your fists – you didn't have two brothers and spend all that time running, jumping, climbing and riding bikes and horses for nothing.'

My house had been burgled and ransacked recently and I hadn't forgotten that either. One of my dogs had been viciously beaten during the robbery; she has been left weakened, vulnerable, defeated by some swine who thought he was great, beating a brave young house pet with a cast-iron frying pan.

My tack had been stolen; saddles, bridles as well as computers, files and instruments, music, archive material, my daughter's violin. A disgusting mess of torn papers, letters, books, prints, maps had been left.

All of this surged through my mind and then, crazily, I also remembered I had a new bridle and a new horse rug – replacement tack – in the boot. I wasn't going to lose another horse rug. The rug became monumental.

Holding the keys in my hand, I ran out and snapped open the tail gate. 'Get out of my car,' I said in a low, menacing growl. 'Get out of my car.' The fellow laughed and stuck his fingers in my face.

'Get out of my car,' I repeated, pulling him by his hair. He stopped sneering and screamed in pain. I kept pulling and pulled so hard, a clump of sweaty hair came away in my hand. He shrieked as I grabbed his shoulder and half hauled him out. The intruder lurched away from the back of the car. I kicked him, maybe three times. I punched him in the face and felt my fist against his teeth. There was blood on my hand. I'm quite sure he didn't bite me. I slammed down the tail gate.

Then, as I turned around his jeering buddies, all middle-class boys with south Dublin accents, who had been chanting 'fat ugly c★★t', roared 'mad ugly bitch, mad ugly bitch' back – but they had stopped laughing.

Now they were indignant. Outraged. It was obvious what they thought. How dare I react with such bad temper? Had I not realised I was supposed to be crying and pleading for mercy?

I swung round and went to pull open the driver's door. A young fellow – young enough, as they all were, to be my son – kicked it closed. I turned and kicked him. Luckily for him, I kicked higher than I had intended and merely winded him. I could feel my foot landing in the soft pad of his stomach.

He fell over, though, and I got into the car and gunned it. No one played at blocking my path this time. On delivering the payment, I drove back to Leeson Street, intending to offer my two cents worth to the guards. But the street was empty.

Cartoon by Martyn Turner.

It's an ugly little story and I'm not proud of acting like a thug. I feel diminished for having been caught up in the sort of moronic, threatening 'fun' that is making driving through Irish streets almost as dangerous as walking them.

SATURDAY, 17 NOVEMBER 2007

Two-fisted Mailer Finally Counted Out

Sideline Cut, by Keith Duggan

One by one, the chroniclers of the Ali era are being counted out. Part of the enduring fascination with the 1970s period of Ali's life surely lies in the circus cast of characters that swirled around The Champ.

There is a brief and hilarious moment in the hugely popular film *When They Were Kings* that shows the late George Plimpton, the erudite American writer, struggling with his pencil and notepad to keep pace as Don King shoots rapid-fire quotations from Shakespeare at him, with the sound of African music reverberating in the background.

In retrospect, staging the Foreman-Ali fight in the middle of the African jungle seems like a wildly extravagant and absurd venture – as the *Los Angeles Times* columnist Jim Murray famously quipped, 'They are holding the world heavyweight championship in the Congo, I guess because the top of Mount Everest was busy.'

An airport employee washes the windows of the viewing area at Dublin airport's new Pier D boarding gate facility. It is intended that the pier will be used initially for short-haul aircraft on routes to and from the United Kingdom and continental Europe. Photograph: Kate Geraghty.

The setting for Ali's comeback bout against the cool and implacable and younger George Foreman – two African American men utterly different in disposition – dazzled imaginations across the world. And while millions had to be content to keep abreast of developments through radio or television, those with the means or good reason to be there were not going to miss it.

Central to the action was Norman Mailer, the literary tough guy and sometime sidekick of Ali who passed away last week aged 84. Mailer was, of course, a self-styled brawler and was accomplished enough at boxing to survive with the former light-heavyweight champion Jose Torres as a sparring partner – though how full-blooded the professional was in his application can only be speculated upon.

But Mailer, of course, was one of the many thousands of people openly and unabashedly fascinated by and in thrall to the charisma and power and beauty of Ali. He spoke and wrote of Ali as a fan and was possibly overawed by the fact that here was someone whose ego and vanity and successes and failures and penchant for humorous braggadocio were displayed in a personality that dwarfed even his own.

Although he became known as the definitive celebrity ringside witness to the triumphs and foibles of Ali, Mailer was genuinely stirred by boxing, a sport and culture that suited his complex, pushy, macho and often eccentric world view, and he wrote with vivid tough-guy tenderness about Ali's predecessors Floyd Patterson and Sonny Liston, who were portrayed as the white and dark angels of the game when they met in 1961.

That had been a hugely emotive fight, an elemental battle between a black American whose persona was acceptable to the prevailing white sensibility and a black American who was portrayed as being scarcely civilised.

Patterson found the effect of losing the heavyweight championship of the world in a single, terrorising minute so profound he disguised himself in glasses and wig and caught a flight to anywhere

– Madrid, as it happened – where he wandered in a daze for several days.

Famously, Mailer managed to hijack the victorious Liston's press conference the morning after by showing up drunk and convinced he alone, given half a chance, could transform a rematch into a hugely lucrative venture. Having arrived without the correct credentials, he was ejected from the room by security people responding assertively to Mailer's dare: 'Carry me out.'

Having inveigled his way back into the room, Mailer proceeded to harangue the new champion with his madcap theory that Patterson had existentially beaten Liston in the ninth round and tried again to advance his theory that he could be the saviour of a rematch. Liston engaged him with a mixture of patience and bemusement and laughed when Mailer accused the champion of calling him a 'bum'.

'Everybody's a bum,' Liston replied. 'I'm a bum too. It's just that I'm a bigger bum than you are. Shake, bum.'

Fifteen years later, Ali was probably the most famous man on the planet and was described by Mailer as America's greatest ego. 'Muhammad Ali begins with the most unsettling ego of all,' he wrote in a famous *Life* magazine essay titled Ego. 'Having commanded the stage, he never pretends to step back and relinquish his place to other actors – like a six-foot parrot, he keeps screaming at you that he is centre of the stage.

'He is also the swiftest embodiment of human intelligence we have had yet, he is the very spirit of the 20th century, he is the prince of mass man and the media.'

Over the years, Ali kept on boxing and slowly got hurt and Mailer had other fish to fry. The spark-eyed, barrel-chested and prodigiously busy writer lived a life that was, in its own way, as full-hearted and messy and vivid as that of his boxing hero.

He had his own furious spats that will be celebrated again now that Mailer has, to the probable disbelief of his detractors, fallen silent. Forget about his bitchy chat-show rows with literary rivals. He went bare-knuckle too. Already, the footage of his mano-a-mano fight with the actor Rip Torn, who attacked Mailer with a hammer on a film set in 1970, has been posted for general enjoyment on YouTube. It is half-riveting and half-comic, and at the end Mailer – then almost 50 years old – sits panting on the grass like a child, points at the younger man and shouts: 'He's hurt worse that I am.' Then he raises his dukes in a way that makes you wonder how he ever survived in the ring with Torres.

Generations of people who were not even born when Ali was in his prime continue to look back at the magnetism of the cast of characters and the depth of meaning those fights seemed to contain. Of course, the racket was probably as corrupt as ever and the commentators of the day probably tend to lionise that time somewhat sentimentally. But it was, clearly, an incredibly rich and unique chapter in sport and it seems a blessing now, in this age of electronic overload, that so many of the best essayists of the day were intrigued enough to tell the Ali story as they saw it.

Stories, as much as the balletic grace and cold power and limitless courage Ali displayed in the ring, have made him the enduring fascination of 20th-century sport. Mailer told them with all the zest and energy he could muster.

When Foreman was finally bested in that epochal fight in Kinshasa, Mailer remembered the end in The Fight.

'Like a drunk hoping to get out of bed to go to work, Foreman rolled over. Foreman started the slow, agonising lift of all that foundered bulk God somehow gave him, and whether he heard the count or no, was on his feet a fraction after the count of 10 and whipped, for when referee Zack Clayton guided him with a hand at his back, he walked in docile steps to his corner and did not resist. Archie Moore received him. Dick Sadler received him. Later, one heard the conversation.

"Feel all right?"
"Yeah," said Foreman.
"Well, don't worry, it's history now."
"Yeah."
"You're all right," said Sadler. "The rest will take care of itself."'

SATURDAY, 24 NOVEMBER 2007

Frank Views from 'A Very Short Fuse'

Sara Keating

Hugh Leonard's reputation precedes him, like a defence guard leading the way. There is the history of infamous spats with peers and rivals to contend with. The barbed wit so fluently and flagrantly exercised in his *Sunday Independent* columns. Not to mention his notoriously protective attitude towards his prolific volume of plays and prose. However, the cat-loving 'curmudgeon' seems more like a tom cat than a tiger. After 81 years of life, the spark of stubborn vitality still flickers around an uncomfortable question, but Leonard is, for the most part, a willing, almost professional, interviewee. It seems that the dual identity of the writer who renamed himself after a character in one of his own plays is more than skin deep.

Leonard has an enormous body of work, which has been widely loved by audiences world-wide but overlooked somewhat in critical circles. Despite the technical experiments of plays such as *Da* and *A Life*, the sharp social satires of *The Patrick Pearse Motel* and *Moving*, the reflected social history of Irish life in *Love in the Title* and *Summer*, Leonard has been largely dismissed as a writer of gentle, middle-class, living-room comedy, as if laughter were somehow easily earned.

However, as Leonard explains, '[the critics] trot out adjectives like "flippant" or "frivolous", but I take my plays very seriously indeed. And as

Playwright Hugh Leonard. Photograph: Eric Luke.

because my most famous play, *Da*, is set there. But I like to think of [the places] in my plays as any-places, anywheres. Brian Friel has Ballybeg and it is rather the same thing in my plays. A single place is common to most of my work, but it is not a real place. What I like to write about is a society that is in flux. Even when I wrote my autobiography, *Home Before Night*, even that wasn't really about me. It was about a place that is vanishing and soon wouldn't exist any more. It doesn't exist any more.'

Changes in the real Dalkey have merely given Leonard fuel for exploring these changes in his fictional work. 'Dalkey used to be a village. Now it's a car park. Joyce could go down Talbot Street and name every shop. You could do the same thing with Dalkey once upon a while, but there's no point in memorising shops now because they'll be gone tomorrow. It has gotten chic – that terrible word.'

Success is another terrible word, perhaps not for Leonard himself, but certainly for a nation of famous begrudgers, many of whom have seen Leonard's commercial success as a reason for dismissing him as a 'popular author' rather than a dramatic artist.

In reference to this begrudgery, Leonard quotes Noel Coward's barb about the 'British hatred of success', but he is happy to admit that he loved the red-carpet treatment he got in the US when *Da* won four Tony awards in 1978 and played on Broadway for almost two years. Reaction in Ireland, however, was 'more muted. There's a great story about that: Brendan Smith (founder of the Dublin Theatre Festival) went to Jack Lynch, who was taoiseach at the time, and said: "Don't you think we should have a guard of honour for Hugh when he comes back with the Tony?" Jack Lynch said: "No. I don't think that's called for – if he was a [member of a] winning hurling team then there would have been reason for it, but it's only a play." I didn't really mind, though. I was the first Irish writer to get a Tony.

for being [criticised for] handling a theme rather lightly or not being a political writer, well I know nothing about politics and have no interest in that sort of thing. As James Cagney used to say, "That's just not the kind of hairpin I am."'

Yet some of Leonard's finest work can be read as a serious engagement with changes in Ireland over the last 40 years, providing an alternative anatomy of the nation through the lives of middle-class urbanites rather than rural-dwelling peasants. 'In my plays,' Leonard insists, 'I think I write about a society that's changing, and not always for the better.'

It is the small community of Dalkey, where Leonard grew up and still resides, that seems to have served as a microcosm for exploring these changes, although Leonard believes that 'the con-nection with Dalkey has been foisted upon me,

Matthew Behan, a member of the 4th Port Dodder sea scouts, on duty at the annual commemoration service for seafarers lost at sea at City Quay in Dublin. The ceremony was organised by the Maritime Institute of Ireland. Photograph: Matt Kavanagh.

It's not up to me to boast about it, but it did mean a lot at the time.'

While the critical success of *Da* was confirmation for the writer mid-career, Leonard could certainly not be accused of over-valuing it. As he succinctly puts it: 'I was doing okay before then.'

Having cut his teeth on television plays in the 1960s – 'commuting to Manchester every week, and sneaking off on Thursdays for a long weekend' – Leonard was steadily writing an original play every year, and an adaptation every other, much of it premiering annually at the Dublin Theatre Festival ('I didn't regard a festival as a festival unless I had something in it').

Anyway, it has always been the audience rather than the critics that Leonard has looked to for confirmation. 'Of course I read reviews. Anyone who says they don't, well, their nose will get longer and longer until it falls off. Of course you are curious about reviews, but only in the commercial sense: you want to know if the public likes it, if the play is going to run. But on aesthetic grounds I don't bother with [reviews] at all. Usually the person gets the meaning totally wrong, and sees another play than the one you wrote.'

Academic investigation of his plays he finds similarly irksome. 'I never read anything [academics] say about my work. I think "That's not what the play is about," and I have to get up in disgust.' Leonard's defences seem to apply to posterity too. 'I don't keep anything: letters, playbills. I pity anyone who tries to write my biography.' And the valiant writer who might try would have an ever-increasing mountain of work to wade through too, as Leonard's new full-length original play – his 25th – *Magicality*, is currently being optioned in London after being turned down by the Abbey ('Fiach [Mac Conghail, Abbey director] said that it wasn't the kind of play that they wanted at the moment, but that they admired it greatly').

In fact, Leonard insists that he is 'busier than I have ever been. I think I'll have to give up the idea of retiring altogether. But my working day has shrivelled and I can only work in the afternoons now. That makes it more difficult. As you grow older you get slower, but your output, for what it's worth, is just as good.' His only regret as he reflects on his life is 'that I haven't done more work than I've done'.

Apart from writing, Leonard is busy 'mending a few fences. I have got a very short fuse, and I'm inclined to blow up. But when [an argument] is over, it's over. Michael Colgan and I were not on speaking terms for a long time, but recently we started talking again. He wanted to get me to agree to do *Great Expectations* at the Gate; I wanted him to do *Great Expectations* at the Gate. We met for lunch, neither of us knowing what the other one had in his mind. But we never discussed what the argument [between us] was and we never will. That's the way all quarrels should be. And there are other fences there too to be mended, but I'm not the one who [broke] them. There are probably two people who wouldn't talk to me at all again, which is not a bad record when you're my age.'

Great Expectations is one of his favourite adaptations for the stage, what with its 'immortal characters' and its involvement of the audience in the story – 'I hate Bertold Brecht,' he says with vehemence, 'an audience should always be involved.'

And his greatest achievement? He cites his 1974 play, *Summer*.

'It was the most difficult play to write. But I brought it off. The German dramaturg Gotthold Lessing said that in a good play every character is in the right, and in *Summer* the characters are all fallible, but nobody is bad. That is an important thing to remember' – and I can't help but think of that fearsome reputation again – 'There are no villains in life.'

WEDNESDAY, 28 NOVEMBER 2007

Finding a Reason for Crying Out Loud

It's a Dad's Life, by Adam Brophy

The younger has two speeds: standard and mayhem. With her fast approaching the end of her third year, we are hoping we can kiss goodbye the terrible twos and start to relax into something resembling a rational relationship with her.

The elder was the same at that age. She would regularly collapse on the kitchen floor and flail and judder until the anger passed. Our approach with her was initially bewilderment, followed by containment. We would sit with her until some evidence of human life would return, by which time the room she was in might have been thrashed.

We are firmer with the younger. When the tantrum starts we attempt to understand the reason and resolve it. That invariably fails and the child is gently escorted to her room, deposited on her bed and told she can return when the screaming has stopped. This has become a part of the dance. She no longer rails against her expulsion, she sits back against the wall and exalts in the remainder of her primal scream. Within minutes she is back downstairs, a little sheepish but able to explain what upset her in the first place.

The first time this type of behaviour was exhibited by her big sister I sat back in astonishment at the force of the anger as it swept through the child. I had been warned about this level of tantrum, but nothing could have prepared me for its actuality. When my shock abated, my concern was that she might hurt herself, but this never quite happened. Instead, she would simply wear herself out to the point of an exhausted, whimpering state.

What shook me was I recognised her anger. The elder is a carbon copy of me in many ways. She looks, walks and talks like me. Even her rage rings bells, but fortunately I have learned not to collapse and howl at the moon in response to some hurt, real or perceived. And so, with the passing of time, has she. When she hurts, I can usually understand why. I may or may not sympathise, but I can put my finger on the reason.

The younger, on the other hand, is an enigma. She comes from her mother's side, and there I have no insight. Now, with a little more experience under my belt, I am no longer terrified by the regular demonic possession of the child, but I struggle to understand it.

Because of this, I overcompensate. I try so hard to be her 'go-to guy' but she bats me away without a second thought as she runs for cover in her mother's skirts. Her mum gets her, I'm just some lanky git who drives her around. I bring her places, I buy her things, I simper to her that we're having special times in the hope that when she's older she'll look back with misted eyes and reminisce to her friends how she and her daddy bonded.

I try way too hard.

The elder saunters up, gives my hand a squeeze and throws me a look as if to say, 'It's all right, Daddyo, I got your back.' Then, last week, the younger didn't want to go to crèche. She was all weepy and stubborn. I checked with her that nothing untoward had happened and it seems she just wanted to stay home. I spoke to the crèche manager and was assured they would keep a close eye on her that day.

That night, picking the girls up, I am told the younger had been speaking about her upset. Apparently, her report went something like this: 'I was crying. I didn't want to go to crèche. Because I miss my daddy.' Result.

A Short Life Lived in a Blaze of Flashbulbs

Quentin Fottrell

If this had been a fairytale, she would have woken up. For one long week, she was a modern-day sleeping beauty. But, for once, we didn't need photographs to imagine Katy French lying motionless in her hospital bed, in a coma, or a deep sleep, her family standing over her, praying that she would wake up.

But this wasn't a fairytale. One week to the day after she arrived at her 24th birthday bash at Dublin's Krystle nightclub in a Rolls Royce, wearing a gold-sequinned dress from Chica and Gucci shoes, she died at Our Lady's Hospital in Navan in the arms of her sister.

Those labels are part of her story. She was a model, after all. What began as an extraordinary rise to fame, in a blaze of flashbulbs and photo opportunities, has become a morality tale for the dying days of the Celtic Tiger. She wanted to live her life in front of a camera lens, amid a ravenous photographic rat-pack largely made up of middle-aged men.

This was a career forged by a brass neck, luck and chutzpah, with a little help from Corporate Ireland. Even her tributes mention the labels she was wearing on the night she celebrated her birthday. 'She lay across the bar in her gold dress like a mermaid for the photographers,' one guest recalled. 'This girl knew what she was doing. She had a game plan. She wanted to be a TV presenter. She saw herself as a brand.'

Beauty . . . and the beast, a vast corporate machine, prying eyes lying in the long grass that she was, perhaps, not so wary of. Newspapers, clothing companies, magazines, drinks companies, TV stations, even the nightclub itself. Everybody had a product to sell and Katy French was It. Her

Katy French. Photograph: Haydn West.

birthday party reportedly cost €50,000. If that is true, which I doubt, she probably didn't pay for it.

She knew what she was doing. On *Celebrities Go Wild* and *The Podge & Rodge Show*, where she spoke about her spat with her former fiancé, restaurateur Marcus Sweeney, who broke up with her after he walked in on her modelling lingerie in his restaurant, she denied it was a stage-managed publicity stunt. Still, the abusive text messages he allegedly sent to her made it into a Sunday newspaper. Before her appearance on *Podge & Rodge*, the show's co-presenter, Lucy Kennedy, did a vox pop item, 'Who is Katy French?' Members of the public probably enjoyed pretending they didn't know who she was. They answered, 'A C-list celeb?' and 'I'd say she don't work on the roads' and, finally, 'Is she a model?'

'Is she a clever minx or just a sphinx without a secret?' Kennedy asked. 'Please welcome controversy-hungry model Katy French . . . whoever she is!' The studio audience cheered. They weren't at home alone in front of their computers, writing anonymous comments on message boards now. Those who get audience tickets for *Podge & Rodge* comprise a large, revolving peanut gallery who desperately yearn to see their least favourite celebrities humiliated and/or publicly flogged.

She also made appearances on *The Late Late Show* and *Tubridy Tonight*, where she told Ryan Tubridy she would like a job like his. She was no longer a model in St Stephen's Green, advertising lager or tequila. She had ambition. That threatens the peanut gallery.

The *Podge & Rodge* clip has been watched nearly 40,000 times on YouTube (and counting). Some online comments say RIP, others are profane, cruel even, making lewd remarks about whether she died from a drug overdose.

The inevitable, sentimental tabloid editorials made the cringeworthy comparisons to her being our own Princess Diana. But Diana was fleeing the media when she died. Katy French was, at the pinnacle of a new phase in her career, chasing it.

Her birthday bash was supposed to be part of *Diary of a Model*, to be screened on TV3.

She was a candidate to host another documentary, *So You Want To Be Famous*, to be screened on RTÉ 1 in January. It is a tongue-in-cheek show. She would have been a participant and a topic. I was supposed to film a talking head piece to camera with her yesterday. I didn't know her, I told the producers, but it still didn't feel right. She was the poster girl for the fame game, after all.

The producers held a meeting and decided to continue with the documentary and 'not refer to her at all during the series'. By airbrushing her out, I said, it doesn't remove her presence. That's ironic, considering the title of the programme – and the fickle nature of the beast. They were making the wrong programme about fame, I said. But the producers were adamant – they were too far into filming and friends of Katy were happy to go ahead. If they were 'friends', I'm not sure they were the kind of friends she needed.

She would have been aghast at the media frenzy: a top story on RTÉ 1's *Nine O'Clock News*, front-page coverage on newsstands all week, even a questionable *Prime Time* tie-in about cocaine with another 'friend'.

The shy, gifted actor Tom Murphy, who died earlier this year, didn't receive this kind of tribute. Nor did Kevin Doyle, the 21-year-old Waterford man who died of a cocaine overdose earlier this week. This was the kind of fame she probably only dreamed of. And yet she never got to experience it.

Katy French didn't have a message. But she searched for one. She joked about vibrators, spoke earnestly about her past cocaine use and travelled to India as a goodwill ambassador for Goal. With her death, the girl who grew up in the sleepy town of Enniskerry became the message. About the perils of fame and, perhaps, other darker forces. She paid a very high price for that. But, as a powerful lesson to young people everywhere, this could be her greatest gift of all.

Survivor Recalls Agony of Chinese Massacre

Clifford Coonan, in Beijing

Zhang Xiuhong is still angry, even 70 years after the event.

'I really, really hate the Japanese. I was raped when I was 11-years-old. I tried to commit suicide three times afterwards,' said Zhang (81), as she recalled the six week-long 'Rape of Nanking', when hundreds of thousands of Chinese were slaughtered by invading Japanese troops who breached the Ming Dynasty city walls of the wartime capital.

The ground assault began 70 years ago this week and is still known as China's Holocaust, and many here in this southeastern city, now called Nanjing, believe the Japanese have failed to atone sufficiently for their wartime crimes.

For their part, many conservative Japanese believe the Chinese are exaggerating the scale of the incident.

'I've repeated this thousands of times. This was in February 1938. I pretended to be dead so the soldier would go away,' said Zhang, who is quite deaf and relies on her daughter-in-law to communicate. 'They raped young girls and grabbed young babies from their mothers and bayoneted them in the behind. They beat me on many parts of my body and I still can't walk well,' said Zhang, now crying as she revisits the period.

The Japanese invasion began on 10 December and the city fell three days later, signalling the start of the 'Rape of Nanking'. Eyewitnesses, both Chinese and western, say Chinese captives were tortured, burnt alive, buried alive, decapitated, bayoneted and shot en masse. Up to 80,000 Chinese women and girls of all ages were raped and many more murdered or forced into sex slavery. The Chinese say the invaders killed 300,000 civilians, while many in Japan say it is far less. A wartime tribunal put the figure at 142,000.

Many right-wing Japanese historians regularly dispute whether the massacre ever took place at all, and the event has left enormous psychological scars in China, remaining a huge stumbling block in

A visitor walks past a sculpture at the Memorial Hall of the Victims in the Nanjing Massacre in Jiangsu province, China, that marks the 70th anniversary of the killings. Photograph: China Photos/Getty Images.

Cartoon by Martyn Turner.

relations between Beijing and Tokyo.

For the communist government in Beijing, the incident is a crucial event in post-revolution history, a milestone in the war against Japanese aggression. There were riots in Beijing as recently as 2005 over regular visits by Japanese leaders to the Yasukuni shrine, which honours war criminals among the country's war dead and is seen as an enormous insult by many Chinese, and attempts to whitewash history in schoolbooks, as the Chinese see it.

Since 2005, relations have warmed considerably between Asia's dominant power, Japan, and its rising superpower, China. While the 70th anniversary is being marked in Nanjing, it has taken on a relatively low profile in the country as a whole, and senior leaders are not attending the main events.

It's a raw tale here in Nanjing. During a news conference to announce details of a new memorial to the victims of the massacre, a Japanese journalist asked what the panel thought about concerns that the figure of 300,000 was exaggerated. This is the kind of question that can wind you up in jail in the EU for denying the Holocaust if you ask about the Nazi extermination campaign which claimed the lives of six million European Jews.

Zhu Chengshan, curator of a new memorial being built in Nanjing to commemorate the incident, fielded the question. 'The Nanjing massacre is historical fact and is only one in a series of outrages perpetrated on China by the Japanese aggressors . . . the figure of 300,000 is historical fact. There is no reason for people to doubt the number,' he said, to loud applause from the Chinese journalists.

The centrepoint of the new museum is a wall with a wreath containing a picture of a victim that changes every 12 seconds to represent how many people died during the six-week massacre.

Many countries who were invaded by Japan during the war, which in China lasted from 1931 until 1945, still feel that Tokyo has yet to say sorry properly, despite billions being paid in war reparations.

A sign of Japanese ambiguity about the issue came in the respected *Yomiuri Shimbun*, which wrote in an editorial yesterday: 'On the number of victims of the Nanjing Incident, the Chinese government has not revised its official tally of 300,000. Indeed, when the Japanese forces wiped out the remaining Chinese soldiers hiding in the city, many executions and violence against civilians obviously took place, according to records and testimonies from the time.

'However, there are theories that the number of victims was about 40,000 and that only a fraction of those deaths were murders that violated international law,' ran the editorial.

'Recently, even some Chinese scholars say scholarly debate should be deepened on the number of victims. Such a flexible stance has started to be aired. The Nanjing Incident is an important area for bilateral joint studies on history conducted by Japanese and Chinese historians. It is necessary for Japan and China to jointly proceed with empirical research toward the final report to be compiled next year,' it wrote.

Such comments are anathema here and there is no denying the power of Zhang's testimony.

'One day three Japanese soldiers came in. We told the Japs (sic) that we are farmers and that father was not a soldier. So the Japs beat my father on

Belfast mayor Jim Rodgers with Travellers Catherine Connors (left) and Margaret Dundon at the Waterfront Hall in Belfast. Travellers' representatives from both sides of the Border said new research stressed the importance of the nomadic part of their culture. Photograph: Paul Faith/PA.

both sides of the face and kicked me into the corner of the house. The second day, the troops burnt all the houses and we had to live in straw huts in the fields,' she said.

'Because of the violence of the rape they tore me down there and it was hard for me to give birth afterwards. I only had one child and it took me three days and three nights,' she said.

'I remember one day when I was in the field, there were piles of rice husks and the Japanese bayoneted the stacks to see if people were hiding in there.

'I was in a small bale and they cut my finger when they stabbed the stack,' she said, holding up her hand to show where the bayonet cut her finger. 'They burned the bigger stacks and I saw people burnt alive.'

Li Gaoshan (83) was a 12-year-old boy soldier during the invasion. Even after 70 years living in Nanjing, the capital of Jiangsu province, he is keen to point out that he comes from Guangdong province.

'There were dead people everywhere in the streets. We didn't dare to go out during the day because of the aerial bombings.

'I escaped when soldiers tried to shoot me in the head. I managed to escape and took shelter with some civilians who gave me civilian clothes.

'We want world peace, and we want the world to know about the Nanjing massacre,' he said.

FRIDAY, 14 DECEMBER 2007

Toys that Talk the Talk

Fiona McCann

Bless me father for I've grown up: it's been 20 years since my last toy shop. Truth is, without children of my own, or even nieces, nephews, or neighbourly offspring, I had no occasion to visit one, and spent much of my adult life unaware that Heelys weren't just evening shoesies and Bratz did not refer to other people's illiterate children.

The last time kiddies' toys played any part in my life, the Minipops were topping the charts and Lolo Balls were *de rigueur*. Since then, I've been living in a relatively toy-free zone until the arrival of my first niece sent me zooming off to Jervis Street like an Evel Knievel Stunt Cycle, in search of modern-day playthings for Iseult.

Despite a strong desire to head straight for the tack and plastic that is my natural home, I did at least begin with a quick nip into the Early Learning Centre in an attempt at responsible aunthood. And lo, as I searched for toys to improve my niece's mind, it turned out that every single toy out there can improve my niece's mind, if you try hard enough to market it that way.

Well. I'm willing to accept the claims that the Honey Bee Tree helps children with their 'fine motor skills' and 'problem solving': after all, if you don't pull out the tiny plastic leaves in time the bees will fall down and then duh, you have a problem — who wants fallen bees on their hands? It does, however, seem to me that the best lesson here would be to teach children to stay away from bees altogether. As I do not wish for Iseult to be stung by angry insects no matter how fine her motor skills, I move on.

The baking and cooking section seems like a place one might learn things of benefit, the kind of skills that could earn her points should she ever appear on *Big Brother* or *Ready Steady Cook*. The first thing I find is a wooden smoothie-maker, a discovery from which I shy away, reflective as it is of the sorry downward spiral of Irish society from fried rashers to squashed fruit. But look! There's also a wooden toaster, which promises not only to help Iseult learn how to 'make friends' and 'enjoy company', but will also 'instil confidence, helping her feel secure and happy and enjoy good self esteem'.

Enjoy good self esteem? Because she can make fake plastic toast? Who knew it was so easy! Enough of the worthy. Toys, I have once again been reminded, are meant to be fun — and not because you're laughing at them — so I gravitate with some excitement towards the Tower of Doom. The Tower of Doom! No esteem-boosting properties here, one imagines – it promises evil, malice and DOOM! I am at once captivated by its menacing exterior until I notice that the packaging is at pains to clarify that the Tower of Doom is made from Forest-Friendly Wood. Well it's hardly the Tower of Doom then, is it? The Tower of Doom to All But Forests! Bah.

The abundance of wholesome playthings has left me cold, and I am in need of the kind of nasty additive-rush that I haven't got since E123 was an acceptable food ingredient. Smyths' toy mecca beckons, where I aim to lose myself in the plastic delights of children's toys and the aisles and aisles of playthings for the 21st-century kid who has it all but wants more anyway.

My, how things have changed since the days of Fisher-Price record-players and space-hoppers. Plastic laptops abound, play kitchens have phones in them, everything is branded and Bratz have taken over the free world. Incidentally, this year you can get the most pose-able Bratz ever! Pose-able? Since when has that been a desirable characteristic for your doll? Come to think of it, since when has Roscommon been the most expensive property on Monopoly? There's little I recognise, although this may be because my vision has become impaired by the plethora of pink. Ah, how far we've come. Now children's kitchens have telephones in them, but girls continue to get pink toys.

Still, in a nod to the joyous gender stereotyping of my youth, I proceed to the baby doll section to find something for my niece.

'Aisles and aisles of baby faces stare glassily at me, lifelike in their vacant expressions and pursed lips, their little plastic baby hands clenched in rigid, vice-like grips' – Fiona McCann samples the toys in Smyths of Jervis Street, Dublin. Photograph: Alan Betson.

Cartoon by Martyn Turner.

All I can say is thank God those waxy-looking baldies are in boxes! Aisles and aisles of baby faces stare glassily at me, lifelike in their vacant expressions and pursed lips, their little plastic baby hands clenched in rigid, vice-like grips. On closer inspection, they all appear to have talking capabilities too, which makes me even more grateful that the batteries are not included. It is a staggering, nauseating array: rows upon rows of Baby Borns, Baby Annabells, Baby Aimees, Baby Petites. It appears toy companies have a little bit to learn about family planning.

What to purchase is another question entirely, and frankly with so much competition out there these days, baby dolls have had to broaden their repertoire in order to capture the attention of your discerning two-to-six year-old. Baby Alive wets and wiggles, as nobody has thought to tell her it's nothing to be proud of, while Fisher-Price My Baby plays peek-a-boo and can hold her teddy all by herself, fair play to her. But can she beat Talking and Singing Lisa, who can speak to you in full sentences despite otherwise resembling a three-month-old baby?

Then there's Dancing Baby With Magic Rattle who does a disturbing shimmy to the strains of B-I-N-G-O. Baby Aoife burps – yes! Burps! – while Chou Chou Mummy Make Me Better (to use her full name) has a pink bruise which disappears and reappears. Hard to top, despite Sneezing Baby's valiant efforts.

The clear non-contender is Lifelike Baby Expressions Doll, mainly because she is the ugliest, most Yoda-looking doll on the block, although her shtick is that her face boasts a range of expressions to put Nicole Kidman to shame. Four, to be exact.

Perhaps I should eschew life-like dolls altogether, and go for something that doesn't even attempt to resemble human form. There's a best-friend robot called Sakura. Apparently, you can tell her your secrets and she won't tell anyone. Hmmm, you think that might be because she's a doll?

In fairness to Sakura, if she does keep mum, she'll be the only thing in Santa's busy workshop that does. These days, you're not a real toy until you can address your owner. Even Girls' World, the free-floating hair-styling head, is talking now. Then there are newcomers Podge and Rodge who have their own stud-farmer dolls on sale that enunciate such delightful early-learning phrases as 'Ya scuttering gobsheen' and 'Axe the back of me sack'.

But somewhere in this morass of all-singing, all-dancing, all-in-your-face toys there are old favourites that have changed little enough to send me spinning into nostalgia. Tiny Tears is still there, and although she has been rebranded as Classic Tiny Tears, it's somehow good to know there are dolls out there that still only cry and wet their nappies. Games like Connect 4, Cluedo and Guess Who? are also still on the shelves, although with newfangled graphics and packaging.

It's also nice to see the Game of Life still doing the rounds, and rumour has it that while new 'Life' elements have been added that include recycling and computer consultant jobs, it still works on much the same premise as it used to. Mind you, in my day, the smart move for a Game of Lifer was to go into journalism, as hacks were the highest paid in the game, reeling in a cool £20,000 – a damn sight more than the lawyers and streets ahead of paltry businessmen. Imagine how such a game would improve Iseult's skills as a fantasist? Maybe I'll buy her a Honey Bee Tree after all.

TUESDAY, 18 DECEMBER 2007

A Lesson for Primary Schools

Fintan O'Toole

Imagine a country so poor that it has no national primary school system. The state doesn't set up schools for children, but leaves the task to parents and local groups.

Teachers and parents spend much of their time trying to collect money for basics like water and heat. We don't have to imagine this country, of course, because – except for the bit about being poor – we live in it. But we are so used to the absurd situation of primary education in Ireland that we forget how crazy it is that one of the most basic tasks of modern states is left to a ramshackle network of over 3,000 private institutions. Maybe

we need the even greater absurdity of forcing parents to pay for the water used in the schools their children attend to shock us into realising that we can't go on like this.

Last week, the Minister for Education, Mary Hanafin, announced 'a new State model of community national school'. As if finally waking up to the impossibility of the current, largely religious, voluntary system, she outlined the development of a new kind of primary school, one that will be under the patronage of a Vocational Education Committee and 'open to children of all religions and none'. This is a welcome development in principle but, in reality, it represents a response so timid that it seems to ignore the very problems that have prompted it. The 'new State model' will amount to a pilot project of three schools, all of them in the Dublin area. And it is envisaged as an addition to, rather than a reform of, the current system. In effect, even the model will apply only in areas where new schools are being planned and where there is a sufficient concentration of population to make a choice of schools practical.

What is completely absent is any acknowledgment that the current model doesn't work any more. It was based on two assumptions. One was that every child belonged either to the Catholic parish or to one of a small number of other faiths for whom special provision could be made. The other was that the parish could act as an informal alternative to the taxation system, raising money from the faithful and using it to fund some of the cost of building a school and most of the cost (apart from salaries) of running it.

Those assumptions no longer apply. The Catholic parish is no longer, in a more diverse society, an adequate synonym for 'the community'. The limited role of the State that was built into the system arose from conditions that have long since disappeared. The State, when the system evolved, was the United Kingdom and most Irish people, for obvious religious and political reasons, didn't like the notion that it would be shaping the minds

Early morning sun climbs into the sky over Sandymount Strand in Dublin as Paula Metcalfe walks her dogs, Jett and Pippan. Photograph: Dara Mac Dónaill.

of Irish children. And primary education itself has gone from being a marvellous modern innovation to being a basic provision.

Nor does the system work in practice. The fantasy that primary schools are essentially private institutions to which the State, in its beneficence, contributes some financial support, translates in reality into grossly inadequate funding. The State spends 4.6 per cent of GDP on education – the OECD average is 6.2 per cent. Less of what it does spend goes to primary education than to any other sector – the capitation grant for a child at primary school is not much more than half of that for secondary school. The result is that most schools teeter on the edge of bankruptcy. Eighty per cent of schools depend on fundraising, not to acquire extras, but to pay for the basics: heat, light, insurance, telephone,

cleaning, and now water. In 200 schools surveyed by the Irish Primary Principals Network last year, the average grant was €25,000 and average running costs were €48,000.

It's not just about money, though. The notion of primary schools as individual, private entities results in a critical lack of management. The State can track every calf born on an Irish farm from birth to dinner plate, but it has no record of the passage of children through the primary school system – where they're coming from, what their needs are, how they get on, where they go to. How could it have, when we don't actually have a national primary system? Meanwhile, at local level, boards of management are asked to deliver a crucial public service without training, resources or support.

Unsurprisingly, they in turn are generally unable to support the school principals whose job of managing, fundraising and in many cases teaching as well, is becoming unsustainable. A report by the Department of Education's inspectorate found 'little or no evidence of collaborative approaches to the realisation of plans that involved parents or members of the board of management'. Yet members of boards of management find themselves personally liable for everything from damages for pupils abused by teachers to water charges. Their altruism is being exploited merely so that the State can avoid its responsibility to provide an education system. If, when they see their water bills, they all decided to resign en masse, would the Government learn a useful lesson?

WEDNESDAY, 19 DECEMBER 2007

Perfect Time of Year to Visit this 'Floating' Italian City

Letter from Venice, by Paddy Agnew

It is a freezing December morning in Venice. We are walking along a little calle (as a street in Venice is called), fortified by a decent cappuccino and on our way to the next tourist appointment, namely a look around the inside of a perfectly restored 17th-century Venetian house at the Querini-Stampalia museum.

And then it happens. As we walk over one of Venice's 400 or so little canal bridges, we hear it quite clearly. Down below us in the rio (canal) a gondola goes by, complete with accordion player and impressively loud tenor. It might be freezing in December, but this guy is belting it out. In the gondola there are two seemingly well-satisfied, oriental tourists – they have seen it at the movies and now they are living it out, the Venetian dream.

Venice, of course, is like that. Or perhaps one should say, still like that. Despite everything, the magic of Venice survives, the magic of a city of beguiling beauty caught not only between land and sea but also between the twin demands of ensuring commercial survival while at the same time safeguarding its unparalleled cultural patrimony. Or put another way, the magic of a city with approximately 60,000 residents and 18 million tourists.

For those who have never been to Venice, there is only one word of advice – go visit it at the first opportunity. There cannot be that many places that deserve a 'Must-See-Before-You-Die' tag, but Venice quite clearly is one. December, despite the cold, is a good time to go since it is one of those rare Venetian moments when there are relatively small numbers of tourists around.

To be in Venice on a warm summer's day is to find yourself stuck in an unending, human traffic jam. In December, however, the cold, the grey sky and the mist all add to the magic of this mysterious place.

For many, Venice conjures up images of gondolas, San Marco, the Rialto and the Grand Canal – in short images of breathtaking beauty. Yet, Venice also prompts images of a decaying city in seemingly permanent crisis, an image that every now and then is reinforced by some terrible disaster. Remember the burning down of the city's famous opera house, La Fenice, 11 years ago. It prompted the great Italian conductor Riccardo Muti to express his frustration, shame and embarrassment when he publicly asked just how did a theatre in the centre of a city famous worldwide for being built on water manage to burn down 'because water couldn't be found to put the fire out'. That unhappy event is behind Venice now. At one point in our ramblings last week, we came round the corner to the welcome sight of the revamped and restored Fenice, apparently doing very good business indeed.

Yet, Venice remains an intractable sort of place. How else do you explain the delays that have bewitched the building of the city's 'fourth bridge' over the Grand Canal. Designed by the Catalan architect Santiago Calatrava, this project was first announced in 1996, and funding of approximately €4.5 million was awarded by the Venetian municipal authorities in May 1999.

Yet when you pull into Piazzale Roma, the arrival point for most visitors, you find the bridge – still unfinished and still apparently under construction. Complex problems regarding the feasibility of the project, the strength of the bridge, its impact on the canal bank and Laguna floor, not to mention an expensive row between builders and suppliers, have all caused huge delays with the project.

All of Venice seems permanently under threat. One night last September bits of the façade of one of the city's most famous buildings, the Palazzo Ducale or Doge's Palace, just fell off, plummeting straight into the canal below. Earlier this month, divers pulled no less than 19 bits of marble that belong to the palazzo's façade out of the canal.

The divers had been sent down by the magistrate called to investigate the collapse. His problem, however, will be to work out whether the bits of marble relate to this most recent incident or any of a number of earlier ones.

Quite literally, Venice is, and for some time has been, falling apart.

In what other major European city do you see warning notices about the high tide on the town walls, explaining to citizens that three grades of sound alarms will ring out according to the state and height of the 'aqua alta' (high tide flood)?

Where else, too, do you see ground floor houses advertised with the comforting assurance that the house is 'esente dal alta marea' (safe from the high tide)?

Perhaps it is a good thing that the city's current mayor Massimo Cacciari is a philosopher by profession. So much has to be taken philosophically in Venice, including the mayor's most recent and provocative declaration that the future of Venice lies on 'terra firma'. That was a reference to the nearby town of Mestre and to the shipyards

and petrochemical complex at Marghera, all of which form part of 'greater Venice' but which are studiously avoided by any right-minded tourist.

The mayor seemed to be suggesting that Venice could not live by tourism alone, but was he serious?

Yet, life in the centre of Venice costs nearly twice as much as on dry land. For those running a business, transport costs are doubled by the water-bound last leg of the journey through the canals. Business, too, can be stymied by the fact that even the most basic building or maintenance project may require up to 35 different approvals from various city hall offices.

In the end, only those in the tourist trade appear to thrive in Venice.

Not, mind you, that they are going to be crying into their calice (cup) this festive season in Venice. If all goes according to the plans of promoter Marco Balich, Piazza San Marco will be vying for a place in the Guinness Book of Records on New Year's Eve when 60,000 people are expected to take part in a massive 'Kiss-In' in the famous square. Balich sees the event as one way of ensuring that images of Venice go worldwide on the night of 31 December.

Forget Venice? No danger of that.

FRIDAY, 21 DECEMBER 2007

Tribunal Attacks Bertie's Dobson Defence

Miriam Lord

Throughout this sorry saga, there is one constant. It has always been the elephant in the room that nobody really wants to recognise, because it is too embarrassing and far too private. Nobody wants to intrude. Yet, on bar stools and around dinner tables the length and breadth of this country, it is the issue that people bring up again and again.

It was Bertie Ahern, who, with a heavy heart and a tear in his eye, first led this lumbering beast into the spotlight. And there, he abandoned it, to nobody's advantage except, perhaps, his own.

Of course we were always aware of the beast's presence – far too big to ignore. But we are decent people and we avert our eyes. It was one of the reasons the Opposition pulled back from an all-out attack when the story of Bertie's strange financial history broke in September 2006.

Call it the Dobson Defence. How can we forget that evening on the news, when a proud Taoiseach stifled his emotions and revealed in painful detail to Bryan Dobson the circumstances surrounding the break-up of his marriage? He didn't want his private affairs made public, and as he spoke, his inner turmoil was apparent.

And the viewing public, the compassionate man and woman in the street, looked beyond headlines and political scalps, recognising the difficulties that can face a man when his relationship falls apart and he must leave the family home.

The Dobson Defence: his money problems were all to do with separating from his wife. Who amongst us doesn't know of someone with a similar story to tell? There were many who listened to him tell his story and thought: 'I am that soldier.' It could never be raised in public, and certainly would never be broached in public by Bertie Ahern, but we are all men and women of the world. So people nod knowingly and whisper to each other about a fella wanting to salt a few bob away for himself, away from the missus and her lawyers.

Not that we are suggesting for one moment that this is what Bertie Ahern was doing when he suddenly developed an aversion to banking his money, running his entire life on a cash-only basis. But a person can't help thinking, and you know yourself . . . These things happen, even to an outwardly successful and undeniably capable man like Bertie.

Yesterday in Dublin Castle, the Dobson Defence loomed large again. As tribunal lawyer Des O'Neill repeatedly pressed the Taoiseach about his bizarre approach to his personal finances back in the early 1990s, Bertie always fell back on the same explanation.

'Because I was separated.'

'That's the way I lived.'

His demeanour in the witness box was far different to how it was three months ago, when he suffered a torrid time in the face of Des O'Neill's forensic examination. Back then, there were times when he seemed a beaten man, a lonely, almost cowed figure. But Bertie was angry yesterday and he fought all the way. He sat hunched, arms folded across his chest, glowering at the senior counsel. The Taoiseach was affronted by his questions, the tone of them and their content.

Bertie Ahern on his way into the Mahon Tribunal. Photograph: Niall Carson/PA.

Cartoon by Martyn Turner.

Bertie had been going through a lengthy separation. Separation – get it? Did he have to spell it out? At any moment, one expected him to repeat the exasperated line he barked at Eamon Gilmore recently in the Dáil. 'Are ya deaf or stupid?' But he didn't. He didn't have to – his snippy remarks and seething resentment said it for him.

If his predicament was due to his personal problems at the time, some of us would have joined him in telling Des O'Neill, as Bertie did, that how he disbursed his money was 'none of your damn business!'

But too much has been heard in evidence thus far, and too many contradictions thrown up, to end the matter there. If Deathly Des ever sounds sincere, it is when he tells Ahern with feeling that he has no interest whatsoever in prying into his private arrangements.

The fact that the tribunal continues to question him, and with stunning determination, is very telling.

Bertie told the inquiry he began using banks again to lodge money and open accounts when the seven-year legal process pertaining to his marital situation was finished. His cash-only existence came to an end. 'I started phasing that out from the time my separation was over.'

It was hard not to wince when highly personal details of Bertie Ahern's private life were aired in the tribunal chamber. How he put this amount of money by to pay for his daughters' education. How that amount was earmarked to pay legal fees. How a different figure was used to pay off his wife's car loan.

When the paltry sum concerning the car loan was mentioned, one of the Taoiseach's staff shook her head in disbelief, a look of disgust on her face. Her expression spoke volumes. It said: how on earth can they be doing this to him?

On one level, the daftness of his situation when he was minister for finance made for highly entertaining listening. Stories of his staff running to the bank to cash his substantial pay cheques and leaving the bundles of cash on his desk were extraordinary. Sometimes, Bertie said, he might stuff it into a drawer.

He was never worried about any of the money going walkies – although as he rarely counted it, it's hard to know if he would have been able to tell. 'I've worked in government offices since 1982 and nobody ever took anything,' he said.

But while his story, on the face of it, seemed plausible in a weird sort of way, questions remained. So his life was chaotic, so what? The difficulty is, and it is one the tribunal is having a problem squaring, that his life was chaotically comfortable. He may have been going through a rough time personally, but he also had money coming out of his ears. Money not consistent with his salary, and that is the only reason he is before the Mahon tribunal now.

His description of living above the shop in Fianna Fáil's St Luke's constituency office was equally entertaining. The top floor apartment was used as extra meeting space by Fianna Fáil councillors and senators and constituency workers.

Electricity from the Van De Graf generator makes Emily Gale's hair stand on end. She is a fifth-year student at Laurel Hill school, Limerick, and was attending Trinity College's open day. Photograph: Mac Innes Photography.

'The only thing I could control was the bedroom.' Cue visions of poor Bertie, minister for finance, eating his toast in his pyjamas of a morning and trying to read the papers, while sundry grassroots discussed party business around him.

Matters got very complicated, and heated, in the afternoon. Bertie's lawyer railed against what he saw as a clear 'breach of the Taoiseach's constitutional rights'. The man himself was far more direct. When O'Neill advanced a hypothesis of his own to explain some convoluted bank arrangements entered into by Ahern – a counterpoint to the witness's explanation – the Taoiseach exploded.

His theory was 'unbelievable'. Not just that, but the tribunal was 'trying to set me up, or stitch me up'. If we didn't know this was a high-stakes game, we did now.

Much now rests on the outcome of today's evidence. One thing is for sure though now: If the tribunal has to shoot the elephant in the room, it will. As of yet, it is still unclear if it has cause to do it.

SATURDAY, 22 DECEMBER 2007

Humbled by an Ancient Light

Eileen Battersby

I ce crunched under foot. The rich farmlands of the Boyne Valley in historic Co. Meath were white under a determined overnight frost that showed little intention of releasing its grip. Cattle slowly stood in the fields, all appearing to be stiff from the cold night that had just passed – the longest night.

Solstice watchers had gathered at Newgrange, the great passage tomb overlooking the bend of the Boyne. On this the 40th anniversary of what has become a defining winter ritual, the communal mood was relaxed. There was no doubt, this would be a majestic sunrise. The conditions were ideal:

One of the 20 people inside Newgrange, Co. Meath, during the December solstice, bows her head as the passage is illuminated. Photograph: Cyril Byrne.

cold, dry and as still as only a perfect winter's morning can be.

By way of the preview for what was to come, the moon had cast a bright, white light over the landscape. All night, it seemed as if the moon was maintaining a vigil, illuminating one of the most famous burial sites in the world.

The monument shimmered with a surreal grace. Throughout the early hours, the moon seemed to glow with a cold allure, while the stars were almost shockingly bright. Tuesday's sunrise had served as an inspired dress rehearsal. But nothing in nature is certain and as if to remind us of that, the following two mornings had been dull. But yesterday showed exactly what can happen if the weather and the gods see fit to agree.

As the moonlight dimmed, a temporary darkness descended but it was never very dark as the hazy mist added to the magic. Early morning has its own beauty. The ground was solid, and the trees and hedges were frozen. It was as if the grass itself was tensed against the cold. As the mist drifted away the tall shadows in front of the monument acquired a more solid form. They are dense, massive stones.

What kind of people were the late Stone Age farmers that settled here and created such a wonder in honour of their dead, and in honour of their Gods?

These ancient people made this landscape; it is as much their legacy as are the passage tombs of Newgrange, Knowth and Dowth. It is impossible not to wonder at their ingenuity, their physical strength, their determination and their faith. Here were a people who looked to the Heavens for hope and for life itself. In the depths of mid-winter, they looked to the heavens for the first signs of a return of life-giving light.

The science has been brilliantly explained. Since M.J. O'Kelly first began his investigations which were to lead to his formal documenting of it, many archaeologists have explored and explained the phenomenon, or rather the inspired merging of observation, astronomy, engineering and religion that is Newgrange. Daylight in winter precedes the arrival of the sun by almost an hour.

Many faces looked towards the horizon. It was easy to identify the newcomers among more seasoned Solstice watchers.

Two small girls accompanying their father for the first time were told that they were very lucky to see this so young. 'I had to wait for what you're about to see.' The girls looked slightly worried. 'Will it be noisy?' asked the smaller one. Dad didn't answer. He seemed uncertain of his camera. The girls waited. The crowd became bigger. Ordinary individuals, no obvious eccentrics amongst us. No characters. No New Age chanting.

There were fewer Santa hats than in previous years, no reindeer headdress – but it looked like Christmas.

At three minutes to nine the sun made its first appearance. Although a glimmer of colour had infused the sky for some minutes, it was not until three minutes to nine that the first blister of amber appeared on the skyline. It appeared to throb, even recede, and then it began to climb, initially almost tentatively. Then it breaks forth, like a bubble. A sense of purpose takes over and watching it becomes compulsive. So much so that it was easy to ignore the large TV screen that had been mounted on the site. Although the intention is to share the phenomenon with a wide international audience, it is incongruous and, as many commented, a distraction.

Inside the chamber, the honeyed beam of amber light begins its journey up the narrow passage. As it moves along it reveals footprints in the sand. It is as if the chosen few inside are retracing the steps of their ancestors.

Solstice and the welcome beginning of winter's slow leave-taking is great theatre, and in common with the greatest theatre, it needs silence. It demands silence. But silence is difficult to experience at Newgrange.

Yesterday, instead of the usual snatches of half-overheard exchanges, microphones made public a conversation between a broadcaster and a Newgrange guide. The old intimacy between Solstice watchers had been replaced by a media moment.

It was ironic though – modern man and his technology attempting to explain a wonder imaginatively fashioned by highly sophisticated late Stone Age farmers. More than five thousand years on, we remain humbled by ancestors who possessed a complex grasp of the physical world as well as a spirituality and humility that continue to elude us, their clumsy descendants.

MONDAY, 24 DECEMBER 2007

Ho Ho It's a Hold-up

Ross O'Carroll Kelly

They've, like, excelled themselves again this Christmas. I'm talking about the lights in Ronan's estate. It's like focking Vegas out here. Mark my words – some pilot's going to mistake this road for a runway and try to land a 747 on it. I'm not being nasty but this crowd will have the hubcaps off it before the wheels even touch the ground.

I'm standing outside the needle exchange clinic on the end of Ronan's block, waiting for a Jo, and I'm laughing to myself at the memory of him this morning, dragging on one of his famous rollies and going, 'Ah, Christmas is for the kiddies but, isn't it?' but then his little face lighting up like a slot machine when I produce that satnav for his

Cartoon by Alan Clarke.

BMX and a pirate copy of *American Gangster*. He's a great saucepan and I'm a lucky man.

Just as I'm thinking this – and also about the fact that the sky is lower around here – I suddenly hear the shuffle of feet, then somebody grabs me from behind and, like, drags me to the ground.

In all the confusion, I'm guessing it's a happy slapping and I'm automatically going, 'Not the face! Not the face!' obviously thinking first and foremost about my modelling contract with Eden Pork and how Luke Fitzgerald would be all over it like a Guiney's suit if anything happened to this boat.

'My face is my living,' I'm going. 'Have mercy!' while at the same time thinking, if they put this on YouTube, that line's going to follow me to the grave.

But there I am, roysh, curled up on the ground and I'm waiting for the punches and kicks to stort, I don't know, raining down on me, but they don't.

All that happens is, somebody handcuffs me, then blindfolds me. A cor screeches to a basic halt and I'm suddenly lifted, carried and then pretty much dumped into the boot.

I haven't a clue what's going on here but it would be fair to say that I'm kacking it – and in a major way.

I'm pretty much visualising every turn the cor makes, trying to follow the route we're taking, but I eventually lose concentration and suddenly we're hitting speed ramps every 20 yards and I'm thinking, we could be literally anywhere north of Westmoreland Street.

After, like, half an hour, the cor stops and the boot is whipped open and all these hands make a grab for me. I'm there, 'Go easy, goys. I've an old rhomboideus major injury – don't want to aggravate it,' but they're not listening. They pull me out of there like a basic slab of meat, then they slow-walk me into what I presume is a house.

I'm trying to work out from the sound of their footsteps how many of them there are and shit? I'm guessing four.

They lead me into a room and, like, throw me down on to a hord sofa. I'm going, 'Ronan, if this is another one of your famous pranks, it's not funny . . .' but they don't answer.

They just leave me there, in total dorkness, with only the chimes of a clock on the mantelpiece helping me keep track of the time, not knowing why I'm being held, by who and, more importantly, where.

It's only when I'm given my dinner at one o'clock, then, at five, a thing called 'tea' – consisting of a slice of ham, a quarter of a tomato, a hard-boiled egg, halved, and two slices of pickled beetroot – that I realise that the people who have me are working class, we're talking serious desperados here, who wouldn't think twice about chopping my head off if they found out I had two gold fillings in my Taylor Keith.

I only manage to get about seven hours' sleep that night.

Senator David Norris (right), who donated his papers to the National Library, with Gerry Lyne, keeper of manu-
scripts, and Aongus Ó hAonghusa, director. Photograph: David Sleator.

It's, like, half-eleven the following morning, pretty much 24 hours after I was taken, that they speak to me for the first time. The door opens and one of them, who must be, like, the leader, goes, 'Story witcher oul' lad?' I'm like, 'My old man? He's a dickhead – that's the story.' 'We're tryina get in contact wi'em,' he goes. 'Why's he not at woork?' I'm there, 'Work? The old man's in the Joy – your place.' They're not happy campers when they hear that. 'I fooken told you we shoulda done it last year, Brian,' one of them's going, and then they stort arguing among themselves.

'Whoa!' I eventually go. 'Can you lot just, like, chillax for an actual second and tell me, basically – double-u . . . tee . . . eff . . .'

'Get that blindfold off um,' the leader goes and suddenly it's, like, ripped off me and it takes a while for my eyes to adjust to the light.

When they do, I actually gasp at the scene of horror in front of me – wallpaper, 1970s furniture, a giant plasma screen television with Sky Sports News on mute and one of those singing fish you buy on Moore Street on the wall over the fireplace.

Then I look at them, as in my actual kidnappers, but I can't see them because they've got, like, rubber masks on – we're talking Bertie Ahern, Brian Cowen, Mary Horney and Willie O'Dea. And they've got Santa hats as well. Oh, and guns.

'What is this?' I go.

Brian Cowen steps forward and he's like, 'You're after been Toiger kidnapped . . .' I'm like, 'What kidnapped?' He's there, 'Toiger kidnapped – cos of, like, the Celtic Toiger an' that . . .'

'That's not why thee call it Toiger kidnapping,' Mary Horney goes. 'It's cos it involves, like, keer-fully stalking the victum beforehand and that.'

Bertie Ahern's suddenly there. 'And we did that, didn't we, Mary? Didn't even know his oul' lad was in-fooken-side. Reet,' he goes, slamming a telephone down on the table in front of me, 'start talking – who'd pay money for you? What about your oul' wan?' I'm like, 'Her? Wouldn't ask that wagon for the time. I'd sooner you took me outside and shot me now.'

'But she writes them bukes,' Willie O'Dea goes. 'My boord reads them. Very good actually. She'd have a few bob, wouldn't she?' I'm like, 'Yeah, but she's tighter than a gnat's orse in a sandstorm . . .' Willie's there, 'Lovely looken boord, if you don't moind me sayin. Nice pair of Easter eggs on it . . .'

I'm there, 'I actually do mind you saying? The woman's a hound. I've flushed better-looking things down the toilet. And you won't get a cent out of her. She hates my guts as much as I hate hers . . .' 'What about woork?' Bertie goes. 'What do you do?' I'm like, 'Pretty much fock-all, I'm proud to say,' but then it hits me and I don't know why I didn't think of it before. 'Oh my God, you know what? The Irish Times will pay up – good bread, as well . . .' Of course, there's, like, total silence. I'm there, 'It's, like, a newspaper?' They all just look at each other. 'Well, I've never heard of it,' Bertie goes.

Mary's like, 'I only know the Heddild,' and Willie O'Dea's there, 'It's a fooken trap, boys,' and he storts making shapes like he's about to deck me.

'Is that what this is about?' Bertie goes. 'Buy yourself some toyim?' I'm like, 'Goys, I swear – it's an actual paper,' and I tell them the phone number and Brian dials it, slowly, while staring at me with, like, total contempt.

Although that's probably just the mask.

'Who'm I askin for?' he goes while it's still ringing and I'm there, 'I don't know her actual name? But they call her, like, Madam?' He's put through and he puts the call on speakerphone. 'My name is Brian,' he tells her. 'I'm a member of a gang called The Cabinet. We've got Ross O'Caddle-Kelly . . .' 'Who?' Madam goes.

'Ross O'Caddle-Kelly! We want 50,000 squids or you'll never see him again.' 'What you're saying,' she goes, in this, like, high-pitched voice, 'it's all gibberish to me. I'm going to put it through to marketing,' which she does.

Of course morkeshing end up asking them to spell out their demands in an e-mail – double spacing, please – using as many bullet points as possible.

But then Bertie loses the actual plot and shouts, 'We're bleedin serious – we're gonna nut this sham!' and they have, like, a total change in attitude. They say they'll test the idea at their two o'clock – kick its tyres, see is it roadworthy – then interface with them again in the pm.

'That means they'll have an answer in the afternoon,' I go, and the four of them seem happy enough with that.

So we all sit around and wait until half-three, when we're supposed to ring back. The five of us sit there and stort shooting the shit. I tell them a little bit about rugby, which they've never heard about before, and they tell me a little bit about Bohemians Football Club, which I never want to hear about again.

'Why are you going to all this actual trouble?' I eventually go. 'I thought your lot just fell down a hole and sued someone when you needed moolah.'

'Look, why does any of us woork?' Brian goes. He's clearly the thinker of the group. 'Put food on the table. We've all got kids. Christmas is an expensive toyim.'

It's weird, roysh, but I remember seeing this documentary once about how people who get kidnapped end up really liking their kidnappers or at least feeling sort of, like, sympathetic towards them, if that's the word? 'Is there any more of that beetroot?' I eventually go. 'I've never tasted it before but – believe it or not – I actually like it,' and Bertie looks at Mary and goes, 'Get him some more beetroot,' which Mary does.

Maybe it's all the talk about kids. I ask them if they know Ronan. I don't even give them a second name. Straight away, they're all like, 'Ah, Ro! Wit the little Ronnie Kray glasses? Ah, he's a great little lad, so he is. One to watch for the future.' I'm there, 'Not any more. He's gone straight. Fallen in love, the lot . . .' 'And you're his oul' lad?' Bertie goes. 'Fair fooks to ye. Here, tell him the boys from the Lawn was askin for him. I'm Martin Doran. That's Paddy Cahill. That's Paul Moyles. And that's Alan Kelly there in the Mary Harney mask . . .'

Call it a hunch but I suspect these goys aren't going to be in this line of work for long, giving out their names and addresses like that.

I wolf down the beetroot and say fock-all.

At half-three, roysh, we ring the morkeshing deportment back.

'The news is not good,' the dude goes. 'We kicked your proposal around – tested its buoyancy, if you will – and we decided we've already spent quite a considerable outlay promoting Ross's column – bus shelters, radio ads, T-shirts and so forth. We've overspent, if anything. Doesn't leave us with any wiggle room, I'm afraid – at least not for this quarter . . .'

It's 20 minutes before the goys realise that what he's basically said is no.

'What do we do now then?' Bertie goes. 'Dump him in the canal?' Jesus, you can see why he's Bertie, can't you? 'No!' I stort suddenly going. 'Don't do it. I've got so much to live for?' 'Give us a fooken name then – someone with munjanah . . .' So I do.

I don't know what he's going to say – and I suspect I'm going to regret it for the rest of my life – but I do. I give them his name and his work number and they ring it . . .

I'm standing outside the Irish Life Mall with my nose up against Eason's window, just like I was told to.

South African Duncan Scott catching a wave estimated to tower eight times his height, off Mullaghmore, Co. Sligo. Photograph: Mickey Smith.

Focking Talbot Street! I felt safer in that room with all those guns. After 15, maybe 20 minutes, I hear a cor horn but I'm too scared to, like, turn around.

'Ross,' a voice goes. 'It's okay, they've gone.' It's him. I walk slowly to the cor. An Audi A6 – you wouldn't focking blame him. I can't even bring myself to say thank you.

'You don't have to thank me,' he goes. 'I mean, I can't imagine how embarrassing this must be for you. Your ex-wife's new boyfriend . . .' I'm there, 'She's still my wife.' He's like, '. . . having to bail you out like that. I mean, gosh, I saved your neck, Ross. You probably feel you owe me some kind of life debt.' I'm there, 'You'll get your 50 Ks back, Cillian, don't you worry.' 'Ten,' he goes.

I'm like, 'Ten?' He's there, 'Yeah – I sort of, like, haggled them down.' Typical accountant.

And he ends up giving it all that, roysh, all the way to Dalkey. 'I want you to forget this. I don't want you feeling like you're under some kind of obligation to me, just because of what happened,' he's going. 'I mean, what was I going to do – let them kill you?' He's got this really smug look on his face when I'm getting out of the cor.

'By the way,' he goes, 'Merry Christmas.'

'Yeah,' I go, giving him the finger. 'Many happy returns.'

Ross O'Carroll Kelly is the alter ego of Paul Howard.

MONDAY, 31 DECEMBER 2007

Dolan an Unsung Icon of Freedom

John Waters

Usually when someone of note passes away – a politician, a writer, an industrialist – it is customary to revisit the social importance of the deceased's work in the form of tribute or obituary.

We witnessed this in recent times following the deaths of John McGahern and Tony Ryan. Last week, however, although one of the most central cultural figures in the Ireland of the past half-century had died, all we heard was that he was a great entertainer.

Joe Dolan was an entertainer in the same sense that Bob Dylan is a singer/songwriter. It is remarkable that we long ago managed to see past these superficialities in the international arena, but have yet to do so in the home context.

Everything said and written about Joe Dolan in the past few days – about his remarkable singing voice, his string of hits in Ireland and abroad, his immense talent for communication with audiences – is important as the detail of something bigger. But this bigger reality is left unstated: that Dolan was one of a handful of key figures in a social movement that transformed Ireland while setting out with more modest ambitions. Other key figures include Dickie Rock, Larry Cunningham, Albert Reynolds, Brendan Bowyer, Fran O'Toole, Big Tom and the Freshmen's duo of frontmen, Derek Dean and Billy Brown. When you scan that list you perhaps begin to understand the nature of the blockage that prevents the full story being told.

Several of these figures, being irredeemably unhip or politically coloured, do not lend themselves to celebration as revolutionary figures. But revolutionary figures they were.

Showbands were unique to Ireland, and for this reason have attracted disdain from the cultural commissars who would have venerated them had there been a direct parallel in some culturally-approved foreign territory. As a consequence of this provincialism, showbands and dancehalls are in popular cultural memory analogous to the Civil War in our political neurology. Though patently central to the social and cultural story, they have fallen foul of a self-induced amnesia, rendered unmentionable by virtue of being deemed incompatible with modern aspirations. This makes for bad history and confused identity.

Among his many contributions, Joe Dolan exploded the idea that being Irish meant you were disqualified from external recognition, communicating that in order to succeed abroad you had only to be excellent and work hard. Who, therefore, can quantify the significance of his pioneering international success in the emerging psyches of U2 and others? In this and a host of other contexts, to attempt a genealogy of the latter-day generation of Irish pop superstars without acknowledging the showbands is like discussing Irish politics without mentioning de Valera. It can be done but it sounds mad.

When I was growing up, Irish pop culture was showband culture and little else. The Drifters, the Miami, the Royal and the Freshmen provided a Big Bang in a society oblivious of its own cultural debilitation. When we talk about the GAA, *The Late Late Show*, *The Irish Times*, the *Sunday World* or the Progressive Democrats, we have no difficulty in underlining – and often exaggerating – the social

significance of each of these phenomena at a certain moment. But we retreat from this mode of analysis when it comes to perhaps the most significant social phenomenon of them all.

The showband/dancehall explosion of the 1960s and 1970s was the most radical and effective force in the breaking of the conservative monolith of post-Famine Irish Catholicism, which, by losing touch with human reality had reduced religion to a form of policing. Showbands were about music and entertainment in much the same way that Bewley's was about coffee. Fundamentally they were about sex, about meeting, romancing and mating, and about extending to the first Irish pop generation the kind of freedom purveyed in the international arena by Elvis, Dylan and the Beatles.

The 7/6 or 50 pence you paid to be admitted to the ballroom was not simply a tariff on the entertainment, or even a levy on floorspace, but an instalment on a licence to have a love life without

Joe Dolan's coffin makes its way through the crowd at the Cathedral of Christ the King in his home town of Mullingar. Photograph: Brenda Fitzsimons.

Cardinal Seán Brady greeting Molly Newman (90) at St Patrick's Church in Carrigallen, Co. Cavan, after a mass for family and locals, during which the Cardinal knelt beside the font at which he was baptised, the day after he was born, on 17 August 1939. Photograph: Alan Betson.

attracting more than cursory notice. It was a nominal tax on freedom and one we gladly paid. (Part of the blame for our poor sense of history must be placed on the unctuously disingenuous nature of most of the chronicles of this era by those who were there. If you want to know what was really going on, read Derek Dean's recent book, *The Freshmen Unzipped*.) Far more than Gay Byrne or Nell McCafferty or David Norris or Mary Robinson, men like Joe Dolan revolutionised Irish attitudes to, in a word, sex.

Joe, like Brendan and Tom and Dickie, was a High Priest of the emerging culture of freedom, ordained with the power to dissolve inhibition and temporarily rescind the law of prohibition so as to enable what we now think of as freedom to take its first faltering steps.

Joe Dolan can be called a liberator in a sense that is only in the faintest degree ironic. May perpetual light shine upon him.

WEDNESDAY, 2 JANUARY 2008

'All We Have Heard in the Last Days is a Pack of Lies'

Mary Fitzgerald, in Karachi

The air inside Benazir Bhutto's Karachi residence is thick with incense and the sound of women keening and weeping. A series of framed cartoons lines the stairs leading to her office. Each of the charcoal sketches features Bhutto herself, and they provide a telling glimpse into the mind of the woman mourned by millions in Pakistan since her assassination last week.

'I have never made but one prayer: "O Lord, make my enemies ridiculous." And God granted it,' reads one. Another shows Bhutto standing in front of a portrait of her father, who was hanged in 1979. 'Every absence is an age,' it reads. The caption above the next declares, 'I can smell a trap in a minute. And I do.'

Grieving guests and members of Bhutto's Pakistan People's Party (PPP) drift in and out of a warren of rooms hung with campaign posters and paintings of Bhutto as a teenager.

For everyone here, there is no mystery over the circumstances of Bhutto's killing at an election rally in Rawalpindi. 'It's a clear-cut case,' says Fehmida Mirza, a PPP assembly member and close friend of Bhutto. 'But all we have heard from the government in the last days is a pack of lies.'

Just over 24 hours after Bhutto's death, Pakistan's interior ministry said three shots had been fired moments before a suicide bomber struck the gathering.

The ministry's spokesman told reporters Bhutto had not been killed by gunfire or shrapnel, claiming instead that she had ducked the bullets before fracturing her skull when the force of the blast slammed her head against a fitting on her

Benazir Bhutto at a Pakistan election campaign rally in Rawalpindi moments before she was assassinated. Photograph: John Moore/Getty Images.

vehicle's sunroof. The government repeated that assertion yesterday despite mounting scepticism.

The PPP has insisted from the beginning that their leader was shot in the neck, and that the bullet exited from the back of her head. Party spokeswoman Sherry Rehman, who was with Bhutto when the attack occurred, and later helped clean her body at the hospital, says she saw two head wounds that bled profusely.

Video footage broadcast widely on Pakistani television since Monday appears to corroborate the PPP's version of events, giving rise to further doubts about the government's account. It shows a clean-cut young man in sunglasses approaching Bhutto's armoured vehicle along with the suspected suicide bomber. Seconds later, the first man fires a pistol at Bhutto, her hair and headscarf blow back and she drops back in the vehicle just as a bomb explodes.

Bhutto's husband, Asif Ali Zardari, said the video was proof the government had tried to 'muddy the water' from the outset. Interior minister Hamid Nawaz Khan said yesterday detectives would examine the video footage, adding the investigation would 'take some time'.

Doctors at the hospital where Bhutto died released an inconclusive report saying the cause of death was 'an open head injury with depressed skull fracture, leading to cardiopulmonary arrest'. Sources at the hospital said staff there had come under intense pressure before issuing the report.

No autopsy had been performed, at the request of Bhutto's family. Her husband insisted it was unnecessary when the cause of death was so obviously a bullet wound.

In a country where conspiracy theories abound, the contradictory accounts of how Bhutto died have prompted a multitude of questions. Some see in the differing stories an attempt by the government to evade responsibility for lax security. Others believe something more sinister is afoot, suspecting officials of trying to cover up the possible involvement of elements within the government or security establishment.

Former director of Pakistan's intelligence services Asad Durrani says the fact that a gunman could come close enough to fire at Bhutto's cavalcade shows there was a serious security lapse. 'The government has made it difficult for themselves,' he told *The Irish Times*. 'I suspect they thought they would be blamed for not providing enough security so they tried to cover their backs, but instead of taking the heat off themselves, they managed the reverse.'

Like many others, Durrani was puzzled when he heard the blast site was washed down with fire hoses within an hour after the attack. 'As well as depriving investigators of evidence, this simply creates more suspicion,' he says.

Mirza agrees. 'Why would you remove evidence like that? What are they trying to hide?' she asks, wiping eyes swollen from days spent crying at Bhutto's funeral in rural Sindh. 'She had been demanding security for months and they did not provide it. Why was that?'

Like everyone else in the PPP, Mirza believes there should be an outside investigation into Bhutto's death – similar to that carried out by the United Nations into the assassination of Lebanese prime minister Rafik Hariri. 'We do not trust any official investigation by Pakistan. How could we trust these people?' she asks.

Outside the high-walled compound (named Bilawal House after Bhutto's teenage son and recently appointed political heir of the PPP) people queue to sign a book of condolences next to a huge framed photograph of Bhutto set on a table garlanded with roses and jasmine.

One of them, a medical student named Aftab Abbasi, proudly shows off a T-shirt identifying him as a member of the all-volunteer force of young men known as the Janisar-e-Benazir (those willing to die for her).

'I blame the government directly,' he says. 'They opposed her moves for democracy so they killed her. This idea that al-Qaeda is responsible is nonsense.'

FRIDAY, 4 JANUARY 2008

Looking for the Right Words in All the Wrong Places

Displaced in Mullingar: Michael Harding

There's a real cool laid-back venue in Mullingar called Danny Byrne's, where you'd need a torch light to find the drink on the table, and a map of the building to find the toilet. It's always dark, with low light from lots of candles.

I was there on a Sunday night. The place was quiet, and dreamy. A young musician sang and played guitar. Two men drank alone at the bar. Young women sat in groups, in twos and threes, dressed as if they expected to meet the prince of all princes.

I sat in an alcove with a friend who had come down from Dublin. We had a view of the bar. He said he couldn't figure out how to date on the net. He thought he might have a chance in Mullingar. I told him I couldn't find Tesco on the net, never mind date women. He kept staring at the girls. After a few drinks our conversation petered out.

It was late. There was a candle on every table, a bouncer who got very attentive when it came to closing time, and one tall girl with short blonde hair and an east European accent at the bar, talking to herself. So I abandoned my friend to his pursuit of love, and headed for home.

The taxi cost me a fiver. There was something on the car radio about another killing in Dublin. The taxi man said nobody passes any remarks any more. 'Death is normal now,' he said.

The following day my friend arrived for breakfast. He had a big grin on his face. 'She was Hungarian,' he declared.

I wasn't impressed.

'Be careful,' I said. 'She might have a husband and three children back in Budapest!'

He said, 'Do you not realise how lucky you are?' I didn't see his point.

'With all these foreigners!'

I asked him did he have a good night.

'We only talked,' he said. 'We talked until five this morning. She was beautiful. But it was difficult to keep it going.'

I said, 'I know the feeling.' I have friends with whom I've tried all year to have one single intelligent conversation.

One day I went to a house with a French man, and ate lamb cooked in yoghurt. It gave me a bellyache. But I didn't tell him in case he would be insulted. That's how tenuous a relationship is when you don't know the language.

Not many in Mullingar are multilingual. Social interaction tends to be shallow and repetitive.

'What is it like in Poland? Do you have much weather? What is the snow like where you live?' It's like a language lesson for beginners; or an interrogation session.

'What do you think of the war in Iraq?' 'Not good. No.' 'No? And what about modern art?' 'Ohhh Good. Yes. I like.' 'And communists? Do you think they tried to create a more compassionate society?' 'A little bit, thank you.'

And there's another difficulty connecting with other Europeans. They keep to themselves, as the Cavanman used to say about the badgers. They don't socialise with the natives too much. Before my friend got on the train he said, 'There's more to life than intellectual blather!' Maybe he's right.

On my way home I noticed that the woman who sold me the Christmas tree was still standing behind the counter in the petrol station, her brown eyes lasering me as I walked in the door. And I still wanted to talk to her, wish her a Happy New Year, or ask her how she enjoyed Christmas.

But it wasn't easy because there was a queue behind, waiting, with bunches of bananas and vacuum-packed rashers and minced meat in plastic cartons. The man ahead of me bought the *Sun*, the

Star, and a Lotto ticket, and then paid for it all with a laser card.

I was holding two bottles of wine, and a blue cheese, and a long loaf of bread. Surely she could see the possibilities. Perhaps I could mention that the Christmas tree that she sold me still looked lovely.

Or at least wish her a Happy New Year! Needless to say I did exactly the same as I did when she sold me the Christmas tree; the same as I do every day when I get diesel, or bread rolls or milk; I handed her my card, and said I wanted 20 cash back, and I signed her receipt, and then I turned away, as if she didn't exist.

SATURDAY, 5 JANUARY 2008

No End in Sight to Norman's Conquests

Richard Gillis

In the shade of a large, overhanging tree, Greg Norman reaches out to put his arm around new fiancée Chris Evert, turning to place a quiet kiss on the side of her head. A small token of affection among many, coming just days after the Australian had proposed marriage to the former 'darling of Wimbledon'. The question was popped over dinner aboard GN1, his private jet, as it flew over the Atlantic from Florida en route to this remote part of South Africa, just north of Cape Town.

That this romantic gesture took place as Norman walked between tee and green during the first round of the South African Open just shows how loved up they are.

On this beautiful morning, Evert (53), is play-ing the role of golf widow. Appropriately dressed in black – lycra – she follows her man around the Pearl Valley Golf Course, a stunning new develop-ment, designed by Jack Nicklaus, set in prime Western Cape wine country. Beside her a young

man is dressed in classic golf casual garb, the line of his chinos spoilt only by the hand gun attached to his belt.

At 52, Norman looks much the same as he did in his heyday, his lean, athletic physique noticeably at odds with the muscle-bound young pretenders prowling the practice range. Evert's presence behind the ropes seems to inspire him: Norman's name is a fixture on the leaderboard this week. He would finish in joint seventh.

The wind off the Frakenheim mountain range blows many of today's young stars off the course. Rory McIlroy takes 83 on the first day, and despite a strong second round misses the cut. Norman's final score of level par is several shots ahead of the other major champions in the field, Ernie Els, Retief Goosen and Angel Cabrera.

It is a considerable achievement, given this is his first pro event since the Dubai Masters in February, a break of nine months. Playing golf has almost become a hobby for Norman, long ago making way for his business career. And, as with the decision-making of any good chief executive, there are financial reasons for his presence this week: Norman would soon officially announce he will be building a second course here at Pearl Valley.

He is, in part, schmoozing a major client: Leisurecorp, the sports arm of Istithmar, the Dubai investment company which owns Pearl Valley. It is the same group helping to fund the Race to Dubai, the European Tour's new, £20 million end-of-season competition which was announced to great fanfare in October.

A few hours later and the focus shifts to Chris Evert, with Norman in support. On the drive that runs up to the clubhouse, they emerge from a Mercedes SUV hand-in-hand and dressed in matching white outfits, so bright they're hard to look at.

They are here to launch a Chris Evert Tennis Centre: four courts built to replicate the four sur-faces of the major championships. It is the second

Greg Norman and Chris Evert. Photograph: Simon Fergusson/Getty Images.

such venture in as many months: the first was in Dubai.

Into the boardroom of the golf club and the couple sit at a large oak table, giggling like teenagers, hands linked under the desk. Evert, who retired from the game in 1989, having won 18 Grand Slam titles, is the warmer of the two, quick to laugh, eyes darting to her partner to encourage his participation. He is more reserved, conscious that this afternoon is her gig.

There is no pretence that the tennis centre is anything but a rich man's playground. However, back in Florida, Evert works with the USTA on developing American talent.

'Point blank, players are hungrier in other countries, notably the eastern European countries,' says Evert. 'They see Anna Kournikova and Maria Sharapova making a lot of money and living a glamorous lifestyle, so they want to get out of

Greg Norman on the 15th hole during the first round of the 2007 Del Webb Father Son Challenge on the International Course at Champions Gate Golf Club, Florida. Photograph: David Cannon/Getty Images.

Russia and come to America, the land of freedom and the land of opportunity.'

Looking back at her career, she says the loss to Virginia Wade in the semi-final of Wimbledon in 1977 was the low point. She should have won, she says, but she allowed the British crowd, pumped up by that year's Jubilee celebrations, get to her.

As she moves her hand, the diamond ring on her finger catches the light and prompts a question about their personal situation. Unaware that Norman had spilled the beans of their engagement in a separate interview a half hour before, Evert is caught off guard.

'Partnership? What is this? A business?' she says in mock indignation.

'He's talking about the marriage,' says Norman, grinning. They laugh as she shows off the ring, and says they will marry sometime this year.

Locals here are quick to notice the irony: more than 30 years ago, in the same country, the bling on Evert's finger attracted similar media interest. That time, in 1973, a similarly impressive ring was given to her by Jimmy Connors, a love match that never made it to the altar.

Instead, Evert married English tennis player John Lloyd in 1979. Following the divorce from Lloyd in 1987, she married former Olympic skier Andy Mill, with whom she has three sons. 'Now I've got four boys,' she says, looking over at Norman.

You sense the playful air owes much to the distance between here and Florida, where the fall-out of their respective break-ups continues, not least in the media.

Evert separated from Mill in October 2006. Last January her relationship with Norman was officially 'outed', with the pair happy to be photographed having lunch at a high-profile Sydney restaurant.

Norman's divorce has been ugly, and public. His wife of 25 years, Laura, was awarded a substantial settlement. The couple's €20 million home in Florida, where they socialised frequently with Evert and Mill, has been put on the market.

A statement issued by Norman's lawyers seemed to sum up his attitude. 'The wife did not teach the husband to swing a golf club,' the petition read. 'The wife did not teach the husband to win.'

It went on to say that Greg Norman's contribution to the marriage 'far exceeded the contributions of the wife'. Would the power relationship between two such high-profile sports people as Norman and Evert be more equal?

The question elicits a surprising response. Unprompted, Norman references his most infamous failure: the loss of the 1996 Masters, when he went in to the final day six shots clear, only to collapse before the grinding brilliance of Nick Faldo's final-round 67.

'Nobody else can understand what it's like to be number one,' says Norman. 'Nobody can understand what it's like to be beaten by Navratilova, or me by Faldo, unless you've been there. Our thoughts and feelings on life are so in synch, it's a very special relationship.'

'Don't let the bastards get you down,' said Faldo to Norman as they walked off Augusta's 18th green that afternoon. The Englishman was referring to the media waiting in the press tent, but the sentiment had a broader application.

Around that time, Norman made the decision to take control of his destiny, a move that has brought him enormous wealth but also in to conflict with some of the game's powerbrokers.

To facilitate his new independence he broke with IMG, the management group founded by Mark McCormack. He came to resent the company's fee structure that saw them take 10 per cent of his winnings and 25 per cent of off-course earnings. His biggest gripe was what he calls their short-term approach.

'I saw value in my own brand, and most management companies only see you as an endorsement-related product. They don't build equity in you, they don't build value over a longer period of time. I saw myself in a different place in

10 or 15 years down the line. I never wanted to be a pass-through entity,' he says.

'They rent players out three to five years at a time until their use-by-date expires and the next set of youngsters come along. It's the same with the PGA Tour, you're there doing your thing for 15, 20 years, then someone else comes along. They don't want to put a whole lot of stock in one individual.'

Tiger Woods, another IMG client, is the exception, having arguably greater power than any individual sportsman ever.

'If Tiger were to come and play the Race to Dubai, it would show that he was doing it for the game of golf and not the individual,' says Norman. 'I've heard that Tiger's management company has said, "You think Tiger Woods is going to play in the Race to Dubai? Dream on!"'

'I get really disappointed when I hear comments like that, because nobody is bigger than the game of golf. No management company, no TV network, no sponsor. You've got to do it for the right reasons.

'I hope he does. He only has to play 11 European Tour events. He's already doing four majors and the WGCs, so that's only three more – you know the numbers. He's probably going to get appearance money for those three others, so it's a stupid statement to make, to tell you the truth.'

The Race to Dubai has been heralded in some quarters as marking a new era in golf, a watershed that delineates the arrival of a World Tour. For Norman it is a case of back to the future: in 1994 he and Rupert Murdoch announced they were going to start a world tour, consisting of 30 events involving the top players in the world rankings. It came to nothing as Norman was outmanoeuvred by Tim Finchem, now the PGA Tour Commissioner.

In Norman's eyes, Finchem derailed the Australian's plan by turning influential American players against him. Once, Arnold Palmer, a personal hero, stood up at a meeting of Tour players and gave a long speech criticising Norman and his plan. The message was the World Tour was more about Greg Norman than the good of the game. All this while Norman was sitting at the back of the room.

The self-interest of the Tour and IMG, he says, stifled a World Tour back then, but big business is driving it now.

'They (The European Tour and Leisurecorp) have seen what's happened in the US where it's become a one-man show,' he says. 'They've seen what's happened with the WGCs, which started off around the world but all of a sudden have been sucked back in to the US.

'I'm not saying I was 100 per cent right, but I never got the chance to work out the situation,' says Norman. 'With the World Tour it was the PGA going behind my back, using their propaganda machine to squash Greg Norman, eliminate the idea and then go and take the same idea and develop it themselves (in the form of WGC events). I'm a member of the Tour and their responsibility should be to their constituents, not just their selfish administration.

'That's how they want to be, (then) I don't need to be in that world. That's why I don't play the US Senior Tour, to tell you the truth. Why should I go out there and support an organisation that has never supported me? I've been out there in the '80s and '90s because I loved to play. I've done enough for the PGA Tour. Why should I go out there and support the Senior PGA Tour, try to lift them up like I did in the '80s and '90s?'

Norman's wealth has been estimated at well over €200 million. His approach to business was coloured by the experience of his hero Jack Nicklaus, the Golden Bear to Norman's Great White Shark. Nicklaus lost money in the 1980s through a series of bad property deals. As a result, the younger man learned to use the power of his name to build his business, but, just as importantly, to use other people's money to do it.

His commercial interests have grown 'in con-centric circles', each using the Great White Shark

brand to enter new markets. There are in the region of 60 courses bearing the Norman name across the world. His GWSE course design business charges $1.25 million (€850,000) for a new layout, and the company has around 40 in production, including four in Dubai. In addition, there is Greg Norman wine, a Reebok clothing line, GPS navigation systems and an interior design business. GN1 is the name of his brand of grass, which was used as the surface of choice at the Sydney Olympics and two Super Bowls.

The growing portfolio of Chris Evert Tennis Centres will doubtless be run on similar lines: Dubai's oil money and Evert's name should be a potent mix.

That evening, at one of the luxury homes that line the Pearl Valley course, there is a barbeque thrown by MacGregor Golf, yet another Norman client. He and Evert arrive quietly after another wardrobe change. They press the flesh with the club-makers and the property developers while steaks are turned over the coals. Then, as quickly as they'd arrived, they are gone, the end of a busy day.

But for Norman and Evert, life as sports' new power couple has only begun.

TUESDAY, 8 JANUARY 2008

Obama Electrifies US with Message of Hope that Echoes JFK and King

Denis Staunton in Lebanon, New Hampshire

By the time Barack Obama arrived yesterday morning at Lebanon Opera House in New Hampshire's North Valley, the auditorium was already full and more than 400 people were left standing outside.

Cartoon by Martyn Turner.

'There's something going on out there, Lebanon. There's something stirring in the air. You can feel it,' Obama declared.

If anyone is feeling what's going on in New Hampshire, it is Hillary Clinton, who has seen a clear poll lead collapse into a double-digit deficit that could doom her hopes of returning to the White House. Obama looks set to repeat in New Hampshire today his remarkable success in Iowa last week, making him the favourite to win the Democratic presidential nomination and the presidency itself.

Both candidates have drawn huge crowds in New Hampshire this week but the atmosphere at their events couldn't be more different. Clinton offers a serious, exhaustive rundown on her policies, taking questions from the floor and even talking to reporters – something she has mostly avoided until now.

Obama's rallies are almost festive, as the candidate jokes with the audience, fires them up to vote and gives them an inspiring message about the potential of ordinary people to achieve extra-ordinary things.

Long before last week's victory in Iowa, Obama had been attracting record crowds throughout the United States, including a rally of 20,000 people in Atlanta last summer. Until Iowa, however, nobody was sure if these crowds would translate into real electoral numbers and most political analysts clung to the conventional wisdom that young people are unreliable supporters because they don't vote.

After all, Howard Dean raised millions over the internet and led in most polls before his 2004 candidacy immolated in Iowa while the dull, establishment figure of John Kerry walked off with the Democratic nomination.

What distinguishes Obama's campaign from Dean's, however, is that he has married the old politics with the new, using websites like Facebook and MySpace and texting young supporters to remind them to vote but also knocking on doors and organising local groups months in advance of the primaries.

For months, Obama avoided specific policy pledges, focusing instead on his core messages of hope and change, even producing campaign posters bearing only the word Hope, without the candidate's name. Under the influence of campaign strategist David Axelrod, Obama made his own biography a central part of his message, suggesting that as the son of a Kenyan father and a Kansan mother, who spent part of his childhood in

Indonesia, he could bring a new perspective to the White House.

At a candidates' debate last Saturday, Clinton accused Obama of raising 'false hopes' among voters without showing a record of legislative achievement to back up his promises. In Lebanon yesterday, Obama responded with a comic riff about John F. Kennedy looking at the moon and deciding it was too far and Martin Luther King telling crowds to go home and dream another day.

'If anything crystallised what this campaign is about, it was that right there,' Obama said. 'Some are thinking in terms of our constraints and some are thinking about our limitless possibilities and the American people are tired of hearing about how we have to be divided and how we have to shout at each other and why children have to be poor and why folks can't have enough health care and why we have to live in the politics of fear all the time and why we have to be afraid of each other. They're tired of that.'

Obama owes his success in Iowa to attracting the support of independents and Republicans and many more are expected to cross over to support him in New Hampshire. Unlike Clinton, who is almost universally loathed among Republicans, Obama attracts little hostility and he claimed yesterday that his conciliatory approach will help him to make real change in Washington.

'If you start off with an agreeable manner, you might be able to pick off some folks, you might be able to recruit independents into the fold, recruit even some Republicans into the fold. That's how you form a working majority for change. That's how you change the electoral map. That's the politics of addition, not the politics of division,' he said.

Clinton's campaign team, led by pollster Mark Penn, have long argued that her high negatives are unimportant because to win the Democratic candidate one only needs to win one more state than Kerry did in 2004. According to this analysis, 45 per cent of Americans will inevitably vote for the Democrat, 40 per cent will vote for the Republican and the election is about winning over the 10 per cent in between.

Obama wants to tear up this electoral map by appealing across party lines and winning support even in traditional Republican strongholds.

'We're on the cusp of creating a new majority in American politics, a new majority that will not just win a nomination, that won't just win a general election but more importantly will allow us to govern, so that we can actually start tackling problems that George W. Bush may have made far worse but had been festering long before George Bush ever took office,' he said.

Until last week, Obama's plan looked, in his own words, like an 'improbable journey' but as New Hampshire votes today, it seems ever more likely that this 'skinny guy with a funny name' is on course to become the first AfricanAmerican US president.

'That's what hope is,' he said yesterday, 'imagining and then working for and fighting for what didn't seem possible before.'

WEDNESDAY, 9 JANUARY 2008

Give Cystic Fibrosis Sufferers a Chance at Life

Orla Tinsley

Just before Christmas my friend asked me if I could have anything in the universe for Christmas, what would it be? I said Johnny Depp and a chocolate fountain, because I didn't want to say what I really wanted, it was too depressing.

What I would have given up my next few Christmas presents for was a cystic fibrosis unit. It sounds like such drivel, but I have never wanted anything more.

On St Stephen's Day 2007, a girl I didn't know called Tammy died. On 29 December 2007, a girl

I did know called Barbara died from the same condition, cystic fibrosis, a disease affectionately referred to as 'the swine' by Barbara. Tammy was 18 and Barbara 24.

Cystic fibrosis is a genetic disease that causes respiratory and digestive problems, osteoporosis, diabetes and other complications.

It's a multi-organ disease and in Ireland there is a 1 in 200 chance that two people who have the gene will have a child with cystic fibrosis. We have the highest incidence in the world and I was one of those figures. I am 20 now and one of over 1,100 people in Ireland living with it.

At the end of November another girl I knew called Tracie died aged 24 from the disease. Her death got one column – 'Tracie feared if care would kill her' – in a newspaper.

That was the weekend after the death of socialite Katy French. In any situation it is devastating to lose someone so young but I found myself not talking about Katy like everyone else, because secretly I felt guilty at the anger raging inside me. Of course it is tragic that she died at 24, but to watch it reported and debated so exhaustively wore me down, so much that I felt like arguing about the girl who has been called 'intelligent and caring'. I never knew her but I was envious of her, or rather the coverage she got after her death.

It made me feel for Tracie, who played music with Phil Coulter in New York, and her family, when she died from an illness she couldn't control. I also thought about my dear friend, sports enthusiast and all round charmer Damien who passed away last year and for my magazine editor, scientist and encyclopaedia-of-knowledge-friend Jean, who passed away last March. I only got to two funerals, and that's just 2007 and just the people I knew of.

Orla Tinsley outside St Vincent's Hospital in Dublin. Photograph: Bryan O'Brien.

Progress has been made on the issue, meetings are being held, talks are ongoing, but we don't need to hear about meetings and conversations. We need a public commitment, a promise that we will have our dedicated unit, and we need it now.

As the public mourned Katy French and the lens on cocaine in Ireland started to get focused, I thought wildly that maybe if I got engaged and broke up with a slightly well-known person, did some lingerie modelling and then died, if I fought off my illness long enough, maybe something would be done.

Maybe the Taoiseach's *aide-de-camp* would come to a cystic fibrosis funeral and see something he would remember, something that he might report back. He might see friends and family congregate, he might hear Leonard Cohen's 'Alleluia' or Tina Turner's 'Proud Mary', funeral songs

A Little Egret takes flight at Booterstown Marsh, Co. Dublin. Photograph: Cyril Byrne.

chosen sometimes years before the funeral took place.

He might see some lucky transplant recipients hovering outside the church, waving and mouthing words from a distance to their still suffering friends that they can't mix with anymore for medical reasons.

And we don't like that word suffering in the cystic fibrosis world, but we are suffering. Watching three of my friends die last year and going on to their tribute pages on Bebo hurts, out of sadness for the event and a personal fear of the unpredictability of life. Each of these people had just as much life as Katy French, and they were making their way through science, through selecting hurling teams, through study. Privately and steadily they mapped their future in a country that seemed to deem them insignificant.

It makes me feel like I need to give up college and get out there and smile for every photo, tirelessly self-promote because physically I cannot do both college and public relations, but maybe if I did then people would notice the tragic ignorance of our Celtic Tiger.

A television programme did a segment that linked Katy French to other celebrities who died young like Marilyn Monroe and James Dean. It made my younger cousin tell me all about the model she never knew until she died and how her classmates are now infatuated.

Maybe it is better for her to be infatuated with the glamorised death of a model than with the gritty realism that people like her cousin are dying, because that is what we are teaching our young people today – get famous and you will be remembered; if you are famous your death will matter.

People with cystic fibrosis take drugs too, and see tireless parties of doctors and nurses and medical students. We drink cocktails, inhale and pop pills everyday, but in a different way from other drug users. It is all relative and people need different things at different times in their life. Some people say they take cocaine to feel the buzz, to feel alive.

I feel very much alive and now I would like the buzz of knowing that the next infection I get might not kill me; that I could have my own room in hospital instead of risking infection from everyone from psychiatric patients to those with broken limbs and common colds.

I would like the buzz that can only come from decreasing our mortality rate from cystic fibrosis which is drastically ahead of Northern Ireland, Britain and the US, in this, the country with the highest instance of the disease in the world.

With cystic fibrosis I cannot choose when to take drugs, shoot up some insulin and I cannot change my fate. But my life and that of my friends can be prolonged. I can also prolong the time I spend out of hospital by ensuring my time in there is well spent.

It is simple: we need a dedicated cystic fibrosis unit with fully-trained staff who are knowledgeable about the disease, not a bed where a nurse tells you that your cough is strange; that you're too young to be on so many drugs and with whom you have to argue for an hour before you get the particular drug you need.

We need our own isolation rooms with en suites so that we can get over whatever infection we have caught, whether that takes us two weeks, three weeks or two months.

We need to know that we do not have to worry about the person with MRSA in the other room infecting us by using our toilet, that we do not have to worry about being heckled for opening the window or being moaned at for vomiting after an operation. We deserve freedom from infection and from the poor, confused woman who you constantly have to guide back to her bed because there is nobody else there to do it.

We need somewhere where you do not have to endure someone else's blood on a tray containing intravenous drugs.

Cystic fibrosis will eventually defeat me but there is no way it is happening yet. A degree, some travelling, maybe falling in love would be nice first.

Or maybe I will become a lingerie model. The possibilities are endless if only the means were there.

THURSDAY, 10 JANUARY 2008

An Irishman's Diary

Frank McNally

Danny Healy-Rae's claim that some pub-goers are now taking up smoking 'for romance' – because it offers an excuse to meet people in the intimate surroundings of doorways – does not surprise me.

I heard a similar thing in Clare a while back, from a man who worried that the smoking ban was having a detrimental effect on traditional music sessions. What happened, he said, was that a female fiddler would go outside the pub for a cigarette break. Then the male whistle player who fancied her would go out too, causing further disruption. If there was a love triangle and – say – the uilleann piper was involved as well, the whole session would be ruined.

As a publican, Cllr Healy-Rae's concern goes beyond mere music. His interest is the well-being, indeed the very survival, of his customers. Thus, he worries not only that some of them are being forced to take up smoking in search of love, but also – as he told this paper – that people are 'catching cold from going outside'. Clearly, this is a romantic tragedy in the making.

So, in an attempt to highlight the problem, I have decided to write an updated version of Romeo and Juliet, set mainly in the doorways of Irish pubs. Here's the first draft (if you'll forgive the pun). I hope to have the script finished in time for this year's theatre festival.

(Author's note: for the internecine feud central to Shakespeare's plot, I thought about using two rival fiddle-playing styles. But passionate as traditional musicians' arguments can be, they rarely result in homicidal violence, even in Clare. So for

realism, it had to be two GAA clubs instead.)

Scene 1: The interior of a pub in Kerry. The Montagues Under 21 football team are celebrating league victory over hated rivals the Capulets, some of whose players are also on the premises. The Montagues' captain, 'Romie' O'Sullivan – known simply as 'Romeo' to his friends – is in conversation with team-mates Ben Foley (aka 'Benvolio') and Mark-Hugh O'Connor ('Mercutio'). Suddenly, through the doorway, his eye is caught by a flaring match struck by Juliet O'Shea (a cousin of the Capulets' oddly-named captain, Tybalt). As she lights a cigarette, Romeo notices for the first time how beautiful she is.

Romeo: But soft, what light through yonder window breaks? It is the east, and Juliet is the sun.

Benvolio: Don't even think about it.

Mercutio: Go west, young man!

Romeo (dreamily): I need to take up smoking.

Scene 2: The doorway, a short time later.

Juliet: Oh, Romeo, Romeo, wherefore art thou, Romeo? (She touches a rose in the hanging basket overhead.) What's in a name? That which we call a rose by any other name would smell as sweet. Not that I can smell anything with these damn cigarettes – they dull all the senses. I know I'm always saying it, but I really should quit.

Romeo (appearing from nowhere): Could I bum one of those off you?

Juliet (flustered): Oh. Yes. Yes, of course. (She holds the packet of cigarettes towards him, pushing a cigarette out with trembling hands. He takes it. Their eyes meet, and they feel a spark between them. Juliet offers Romeo her cigarette as a light, but the spark has got there already. Romeo takes his first drag, trying not to choke.)

Juliet (to herself, smiling): Imagine. If I'd quit smoking, this might never have happened.

Scene 3: Six weeks later, in the pub's new beer-garden. It is late. Although an Arctic wind whips through the open-air facility, Juliet lingers over yet another cigarette with Romeo, who now has a 40-a-day habit. Mercutio and Benvolio stand

Young Scientist of the Year Emer Jones from Presentation Secondary School in Listowel, Co. Kerry, with her project on emergency sandbag shelters, at the RDS yesterday. Photograph: Alan Betson.

nearby, having also taken up smoking in the hopes of getting lucky.

Romeo (to Juliet): Parting is such sweet sorrow, that I shall say goodnight until it be tomorrow.

Publican: Have ye no homes to go to?

Juliet (coughing badly): Here's my lift.

Scene 4: Another pub doorway. The Capulets and the Montagues have met again, this time in the championship. The Montagues have suffered a heavy defeat, after a catastrophic drop in fitness levels, caused by smoking. Worse still, Juliet is in hospital with pneumonia. Romeo and his friends stand under a cloud of smoke, drowning their sorrows. Enter Tybalt and team-mates.

Tybalt: We meet again, losers! And now you pay for what you did to my cousin. (They fight. Tybalt fells Mercutio with a beer bottle.)

Mercutio: A plague on both your houses! (He

dies. Romeo slays Tybalt, earning a six-week ban from all club matches. This is later suspended pending an appeal to the games administration committee.)

Scene 5: A convalescent home. Juliet has recovered from her illness. But in an attempt to kick the smoking habit, she has enlisted the services of a hypnotist, who has put her into a death-like trance for 48 hours. Not knowing this, Romeo thinks she really is dead. He leaves the home scarred for life, gives up smoking, and vows never to darken the door of a pub again.

Scene 6: The publican stands behind the counter of his empty bar. It has just opened for the day, but he knows there will be no customers.

Publican: A glooming peace this morning with it brings/The sun for sorrow will not show its head/Go hence to have more talk of these sad things/Some shall be pardoned and some punish-ed/For never was a story of more woe/Than this of Juliet and her Romeo.

(Exit publican, locking door and placing 'For sale' sign on window.)

MONDAY, 21 JANUARY 2008

When You Can't even Trust a Stereotype

LockerRoom: Tom Humphries

A few weeks back I was in town and ran into Adekunle Gomez, whom I hadn't seen – well, let's see, certainly since late in the last century. Years ago Ade and myself tried our hand at running an African disco.

Ade had the music. I had the use of the hall. I was to promote the idea to college kids, young people whose idea of a cultural night out didn't extend beyond the traditional disciplines of drinking and shifting. Once the kids got the idea that African music didn't preclude drinking and worked quite a charm when it came to the shifting, all was well. And there was a little fad for the music.

Funny thing is – and I'd feel guilty admitting this to Ade (although I'm sure he's used to chancers like me by now) – that while I owned and still have on the iPod music by people like Remi Ongala and King Kiki, and enjoyed the soukous of outfits like Orchestra Makassy, I never developed the interest any further or deeper. Apart from being able to throw in the odd name and recognise the odd riff, that's where my expertise ends.

But of course I'm a white, European male

Lizzie Swanwick, aged 16, from Alexandra College in Milltown, Dublin, and Roland Omisore, aged 15, from Old Bawn Community School in Tallaght, Dublin, on stage during the Science Made Simple show at the Young Scientist exhibition in the Royal Dublin Society. Photograph: David Sleator.

A group of Irish schoolchildren take part in the opening ceremony of the Dublin Chinese New Year festival at City Hall. Photograph: Niall Carson/PA.

type, and in the back of my mind I think that the trick of being able to name two or three disparate African artists makes me one with my brothers. If a journalist should always have a keen sense of the superficial, then you are reading a man at one with his calling.

When we spoke, Ade was heading home to be at the African Cup of Nations. Naturally I enthused about this and encouraged him to do some writing and reports on the matter when he got there.

When we parted, though, I came away with a keen sense of *déjà vu*. I felt the same as I had felt years ago over the African music disco business. I was very enthused and positive and keen to display my minuscule shards of knowledge and the fact that I consider African football to be a good thing, but my knowledge is shallow and sketchy.

Years ago, when I got into this business, one of the first paying gigs I had was to write little preview boxes for the 1990 World Cup. If there were rules for the coverage of African soccer, they were rudimentary and old school. The writer would examine in detail the prospects of all European and South American contenders, and then proceed to treat Africa as one all-purpose country. Cameroon being the exception, of course, because Roger Milla was then the oldest man in the world and we all found him perfectly charming.

Then there would be some general aspirational stuff and a little schoolboy sociology. Writers noted breathily that African countries were always about to take their place on the world stage. Nigeria, in particular, was just about to realise its immense potential and express that realisation through football.

African countries always won many friends with their natural athleticism and refreshing approach to the game. They were the future of world football, but could, tut tut, only be confirmed as such when they learned discipline. Old, un-reconstructed types referred to the 'dark continent'.

African football was always refreshing. The smart young writer would comment approvingly that they love their football, them Africans.

On a more serious note, however, he would notice that there are no cities in Africa, a lack which gives them a tremendous advantage: everybody runs everywhere barefoot and this makes them very hardy. All pieces would end with the convivial thought that it was time for them to arrive. Any sociologists still standing would refer to the teams representing individual countries by their nicknames. The Eagles! The Lions! The Elephants!

All this time later it is interesting to see how things have changed. That is, not very much at all. The African Cup of Nations which began yesterday is still filtered through European media as a novelty package with a level of seriousness about it not commensurate with us clever European folks whose continental tournament later this year will be filled with so many exhibitions of extemporary dullness that we will be able to laud ourselves yet again on our tactical nous and sophistication.

We always like to think that we are five to 10 years ahead of the best of Africa. Maybe this tendency to patronise is no bad thing. It might help preserve a necessary distance. When European and African football mingle, the result is always the same. European involvement in African soccer has

Wayne O'Donoghue (in the rear seat) leaves Midlands Prison, driven by his father, Ray O'Donoghue, and accompanied by his solicitor, Frank Buttimer, after serving three years for the manslaughter of Robert Holohan in January 2005. Photograph: Alan Betson.

by and large been a contamination, a sporting extension of the old colonialism and imperialism. We have taken the continent's best players when our own have become too uppity and demanding. We have endeavoured to coach out of them the natural talent which attracted us to them in the first place. We go to some lengths to purchase African players and then act surprised and hurt when they turn out to be, well, African, and would like to return home to play for their African countries in events like the African Cup of Nations which self-ishly they stage during the Premiership season.

They just don't understand.

In exchange for the best of their players, we have sent to Africa the most affordable of our coaches. Most of the sides competing in Ghana over the next few weeks are coached by Europeans, and our besuited chaps have infected African football with such discipline and sterility that you have to stop and wonder if the whole debate shouldn't have been about what European sides needed to shed so that they could just lighten up and enjoy the game.

Yesterday it all kicked off for the 26th time in Accra. The African Cup of Nations! Ghana entertained Guinea in the opening game, and though a shock hadn't been ruled out the pressure was on Ghana. Those of us who are Leeds fans and who loved in an aching, almost physical way Tony Yeboah will always have a soft spot for Ghana.

Indeed, back in Tony's heyday (which was considerable), he played on a Ghanaian side which seemed to sum up African football for everyone at the time. Leading Germany (no less) by a goal to nil at half-time in a friendly in Bochum, the side (which also boasted Abedi Pele) fell to doing what Dutch teams had been doing for many years before that: they argued, so the story goes, over their match bonuses. The squabble was unresolved as they went back out on to the field. They managed to lose 6-1.

Yesterday, as we ploughed through this job of scribbling while stealing glances at the progress of the game, we rooted first and foremost for the story. For Ghana and Guinea to produce a game that would fit into the recent sterility of Nations Cup games and thus happily buttress the arguments being poured into this column like wet cement.

Of course they would do nothing of the sort. It was only two goals to one but the football was wonderful and Ghana won it in the end with a shot from Sulley Muntari who makes his money at Portsmouth but who, having scored such a screamer during the transfer window, could be with a big-four club by February.

Muntari's goal and much of the play that preceded it were a disgusting display of arrogance by a home side that seemed prepared to make a fool of this columnist in particular. So be it. Both sides were managed by Frenchmen.

Obviously, the tempering influence of European soccer on the African game is a good and joyous thing. All other opinions should be discounted. Grrrr.

TUESDAY, 22 JANUARY 2008

Demented Notions of Patriotism

Fintan O'Toole

When Fianna Fáil is in a corner, it tends to reveal itself. An underlying, and perhaps unconscious, world view emerges. It can be summed up in three words: *L'etat c'est nous* – we are the State.

If the mystical mood is upon them, 'the nation' can be substituted for 'the State'. The belief is rooted in history and ideology, in the sense of being the republican vanguard that really represents the essence of the Irish people. Reinforced by the experience of being an almost permanent party of government, and stripped of its historical and ideological meaning, it becomes the epitome of

Fine Gael leader Enda Kenny being interviewed outside Leinster House in Dublin. Photograph: Cyril Byrne.

banana republicanism – the dictator's equation of criticism with treason.

Just as everything in history is repeated, the first time as tragedy and the second as farce, this notion reached its apogee of comic bathos last week when Mary O'Rourke was on Newstalk radio's *Breakfast Show*, talking about Enda Kenny's temerity in criticising the Taoiseach the day before he departed for Africa.

She told Ger Gilroy: 'Can I say on Enda Kenny, I cannot believe a leader of a very proud party called Fine Gael committed such a disloyal treasonous act. The Taoiseach was out of the country. He was flying the flag for Ireland. As I sit here at my desk, I've a small Irish flag on my desk to remind me of the honour of being a member of the Oireachtas. He's doing business for Ireland, he's flying the flag . . . What has enraged me,

absolutely enraged me is the idea that you could commit such an act of treason that you would seek to pull him down while he is away doing the Government's business, the country's business.'

As a comic turn, the notion that it is treasonous to raise the awkward issue of Bertie Ahern's finances and tax affairs when he is outside the jurisdiction (including, presumably, when he is in Manchester) is good for a laugh. But this 'hit me now with the green flag wrapped around me' posture has a serious side.

For when you put this notion of treason beside the Taoiseach's own notion of its opposite – patriotism – you get some idea of the brazenness that besets us.

It was Ahern who described Charles Haughey as, of all things, 'a patriot to his fingertips'. When a man who prostitutes the most important office of

State for money is a great patriot and anyone who dares to criticise the Taoiseach's finances is a traitor, the topsy turvy morality of the party stands forward, naked and unashamed.

When the party is the leader and the leader is the State, these demented notions of patriotism and treason make some kind of weird sense. Let's remember what, in this world view, is not treasonous. It is not treason to line your pockets with private donations while you're in well-paid public office.

It is not treasonous to evade the tax and exchange laws of your country, as Haughey did, by stashing that money in the Cayman Islands. It is not treasonous to accept large sums from private citizens while you are minister for finance. Or to withhold evidence from a tribunal established by the Oireachtas until it discovers it for itself. Or to be unable to produce a tax clearance certificate. Or to state, quite bluntly, that you appoint people to State boards because they are your friends. But it is treasonous to criticise any of these things.

This notion goes back a long way, to the days when anyone who didn't agree with militant Irish nationalism was by definition 'anti-national' and 'unpatriotic'. But it was the Haughey generation that made it a high crime of State to disagree with Fianna Fáil about things other than the national question.

O'Rourke's late brother Brian Lenihan, as early as 1963, told a party meeting in Roscommon that, in relation to a forthcoming budget, 'they would meet criticism but he wanted them to remember that most, the vast majority of people from whom criticism would come, were antinational. One found that the people who supported Fianna Fáil came from a national background'.

Later, Tom McEllistrim famously said of criticism of Haughey by Des O'Malley: 'That's treason.' Seán Doherty justified the tapping of the phones of Bruce Arnold and Geraldine Kennedy on the grounds that they were discussing 'treason'.

The resort to this rhetoric now is certainly a token of desperation. But it does explain the failure of even one senior figure in a party that prides itself on its patriotism to condemn either Ahern's acceptance of money from private donors or the extraordinary stories he has told both the public and the Mahon tribunal.

If the leader of Fianna Fáil embodies the State, then by definition he cannot dishonour the State. No amount of grubbiness, no extreme of evasion, can be seen as disloyalty to Ireland, because that quality belongs innately to those who are outside Fianna Fáil. And when patriots are traitors and traitors patriots, how can public morality mean anything?

This is, of course, the utmost codology. That we have to take it at all seriously is, in its own way, a kind of humiliation. But it is, risibly and shamefully, a fact of our strange political life.

TUESDAY, 29 JANUARY 2008

Slayings Continue in Kenya as Gangs Hunt down Victims

Rob Crilly, in Naivasha

The gang was baying for blood and wouldn't believe Peter Oduri as he tried to deny being a member of the Luo tribe. But the 10 youths armed with pangas knew how to check. They pushed their way into the tiny shack and forced him to strip naked, whooping with delight when they saw the evidence. Oduri had not been circumcised, marking him out as a Luo living far from home in the small market town of Naivasha.

'They cut him down with a panga to his neck,' said his brother John, speaking in the safety of the town's police station.

The attackers were from the Kikuyu tribe, which has launched a string of revenge attacks in the past week as Kenya descends into a new round of ethnic violence. Some 800 people have died

So keen were the people behind the new Gael Coláiste secondary school in Arklow, Co. Wicklow, to get it built that they decided not to wait for the ESB to remove two electricity poles in the way of construction. The poles were taken down subsequently. Photograph: Garry O'Neill.

since President Mwai Kibaki was sworn in at the end of last month after a ballot dismissed as flawed by most observers. Raila Odinga, the main opposition leader, insists the election was stolen from him.

The violence has transformed a country once seen as a haven of stability and economic growth into a cauldron of ethnic tension. At first opposition supporters, drawn largely from the Kalenjin and Luo tribes, had targeted Kikuyus from the same ethnic group as Mr Kibaki.

The lakeside town of Naivasha, about 55 miles from Nairobi, had escaped the weeks of clashes until Sunday morning. The Kikuyu gangs arrived at about 8.30am and began hacking and torching their way around the town in a day of revenge.

Mr Oduri, his tatty clothes still spattered with blood, said the attackers were from out of town. They were guided by locals from house to house, seeking out opposition supporters. 'They were hunting Luos,' he said.

At least 22 people were killed in the town during the weekend. Most died after they were chased into shacks which were then set alight, said Grace Kakai, a police commander.

Yesterday, Naivasha remained tense. Smoke still rose into the sky from Kabati slum, the scene of the worst trouble on Sunday. Volleys of gunfire echoed around the town as police fought running battles with youths.

At one point rival tribes confronted each other close to the flower farms that make this area one of Kenya's richest. Police fired tear-gas and live rounds to keep them apart. The attacks in Naivasha provoked a series of tit-for-tat exchanges elsewhere.

Hundreds of Luo demonstrators took to the streets of Kisumu, an opposition stronghold in western Kenya. They set light to barricades and began looting shops. Eldoret in the Rift Valley saw similar scenes.

The latest violence shows the huge task facing Kofi Annan, former secretary general of the United Nations, as he attempts to mediate between Mr Odinga and Mr Kibaki.

THURSDAY, 31 JANUARY 2008

The Irish Breast Uncovered

Ann Marie Hourihane

It would be wrong to use this column to undermine the gaiety of the nation, and it would be irresponsible to chip away at said gaiety, pleasure by pleasure.

However, this week, with news of the job losses at the Allergan plant in Arklow, it does seem opportune to dwell a little on the subject of breasts. Allergan manufactures breast implants, amongst

Thomas Mitchell, chairman of the newly formed Press Council of Ireland, speaking in the former House of Lords in the Bank of Ireland, College Green, Dublin, at the launch of the council. Seated with him are (left) the then justice minister, Brian Lenihan, and the Press Ombudsman, John Horgan. Photograph: Brenda Fitzsimons.

other things. Mind you, in this culture it is always opportune to dwell on breasts. Never has so much been exposed by so many to, well, everyone else.

At one point Irish women had to do their very best to pretend that we did not have breasts as they were an occasion of other people's sin. We had to swathe them in wool and wear our overcoats indoors in case we started a riot, or upset the priests, who were notoriously sensitive in these matters.

In the 1960s and 1970s breasts became unfashionable, and were, therefore, a cause of shame both on the grounds of Irish morality and – much more woundingly for the young – international fashion.

In the 1960s Barbara Windsor built a career on exposing her breasts in the most inappropriate circumstances. Younger readers should note that in those days Barbara Windsor was a comedienne, not the great dramatic actress she is today. Her breasts were funny because they were unavoidable.

Even in the 1980s breasts were strictly for evening wear; it was just about permissible to stick a bit of diamante in your cleavage after dark, but the breasts, like Cinderella and vampires, were usually home before it was bright. (Often in somebody else's home, but that's another story.)

The point here is, whatever happened to cocktail hour? Now, though. Now. Now breasts are exposed, in the most casual manner, in the most surprising circumstances. Like the bank, for example. And the supermarket. And the reception area of very respectable offices. And the newsagent's.

Even as a female it is hard to know how you are supposed to react to an eyeful of someone else's cleavage at 10.30 in the morning.

It is difficult not to be curious when, as an anonymous bystander, you can see straight down someone's blouse to the lowest point of a stranger's bra. The ubiquity of the exposed breast makes dirty old men of us all – even if you are female.

There are surely many reasons for the fact that the Irish breast has never been so visible. The booming economy used to be just such a reason.

Breasts, like short skirts, have frequently been taken as a sign of economic plenty.

The sexualisation of our culture, where the female ideal is taken directly from the porn industry, is surely another.

This is not the place to explore the reasons why our beautiful young women seem determined to look like very tanned, dollar-a-night lap-dancers. But the acquisition of brand new, surgically-enhanced breasts has also had an impact on the amount of cleavage shown in public. There is a crude term for this phenomenon: Pay And Display.

Yet the breast thing is bigger than that. Breasts have broken through the barriers of the sexual context, they have left even flirting far behind them, and hit the main street. By this I mean that the exposed breast is everywhere, all the time. Even women who are not dressed to impress, or to seduce, who are just going about their daily business, have those top buttons undone. Maybe it's a form of aggression. As one man put it: 'You're meant to look but you're not allowed.'

Last year Britain's home secretary Jacqui Stephen scored a first in the House of Commons when she delivered one of the first speeches of her new appointment with a television camera pointing straight down her top. You can see the logic of her position. She's a substantial woman, in a man's world, and the fashion advice in those circumstances is to wear a big necklace and emphasise your femininity. Mistake.

For the exposure of younger women's breasts I blame the porn industry, and the eternal female desire to please.

For the exposure of older women's breasts I blame Trinny and Susannah and the eternal female desire not to be left behind. We all know the Trinny and Susannah tactic on this: you're over 35, you've put on a bit of pud, your waist is gone, for God's sake get a good bra to hoik them up a bit, and show that you're still game.

While many of us would sympathise with – nay, live by – this world view, it does have its limits.

When Trinny and Susannah say that we should show a bit of cleavage because it 'hints at what could yet be revealed' it might be worthwhile considering if your colleagues and bosses and customers want to be thinking about what yet could be revealed, especially if you are, for example, a lawyer.

Behind all this breast exposure is a new and troubling distrust of the male imagination. Someone should sit down and talk to the men who were young in the 1950s, in the days of the Sweater Girls. They managed, you know.

FRIDAY, 1 FEBRUARY 2008

Low Lie the Illegal Irish and God Help those who Fall Ill

Letter from Boston: Kevin Cullen

Eddie Treacy was a man of simple pleasures. He didn't ask for, nor expect, much. Once, he told his great pal, Muldoon, that he'd be happy if he died in his own bed and they played 'The Fields of Athenry' at his funeral. Eddie and Muldoon laughed at that, because they were young and young men don't think they'll die.

Last week, Eddie Treacy died in his own bed, in the Dorchester section of Boston, and they played 'The Fields of Athenry' at his funeral here in the American city where he lived in the shadows. He was 33-years-old and he had an eminently treatable form of pneumonia. But he was also living in Boston illegally, one of the thousands of Irish who live in a country increasingly hostile to those who are undocumented.

He left Athenry and came to Boston eight years ago, joining his brother Michael as part of the last great wave of young Irish to come to the most

Irish city in America. After 160 years of steady immigration from Ireland to Boston, the boom created by the Celtic Tiger and the crackdown created by 9/11 have conspired to make Boston and the rest of America far less desirable a destination for the young, undocumented Irish.

But Boston is still Irish enough to be a comfortable and comforting home for young men like Eddie Treacy. There's plenty of work. The GAA pitches in the suburb of Canton hum at the weekends. And there's good brown bread and scones to be had at the Greenhills Bakery in Dorchester every day. Michael went home, but Eddie stayed on. He liked it here.

Eddie was a master carpenter and made a good living. For a young man, he was decidedly old school, using a simple tool called a square. Eddie only needed one measurement for a job. Others would punch away at calculators, but Eddie would do the calculations in his head, and hand off the wood, cut precisely, like a diamond.

After a day's work, Eddie would make his way to the Eire Pub for a few jars. If the stool next to Muldoon, a plasterer from Galway, was open, he would take it. 'How's Mul?' Eddie would ask. 'How's Eddie?' Muldoon would ask back.

And then they would silently watch the news on the TV, or step outside for a wordless smoke, watching the rush-hour commuters stream toward the suburbs. With Eddie, there was no need for long yarns or running commentary. Eddie was a rare Irishman in that he was a great listener, not a great talker. If he agreed with you, he'd nod, almost imperceptibly. If he thought you were a chancer, he'd raise an eyebrow, a silent indictment.

Like other illegal immigrants, he wanted to legalise his residency. He would have paid anything, done anything. But there was no way. The immigration system in the US is broken, and there is no will to fix it.

Eddie kept his head down, and kept to the shadows. It's unclear if it was just stubborn pride or a fear of being deported that kept him from going to a hospital to treat the pneumonia that killed him. Maybe he just didn't realise how sick he really was.

Sister Marguerite Kelly, a nun from Ballinasloe who works with immigrants in the Irish Pastoral Centre in Boston, sat at Eddie's wake and shook her head.

'The young people, the undocumented, a lot of them are afraid to go to the hospital,' she said. 'I don't know if that's what happened with Eddie, but it happens a lot.'

Gerry Treacy hadn't seen his brother in eight years, and when he finally did Eddie was lying in a casket inside the Keaney Funeral Home on Dorchester Avenue. 'He was a quiet lad,' Gerry Treacy said, softly.

Next to the open casket, there was a photo of Eddie, in a jaunty pose, a cowboy hat on his head, a thin cigar in his mouth. He looked like the Sundance Kid. In front of the photo, there was a sliothar. Eddie was a great man for the hurling. He hurled for the Father Tom Burke club in Dorchester and managed the club's juniors.

Brendan McCann, a senior at Boston College High School, whose father emigrated from Co. Antrim some 30 years before, stood near the altar and played 'The Fields' on his fiddle as they wheeled Eddie's casket down the aisle of St Brendan's Church.

After Mass, about 200 people posed on the front steps of the church for a photo to send to Eddie's mother, Ann, in Galway so she would know that Eddie mattered here. Many of the young men standing there, shivering in the cold, had given up a day's wages to pay their respects.

Then everybody went round to Sonny's, the pub that sponsors the hurling teams Eddie played for and managed. Muldoon raised a glass to his friend. 'We'll never see the likes of him again,' he said.

On Monday night, as President Bush gave the State of the Union address, telling Congress and the American people that they need to find 'a sensible and humane way to deal with people here

illegally,' Eddie Treacy's body was in the cargo hold of Aer Lingus flight 132, somewhere over the Atlantic, heading home.

Eddie Treacy was buried yesterday in the fields of Athenry.

SATURDAY, 9 FEBRUARY 2008

The Next President?

Denis Staunton, in Washington

On Thursday afternoon, John McCain stood before hundreds of conservative activists in a packed Washington ballroom and asked them to put aside their long-held antipathy and unite behind him. Two hours earlier, Mitt Romney had told the same audience that he was leaving the presidential race, effectively clearing the way for McCain to become, at 71, the Republican Party's nominee for president.

Some of the activists booed McCain as soon as he appeared onstage and others gazed sullenly ahead in disbelief that a man they have viewed for years as the sworn enemy of the conservative movement is about to become their party's standard-bearer.

Just six months ago, with his campaign broke and in disarray after most of his senior staff had resigned or been fired, McCain was almost universally dismissed as a dead man walking in the presidential race.

'His poll numbers plummeted, the fundraising dried up and he was really written off as a candidate for most of 2007,' says Grant Lally, a member of McCain's legal team and his campaign's vice-chair in New York. 'It's really by dint of his hard work and his decency and his sincerity that a lot of people in the Republican Party who had walked away from him gave him another look and came back into the fold.'

McCain, who had started out as his party's front-runner, burned through $24 million (€16.5 million) in the first few months of last year, hiring teams of consultants and flying the media around the country to campaign events. By the summer, he was travelling by bus and staying in cheap motels as he campaigned in New Hampshire, sometimes before audiences numbering less than two dozen people.

'A lot of people disappeared. A lot of people signed up to other campaigns,' Lally says. 'I hosted an Irish for McCain fundraiser at the very end of June of 2007 and it was very tough to get people to come to the event or to write cheques to support Senator McCain. By contrast, at that point, Rudy Giuliani had raised $60 million for his campaign and Mitt Romney was raising inordinate amounts of money.'

Last November, with the first caucuses and primaries looming and $500,000 in debt, McCain applied for a $3 million overdraft from a Maryland bank, offering his fundraising lists as collateral. The bank told him that, because of his age, he would have to take out a life insurance policy in case he didn't survive the campaign.

McCain has not only survived but thrived on a punishing schedule of 18-hour days packed with events, campaigning harder than the younger rivals he has dispatched one by one. Losing his front-runner status seemed to liberate McCain, and as he recaptured the straight-talking, irreverent style he adopted during his 2000 presidential run, Americans saw the side of him they like best.

'John McCain is always strongest as the underdog and when he faces adversity he fights hardest,' says Lally.

Near-death experiences are nothing new to John McCain, who has survived three plane crashes, a fire aboard an aircraft carrier that killed more than 100 men, a bayoneting by a Vietnamese mob and years of torture and beatings in a Hanoi prisoner-of-war camp. He is still unable to lift his arms to shoulder level or to comb his own hair on account of broken bones left untreated by his Vietnamese captors.

The son and grandson of admirals, McCain spent much of his childhood moving from one naval base to another, and when he left school he

John McCain, Republican Party nominee for the US presidency, campaigning in New York before the Super Tuesday primaries in February. Photograph: Mario Tama/Getty Images.

went to the United States Naval Academy in Annapolis.

'He says he didn't like going to the Naval Academy, but I was unaware of that,' his 96-year-old mother Roberta recalled in an interview last month. 'In our day, a boy, if his father was in the navy, he just went to the Naval Academy. In my mind, it was just automatic.'

Rebellious and stubborn, McCain was seldom out of trouble at the academy and came close to being expelled for receiving too many disciplinary actions. He graduated fifth from the bottom of a class of 899 in 1958; John Poindexter, one of the key figures in the Iran-Contra scandal during the 1980s, came first.

McCain became a naval pilot, flying attack aircraft, and in 1964 he married Carole Shepp, a divorced mother of two children. In the spring of 1967, he was sent to Vietnam aboard the aircraft carrier *USS Forrestal*, receiving shrapnel wounds a few months later when a rocket was fired accidentally on board, causing a fire that killed 134 men.

On 26 October 1967, McCain was flying a bombing mission over Hanoi when his plane was hit by a surface-to-air missile. As he ejected from the aircraft, he struck part of the plane, breaking his left arm, his right arm in three places and his right knee and was knocked unconscious.

He plunged into a lake in the centre of Hanoi and, when he came to, he was being hauled ashore by a group of angry Vietnamese civilians.

'A crowd of several hundred Vietnamese gathered around me as I lay dazed before them, shouting wildly at me, stripping my clothes off, spitting on me, kicking and striking me repeatedly,'

he wrote in his memoir, *Faith of My Fathers*.

'Someone smashed a rifle butt into my shoulder, breaking it. Someone else stuck a bayonet in my ankle and groin.' An army truck arrived and took McCain to Hoa Lo prison, known to prisoners of war as the Hanoi Hilton, where he was interrogated and told that he would not receive medical treatment until he gave them information about his aircraft and future targets. After the Vietnamese discovered that McCain's father was one of the most senior officers in the US Navy, they took him to a hospital where he was given blood and glucose and several shots but received no treatment for his injuries.

McCain spent two years in solitary confinement and at one stage the beatings he received became so regular and intense that he agreed to write and record a false confession, describing himself as an 'air pirate' and denouncing US policy. He deliberately used stilted, communist jargon to

Elephant mother Yasmin, with her new born (un-named) son at Dublin Zoo. Photograph: Bryan O'Brien.

signal that the confession was coerced but was so ashamed of having broken the navy's code of conduct that he tried to hang himself in his cell, only to be interrupted by a guard.

He refused to accept an early release, insisting that those Americans captured before him should be freed first. It was not until March 1973, after the Paris peace accords ended the direct involvement of the US in Vietnam, that McCain was released.

Returning to the US, McCain discovered that his wife had been badly injured in a car accident and was using crutches. They resumed their life together for a few years, but by the late 1970s McCain had started seeing other women and they divorced in 1980.

Too severely disabled to return to a combat role, McCain became the navy's liaison with the US senate, developing an interest in politics and an admiration for Ronald Reagan.

At a party in Honolulu in 1979, McCain met Cindy Lou Hensley, a teacher from Phoenix, Arizona, where her family owned a large beer distribution business. She was 18 years his junior, but they discovered when they married the following year that each had lied about their age, she pretending to be three years older and McCain knocking four years off his age.

Cindy's father's wealth and political connections helped McCain to secure a congressional seat in Arizona in 1982, and he won Barry Goldwater's senate seat in 1986. His first senate term was overshadowed by a scandal that linked him to the collapse of a savings and loan association owned by Charles Keating, a generous Republican donor.

McCain, who had received more than $100,000 in donations and a number of private plane trips from Keating, was accused with four other senators of trying to pressure regulators on Keating's behalf. A senate investigation found that McCain had exercised poor judgment but he was not prosecuted.

As McCain struggled to rescue his reputation, his wife was secretly enduring an ordeal of her own

as she became addicted to the prescription painkillers Percocet and Vicodin following a back injury.

'When people think of drugs, they envision some guy in the street with cocaine, which, quite frankly, was my arrogant attitude as well,' she told *Harper's Bazaar* last year.

'That was the darkest period of my life. I was in pain, took too many pills, and, like many women, just fell into it.' Cindy started stealing painkillers from a charity she ran, which sent medical teams to Third World countries, and she was investigated by federal authorities. Cindy had three children with McCain, but after a number of miscarriages, she adopted a Bangladeshi girl she met during a field trip to India with her medical charity, calling her Bridget.

During McCain's 2000 presidential bid, supporters of George W. Bush in South Carolina spread a rumour that McCain had fathered a biracial child with another woman. Googling her name recently, Bridget learned about the rumours.

'Over the years, I was always afraid that someone at school would say something, but they didn't,' Cindy said. 'It just never clicked that she'd look herself up on the internet. She was so upset, took it so personally. John and I tried to make Bridget understand that people who say things like that are very wrong; it's not what we – nor most people – are about.'

Despite suffering a stroke in 2004, Cindy has been an almost constant presence on the campaign in recent months, adding a touch of elegance to McCain's rough and ready events.

McCain prides himself on his readiness to voice unwelcome truths, christening his campaign bus the 'Straight Talk Express' and bragging about his refusal to pander to public opinion. His support for comprehensive immigration reform, which would have allowed most of the 12 million undocumented immigrants in the US to remain in the country legally, has alienated much of the Republican base.

Groups such as the National Rifle Association and anti-abortion organisations will never forgive him for sponsoring campaign finance legislation that limits their role in elections. And many congressmen resent the role he played in exposing Jack Abramoff, a corrupt Republican lobbyist who pleaded guilty to a number of felonies in 2006.

He has been the strongest and most consistent supporter of Bush's surge strategy in Iraq, but he stood against the president in opposing the use of torture on terrorist suspects. And he has angered the oil and motor industries with his demand for tougher environmental standards and a new international agreement on combating climate change.

McCain's temper is legendary in Washington and numerous lawmakers have faced his foul-mouthed diatribes, only to receive a letter of apology the following day.

McCain served up a more measured dose of straight talk when he addressed the American Ireland Fund dinner in Washington three years ago and, with Gerry Adams in the audience, launched a blistering attack on Sinn Féin and the IRA.

'Stealing from banks and slaying men in the streets to settle personal grievances are not the acts of freedom fighters. They are the work of a small minority trying to hold back the forces of history and democracy, and they hurt the very people for whom they claim to fight,' he said. 'Whatever your views about the historic cause they claimed to have served or the methods they employed – which were, in my opinion, indefensible – no one can honestly claim today that the IRA is anything better than an organised crime syndicate that steals and murders to serve its members' personal interests.'

Although he traces his ancestry to Co. Antrim, McCain's interest in Ireland is relatively recent and he initially opposed Bill Clinton's engagement in the North. He warmed to the peace process later, however, and is now an admirer of all things Irish, including the books of William Trevor and Roddy Doyle.

'A McCain presidency would be great for Ireland,' Lally says. 'John McCain loves Ireland.

He loves Irish America. He's part of Irish America and he identifies very closely with Ireland. He knows his family roots very well. He knows they go back to Ireland and Scotland and he's very familiar with the Irish peace process. He knows Bertie Ahern. He's met Ian Paisley and all the leaders in the Irish political world. He's very comfortable with the Irish political leadership.'

If McCain wins in November, he will be the oldest man ever to be elected to the White House but also the president with the most remarkable and compelling personal story. He is the Republican candidate Democrats fear most on account of his appeal beyond the Republican fold.

Despite his differences with the Republican mainstream, a McCain presidency would be uncompromisingly conservative, cutting government spending and taxes, appointing conservative judges to the supreme court and keeping US troops in Iraq.

He would bring to the White House a sensibility seldom found outside the military, an old-fashioned sense of honour and a patriotism shaped by his captivity in Vietnam.

'In prison, I fell in love with my country,' he wrote in his memoir. 'I had loved her before then, but like most young people, my affection was little more than a simple appreciation for the comforts and privileges most Americans enjoyed and took for granted. It wasn't until I had lost America for a time that I realised how much I loved her.'

FRIDAY, 15 FEBRUARY 2008

Bloody and Unbowed

Michael Dwyer

Daniel Day-Lewis has spent the past two months caught up in the whirlwind of the awards season, travelling from one ceremony to another and collecting prize after prize for his towering performance in *There Will Be Blood*.

Daniel Day-Lewis in **There will be Blood**. *Photograph: Melinda Sue Gordon.*

The tour comes to an end on Sunday week at the Academy Awards ceremony, where Day-Lewis well deserves to collect his second Oscar as best actor, which he first received in 1990 for his extraordinary portrayal of Christy Brown in Jim Sheridan's *My Left Foot*.

One of the finest films in years, *There Will Be Blood* is a riveting, intense drama directed with tremendous accumulating power by Paul Thomas Anderson (*Boogie Nights, Magnolia*).

Spanning the period 1898-1927, it stars Day-Lewis as a cold, self-made, hands-on businessman who makes his fortune from oil, regardless of all those he exploits in his acquisitive greed. In a performance of staggering depth and complexity, Day-Lewis portrays this misanthrope in all his sly charm, steely determination and volcanic ferocity.

When we meet, Day-Lewis is back on home ground in Co. Wicklow, where he lives with his wife, writer-director Rebecca Miller, and their two sons, Ronan and Cashel. He is on the school run and he suggests that we meet in the bar of Ardmore Studios in Bray, where he has happy memories of filming *My Left Foot* and Sheridan's *The Boxer*.

We have the bar to ourselves, and Day-Lewis is in engaging, expansive form as we talk for an hour and a half. He's glad to be home.

'It was with great relief that I touched down at Dublin airport,' he says. 'As lovely as the last few weeks have been, when you've trotted up and down a few red carpets and disgorged a few incomprehensible soundbites, you can feel that you've ceased to recognise yourself to some extent.

'It was hard to get back to normal life. That's where the real divide exists. It's not between the world of the work and the world of one's home life. It's really in that aspect of what they call the industry, which can be quite startling if you're not used to it. Jump back into that after a couple of years and you've forgotten what it's like.'

That includes doing the international interview circuit, which he has undertaken because he is so supportive of *There Will Be Blood*, even though it entails the rehashing of myths about his process as an actor and how he immerses himself in the roles he chooses to accept.

'The mistake you make is thinking that you can begin to set the record straight. The only response, really, is no response at all, and yet when you do not respond, rumour becomes confused with fact and the claims get wilder and wilder. Therefore, it appears that I invite that kind of stuff.

'You keep out of the way as much as you can, and that probably lends a specious aura of mystery to the whole thing. Then, when you engage in it, it seems like you're on an orgy of self-promotion. There doesn't seem to be any balance you can achieve that isn't going to have them sharpening their knives.'

In his native England, the media are always keen to remind Day-Lewis that he has not made a film in the UK since *A Room with a View* in 1985. 'I daresay over in England they feel every five years or so that I should be chopped back down to size.

'It was never my intention to avoid working in Britain. There's still that fascination and repulsion for American cinema. The British attitude is conflicted, to say the least. They like to be included in the big party, but they can't quite seem to get things on a sure footing for themselves. They're between the devil and the deep blue sea, really.

'All the flag-waving puts so much pressure on any British production that comes along. It's like the Falklands war when you make a film there. The people who make the films should be able to release them in the same way other films are released, without any added pressures. And they are making some very good British films. *This Is England* is a very fine film. *London to Brighton* was another one, so is *Control*.'

Then there was his recent *New York Times* interview, which claimed that after seeing *Taxi Driver*, Day-Lewis realised that he longed to be a great American actor.

'I had to excuse myself to so many people after that was published. Can you imagine me ever making a claim to be or to wish to be an American actor? It's completely ludicrous. The article was all done with good will, so it's hard to argue the point. But it's something that never occurred to me.

'When I was coming up and watching films, Ken Loach would have been one of the formative influences in my life, as before him were Lindsay Anderson, Karel Reisz and Tony Richardson, who were all part of the British social realist movement. I absolutely devoured all those films.

'There was a sense of discovering the exotic when I saw Martin Scorsese's work and Robert De Niro's work for the first time, having already seen the films of Clift and Brando. It never occurred to me that I might ever be a part of that world. At that time, very few actors from our part of the world had a chance to work on American films, and it seemed like our future would be predominantly in the theatre. And we accepted that, even though there was a secret wish to be part of cinema.'

Now 50, Day-Lewis was 33 when he won his Oscar for *My Left Foot*. What would winning again this year mean to him?

'It certainly would make me very popular at Paramount Pictures! Of course, when you get something like that for the first time, it feels unique, an unrepeatable experience. There's a particular kind of bewilderment that goes with an experience like that, especially when you're young.'

I recall meeting him at a party on the night he won his previous Oscar and how he described hearing Jodie Foster announce him as the winner as 'like being hit by a car'. He responds: 'It is a wonderful experience, but it's quite shocking as well. Who knows what's going to happen this year. There are so many good films and great performances. It's impossible not to seem as if you are on a campaign trail for it. George Clooney is very open and charming about it, and talks about kissing babies and so on. He's prepared to do his bit.

'But it does seem strange to me, having done a piece of work which you then invite people to look at and make up their minds about, that you then go on an almost entirely separate venture which involves trying to charm people into thinking that you're terrific. I just don't really understand that.'

Paul Thomas Anderson has said that he wrote *There Will Be Blood* for Day-Lewis and wouldn't have made the film without him. 'It's probably easy for him to say that now,' Day-Lewis laughs. 'My feeling is that he probably wrote it partly with me in mind, but I think he didn't chain himself to the idea of one actor to the exclusion of any other. But he certainly didn't need to sell it to me.

'I was astonished by the audacity of it, the depth of the writing, the beauty of the language, and the sheer honesty of it. I felt there was something truly unconscious about it, a freedom to the writing, which was nonetheless beautifully ordered and sculpted, because he is a great craftsman, too.

'I sensed that, as a writer, he had begun to explore that world that he was imagining through the experiences and the eyes of that character . . . I felt he understood that world from the inside. I felt a kinship with that and the work that I do.'

There Will Be Blood is set early in the last century, but its themes are just as relevant today, when greed for oil and religious zealotry are at the root of so much conflict in the world.

'Those echoes are apparent in the film, but for us, the work is a much more selfish endeavour than that. It's focused very narrowly on a very specific period in time, a very specific culture, and very particular lives within that culture. I don't think any of us was consciously working towards any kind of commentary on the world today.'

Does Day-Lewis believe, then, that movies tend to be over-analysed? 'Sometimes I think that's true. In the case of our film, most of the discussion about it has been quite vigorous, and I'm glad that the film has made people want to talk about stuff that is important. There's nothing better than that, really.

'Film has become such a central part of our culture now that I think sometimes too great a weight is placed upon it in terms of scrutiny and analysis. There's a lot of rather specious professorial stuff that swirls around films, I think. At the same time, God bless people who do study films, because it keeps alive the possibility that you're working on something important.'

Another central theme of *There Will Be Blood* is capitalism as personified by Plainview, and he has his equivalents in the modern world who, no matter how much wealth they have, are intent on accumulating even more.

'Power may be part of it,' Day-Lewis says, 'but my feeling is that the fever becomes an end in itself. People always imagine that Los Angeles is founded on the film industry, but it's not. It's founded on muck, on oil. The early photographs of the city show a forest of oil derricks with tiny houses lined between them. All the thoroughfares would have been swamps, with crude oil and overspills running down the streets. The whole place was founded on pollution.

'When Plainview is camping in his mansion, it's an echo of his way of life in the silver mining days. Because of the nature of that work, most men would have been brutalised by it. Most would have been broken by the experience, and of those who survived, most would have done so without any reward whatsoever.

'Those few who actually were rewarded with great showers of gold, like Plainview, seemed like they were still rooted in the savagery of those days when they were groping in the dark at the bottom of mineshafts, living like animals and having abandoned their wives and children for months and years. The only thing that sustains them is the fever.

'At a given moment, down in the dark they will see something glitter, and the pulse starts to beat faster and that may carry them to the next lease on a piece of scrap land and just enough money to dig another hole and maybe that's going to be the big one. In the process of developing those leases, of course, they have had to betray many people and they themselves probably have been betrayed very often.

'So deceit and brutality, and physical hardship and spiritual anguish, are very much part of their experience. They are irretrievable by the time they build these great pyramids to themselves, like the Plainview mansion.'

Having spent so much time deep inside Plainview's skin, how did Day-Lewis feel when shooting ended and he had to leave the character behind?

'More than anything, I suppose, I felt a great sense of sadness. That isn't exclusively sadness at putting aside a life that has engaged your curiosity for a long period of time, but the entire experience, largely thanks to Paul, had been such an invigorating one. It always seems like you're in an experiment that could go horribly wrong.'

One of the most daring aspects of the film is the 12-minute opening sequence, which employs all the elements of pure cinema – the acting, the direction, the camera movement, the production and costume designs – to speak the language of film without using any dialogue.

'That was an intoxicating sequence. We shot that in the first few days and it tells you everything you need to know about that man at that time in his life, without saying a word.

'The sensation I felt as I read it was the same as the first time I read Jim's script for *My Left Foot*. It described Christy's foot in a lengthy opening sequence, reaching into his record collection, choosing a record, putting it back and picking another one, switching the turntable on, putting it on the turntable, and then delicately placing the needle on a particular place, and changing the needle. That whole sequence was without dialogue, and I remember the very powerful visual sense Jim was able to create.'

Next month Day-Lewis will be taking care of his sons while their mother directs a new film, *The Private Lives of Pippa Lee*, which stars Robin Wright Penn, Keanu Reeves, Alan Arkin, Maggie Gyllenhaal and Monica Bellucci.

'It's a wonderful cast,' Day-Lewis says. 'It will be shot in Connecticut. I might get to swing a hammer because there are some sets to be built. That could be the perfect antidote to all this. I am in the craftsmen's union. After I worked on building the house in *The Crucible*, the union invited me to become a member. I'm very proud of that.'

Day-Lewis subsequently received the Oscar for best Actor for his role in There will be Blood.

SATURDAY, 16 FEBRUARY 2008

Chasing Lynn

Simon Carswell, in Cabanas, Portugal

Cabanas is a quiet, sun-soaked Portuguese fishing village on the Algarve coast to the east of the region's capital, Faro. If you were trying to avoid €84 million in bank claims, 126 High Court writs and angry investors, this little oasis would be on your shortlist for a place of refuge.

You can see why solicitor Michael Lynn saw potential for a property development in Cabanas. The eastern Algarve is very different to the resorts west of Faro, which are largely overbuilt and packed with holidaymakers. Cabanas is sleepy by comparison.

Five years ago the man from Crossmolina in Co. Mayo set out to build his first overseas holiday development at Cabanas through his Dublin-based property company, Kendar. He recognised that the attraction for investors would be huge – there are few places on the Algarve where you could buy an apartment for €220,000–€300,000 about 200 yards from the sea. He planned to build 272 apartments and 10 houses.

Solicitor Michael Lynn going to the High Court. He later fled the country. Photograph: David Sleator.

By the time Lynn's legal practice, Capel Law, was shut down by the Law Society on 15 October 2007, amid concerns about his property business and his dealings with a multitude of Irish banks, only the first of three phases had been built at Cabanas – 76 apartments. Customers had paid substantial deposits on many of the remaining apartments in phases two and three of the development, called Costa de Cabanas. Many investors are now confused about what's going to happen next since the high-profile collapse of Lynn's property group in October. They are unsure whether they will get their money back or get a new holiday home in the Algarve.

In the meantime, Irish banks are going into the High Court on an almost daily basis seeking judgments against Lynn – and in some cases against his wife, Bríd Murphy, as well – for multi-million euro loans drawn down by the 39-year-old solicitor and property developer. The case taken by the Law Society, which regulates the legal profession, is ongoing in the High Court. It is still investigating Lynn and his practice, while legal papers in one case against him have been referred to the Garda Bureau of Fraud Investigation, which is also examining his affairs.

Lynn was nowhere to be seen at his Portuguese development this week and his whereabouts are unknown. He was meant to have appeared in the High Court in December for two days of questioning by the Law Society, but failed to show. A warrant for his arrest was issued, but because the Law Society's case against him is a civil matter, no extradition proceedings could be brought against him. An individual can only be extradited in criminal proceedings, though the Law Society has argued before the High Court that his failure to appear for his cross-examination could constitute criminal contempt.

The Law Society had intended to quiz Lynn on his property dealings, and in particular on his drawing down of multiple mortgages using solicitors' undertakings, a trust mechanism used by solicitors in residential property transactions. To speed up deals and to reduce costs, banks provide loans on the basis that one solicitor involved in the transaction undertakes to register the loan security on the property at a later date. It has been alleged that Lynn used undertakings to draw down multiple loans and build up such massive debts.

Lynn's disappearance means he cannot be quizzed on how he amassed so much in loans to grow his property business in nine countries. He had been attending court regularly since the controversy emerged in mid-October after a solicitor in his practice, Fiona McAleenan, tipped off the Law Society.

There was no sign of Lynn at his properties in the Algarve this week. The shutters were down and the curtains drawn at his home in Quinta do Perogil, an estate that overlooks the town of Tavira. He was reported to have stayed here over Christmas.

Robert and Sheila Lee live in Lynn's house in Aldeia das Ferrarias, near the resort of Quinta do Lago in the western Algarve. Robert used to work for Lynn's Portuguese business as a project manager. Speaking at the house yesterday, Sheila said she had no idea where Lynn was and had not seen him since his wedding in Ireland last year. She said she was amazed at what has happened to Lynn in Ireland.

Not far from there, Lynn's apartment in Al-Sakia Village showed no sign of life. This was where Lynn accommodated staff who worked at the Kendar office in nearby Vilamoura. The office was also closed this week. Its windows have been painted white and a 'for rent' sign has been posted on the door.

Property sources on the Algarve said Lynn paid his Portuguese staff exceptionally well. One agent said Lynn offered a colleague more than three times her monthly salary to move to his company but she declined. One source said he was originally involved with local investors in the Cabanas development but fell out with them and they subsequently parted company.

'[Lynn] was in here with his wife a month or two months ago,' said a barman at Pedro's restaurant in Cabanas, a five-minute walk from the property development. 'He usually came in to eat most days when he was here but I haven't seen him for a month or two.' Lynn was spotted at Newark airport in New Jersey in the middle of last month after arriving on a flight from Lisbon. He reportedly told immigration officers in the US airport that he was on a three-day visit to the US and intended returning to Lisbon.

He was also seen last month in Tavira, five kilometres along the coast, west of Cabanas. At that time, he was spotted with Nuno Paulino, an accountant originally from Lisbon who has been in charge of Kendar Portugal since last year. The company is now called Vantea, having changed its name on 16 January last. The company's web address, *www.vantea.com*, brings visitors to *www.costadecabanas.eu*, which advertises the final two phases of the Cabanas project but carries no details of who owns Vantea or the names of the people managing the development.

The website tells potential investors that they must pay a €5,000 deposit for a property at Costa de Cabanas and 21 days later they must sign a contract and pay 30 per cent of the total apartment cost. The remainder must be paid on completion.

For some time, *The Irish Times* had been trying to contact Nuno Paulino to find out whether Irish investors would get their deposits back, but he failed to return calls or e-mails. On Thursday morning, this newspaper caught up with him as he arrived at the Cabanas sales office.

Speaking publicly for the first time, Paulino claimed Lynn was no longer involved in Costa de Cabanas and had sold his shares in Kendar Portugal last year.

'Michael Lynn sold his shares in the company and he resigned as manager in the third or last quarter of 2007,' said Paulino. Asked if Lynn received any money for his shares in Kendar, Paulino said: 'Supposedly yeah – he should have.'

He said Vantea was now owned by two Portuguese companies, Nota Breve and Numero Misto. He claimed Portuguese investors owned the companies but refused to name them.

Nota Breve and Numero Misto are 'sociedades anóminas' (SA) or anonymous societies, which are not required to publish the names of shareholders. Official Portuguese records show that Lynn transferred his interest in Kendar Portugal to the two SA companies on 6 December 2007 – the week before his disappearance in Ireland.

Paulino said Nota Breve and Numero Misto were 'normal companies' and 'not covering up anything', yet he still would not reveal their shareholders. The companies' registered address is an apartment in the tourist resort of Alvor, which is in the western Algarve. No one answered the door at the apartment yesterday.

Paulino said that, despite Lynn's financial difficulties, he wanted to protect his staff and clients by completing the Cabanas project. He claimed that even in the event that the project is not completed and investors do not receive properties, they would be able to register their interest in the land at Cabanas. He also claimed that the company still had the support of Millennium BCP, Portugal's largest bank, and local people. 'These new investors are represented by myself. We needed something behind us to finish the project. They are Portuguese, based in the Algarve,' he said.

Paulino hasn't seen Lynn since last month. 'I saw him when he was here in Portugal at the beginning of the year.'

No work has yet started on the second phase of Costa de Cabanas, even though investors were told before Christmas that work was due to start imminently. Paulino said he hoped 'infrastructure work' would start over the next six months and that the remaining apartments and houses would be built over the following 24 months. He claimed the company was still assessing tenders from contractors.

'We are still trying to commit with deadlines. There was a one-month delay. We had expected to start in December. The contract is ready to be signed. We are deciding who will have the best offer,' he said.

Referring to Lynn's problems in Ireland, Paulino said Kendar Holdings, 'the mother company' of the group, had collapsed, leaving its European subsidiaries as 'orphans'. Despite this, he said, Vantea would open a new office next to the town hall in Tavira to sell properties in the Algarve. It was outside this office that Lynn was seen with Paulino last month.

Investors are growing frustrated at the delays in the Cabanas project. A group of 36 investors who bought in the second and third phases of Costa de Cabanas off the plans have hired a Portuguese lawyer, Alves Caetano, who has offices in Vilamoura and Quarteira. He is planning to register a claim against the land in Cabanas to protect the investors' money.

Under Portuguese law, investors can claim double their money back from a developer if the project is not completed as agreed. This would give investors a strong hand in ensuring it is completed. Also, 2 per cent of the company is owned by Kendar in Dublin, Lynn's 'mother company', as Paulino put it. A liquidator was appointed to Kendar earlier this month and he may be able to have some say in the assets of the Portuguese company.

One Dublin woman who paid a deposit on an apartment in Cabanas said she and her husband had also paid the full amounts for properties 'off the plans' in two other Kendar projects, Amber Square in Hungary and in the Bulgaria ski resort of Bansko. She said they paid the full price in advance because friends had bought properties from Kendar and had made a substantial profit on their investments.

The investors would have been impressed with Lynn's strong network of auctioneers and sales agents, high-profile publicity campaigns, and what appeared to be a large Dublin law practice, she said.

'In the cold light of day we were very naïve. We took it in good faith that they were going to be built. We are shattered, absolutely shattered over what has happened,' she said.

No investor who spoke to *The Irish Times* wanted to be identified. One said he had bought in the first phase of Cabanas and had encountered no problems receiving rent from the management company in charge of the development, but he was owed money on the second phase.

Cabanas was one of Lynn's most valuable projects. A Kendar document dated 18 April 2007 showed the company had taken €12.1 million from investors in the first phase of 76 apartments. Last summer Kendar received loan approval of €25.6 million from Portugal's largest bank, Millennium BCP, to build phases two and three. Of this, €6 million was provided to Kendar Portugal the day the loan deal was agreed, according to a Portuguese title deed obtained by *The Irish Times*. It is not clear where this money has gone, however. According to the affidavit filed by Lynn in the High Court on 19 November last, the largest cash balance in any of his 10 accounts with four Portuguese banks was €924,349 in an account in Millennium BCP.

The deed valued the land on which phase two would be built at €15 million and the phase three property at €12 million – about four times more than what Lynn paid for the land. Given that the firm was charging an average €250,000 a property, the final value of the entire project could have been far in excess of €50 million. This may also explain why the company is so eager to complete the development.

Matters have changed drastically since then. Irish banks are trying to untangle the complex web of property deals and money transfers around Lynn's companies. The situation has been further complicated by the free flow of money between Lynn's law practice and property business, which are being investigated by a variety of parties.

The high court heard on Monday that €13 million was moved from Lynn's law practice to his property business last year, while €5 million came back to the practice. This flow of money concerned the Law Society deeply when it investigated Lynn last September – solicitors are forbidden from using client accounts for personal transactions. A substantial deficit in Lynn's client account prompted the Law Society to shut down his practice and seek a High Court order freezing his assets. This precipitated the collapse of his entire property group.

There appears to have been little separating Lynn's law practice and his property business. They had common staff, with the same individuals signing cheques for both the legal practice and Kendar. Their offices were next to each other in the ultra-modern Capel Building near the Four Courts, where Law Society officials are still sifting through Lynn's papers.

A separate company also linked the practice and business. Some investors said they were advised by Kendar or its agents to seek legal advice from a firm called Overseas Property Law (OPL) in Dublin. One investor said OPL demanded €2,000 up front for the advice and was not informed by Kendar that OPL was in fact part of Michael Lynn's law practice.

Many investors paid well over the odds on deposits for apartments in Cabanas. One investor said he paid a deposit of €100,000 to avail of a reduction in the overall price of the property.

About €84 million is now owed to Irish financial institutions by Lynn and his property companies. Millions more are owed to investors. Lynn said in his affidavit that his assets, mostly his 148 properties, were worth €52.4 million. This leaves a shortfall of at least €30 million. The affidavit, which lists 154 bank accounts, sheds little light on where this money might be. The top 20 cash balances in the 154 accounts total only

Karen Fitzpatrick models a full-length, silk, halter-neck dress for Brown Thomas. Photograph: Bryan O'Brien.

€3.5 million and the affidavit does not list balances on many accounts.

Banks have been scrambling to register first claims against him and his properties since Lynn's house of cards fell last October. Some have examined his overseas assets to see whether they can make claims against them. Last month ACC Bank obtained a European Enforcement Order, which enables it to take steps in countries where Lynn has properties to recover debts due in Ireland.

However, it will be extremely difficult for the banks to 'follow the money' around Lynn's labyrinthine business empire or trace the links between his companies. His affidavit lists 72 bank accounts across continental Europe, including two in the names of 'Caviarteria Technologies' and 'Merola Consulting' in Liechtenstein, the European principality well known for its impenetrable secrecy laws.

One source who had dealings with Lynn said he had been setting up an overall parent company for his group in Luxembourg, the ownership of which is held in bearer shares, when the Law Society launched its investigation. Such shares are like cash, which is essentially a type of bearer bond – whoever physically holds the bearer shares owns the company. This will make it exceptionally tricky to decipher Kendar's ownership structure.

Other individuals working in Lynn's law practice and property business have been drawn into the legal proceedings against the solicitor. The court was told last Monday that Liz Doyle, an employee of Kendar and Lynn's PA, who helped Lynn manage the company while he was away on business, had been added as a defendant to the action being taken by Irish Life & Permanent, which is owed €10 million. The group is also suing Fiona McAleenan. Doyle and McAleenan deny any wrongdoing.

A number of investors who spoke to *The Irish Times* expressed surprise that few investors have issued proceedings against Lynn and that little has appeared in the media about their plight. Several investors expressed disbelief that the banks did not spot the warning signs earlier and that it took an employee of Lynn's practice to blow the whistle. However, one lawyer representing a bank owed money by Lynn explained that, while he may have over-borrowed on his properties, bells did not sound in the financial institutions because Lynn managed to keep up repayments on all of his loans, some of which were interest-only mortgages.

One source who had dealings with Lynn in recent months said that even when his business empire was crumbling around him and banks were queuing up to sue him, Lynn still had 'a remarkable capacity to absorb a huge amount of stress'. This was borne out as he attended court for more than six weeks.

Things quickly changed as the cases against him progressed. His legal team said he wanted to co-operate with the investigations and the civil actions against him but he was fearful of incriminating himself by providing information that could be used against him in any future criminal proceedings. He outlined this in his affidavit, which is still the only detailed document he has filed in any of the cases against him.

This may have been why he failed to appear for cross-examination on Tuesday, 11 December. Since his disappearance, the courts have become even busier. The number of High Court proceedings against Lynn has risen to 126, with most banks issuing multiple writs over their loans to him.

In his absence, the court has allowed the banks to serve their writs to his home in St Alban's Park, Sandymount, Dublin 4. The house was empty and in darkness on Tuesday. Lynn's home, like many of his Irish properties, will be sold to repay some of his debts.

Lynn remains at large. There have been sightings of him in eastern Europe and even reports of him in Brazil. International police were alerted last month about the outstanding arrest order against him. He faces arrest if he returns to Ireland.

His investors are watching developments in Cabanas closely. A Dublin woman who paid a deposit on an apartment in Portugal is waiting for positive news about Cabanas, while she and her husband are forced to repay a substantial bank loan drawn for the investment. 'We are adults – we took a chance and we got burnt.'

SATURDAY, 16 FEBRUARY 2008

The Georgian Guardians

Robert O'Byrne

When the Irish Georgian Society was founded almost 50 years ago, the nation had no great love of its architectural heritage. Thankfully, times have changed.

It has become something of a truism to say that Ireland and her citizens are today utterly changed from what they used to be. But nothing better brings home the reality of this observation than an examination of our recent past. It is, for example, astonishing to discover that when two private individuals, Desmond and Mariga Guinness, officially established the Irish Georgian Society on 21 February 1958 (50 years ago on Thursday), the nation's heritage of 18th-century architecture was viewed by most of her citizens with at best indifference, at worst overt hostility.

The incident that spurred the Guinnesses into action serves to illustrate just how bad the plight of our Georgian heritage then was. In July 1957, the demolition of two superb 18th-century houses on Kildare Place, a small piazza adjacent to the Dáil, received authorisation from the government, which owned both buildings. No. 2 Kildare Place had been designed by Richard Castle and executed after his death in 1751 by John Ensor; its equally distinguished neighbour was of a slightly later date.

Both of these splendid houses were in excellent condition and there was no reason for their destruction other than a disinclination on the part of the State to maintain the properties. Had they survived, they would now be worth millions, an asset to the

exchequer and to our tourist industry. But as a correspondent wrote in the *Irish Architect and Contractor*, 'In the year 1957, when financial stringency decrees that 50,000 of our people must leave in order that our balance of payments be preserved, our Government allows the wilful destruction of £40,000 of Irish public property which from a point of view of history and tradition is priceless.'

Desmond Guinness still remembers that the first he knew of the intended Kildare Place demolition was when, emerging from the Shelbourne Hotel, he saw workmen removing the houses' roof slates. Immediately he wrote a letter of protest to the editor of *The Irish Times*, proposing that rather than being wantonly destroyed, the houses should be preserved and used to display properly the neighbouring National Museum's fine collection of 18th-century furniture, at that time squeezed into a couple of rooms and 'stacked as though in a saleroom for lack of space'.

An editorial in the same edition of this newspaper concurred with his suggestion and decried the official 'barbarous decision to destroy the two handsome houses'. And in his Cruiskeen Lawn column, Myles na gCopaleen felt driven to ask whether the clearance of Kildare Place meant 'that there is no regard by the State to what may be called the nation's soul?' All protest was to no purpose – the government had made up its mind. In August 1957 the two houses were pulled down and an ugly brick wall erected in their place. Half a century later it is still there, leaving Kildare Place a barren, wind-swept spot.

Though a few people mourned the unnecessary loss of these fine buildings, probably more concurred with the minister of state quoted as saying, 'I was glad to see them go. They stand for everything I hate.' For much of the last century Georgian architecture was widely perceived in Ireland as being something alien, the product of a foreign culture imposed upon this country.

In 1970, Tipperary County Council wished to demolish the early 18th-century Damer House in

The River Nore and surrounding countryside in winter. Photograph: Dylan Vaughan.

central Roscrea, Co. Tipperary, and replace the building with a municipal car park. The Irish Georgian Society campaigned against this proposal and volunteered to undertake a programme of restoration. This offer was eventually accepted, but even when the work had been completed a local councillor could still see fit to denounce Damer House as a 'bastion of British imperialism' on which no public funds should be squandered.

Is it any surprise that in such a climate so many significant properties, part of this nation's collective heritage, the work of Irish builders and craftsmen, were wilfully swept away? Though much remains, it is easy to forget how much has been lost in the past half century, very often, like with the Kildare Place houses, through acts of breathtaking vandalism. In 1946, for example, the Land Commission, which had already carved up the Hazelwood estate in Co. Sligo, sought a buyer for the old house, a superlative Palladian building dating from the early

1730s. It was a condition of the sale that the new owner should demolish Hazelwood, remove all materials and level the site. (Curiously, the house somehow survived this intended fate and is now scheduled for restoration.)

The commission's unsympathetic approach to Ireland's Georgian heritage was typical of the public sector, but the private was no better. At the end of the following decade, not long after the Irish Georgian Society was founded, Elizabeth Bowen, one of this country's finest novelists of the 20th century, finally gave up the fruitless struggle to maintain her family home, Bowen's Court in Co. Cork. She sold it to a local man in the belief that the house, a fine example of mid-18th-century design, would continue to be cherished. Within two years her former home had been pulled down.

'It was a clean end,' she later ruefully observed. 'Bowen's Court never lived to be a ruin.' But the house should never have had to be a ruin, and nor should it have been pulled down. Elizabeth Bowen was obliged to sell because she could not afford to live in the house any longer; because the State gave no support in ensuring its survival; because, as Desmond Guinness wrote in the Irish Georgian Society's spring 1960 bulletin, 'we are the only country in Europe that has not yet developed its architecture as a tourist asset'.

Right from the start, the society argued that this nation's Georgian buildings should be cherished and protected, not merely for their inherent beauty, but as a valuable asset in the business of attracting tourists to Ireland. Nobody, after all, has ever travelled here to admire our extensive collection of dormer bungalows and suburban housing estates. It has always been apparent that the majority of visitors to this country relish our exceptional heritage of 18th-century architecture. In fact, for a long time the only people who seemed not to appreciate its worth were the citizens of Ireland.

On 31 December 1959, the architectural correspondent of this newspaper wrote, 'It is well-known that, as far as the central city is concerned, the days of Dublin's Georgian heritage are numbered and that when these decayed and obsolete monuments of a past age come to be demolished, many of their sites will be redeveloped with buildings much larger in bulk and greater in height than the present ones.'

That unhappy prophecy soon came to pass when, in 1961, the ESB announced its intention to demolish a terrace of 16 Georgian houses on Lower Fitzwilliam Street and the fight to save the capital's legacy of 18th-century architecture commenced.

Today the fight is largely over. During the past 50 years, the Irish Georgian Society – which remains a small, voluntary organisation entirely funded by the generosity of a few thousand members worldwide – has engaged in many battles. Some of these it won, others it lost. The victories include saving several key 18th-century monuments such as the Tailors' Hall and St Catherine's Church in Dublin; rescuing properties such as Damer House, Roundwood House in Co. Laois, and Doneraile Court, Co. Cork; and, above all, ensuring the preservation of Castletown House, Co. Kildare, which is Ireland's earliest and greatest Palladian house.

Unfortunately the defeats were equally numerous and can be recalled wherever the pathetic remnants of a once fine house or an ill-sited, ill-conceived and poorly executed building are found throughout the country.

Attitudes, both public and private, have changed, and legislation, along with its implementation, has greatly improved. When it comes to questions of heritage, Ireland and her citizens are now very different from what they used to be. But it would be a mistake to imagine that the cause that originally inspired the establishment of the Irish Georgian Society half a century ago has become redundant.

In the very first year of its existence, the society expressed grave concern over the fate of Vernon Mount, an irreplaceable late-18th-century villa with painted interiors that stands on the outskirts of Cork city. Vernon Mount is now in such poor condition that it has been placed on the World Monuments Fund's 2008 list of 100 most endangered sites and, just as was the case 50 years ago, the Irish Georgian Society is campaigning to ensure the house's future. The fight for Ireland's heritage is by no means over.

SATURDAY, 16 FEBRUARY 2008

Down on the Piste

Róisín Ingle

We all, in our own ways, prepared for the skiing holiday to Switzerland. There were those who worked out a complex range of lunge exercises, to simulate as closely as possible the activity on the slopes.

Lone surfer Tom Doidge-Harrison of Kilshanny in Lahinch, Co. Clare, riding a giant wave near the Cliffs of Moher. Photograph: Mickey Smith.

There were the ones who dusted down the rollerblades and went for long skating sessions in the Phoenix Park. And there were others who stayed up the night before the holiday and learned all the two-letter Scrabble words off by heart. At least when lying on my back on the nursery slope, being laughed at by small children, I could take solace in knowing that ug, ky and ob would pass muster on the board later that night.

Out on the snow, as soon as I put on the torture shoes – sorry, ski boots – I knew the skiing part of the skiing holiday was never going to be successful. When the last clasps were fastened on the boots, and I snapped myself on to the skis, I was overcome by a need to get these yokes off me nowwwww . . . You know, when somebody drags their nails down a chalkboard, how irritating that is; wearing those boots was like that, but also like

wearing leg irons at the same time and being kicked repeatedly in the shins.

Momentarily there dawned the realisation that I was unable to remove the boots myself. Eventually, my fellow novice skier figured out how to unleash me from the boots of doom, and I sat in my stockinged feet on the snow beside the cross-country skiing track, which seemed to mock me. I would go no further, I vowed.

I wasn't wearing waterproof trousers. And my bottom was rapidly going numb. So after a while there was nothing for it but to allow someone to strap me back into the contraptions and shuffle at an almost imperceptible speed towards the gently sloping hill.

Once at the nursery slope – ah, it's called a nursery slope because there are what look like actual live babies skiing expertly down here – we were propelled up a travelator, which kindly spat me out at the top, causing me to fall, which in turn triggered a messy pile-up of three-year-olds, who, before you could say Eddie the Eagle, dusted the snow off their snazzy outfits and swish-swished down the hill.

I lay there on my back, like a ski-shod beetle, until I was rescued by a woman whom I immediately thanked by sliding in her direction and causing her to take a tumble. As I slid past her towards more infant Olympic athletes, I wondered whether it was cold enough for tears to form icicles, because that would have been the final indignity. Oh no: that would be the part where it took half an hour to get the boots off.

My first skiing experience wasn't helped by the fact that there were no lessons available in the whole of the resort. This turned out to be a blessing in disguise. Much as Michael Jackson declares to Paul McCartney, 'I'm a lover, not a fighter' in the classic duet 'The Girl Is Mine', I've discovered I'm a sledder, not a skier. And it suits me fine.

I have distant memories of sledging down the Dublin Mountains, back in the days when we got actual snow instead of icy slush. We dragged our bright red plastic sleds as far as our little legs would take us and then sleighed down the rocky slopes at breakneck speed. Once, I was going so fast I sleighed right down to the car park and under a car, narrowly escaping being knocked out by an exhaust pipe. Happy, if not exactly safe, days.

So I feel what I am doing here is a public service for all those who have tried and hated skiing. Don't go skiing, is what I say, go sledding instead. The benefits are endless. You get to go on the big chair lift, just like the skiers, but in an added bonus you get to not fear for your life when you fall out of the ski lift. Two legs good. Two legs trapped in boots and skis, very bad.

You get to walk through a pine forest, where everywhere you look, untouched snow sits like perfectly cooked meringue. You get to feel like you are five years old as you stand at the top of a hill, sit on your padded sleigh and let yourself go.

You get to experience the exhilaration of whizzing around tight corners, your feet acting like brakes, as you wonder whether this will be the corner when you finally go over the edge. You get to go over the edge, like James Bond, rolling over five times until you stop, still alive, pink with excitement and able to get up again without the help of a crane. Sledge, don't ski. You know it makes sense.

FRIDAY, 22 FEBRUARY 2008

How to Map Kosovo along the Same Lines as Northern Ireland – an Ulsterman's Guide to Recognising the Stark and Varied Terrain of Kosovo

Newton Emerson

Q: I know the Kosovo Albanians are Muslims. But are they Protestant or Catholic?

A: The Kosovo Albanians occupied an ancient province of Serbia many centuries ago, so they are essentially Protestant. However, you do realise that they have been fashionably oppressed, so they often sound Catholic.

Q: What about the Serb minority in the north? Would it not be fair to say that they could be the Protestants?

A: Only if Kosovo is compared to the whole of Ireland. If Kosovo is compared to Northern Ireland, then its unwanted Serbian enclave is really much more like Derry.

Q: Does this mean Albania is Britain and Serbia is the Irish Republic?

A: If Kosovan independence is a final settlement, then Albania is Britain. However, if its independence is a step towards a Greater Albania, then Serbia is Britain. And Yugoslavia was the United Kingdom.

Q: So which side am I on?

A: Some Irish republicans side with Serbia out of pro-communist nostalgia. And some unionists side with Serbia out of nonconformist solidarity. Apart from that, you're on your own.

Q: What about all those Union Jacks the Kosovo Albanians were waving in the street? Does that mean anything?

A: Yes. It means they'll have plenty of Union Jacks to burn in the street when the money runs out.

Q: Is the Kosovo Liberation Army the IRA or the UVF?

A: The KLA's political wing is now in government, so that makes it the IRA. On the other hand, it is heavily involved in organised crime, so really it could be either.

Q: Does prime minister Hashim Thaci combine the roles of Ian Paisley and Martin McGuinness?

A: Mr Thaci is the president of Kosovo's largest nationalist party and he is also a former leader of the KLA. Therefore, it might be more accurate to say that he combines the roles of Gerry Adams and Martin McGuinness.

Q: Hasn't Mr Thaci been convicted of terrorist atrocities?

A: That question is anti-Thaci, anti-Kosovan and unhelpful to the independence process.

Q: Could the Kosovo Albanian groups inside neighbouring Macedonia be compared to Orangemen in Liverpool or Celtic supporters in Glasgow?

A: For Macedonia's sake, let's hope not.

Q: Kosovo has roughly the same area and population as Northern Ireland. Is the world's media likely to point this out?

A: No. Under international reporting rules, Kosovo can only be described as 'smaller than Wales'.

Q: So an independent Kosovo doesn't set any precedent for an independent Northern Ireland?

A: What Britain and America are actually backing is 'supervised independence'. And sure don't we all know that Northern Ireland set that precedent a while ago.

Q: Isn't the Kosovan parliament quite like Stormont, when you think about it?

A: It has a 120-member assembly with guaranteed Serb minority representation, so yes. But the minority parties keep walking out in a huff, so no.

Q: Then surely that means that the Kosovan Serbs must be nothing if not Protestant!

A: No. The Kosovan Serbs are eastern Orthodox.

Q: This is far too complicated – perhaps I should turn the question around. Which side are the Kosovars on?

A: Why, yours of course. In Pristina, you will find they speak of little else.

TUESDAY, 26 FEBRUARY 2008

'You've Got Cancer, Buddy'

Deaglán de Bréadún

It's the last thing you want to hear. You've got cancer. Except it's not said like that; the wording is more polite and considerate. But the bad news still has to be broken and, no matter how it is dressed up, you are left with the realisation that the Big C is inside you, working away.

I was on assignment for this newspaper down the country when I pulled into the side of the road to ring up for the test results. I had a news deadline to meet and was hardly concentrating when I made the call. A previous biopsy had come up with nothing: why should this one be any different?

Suddenly, I was all ears. They had taken eight tiny 'cores' out of my prostate and one of them came up cancerous. A door opened on a whole new world of terminology. Something called 'the

Deaglán de Bréadún. Photograph: David Sleator.

Gleason score' stood at six; this turned out to be a system for grading cancer tissue from two to 10.

In time I discovered that being diagnosed with cancer does not have to be the end of the world. But I had grown up in an environment where 'cancer', 'incurable' and 'terminal' were pretty well synonymous.

I placed my mobile phone on the car seat and considered the situation. A few minutes before, I was pootling along without a care in the world. Now my whole perspective changed and there I was, staring into the jaws of eternity. Looking back, I am tempted to smile at the melodramatic thoughts crowding into my mind. My life seemed to be over: goodbye to family and loved ones; no more beautiful scenery; that long-planned return trip to Rome would never happen; I would never read any more books by Dostoyevsky. A lot done, more to do, as it were, but time had just run out.

It all seemed so terribly unfair. But I went ahead, finished my assignment, filed my copy to the news desk and drove on home. I woke up the next morning feeling as perky as usual, until an invisible hand grasped me around the throat and a voice whispered inside my brain: 'You've got cancer, buddy.'

Those early days were the hardest part. Had the malignancy spread beyond the prostate into the bone? A bone scan was arranged at Tallaght Hospital and, following a tremulous wait, the news came through that the result was negative. Hallelujah.

My experience of the health service was almost entirely favourable, barring a few minor irritations. Everyone I dealt with – doctors, nurses, secretarial and administrative staff, therapists – was kind, considerate, efficient and, above all, humane. This is not to deny that others have legitimate complaints.

I had never been seriously ill before and was deplorably ignorant of the world of medical science. I hardly even knew what my prostate was for and it came as a pleasant surprise to discover that it was 'about the size of a walnut' and played a major part in the reproductive process.

If there was a book in this, I already have the title: Me and My Walnut. There were other surprises to come. I thought the medical people would decide what form of treatment I should undergo, and was intrigued to discover that this was being left up to myself to a considerable extent. My choices boiled down to surgery or radiotherapy. A third option, 'watchful waiting', was ruled out under the circumstances. Best to deal with the problem right now.

Several long nights of the soul followed as I weighed the options. Various friends and acquaintances who had tried one or the other gave their opinion. I was beginning to discover that every cancer patient is unique and what's best for one isn't necessarily right for another.

Go for surgery, some said. It's more final, complete and definitive: 'If thy prostate offend thee, pluck it out.' Others recommended radiotherapy as the kinder, gentler option, where the risk of side-effects was considerably less. A key point to be considered was that, if surgery failed, you could still have radiotherapy, whereas if radiotherapy failed, surgery could be quite problematic.

Cancer is a great leveller, affecting high and low. Senior US politicians such as John Kerry, Colin Powell and Rudy Giuliani have all been afflicted. A quick perusal of the internet revealed that Kerry and Powell took the surgical road, whereas Giuliani chose radiation.

A kind friend gave me an article by the head of a multinational company, describing his happy experience of radiotherapy. So far, so reassuring, until I noticed the date on the article: 1996. Was the guy still alive? A rapid trawl of the web revealed that he was.

In the end, after prolonged consultations, I decided radiotherapy was the best option. It seemed to suit my particular circumstances best, although many men have opted for surgery and never regretted it.

Happily, all the indications were that my tumour was confined within the prostate. Prostate cancer has few symptoms, although frequent urination may be one. Some men show no symptoms at all. In my own case, alarm bells started ringing after a routine prostate-specific antigen (PSA) blood test.

Cancer, by definition, never comes at a good time. I was particularly busy and hated being distracted. In addition to my new role as a political correspondent with The Irish Times, I was also actively involved in the National Union of Journalists, as well as updating a book on the Northern Ireland peace process for a second edition.

But when cancer strikes, everything else takes second place. Scrambling my way up the learning curve, I discovered that radiotherapy is a form of X-ray treatment which destroys cancer cells by damaging their DNA. Normal tissues can also be damaged during treatment but are usually able to repair themselves. Cancer cells lack this ability to recover because they are more disorganised structures.

This conjures up a pleasing image of cancer cells as marauding drunks who are finally expelled from the pub at closing-time and find themselves with nowhere to go for the rest of the night. Radiotherapy is like the head bartender who kicks out the drunks and locks the door tightly behind them. And so it was that I found myself making a daily pilgrimage to St Luke's Hospital in Dublin to have my prostate 'zapped'.

There were 37 sessions which extended over a

period of about eight weeks. The side effects included tiredness and difficulty passing water but it was far from a harrowing experience.

I learned a lot from my daily visits and from sitting around waiting my turn. I always knew cancer had a broad reach but was still surprised to meet so many people that I knew. The Equality Authority could never support an anti-discrimination case against cancer, which does not distinguish between old and young, black and white, citizen and immigrant, rich and poor, male and female.

It was touching to see young children, some of them from immigrant families, going for treatment at the same time as me. One could not help being moved either by those women patients who had cut off the fine, flowing tresses they had so proudly groomed over the years. Their bravery was inspiring.

I also became quite attached to St Luke's Hospital, which I affectionately dubbed Cancer Central. In my youth it was a name that struck terror. If you heard someone was 'above in Luke's' you felt sure that person was a goner. But surely there is no hospital in Ireland with a more beautiful setting, in the heart of leafy south Dublin.

Squirrels gambolled in the grounds as I parked my car each day prior to treatment. It's a pity the place is being closed down and sold off. The site should be retained as a medical facility, perhaps for convalescent purposes.

My treatment over, I am back at work full time and getting on with my life. Continuing tests will show whether I have kicked the Big C but the outlook is very promising and the medical people are highly optimistic.

If I have a criticism of the health services, it is this: there should be more alerts and a greater awareness of prostate cancer. A man is one-third more likely to get it than a woman is to get breast cancer. Men who are in middle age or older should ask their doctors about a PSA test or call Action Prostate Cancer on 1800 380 380. Guys: get that tumour before it gets you.

THURSDAY, 28 FEBRUARY 2008

Let's Record Gratitude for Van's Monumental Talent

David Adams

Good fortune indeed, if at least once in your life you happen upon a piece of music so magnificently beautiful and unique that it completely overwhelms you. You are immediately lifted up by it and swept away on a wave of deep-found, previously untapped emotion. The sense of wonderment is so great, and the sensations unleashed so profound, that you are incapable of any reaction beyond open-mouthed speechlessness and tear-filled eyes.

Insofar as it is describable at all, that is how I felt when I first listened to the Van Morrison album, *Astral Weeks*. I had known of Van when he was the lead singer with Them, a Belfast band that had made the upper reaches of the British singles chart on a few occasions, but I hadn't heard any of his solo work. It is ironic then that circumstances had me resenting *Astral Weeks* even before I had listened to it.

One of my many flatmates in a sweaty, over-crowded bedsit in England had borrowed a favourite album of mine, *Let it Bleed* by the Rolling Stones, to take to a party. By party's end the Stones album had disappeared, so he helped himself to *Astral Weeks* and brought that home instead. I was annoyed at having lost *Let it Bleed*, and my mood didn't improve when presented by way of replacement with something that has one of the most unattractive covers I have ever seen.

With a circular photograph of Morrison superimposed over some indeterminate greenery and all enclosed within a broad black border, the sleeve gave the appearance of having taken about 20 minutes to design. I thought it looked like something straight out of the discount bin at a Woolworths' record counter.

A few nights after acquiring it, I put *Astral Weeks* on the turntable and braced myself for the worst. How can I begin to describe the music that then emerged to envelop me? It was a wondrous fusion of jazz, rock, folk and blues, with an extra something magical added to form a distinct genre all of its own.

Sometimes-mystical lyrics of hope, dismay, joy, sadness, introspection, reflection and much, much more were wrapped up in melodies to die for, and delivered in perfect harmony by Morrison and his occasional supporting vocalists, in faultless marriage with superb instrumentation.

Here too was the guttural and, to a stranger's ear, often barely intelligible Belfast accent, unashamed and defiant, not hidden or masked as we had been taught was best, but proudly given full authentic voice, and yet somehow forged anew to be a thing of beauty.

The songs evoked such colourful imagery that the overall sense was of impressionist art set to music, with a kaleidoscope of characters, situations and emotions all piled on top of one another to create a disjointed yet at the same time perfectly coherent narrative, sprinkled throughout with nostalgic snapshots of Belfast.

To top it all, Morrison's singing was a master-class in vocal intonation, with him sometimes repeating a single word or a phrase over and over again, yet never failing to infuse it with different meaning on each rendition. I almost cried when I first heard 'Madame George' and 'Ballerina' – those tracks still have the same effect on me today.

It is 40 years and many brilliant Van Morrison albums since *Astral Weeks*, but he has never managed its equal. There is no shame in that, for neither has anyone else. Bob Dylan is my favourite artist of all time, but if I had to choose my favourite album, it would undoubtedly be *Astral Weeks*.

A few weeks ago, Declan Lynch of the *Sunday Independent* wrote a lovely column in praise of Van Morrison. He described him as the greatest artist of any kind that Ireland has ever produced, and

wondered why he has never had the appreciation he deserves. I agree with every point he made. Morrison's home town of Belfast hasn't even named a street or a building after him, much less thought to offer him the freedom of the city.

Painfully shy, even brusque at times, Morrison has few friends outside of the music industry, and possibly very few inside it as well. Much to the chagrin of the media, he has always steadfastly refused to play the part of the archetypal 'rock legend' or, God forbid, act the celebrity.

A determinedly private individual, he has steadily maintained that his music does the talking

Frank Dunlop at Dublin Castle after finishing his evidence to the Mahon Tribunal. Photograph: Collins Photos.

for him: quite simply, he has nothing of any importance to add. This attitude has certainly not endeared him to the types that lobby on your behalf for awards to be presented or statues erected.

Still, Morrison has every right to be as reclusive as he likes; it really is none of our business, and certainly should have no bearing on how we view his art. We are entitled to buy his music, but not his soul.

It would be fitting in this, the fortieth year since *Astral Weeks* was released, if Ireland, North and South, were to honour Van Morrison. It is high time we paid proper tribute to this colossal genius of ours.

WEDNESDAY, 5 MARCH 2008

Only Old Brashness Remains as 10 Years in Tribunal's Spotlight Take Huge Personal Toll

Paul Cullen

On 9 October 1998, when he received his first letter from the planning tribunal, Frank Dunlop was a successful and wealthy public relations adviser with contacts in the highest reaches of power.

His teenage son Cathal had died of an illness just four months earlier, but otherwise he was on top of his professional game. And just in case adversity came his way, he was equipped with 'balls of iron and a spine of steel' to withstand any attacks, as he had boasted during a planning controversy a short time earlier.

By yesterday, almost 10 years later, when the former government press secretary was told the tribunal had finally finished with him, all had changed utterly. The years up in Dublin Castle have taken a huge personal, financial and emotional toll. His business is long gone, as is his good name, and he hasn't worked formally for years. When not on the golf course, he studies law. Only the old brashness remains.

'I don't give a hoot whether people think I'm arrogant. I've a life to lead. At my age, you can't reinvent myself,' said the 60-year-old yesterday, taking a break from his Master's studies in Trinity College's Law department.

Dunlop remains the only tribunal witness to 'fess up' to his involvement in planning corruption. In April 2000, under pressure from tribunal lawyers to explain the flow of money in his accounts, former chairman Mr Justice Feargus Flood invited him to 'reflect' on his evidence overnight.

Reflect he did. A different man arrived in the witness box on 19 April that year – Spy Wednesday.

Haltingly at first, he revealed the details of payments to 15 different county councillors ranging in size from £500 to £48,500. Whereas previously he had insisted there was a distinction between bribes and 'legitimate political donations', Dunlop now acknowledged for the first time that most of the payments were intimately connected with the councillors' stance on the rezoning.

For the first time, a key 'insider' was 'coming clean' about the dubious details of brown paper bag politics. As the day wore on and Dunlop added yet more names to the list of politicians handed to Mr Justice Flood, the shock waves reverberated around Dublin.

After that momentous day came the collapse. Dunlop spilled all the beans to the lawyers in private sessions over the succeeding months, but his health suffered and his business contacts dried up.

'Clients finished their contracts, retainers ended. As for the speed with which that happened, I'll make individual judgment elsewhere,' he says, referring to a planned book on his involvement with the tribunal.

'True friends weren't a problem; they remained. As for the rest, the flotsam and jetsam of human life, the people you meet on the journey through life, some were spineless and others were hypocrites.'

Of late, he says, some of these erstwhile friends have been knocking on his door again, but 'too much water has passed under that particular bridge'.

He says he hasn't worked in years, apart from 'the odd small background advice'. He lives off his 'wise investments', notably his 5 per cent stake in the lucrative Citywest business park in south Dublin.

Is he comfortable? 'What is comfortable? I still live in the same house we've had for the past 30 years. I still drive the same kind of car. The only pity is that I didn't pick myself up quicker.' This is in spite of the fact that he has paid out more than €2 million in legal fees and could face more bills in the future.

He wrote a book, *Yes Taoiseach*, about his time as government press secretary, in 2004, which sold more than 20,000 copies in hardback, and a new memoir is planned for Christmas 2009. He plans to do a doctorate after he completes his current studies – and no, he's not planning to go to King's Inns to become a barrister.

He says he feels for Bertie Ahern 'to a point' in relation to his entanglement with the tribunal. 'When you look at it objectively, he's there for one reason only, a piece of hearsay by Tom Gilmartin, and hearsay is not allowed in court.'

He doesn't regret having 'reflected' on his evidence as asked by Justice Flood, but admits to finding it 'bizarre' that his revised evidence is repeatedly called into question by the tribunal and outside the inquiry.

'Why would I bother to make it up? The world and its mother knew that certain things were happening, that a block was not laid upon another block in Dublin since the 1960s without some sort of inducement being paid.'

Ordinary Lives Compelling to the End

Ruadhán Mac Cormaic

It was just after 10 o'clock and the courtroom, made so intimate and stuffy these past few weeks by the sheer press of people, still had the airy, spartan feel of morning.

The jurors' chairs were empty, and even the registrar had yet to arrive. It was quiet, too, but for the tap-tap of a laptop at the back and some faint patter from the gallery above. A few detectives passed in and out, lugging the familiar props – brown labelled bags, stacks of files and folders, an ensuite door – and setting them down in their usual place.

As always, Brian Kearney had arrived early. He sat in his seat by the witness box, accompanied by his daughter Aoife and brother Niall. Just now he was listening as Aoife told a story, smiling here and there and letting out the odd laugh. Less than an hour before the judge would begin his charge to the jury – the final act before jurors would retire to consider whether Kearney murdered his wife – he looked relaxed, at ease. Wasn't this the first time we had seen him laugh?

And then the McLaughlins began to file in; first Deirdre, then her sisters Caroline, Niamh, Brighid, Aisling, Ann Marie, brother Owen and their parents. Kearney's demeanour changed in an instant. He sat rigidly now, at an awkward angle to the court. He picked a fixed point on the wooden ledge and stared inscrutably ahead.

The McLaughlins, for their part, studiously avoided looking at the man they called 'Mr Kearney'. Usually the accused sits alone in these situations, but at his trial Kearney's extended family lined up alongside him every day, leaving an uneasy proximity between the two families. They know each other well, and yet to look at them they might have been strangers.

How did it come to this? How did the story that began 17 years ago, when Brian Kearney met Siobhán McLaughlin at work in Mulhuddart ('She was 21, I was 31. I thought she was older. She looked so in control of the place.') end here, he facing a life in prison for her murder?

From a distance, the Kearneys must have seemed enviable neighbours in early 2006. They lived with their three-year-old son in a fine home in an attractive Goatstown estate, just around the corner from where Kearney's parents lived. Building work had finished on the new house in the garden, and as well as his successful electrical contractors business there was an income from the other south Dublin properties Brian jointly owned with his own family. The couple ran a €2 million Majorcan hotel, and had looked seriously at fulfilling the long-held dream of owning a yacht on the Mediterranean.

But below the surface, the Kearneys had their troubles. Siobhán had initiated moves towards a legal separation and, on the advice of her solicitor, had started keeping a diary, which she kept hidden in the hot press at Carnroe. Her plan was to move into the new house. One of Siobhán's closest friends told the court that she noticed a week before her death that her friend wasn't wearing her wedding ring, and we know that Siobhán worried that she couldn't devote enough time to the boy because of her hotel work, and felt Brian was putting pressure on her to return to Spain.

For his part, Brian was overstretched on borrowing – €844,456, according to forensic accountant Toni Massey and, according to the prosecution, the most logical option – the sale of the family home – would be closed off to him if the separation went ahead.

There were hints, in evidence, that relations between Kearney and the McLaughlins were strained even before he was arrested. Aisling McLaughlin recalled arriving at Carnroe at about 10.45am on the morning Siobhán died. When

The family of Siobhán Kearney leaving the Dublin Central Criminal Court after her husband Brian Kearney was convicted of murdering her. Photograph: Aidan Crawley.

Kearney arrived half an hour later, 'I told him to get out, but my mother told me to stop', Aisling told the court.

Later that morning, when the McLaughlins were talking in the kitchen and one of Kearney's brothers came in to boil the kettle, he was told to leave the room.

Brighid felt there was something odd in his reaction to his wife's death. And why, asked Dominic McGinn for the prosecution, did Brian not ask what was wrong when Siobhán's mother phoned him from his own home to tell him to get home straight away?

In court, it was clear from day one that the McLaughlins were convinced of Kearney's guilt. But it was another matter to persuade the jury beyond reasonable doubt.

The prosecution's case, resting substantially on circumstantial evidence, involved convincing jurors not only that the accused had a motive and an opportunity to kill his wife, but that murder by Kearney was the one inescapable conclusion to draw.

Simply put, the motive was money. Although Kearney had assets – of almost €5 million – he was overstretched on borrowing and was under pressure from the banks to reduce his loans. Hotel Salvia had been on the market for some time but was refusing to sell. That left as the most logical course the sale of Carnroe, and for the family to move into the house they had built next door. 'The difficulty was, the separation wouldn't fit it,' as Dominic McGinn put it.

By combining State Pathologist Marie Cassidy's evidence on the time of death with the

Kidney transplant hopeful Lana Devine, aged 4, from Kells in Co. Meath, at the Mansion House in Dublin for the launch of Organ Donor Awareness Week 2008. Since Christmas 2004 Lana has been receiving peritoneal dialysis six nights a week; an organ transplant would enable her to live a normal life. Photograph: Bryan O'Brien.

intruder alarm log, the prosecution was able to narrow the spectrum of possibilities. Prof Cassidy put the time of death at 9am, with a range of three hours either side. But we knew there was no sign of a break-in and, importantly for the prosecution, Kearney accepted in a Garda interview that his wife died when only he and his son were in the house.

That left two options: either Siobhán killed herself, or she was murdered by her husband. To disprove the suicide theory, the prosecution relied on scientific evidence and testimony showing the short- and long-term plans Siobhán had been putting in place.

And plans there were. Apart from instigating moves towards a legal separation, she was working to secure a school place for her son and making arrangements to hand over management of the hotel in Spain. She had a hair appointment at a local salon for later that morning, and another meeting at the Citizens Advice Centre for the following month. The night before she died, Siobhán sent a chatty e-mail to her sister-in-law, Alessandra Benedetti, saying how excited she was by their impending visit. 'Not something someone would write if they were going to kill themselves,' said McGinn.

The prosecution leaned heavily on Prof Cassidy's evidence, and in particular her finding of deep bruising to the neck area and three separate fractures to the Adam's apple, factors which she said were 'more usually a factor suggestive of manual strangulation, less common in ligature strangulation and unusual in low-level suspension'. Prof Cassidy also hypothesised that the victim had been strangled on the bed before the flex was applied to her neck.

There was then the testimony of Dr Neal Murphy, an engineering lecturer at UCD, whose tests on the original vacuum cleaner flex showed that it would break after five to seven seconds if an object of Siobhán's weight was applied to it.

And then there was the key, which was found just inside the locked bedroom door by those who arrived that morning. Why, if she was going to kill herself, would Siobhán Kearney lock the door, take the key out and throw it on the floor? More plausible, to the prosecution, was that Brian Kearney slipped it under the door after locking it from outside.

Moreover, why was there no noose around her neck when her body was found, and why was the flex not tied to any anchor-point in the room?

Defence counsel Patrick Gageby SC made strong criticism of forensic scientist Dr Michael Norton's evidence on the vacuum cleaner flex. Whether valid or not, it was clear that Dr Norton – a nervous witness whose hand tremor made his reconstruction of the flex loops confusing – presented something of a problem for the prosecution. In the absence of the jury, they tried to have the demonstration redone before the jury by Det Insp Martin Cummins, but the judge refused permission on the basis that it added nothing to the case.

The contents of Siobhán's diary were also the subject of legal argument not witnessed by the jury. Denis Vaughan Buckley SC, prosecuting, had originally indicated he would try to have its contents admitted as evidence, but changed his mind the next day, apparently due to what Mr Justice White called 'an excess of caution' caused by fear that the Court of Criminal Appeal might not look kindly on its introduction.

Also in the jury's absence, Mr Gageby last week tried to have the case withdrawn because there was insufficient evidence and pointed out that, according to Prof Cassidy's time of death, Siobhán could have died after the accused left the house. The judge refused the application.

When yesterday's verdict was delivered, there was barely room to stand in court No. 3, a reminder, if it were needed, of the hold this short but gripping trial has had on the public mind. In some ways this case was different; both legal teams and the judge alluded to the couple's wealth, and it's not every day that a drama such as this plays out at the Central Criminal Court.

But in another sense it was perhaps the banality of the mosaic pieced together over the past fortnight that was most compelling. The exhibit list was an inventory of everyday suburban life, and the pictures of the dead woman's body stuck in the mind above all for the odd juxtaposition of violent death amid everyday suburban detail: a Dyson vacuum cleaner, a flip-flop, the red tartan pyjamas.

As the judge requested, there was no triumphalism in court yesterday afternoon; no yelling and no pumping fists. But perhaps it would have been that way even without his asking. By 3.45pm on day 13 of an unbearably intense trial, too much energy had already been expended, and too much emotion put on the line.

Too much had been lost.

THURSDAY, 6 MARCH 2008

God's Man for the Hour Finally Became a Liability

Susan McKay

His big menacing voice boomed through my childhood. We'd hear that bullish roar across the school fields behind our house. That was in the 1960s, when he preached hellfire and damnation for the unsaved in his church on the edge of the local housing estates, on the farther outskirts of Derry's Waterside. God was not mocked. Oh for a tempest of power!

We'd hear it as well on the television in the evenings, dire daily warnings of apocalypse for the beloved province. Savage denunciations of O'Neill, then Chichester Clark, then Faulkner. Traitors all, and all destroyed by Paisley. Many years later, Trimble was the last to topple. The Lord has wrought a great deliverance!

Some of the boys I went to school with heard that voice too. They heard a call to arms. They were among the crowd that headed up the road to Burntollet with nail-studded cudgels to meet the students from People's Democracy. One of them had his hand blown off planting a bomb. Others spent years in jail among the loyalist paramilitaries who thought it was their duty to serve God and Ulster by killing Catholics.

It used to be said of loyalists in full, violent spate, 'the blood is up', and no one knew better than Paisley how to rouse them. It has been well said of him that he was always willing to fight to the last drop of everybody else's blood.

His appeal in the early years was greatest among those at the bottom of the unionist heap, who were reared to defer to their betters and to know their place. One Orange Order landlord in the 18th century spoke approvingly of the 'stout fellows somewhat lawless' who, in the matter of loyalty, 'could not be outdone'. Any notion of class solidarity with Catholics was stamped on. Catholics were the enemy.

Right from the start, Paisley sneered at O'Neill's plummy big house accent, declared himself one of the 'nobodies'. He wasn't, of course. He was a shrewd and self-interested politician. He encouraged a furious sense of grievance among his followers, as well as cultivating the atavistic sectarianism that allowed them to look down on Catholics at the same time as fearing their treacherous intentions.

The notion that 'we are the people' included the notion that Paisley was our Moses, God's man for the hour, leading his people, assailed on every side by their foes, to salvation. The poet John Hewitt saw that Paisley could not have risen with the rabble alone behind him. His 'coasters' from the comfortable middle classes played their part, confiding in the club: 'You know, there's something in what he says.'

He made it impossible for other unionist leaders to move forward, split the party, then set up his own 'democratic' one. He sowed dissent among the God-fearing Presbyterians to the point that their church split and he was able to set up his own 'free' sect.

Teachers Cathríona Ní Chathail and Olivia Carnelia at the TUI Congress 2008 in Wexford. Photograph: Patrick Browne Jnr.

The first time I went to hear him preach was in the 1970s in a marquee in the Waterside. I brought my southern boyfriend. We went for idle thrills, but his repeated threats to string up the apostates at the back of the tent had us ashen-faced by the time it was over.

He was a dictator. He threatened 'the mailed fist'. He marched armed men up mountainsides. He claimed when Thatcher signed the Anglo Irish Agreement with Garret FitzGerald that she would 'wade knee-deep in the blood of loyalists'. He said the peace process was 'the worst crisis in Ulster's history', and the Good Friday Agreement was a 'partnership with the men of blood' and a 'prelude to genocide'.

He loved to tower over the brink while others plunged into the abyss. The emergence of the Provisional IRA was perhaps his first self-fulfilling prophecy.

Nearly three decades of bloodshed later, he was warning that 'they', meaning the authorities, had better let the Orangemen down the Garvaghy Road, because otherwise 'anyone with any imagination' knew what was going to happen. What happened was the firebombing of a Catholic house in Ballymoney, resulting in the burning to death of three children. – which Paisley duly condemned.

And then, after all the obdurate years of 'Never! Never! Never!' and 'No surrender!' Paisley agreed to share power with those who make up almost half the population of the North. There was nowhere else to go.

'Today we have begun to plant and we await the harvest,' he said. It was as if he had either just come off some powerful drug, or just gone on one.

For years, politicians in the Republic treated Paisley as a buffoon. In recent times, the Taoiseach has come to like him a lot, for the same reason that

Tony Blair did. They looked brighter in the great beam of his approving smile, less tawdry than in the light of other exploits.

There is no doubt he would have hung on had he not been pushed. It wasn't because the grass-roots feels betrayed by powersharing, though. Most have taken to it perfectly well. His determination that the House of Paisley would continue to dominate the DUP played its part in his downfall.

Like the IRA for Sinn Féin, he had simply become a liability.

SATURDAY, 15 MARCH 2008

Tale with no Happy Ending

TV Review by Hilary Fannin

'Pussycat, pussycat, where have you been? I've been to London to visit the queen. Pussycat, pussycat, what did you there? I frightened a little Maoist under her chair.'

So riffed Cathal Ó Searcaigh, having inquired of a young Nepalese friend whether there were Maoists in his local village and having received the answer that there were, indeed, many 'Maoists' of the little furry, long-tailed variety, the kind that scuttle under chairs. Language is tricky, understanding other cultures is tricky, accepting mores and traditions that are not your own is tricky. The politics of desire is extremely tricky.

Fairytale of Kathmandu was finally aired on RTÉ this week, allowing the viewing public to see what all the fuss on the airwaves and in the papers has been about these last few weeks. Just on the off-chance that you have had your head firmly lodged in your coal scuttle, let me fill you in on the story so far. Two years ago, film-maker Neasa Ní Chianáin accompanied her friend, Irish-language poet Ó Searcaigh, to Nepal, a place he considered to be his spiritual home, where he took up

residence for three months each year in the Buddha Hotel to write his poems and cruise the streets for attractive young men to patronise.

Ní Chianáin's film (which, almost incidentally at this stage, is beautifully shot), follows Ó Searcaigh – along with a bunch of acolytes, his gang, young men he has befriended over the years – as he sojourns in that misty, far-off land. Along the way, after trekking in the mountains with the poet and observing him peruse the dusty city streets for bicycles and clothes to gift to his young associates, Ní Chianáin's hitherto sentimentalised portrait of 'the guru of the hills' sours into disillusionment. Witnessing the frequency with which Ó Searcaigh invites new 'friends' to stay in his room for the night, she begins to suspect that the poet's beneficence comes at a price. Her romantic illusions about her Donegal neighbour are shattered as this idealised artist in his pill-box hat turns out, surprise surprise, to be a sexual being, a man using his power to gratify his own desires.

And bang, the fuse is lit: now, instead of a mellow paean to the poet, dripping with sensitivity and shod by the natural shoe shop, we have a stomping beast of a documentary featuring sexual tourism and exploitation and, in the leading role, an over-indulged, libidinous westerner tripping around the Himalayan foothills with his parasol under his arm, like an archetypal colonialist looking for a little something to sweeten his tea.

Fairytale of Kathmandu is a depressing film on many levels, but primarily because of Ó Searcaigh's desperate self-delusion. The man is incapable, it would seem, of understanding how his actions impinge on those around him and unable to recognise the inequality, the disparity of power, that make the sexual relationships he has with young Nepalese men (all, as the programme admitted, over Nepal's age of consent) so difficult to condone.

'I prefer to give money directly to the boys,' he said, with no hint of irony.

A man lauded for his talent, courage and openness about his sexuality, Ó Searcaigh is clearly unable to resist the temptations of omnipotence ('He is like a god to us,' smiled one of his friends) and behave with judicious restraint in an impoverished country among vulnerable young people.

But, however distasteful and exploitative Ó Searcaigh's conduct, these are relationships he honestly admitted in the paltry few minutes on film Ní Chianáin allowed him to defend himself, once they were back in Donegal. ('I wanted to talk, but I didn't know how,' was Ní Chianáin's fey excuse for not confronting him during their time in Nepal, which goes to the heart of the film's weakness.)

It is also depressing that we are being asked to share in Ní Chianáin's naïve shock and distress. Had she thought about it before she boarded the plane, clutching Ó Searcaigh's eloquently revealing volumes of poetry, it might have occurred to her to look at her friend's life (a depressive mother, a repressive society, a first love shattered when the man he loved left him for a woman) and conclude that his complex sexuality wasn't going to be contained by his fez.

I don't condone Ó Searcaigh's actions, and my instinct towards the man and his pompous egotism is not friendly, but I was made uneasy by the film's incautious emotional appeal, and its possible consequences both for Ó Searcaigh and the young men now tainted by his largesse.

In a film that questions the nature of consent, perhaps Ní Chianáin herself has questions to answer (some Nepalese friends of Ó Searcaigh's have expressed anger that their consent for inclusion in this film was never sought, and it has been suggested that others felt coerced into making condemnatory statements after Ó Searcaigh's departure from Nepal). 'I searched their faces for answers,'

Participants at an Easter Sunday ecumenical Sunrise Celebration at first light at the Papal Cross in the Phoenix Park in Dublin. Photograph: Alan Betson.

Ní Chianáin said of the young Nepalese men at one point in her film, attempting to unravel the complexity of the interactions she had witnessed.

But maybe there is no such thing as an answer in this intricate web of motives and needs, and possibly more care should have been taken before the life and career of this delusional man was thrown on to the smouldering coals of our collective outrage.

This is a truncated version of Hilary Fannin's television review of 15 March 2008.

THURSDAY, 20 MARCH 2008

An Irishman's Diary

Frank McNally

At the risk of appearing heartless, I live in hope that the trauma Paul McCartney has been through lately may inspire him to turn back the years and produce a classic divorce album.

Dylan did it, after all. Springsteen too. Maybe it's too much to expect that a *Blood on the Tracks* will emerge from the McCartney-Mills saga, the climax of which was a jug of water on the defence lawyer. But I'd settle for something even half as good. As a starting point, perhaps Sir Paul could write a darker, pain-filled version of one of his old Beatles hits, entitled: 'When I'm 65'.

On the other hand, it's possible that the divorce settlement was just too much of a victory to benefit him artistically. He has escaped the marriage's train-crash with his public image intact (at least by comparison with his ex-wife's), not to mention his fortune. So he may, paradoxically, be happier now than he has been for some time.

This could be very bad news for music fans. A reprise of his 1980s hit, 'We All Stand Together' – complete with the Frog Chorus – might well be in the offing. Indeed, if that song too were slightly re-written (perhaps as 'We All Can't Stand Heather'), it would probably give him another Christmas No. 1.

The link between domestic happiness and the death of creativity is no doubt overstated. But if it is a myth, the Beatles did more than any other band in pop history to perpetuate it. Looking back on a chronology of the group's career, the marriages of John and Paul – occurring within eight days of each other in 1969 – now have the ominous ring of other events from that era, such as the crushing of the Prague Spring, or the fall of Saigon.

True to form, the messy break-up of the great songwriting partnership inspired a few final high points. Once they were happily married to other people, however, the music went sharply downhill. Maybe it wasn't all bad. But listening to many of the Fab Two's post-Beatles records, one had the uncomfortable sensation of intruding on personal bliss.

Around the same time Lennon and McCartney were being diagnosed with terminal happiness, Bob Dylan was copper-fastening the perceived connection between suffering and high-quality songwriting. Never had so many music fans been so selfishly grateful for other people's pain.

Ending his decade-long decline, Dylan's divorce inspired a short golden era spanning the brilliant *Blood on the Tracks*, the very good *Desire*, and the more-than-decent *Street Legal*. By then, time had healed his wounds and he was about to find religion, leading to another artistic slump. But his misery had been good while it lasted.

The idea that turbulent lives are a requisite for creativity extends well beyond music. From Van Gogh to Dostoevsky, it covers most art forms, with the possible exception of clock-making (see below). It also extends beyond individuals and groups, to embrace whole countries.

Summing up the philosophy in *The Third Man*, Orson Welles as Harry Lime cast 15th-century Italy as a national version of the Beatles, with Switzerland – past and present – as Wings: 'In Italy, for 30 years under the Borgias they had warfare, terror, murder, bloodshed – they produced Michelangelo, Leonardo da Vinci and the

Captain Aisling Campion and her Loreto High School teammates celebrate their 2-1 victory over Alexandra College in the Leinster Schools Hockey Senior Cup final at Grange Road, Dublin. Photograph: Matt Kavanagh.

Renaissance. In Switzerland, they had brotherly love, they had 500 years of democracy and peace, and what did that produce? The cuckoo clock.'

Even if the creative power of suffering is not a myth, of course, it may be too late in Paul McCartney's career for a messy divorce to save him. Besides, there is also the fact that his first wife remained the real love of his life, even during that short period of calm after he re-tied the knot in Castle Leslie.

Yes, his 2007 album, *Memory Almost Full*, included a love song dedicated to Heather. But fans with too much time on their hands quickly pointed out that *Memory Almost Full* was an anagram of the phrase 'For My Soul-Mate LLM' (Linda Louise McCartney, in case you didn't know). And although the song-writer denied this was deliberate, insisting the title was inspired by a message on

his mobile phone, he was clearly not unhappy about the coincidence.

It is one of the misfortunes of the McCartney-Mills debacle, arguably, that he is the singer-songwriter, not she. Ms Mills is in the ideal creative place right now: hurt, angry, wanting to spill her guts out; while at the same she is insulated – by €31 million – from any pressure to produce a commercial record.

You can imagine her writing something like Dylan's 'Idiot Wind', with its ranting intro: 'Someone's got it in for me/ They're planting stories in the press'. It's slightly harder to envisage her running through the rest of BOTT's emotional gamut – such as the forgiving 'If You See Her, Say Hello' or the jauntily wistful 'Buckets of Rain'.

But with so much turbulence in her life, all she would have needed was a good voice and some songwriting talent. In which case, yet another wedding album – with its glossy smiles and perfect hair-dos – would now be undergoing transformation into an album of a different kind, for the greater glory of music.

FRIDAY, 21 MARCH 2008

Proud Day for Bertie as Former Secretary Breaks Down in the Witness Box

Miriam Lord

Bertie Ahern must be a very proud man today. His Ministers must be so proud of him too. It's such a pity none of them could make it to Dublin Castle to watch Gráinne Carruth give her evidence.

They would have seen a woman, alone and trembling in the witness box, battling back the tears as she whispered in tones so anguished they were barely audible: 'I just want to go home.' It was so pitiful, it's just a pity Bertie wasn't there to see it.

He might have stood up and shouted like a man: 'Let the girl go. It's me you want!' But that only happens in the movies.

The Taoiseach was unavailable to the media yesterday.

If he had been in Dublin Castle, he would have witnessed the distress of his former secretary, loyal servant to the last, struggling to maintain her composure in the face of strong but fair questions about his finances.

His finances.

If Bertie had been there, he would have witnessed her obvious discomfort as she continued to insist she cannot remember three occasions in 1994 when he gave her big wads of British currency and told her to tip across to the bank and change them into Irish punts.

Gráinne Carruth, who earned £66 a week

back then, would have gone into the bank on each occasion and handed the teller bundles of money that were far in excess of her annual salary.

Six thousand, five and a half thousand, four thousand. In sterling. In cash.

But she just can't remember. She can't remember the foreign exchange element of the transaction. She can't remember splitting up the resultant punts and lodging separate amounts into Bertie Ahern's account, and into accounts in the names of his two daughters.

All she can recall is that she used to cash her boss's pay cheques and lodge a few bob from them, upon his request, into his daughters' accounts. 'I always remember just the girls.'

These were the days when people had passbooks, and transactions were recorded as they occurred. Bertie would hand Carruth the girls' building society books before sending her over to the Irish Permanent.

But of the amounts she banked on those three trips, by far the largest ones went into her boss's account. Carruth, to this day, still can't remember he had one.

'So you would have had three passbooks then, would that be correct?' asked Judge Keys.

'I only remember the two,' replied Carruth in a faltering voice.

A few people laughed in the public gallery. But for the most part during her evidence, the audience just watched and listened in amazement.

To the even most casual observer, Carruth's obvious agitation would have been apparent. She was forced to accept, in the face of the documentary evidence, that she had converted sterling and lodged some of it in Bertie Ahern's account. All she could say, the only thing she could say, was that she couldn't remember.

Truly, the Taoiseach, had he been at the Mahon tribunal yesterday, would have been proud of what he heard.

For he has told the tribunal, Dáil Éireann and the Irish people that he never had any dealings

Cartoon by Martyn Turner.

with foreign currency (apart from that one un-solicited whip-round in Manchester). And Carruth, the woman who once worked in his office, was able to repeat what she has told the inquiry all along: as far as she remembers, she only ever cashed his pay cheques for him. She never saw or handled sterling.

The tribunal proved that this is not true.

'I can't dispute it. It's here in black and white in front of me. I don't recall it, but it is here in black and white in front of me,' was the best she could manage. 'I don't believe I ever told an untruth,' she said forlornly.

However, Carruth, echoing a phrase already used a couple of times by her solicitor, accepted that she changed sterling for Bertie Ahern 'as a matter of probability'. But this mother of three young children, who gave up her job as the Taoiseach's constituency secretary in 1999, is not in the same league as Bertie's cohort of amnesiac businessmen; that swaggering stream of pin-striped amigos who have blustered in and out of the wit-ness box, brazenly vague and forgetful, and not in the least bit bothered that nobody is buying their tall tales.

(For those of you looking for something to do on Good Friday, here's a suggestion: Google 'Mahon tribunal'. On the left-hand side, click on 'transcripts' and look up 3 April 2006. Marvel at the evidence from Tim Collins, Bertie's close associate who gave entertaining evidence last week.)

Carruth isn't like Celia Larkin either, who couldn't remember much when she appeared, but clothed her memory lapses with a certain style, addressing the tribunal's lawyer on first name terms and airily dismissing his rising incredulity with icy disdain.

No, unlike the others, Carruth was not able to hide the fact that she didn't want to be in the witness box. She radiated unease and apprehension. She only spent an hour and a half on the stand, but it will rate as one of the most uncomfortable tribunal sessions that observers have had to sit through.

At one point, she was asked why she changed her solicitor. At the outset, she had the same solicitor as Bertie Ahern. She met this solicitor to discuss what she knew before she went to talk to the tribunal in private session two years ago.

Carruth told Des O'Neill, who managed to be both solicitous and incisive yesterday, she 'was upset and this was coming on a daily basis to my door and I just wanted it out of my house and my husband, my husband found Mr Millar'.

A change of solicitor so, for Carruth, as any citizen is entitled to. Her husband, as he is entitled to do, found Hugh Millar, who took on her case.

Millar also represents Celia Larkin and businessman John Kennedy, who attended Bertie's famous whip-round dinner in Manchester.

One wonders if the highly regarded Millar had a Humphrey Bogart moment when he heard the identity of his new client: 'Of all the legal joints, in all the towns, in all the world, Gráinne Carruth's husband walks into mine.'

Perhaps the most telling moment of the morning came when O'Neill asked Carruth why she hadn't contacted Ahern when she finally saw the documents linking her to the sterling transactions. After all, she couldn't remember a thing.

She said she didn't contact Bertie because her children are her main priority. O'Neill, gently, pressed the issue. Did she not want to clarify matters 'of crucial importance' to her and her family? Why didn't she call Bertie? Carruth's voice began to crack.

'Because I'm hurt.'

'Because why?'

'I'm hurt.'

'You're hurt?'

Bertie Ahern's former office secretary began to cry.

'And I'm upset.'

'Yes,' soothed Des. 'And what is upsetting you about your evidence before the tribunal today?'

'Because it's taking me from my family, and that's why I'm upset,' sobbed Carruth.

'Is there any other reason, Ms Carruth?' asked Des, softly.

There was a tortured pause.

'I just want to go home.'

A proud day for Bertie. A proud day for his Ministers, and the rest of his parliamentary party inbertiebrates.

Brian Cowen is in Vietnam.

SATURDAY, 22 MARCH 2008

Not So Super Sweet 16

Kathy Sheridan

Some weeks ago, while scratching around for a theme for a talk I was giving to a fund-raising lunch, it occurred to me that the project involved – the wonderful Tallaght-based education centre, An Cosán – was 22 years old, the same age as my youngest daughter.

A call to the project's CEO, Liz Waters, elicited a typical day in the life of a girl considering the monumental step of a return to education with An Cosán. She probably sits around most of the day in a rented flat, alone with her child, with no one to babysit and no money for a babysitter anyway. She can't afford a mobile phone although she has one anyway, but never has credit for it.

She eats rubbish, probably from the chip van, almost certainly smokes, probably has no relationship with the baby's father and struggles constantly with loneliness. Life is an endless struggle to make impossible ends meet. She resorts to the moneylenders for Christmas, first communions and confirmations. If she lives at home, it's intolerably over-crowded and often involves family relationship problems. She sees the doctor regularly for recurring stress-related physical ailments, 'flus, tummy bugs, chest infections. If she seems hard and tough, it may be because 'too long a sacrifice makes a heart of stone'.

And then you think of your own daughter and her friends, with all their myriad choices about where and how to live their lives. If they drop out of college, do you go on supporting them? At what point do you say enough is enough? Are we too full of guilt to ever reach that point? In the 22 years since An Cosán's birth, during which we have hurtled from stagnancy and recession to insane over-indulgence, have we implanted a dangerous sense of entitlement in our privileged Celtic cubs?

By way of example, I took the generally well-heeled audience on a shopping trip through the eyes of a typical, affluent 14-year-old private school girl in Dublin, a trip which went something like this.

First stop, Brown Thomas. False tan, fake eyelashes and nails are necessities for a night out and are therefore called upon at least once a week. A typical trip could include a trip to Benefit for a 'Bad Gal' mascara (€25), foundation (€30) or false lashes from MAC (€15).

The nailbar is another option at €20 for a file and polish. The only fake tans to buy are St Tropez or Fakebake – about €30 a bottle.

No self-respecting cub is without a Juicy Couture tracksuit, €185 (top) and €140 (bottoms); Ugg boots at €200; a Louis Vuitton pouchette, a snip at €210; a Juicy Couture tote bag €265; and Juicy Couture dress €280.

An online order from Abercrombie and Fitch is a regular splash, with a typical spend being €300 to €400 every few months.

On Saturdays, the Dundrummies hit the Dundrum Town Centre where they while away an afternoon shopping and checking each other out over a Starbucks non-fat soy latte, sushi from Yo! Sushi for lunch, a Butler's hot chocolate later on and a trip to Movies @ Dundrum.

A shopping trip around Zara and H&M is a

'Oh my God, oh my God, oh my God…' actress Aoife McGuinness poses as the spoilt teenager. Photograph: Alan Betson.

regular event just for a new 'going-out top'. For something truly important, like a pair of jeans, it's straight to BT2 for Sevens, True Religion or Sass and Bide, all more than €200. After all this, says my informant, Mum pulls up in the Range Rover and they zoom off.

Lest you imagined that 14 is too tender an age to be so high-maintenance, then be aware that

Fans of the **Father Ted** *television series enjoying themselves at the Fr Ted Festival on Inishmore island, off Galway. Festival events included a Priests v Nuns five-a-side, Buckaroo speed-dating, the Lovely Girls competition and the Craggy World Cup Finals. Photograph: Bryan O'Brien.*

there is a southside nail boutique, for instance, that offers a 'Little Princess' package for under-13s; €25 for a polish and a soak.

These, roughly, are the same girls to be seen in their droves at 'Wezz' disco every Friday night. The pre-drinks rituals lead to a lot of drunk teenagers outside – before, during and after.

The point is that many of these little girls obviously have 'mates' for parents. They have the kind of financial freedom and sense of entitlement that hard-working people three times their age will never achieve, thanks to their 'mates'. Yet observe them trudging through the marbled halls of Dundrum Town Centre and the most notable thing about many of them is a kind of sullen boredom. Of course some of that can be put down to raging hormones, but you find yourself wondering – what would you give a girl like that for Christmas? And how many averagely well-off parents and their children now perceive all this to be the norm?

It all started with the children's parties; with the pricey entertainers and the increasingly upmarket goody bags until they became the norm. Then came the limos, the helicopter rides, the hotel lunches and the cases of champagne for the First Communions.

That morphed seamlessly into the generation that swoons over *My Super Sweet 16* (an American TV hit with viewers aged zero to 25, which featured an Irish family last year), where children are indulged with designer gowns and fast cars on their 16th birthdays, encouraged to bully their less well-off 'courtiers' with threats of exclusion from the marvellously narcissistic party, and are given a power and status they haven't even begun to earn or understand.

And how do you follow that for an 18th birthday party? Well, you need a dress or two (because duh, you can't wear the same one twice in a birthday season), from Alila, Dolls and Chica, costing anything from €600 up. And if that's a dilemma, here's a worse one. Do you supply alcohol or meekly condone its presence when you know that half the guests haven't even reached the legal drinking age? If the first, do you consult all the parents first in the event of some stomach-pumping being required at some stage?

We can draw a veil over the school debs, a well-documented blow-out to which entire magazines are dedicated, although their extravagance seems under-stated now compared with all that goes before and after.

Twenty-first parties are staged on the scale of mini-weddings, while weddings themselves have become such overblown three-day extravaganzas, the drive for perfection so obsessive, the Bridezillas so repellently narcissistic, the whole event so staged, that it has become a branch of theatre rather than a public commitment to love and cherish. It's worth noting that Dadzillas are a new entrant in the weddings category (i.e. fathers of the bride who fancy themselves as event organisers).

As for the guest, the professional advice in this magazine a few weeks ago was that they have the right to say no thanks to an invitation to bankruptcy. But that is to ignore the problem – that weddings have become so ridiculously demanding that a young professional whimpered recently that she'd prefer to get a summons than a wedding invitation.

Hand in hand with this has come a parental insistence on the rightness of their child's decisions or actions. When they set their children off on an early-life assault course of Suzuki violin and Kumon maths, they probably didn't know that the same child would still be dithering about how precisely to make a living for themselves at 25.

One of the great parental challenges now is to discern the difference between lazy choices and courageous dreams where our children are concerned. Are we slowly stunting them with our airy promises of unconditional support, no matter what; with the implied assurances that we can always fix things for them when their impulsive decisions or unwillingness to get stuck in bring the inevitable fall-out? And what becomes of the pampered young bride when the little scion arrives? Southside lore suggests that she chucks in the job

and summons night nannies, day nannies, cooks and cleaners to enable her to survive this uniquely demanding and exhausting sacrifice.

After our lunch, an accountant mused that with the economic slow-down, the 'Dundrummies' are being reined in as we speak, leading perhaps to fewer 'mates' of the parent-child variety. But has the damage been done? Has the national guilt-trip over house prices for first-time buyers, for example – the pressure on ageing parents to re-mortgage to help out their children – created another monster?

A friend tells a true story about a 30-something who had been living at home and announced to his parents that he was moving in with his girlfriend. That's grand, said the parents. But the girlfriend, said the son, had a heavy mortgage on the apartment. Umm, that's life, said the parents. But the son ploughed on undeterred. Since his room in the family home would be empty, he thought it was only fair, surely, to allow him to rent it out so he could make a contribution to the mortgage!

Astonishingly, two weeks later, when the parents had begun to exhale again, a pleasant lady with several suitcases and a tenuous grasp of English turned up at the door.

Is this the corollary of our efforts to lavish our children with money, possessions and choices that we never had? Did we forget about the bit in-between that makes acquiring your own mortgage a singular event, something extraordinary and liberating?

Sure, we've moved from barefoot school-children to the high-maintenance, Heat generation in the blink of an eye and what sane person would want to go back? And of course, it's more fun being a 'mate' to your children and a lot less trouble. It cuts out the relentless battles over study times and Saturday night curfews. And if you and your 'mate' fall out, you can always flounce off, unlike old-fashioned parents who have to stand their ground, now and forever.

But it can be salutary to be discussing these matters in the surrounds of a five-star hotel, where a young client of An Cosán bravely takes the podium to talk about achieving her dream of a certificate in childcare. And all credit to her generous audience, the irony escaped very few of them.

SATURDAY, 22 MARCH 2008

Our Assembled Pond Came to Enchant our Springs

Another Life, by Michael Viney

But for the jelly-moulds of frogspawn shivering at the surface, our garden pond is now virtually invisible: one false step and you'd be up to your knees. Beneath the mattress of twining meadow-grass and spiky rushes, a jungle of stems crowds the water – still seething, no doubt, with small aquatic animals stalking each other through the dark.

All this dates from my attempts to 'furnish' the newly made pond a dozen years ago: anything to take the bare look off a bottom of black plastic. A few shovelfuls of soil, a few buckets of plants and roots from the lake with their attendant eggs and larvae, a few dollops of spawn from a pool up the hill and the trick was done: sit back and wait for an ecosystem! When the fog of green algae had cleared, the assembled pond soon came, indeed, to enchant our springs. Perhaps 100 frogs gleaming and churring in the water, their orgies piling it with spawn. A steeper sun discovered great water beetles gliding after tadpoles or the courtship ballet of gilded newts. At the surface, the scribbling of whirligig beetles, the dimpling of featherweight pond skaters, a first damselfly unfolding crimson tinsel. Collins' *Field Guide to Freshwater Life* had me peering after sprites and goblins; a microscope would have captured me for ever.

The plants unfolded with enthusiasm, jostling for sun. A yellow water-lily stolen from a marsh eventually gave up its struggle for space as pondweeds, bogbean and water mint crowded together at the surface, and grasses and mosses crept

in from the edge. The bogbean is still a delight in May and June, holding up pink-and-white flowers like fringed, orchidaceous hyacinths. They decorate, for a while, a pond that wants so much to be a fen, if not, in some long, mossy future, a little bump of bog.

I did fight this for a few years, laying into it each autumn with an ancient, long-handled, iron claw (the original muckrake) to drag out heaps of vegetation (duly left to drain so that accompanying creatures could hop, skip or slither back in). All I wanted was a little open water, some lively glitter and ripples, a bright mirror on dull days. But the effort finally was too much hard work, and natural succession has been left to take its course. The frogs have dwindled in number; the newts are no longer on show.

So that's one sort of result in faking nature – but native nature, as it were, and doing, in the end, small harm. Most garden ponds, however, are made in suburbs remote from wild marshes and lakes. This may be just as well, but it has set up a brisk garden-centre trade in decorative water plants, many imported from abroad. Aquarium hobbyists, too, seek to make their fish at home among suitably feathery, oxygenating fronds. In consequence, some aquatic plants now figure among the worst of Ireland's invasive species.

Don't ask me how they escape from ponds and aquariums, but they do: thrown out in the wrong place, whirled in the wind, flushed down the loo. Water plants spread mainly vegetatively – from fragments of themselves – and their urge is to go on spreading as far as space and conditions allow.

The spiralling fronds of curly waterweed (*Lagarosiphon major*) from southern Africa, positively bubble with oxygen. First found in Lough Corrib in 2005, it now notoriously covers 10 hectares of Rinneroon Bay, near Oughterard, its dense stands filling the water to a depth of several metres, clogging engines, strangling divers and threatening the ecology of Ireland's premier trout angling lake. There's a task force bent on finding ways to control it.

Parrot's feather (*Myriophyllum aquaticum*) looks like one of those beautiful tall mosses in the ditches of conifer plantations, but grows as dense floating mattresses that can, in official disapprobation, 'impair recreational exploitation of infested waters'. It is widely grown in garden ponds and has been spotted at five new wild sites in the Republic since 2000.

With the common name of fairy moss, but actually a floating aquatic fern, *Azolla filiculoides* is a free-floating plant with lovely pink edges to flat, lacy leaves (press them under water and they bob straight up again). I can quite see why anyone should want it in their pond, but it can spread forever on calm water and pile up in dense, rotting rafts. Coming from the warmer parts of America, and already in Ireland, it is one of those undesirable aliens that climate change could turn into a eutrophicating menace.

Visit *www.invasivespeciesireland.com* and you can find your way to more 'most unwelcome' water plants, either here already or just waiting to arrive. You are begged, by relevant agencies north and south, not to buy invasive aquatic plants and to dispose of garden waste 'in a responsible manner'. That goes for aquariums, too.

SATURDAY, 29 MARCH 2008

Endangered Species

Lorna Siggins

Sally Barnes must have been a wild Atlantic salmon in one of her former lives . . . a finned athlete surmounting a weir on a river in full spate. Swimming against the flow seems to come very naturally to her, whether

Newt by Michael Viney

she is questioning a cosy consensus on the merits of the drift-net ban, or speaking her mind about farmed fish.

The Ayrshire-born founder of Woodcock Smokery in Castletownshend, Co. Cork, famous for its top quality smoked salmon, knows her pectoral from her dorsal fin, her pelagic from her demersal, having taken the supreme accolade for her fish products at the Great Taste Awards in London in late 2006. A few weeks later, she faced a crisis when the Government caved in to EU pressure and issued the drift net ban that threatened to put her out of business.

Small wonder that there was a packed audience for a talk she gave recently at this year's Irish Skipper conference in Salthill, Galway. Many of the 4,000 dayboat catchers and fish farmers passing through from all compass points on this country's 7,500km coastline will have been aware of Barnes's highly critical voice when the Government proposed banning all drift-netting for salmon just over a year ago.

'As one skipper said to me, we're going to have to find something else to catch, Sally . . . We're used to diversifying, but who is going to look after you?'

It's that sort of empathy between catcher and artisan that has made Woodcock Smokery such a success. Attuned to the struggles of those trying to survive in an industry which is subject to a very politicised, overly bureaucratic and mismanaged EU policy, Barnes knows and understands her own community – and recognises that most skippers and crew are not the criminals that Government and EU officials would make them out to be.

Irish drift-net fishery has been a 'victim' and not a cause of the decline in wild salmon stocks, Prof Noel Wilkins, former head of the National Salmon Commission has said, warning that the ban would 'replace one set of problems with another'. His successor, Joey Murrin, has recently tried to highlight several of these problems, including the lack of monitoring on rivers. Barnes agrees that the

Government's failure to implement measures crucial to the survival of fragile stock has transferred a resource caught offshore to one caught inland by unscrupulous anglers.

'Unfortunately, there is now rampant poaching on river systems,' Barnes says. 'And what happened to the promise to restore river systems, to eradicate pollution, to protect spawning beds, and to have a proper system of control inland?

'I've been offered fish by anglers, of course, but I've said I won't take anything caught illegally. In any case, there is nothing quite like the quality of the salmon netted offshore. The fish has metamorphosed when it returns to its river, it has lost so much fat in that journey that it is not worth killing to eat . . . and the effluent in rivers is such that you couldn't stand over the meat.'

Barnes's family and neighbours were her initial quality controllers, when she first began smoking fish over 25 years ago. She has told the story often – how her husband Colin, now a whale-watching skipper, would bring home enough fish for several weeks when they did not have a freezer.

It was the three weeks' supply of mackerel that finished her off. She took out an old tea-chest, put a hole in the bottom of it, and began her first smoking experiments. 'The fish kept falling into the sawdust, however, so we managed to secure a kiln in exchange for some credit owed to us.' The mechanical Afos kiln allowed her to smoke both 'cold' and 'hot', as in curing or cooking. She studied food production with Open University, and followed that with oceanography.

In 1996, a trip to Turin won her over to the Slow Food Movement, of which she is an ardent member. She nominated wild Irish salmon for the Slow Food 'Ark of Taste', which was created in 1996 to catalogue foods that have been forgotten or marginalised and are at risk of disappearing. For that, she earned a reprimand from conservationists who were by then campaigning for a drift-net ban. 'Slow Food came under pressure over that, to the extent that that nomination is currently suspended.'

Inishturk fisherman Bernard Heaney with his catch of the day. Photograph: NUTAN.

Barnes will not work with farmed salmon, nor will she try to hoodwink customers with loose but legal labelling – there is a lot of confusion among consumers about 'organic' salmon, for instance, or calling fish 'Irish' if it is smoked here but caught elsewhere.

One solution for islanders and indeed artisan producers such as herself, Barnes suggests, is to develop a market for other catches. Mackerel, herring, kippers, haddock and tuna also appear under the Woodcock label, but salmon comprised half of the 10 tonnes of fish preserved by her annually.

Over the past season, she has secured a limited supply of sea-caught fish from Scotland. 'And what about developing more ranching?' she asks. Ranching has been tried on a limited scale here, but its success depends on having little or no coastal fishing interfering with the harvest of returning fish.

It involves breeding smolts in hatcheries, keeping them in nets in estuaries to allow the smell of the river to be imprinted on their memories, and then releasing them into the wild. It has proved to be very successful as a more natural form of salmon rearing and restocking in Iceland, Norway, Scotland and Alaska, and even in Spain and Portugal.

Barnes also believes that the pressure on skippers to move into larger vessels for trip fishing has had a dramatic impact on the fresh fish market at home, although premium prices abroad are also an influencing factor. Because of high fuel prices, trip fishing boats stay out for three or four days at a time rather than returning with their catch. Sally Barnes would like to see more day fishing, and believes island communities have an opportunity to market a fresh daily catch.

Comhdháil Oileáin na hÉireann, the Irish Islands Federation, published an enlightened marine policy as part of an overall submission to Government on the future of offshore economies late last year. Projects such as holding tanks for storing lobster in recirculated seawater beyond the short summer season have been proving successful on Inis Oirr, for instance.

Barnes believes that smaller island fleets could develop their own niche market in daily-caught fresh fish.

'I did a diploma in social studies way back,' she says, 'and I realise that island economies don't need the massive big factory planted there with some State agency's encouragement, benefiting no one; in the long term when it shuts. Islands need small pieces of activity, based on developing skills which help to consolidate communities.'

She has been talking to islanders on Cape Clear about setting up a smokery there, which would depend on day-caught fish and which would sell under her label.

SATURDAY, 29 MARCH 2008

Back to the Barrow

Olivia O'Leary

One late August day I was swimming with my sister above the weir at Clashganny. The sun glanced off the water. Under the bank, fat blackberries dipped down into the river. Suddenly beside us was the wet dark head of an otter. He paddled along quietly. So did we. River etiquette, as Mole and Rat would tell you, forbids any sort of comment on the sudden appearance or disappearance of one's friends.

This is summer for me: long lazy hours by the river; friends strolling down the towpath as day wears on. We swim over to the weirs and lie back on the mossy stones, letting white water bubble over us. All around is the dizzying roar of the water, the silty smell of its churn. The bank faces west or southwest, so on good days it stays warm until sunset, when the river turns gold and the fish are jumping and there's an echo all down the valley.

Even when it's raining, which it was most of last summer, you can still lose yourself down here. It's

quiet. People have all the courtesy and reserve of an area that has never had to rely on tourism. They'll leave you alone. You won't meet half of Dublin. There's no sparkling sea. There are no public gulls. This is intimate, the heart of the country.

The Barrow Valley is where I'm from, south Co. Carlow. The river defines the county on the west; Mount Leinster and the Blackstairs define it on the east. In between, you can go swimming, canoeing, boating, cycling, climbing, riding, golfing, but, most of all, this is country made for walking.

I'll describe the most beautiful walk, also the simplest. It runs all along the grassy towpath of the Barrow and Grand Canal waterway and brings you through some of the most beautiful riverscape in these islands.

It starts at Ballytiglea Bridge, above Borris, and ends in St Mullin's, at the southern tip of the county, a walk of about 18km but one that can be easily divided into three sections of about an hour point-to-point, or two hours if you double back. The way is flat. Waterways Ireland keeps the grass mowed, so it's very easy to walk. And all the way, except when the river cuts through Graignamanagh, you'll be away from roads and cars and noise. It will be as though a door has shut behind you and you'll be tempted never to open it again.

Heading south from Ballytiglea, you'll have Borris House demesne for a kilometre or two on your left. You'll pass Borris Lock and come to Bunnahowen — we learned to swim there, in the freezing Mountain River, and then, as we got stronger, floated out under the old stone bridge into the deep and warmer Barrow. It was our down-home version of a plunge pool and hot tub.

The next lock you come to is Ballinagrane, its long weir, like all weirs, guarded by a hungry heron. It'll push off resentfully as you approach, but it'll be back as soon as you round the corner. On then to Clashganny, one of the few places where a car is allowed near the line, so someone can pick you up if you're tired.

Bring your togs, because Clashganny (or Sandy Valley) is a perfect place to swim. Above the lock and opposite the weir there's a full-time lifeguard in July and August. Here, there are steps down to the water and, on the weir side, a breakwater to dive off.

The next leg of the walk is from Clash to Graignamanagh. There are deep woods above you all along the left. The river splits off for Clohastia on the right – you can hear the weir.

You'll head along the quiet canal bank to Ballykeenan, the only double lock on the river and the deepest. There the river rejoins you – you'll see the ancient eel weir on the other side of the island and you'll bowl along the stretch to Graignamanagh.

Take a bit of time in Graig. Cross over the graceful Palladian bridge built by a pupil of George Semple in the 18th century and walk up to the 13th-century Duiske Abbey. The biggest

Cistercian foundation in Ireland, it was restored in the 1970s to its original soaring roof height. The old floor tiles with their *fleur-de-lis* pattern can still be seen, as can the magnificent Romanesque processional doorway.

Before you resume your walk, I might as well warn you. Last time I checked, there was nowhere to eat in St Mullin's and nowhere to drink if Blanchfield's pub is closed, so grab something in Graig. You can have a great coffee and sandwich at Coffee on High, on High Street, a good carvery lunch in the Duiske Inn, on Main Street; two good Chinese restaurants, one on Main Street and one in Tinnahinch.

New on the Tinnahinch side of the bridge is Boats, a bistro with an Italian chef, open from the end of March. It will serve food from 11am with a lunch-type menu until 7pm and after that a more sophisticated dinner menu.

Olivia O'Leary by her beloved River Barrow. Photograph: Michael Brophy.

Graig is an old canal port, and the boats and the ducks gather on either side of the bridge. You'll be tempted to stay, but press on down the towpath past Upper Tinnahinch Lock and you come into one of the loveliest stretches of the river. You'll pass the ruined Butler Castle at Tinnahinch and walk on down to where the woods rise high on either side and the town and the traffic die away.

The river is wide here, and the woods are deep and full of life. I've watched a stoat on the towpath rise to its hind legs and sniff the air as I waited in the shadow of the trees. Walking along here in the dusk, I've seen grey owls swoop low over my head. There's a rustling in the undergrowth all the time as you walk along, and you wonder how many wild things are watching.

Three locks on, you'll reach the end of the canal way at St Mullin's, with its Dutch-looking lock house and its little harbour of boats. Now you'll be conscious of mudflats, of the river changing. Though the sea is 50km away, from here down the river is tidal. If you're lucky as you arrive around the bend, the tide will be in, the water brimming and all the deep dark beauty of St Mullin's on show. Your walk is ending not just with a pretty village but with a wealth of history.

Here, towering above the river, you'll find a Norman-period motte and bailey built in even earlier pre-Christian remains. In the graveyard, you'll find the base of a round tower and the remains of four churches said to have made up the monastery of the 7th-century local saint, St Moling, the man who is said to have got rid of the infamous borumha, or cattle tax. (The *Book of Moling*, which details his exploits, is displayed in the same case as the *Book of Kells* at Trinity College Library.)

Moling's Holy Well is nearby, and locals visit it on his pattern day, in July, and also visit the graves here of many of the 1798 dead. Traditionally, this graveyard is said to be the burial place of the kings of Leinster, including Art McMurrough Kavanagh – a gravestone marks the spot.

This is Kavanagh country, and you have a chance to hang out at the McMurrough Kavanagh seat, Borris House, this July when it hosts Blackstairs' Opera in the Gardens (all details when finalised on *www.blackstairsopera.com*). You can picnic beforehand in the gardens and see the whole of the Blackstairs range and Mount Leinster laid out before you. It's magic. So is the opera.

TUESDAY, 1 APRIL 2008

Even in Death, Controversial Belgian Author Keeps Debates Alive

European Diary, by Jamie Smyth

The life of Hugo Claus, one of Belgium's most renowned authors, was celebrated at a ceremony in Antwerp last Saturday following his death by euthanasia on March 19th.

Claus (78), who suffered from Alzheimer's disease, wrote more than 20 novels, at least 60 plays and countless poems. Often called the Lion of Flanders, the title of one of his films, Claus was best known for his 1983 seminal work *The Sorrow of Belgium*, which depicted how Belgians reacted to the Nazi occupation during the second World War. This controversial work drew on Claus's experience of growing up in Flanders and played a large part in undermining the myth of widespread resistance to Nazi occupation that was fostered after the war in Belgium.

Never one to shy away from difficult issues, he tackled the connection between the Belgian monarchy and its brutal colonial past in the Congo in his 1970s play *The life and works of King Leopold II*.

He also admitted his own ambivalence about his nationality, declaring in a magazine interview: 'I insist on being Belgian . . . I want to be a member of the pariah nationality, the laughing stock of the French and an object of ridicule for the Dutch. It's the ideal situation for a writer.'

But despite his scathing criticism of Belgium, Claus received warm tributes from both the Flemish and francophone communities following his death.

'In his works he gave us a mirror on our lives,' said former prime minister Guy Verhofstadt, who was a close friend. 'Certainly a hard image, often unpitying, which helped us understand who we really were.'

Even in death Claus courted controversy by reopening a bitter debate about the practice of euthanasia in Belgium. Legalised in 2002 by the previous government led by Verhofstadt, euthanasia is chosen by 500 people every year as a means to end their lives.

'He himself picked the moment of his death and asked for euthanasia,' not wanting to extend his suffering, his wife, Veerle De Wit, said in a statement to the media.

Verhofstadt also spoke of the 'inevitable and unbearable torture' suffered by Claus, who for 60 years had no difficulty in finding the phrases to express himself. 'I can live with the fact that he decided [to end his life]. Because he left us as a great glowing star, right on time. Just before he collapsed into a black hole,' he added.

Stung by positive media reaction to Claus's decision to practise euthanasia, the Catholic Church in Belgium hit back from the pulpit. Cardinal Godfried Danneels of Brussels denounced euthanasia during his homily on Easter Sunday. 'Avoiding suffering is no act of bravery . . . Our society seems unable to cope with death and suffering.'

Brother René Stockman of the Congregation of Brothers of Charity also criticised the media's coverage of Claus's decision to take his own life.

'Only God can decide on matters of life and death,' he wrote in an open letter.

The Flemish Alzheimer League said it respected Claus's decision but believed 'the media coverage of his death neglects other options for Alzheimer patients'.

Belgium became the second country – after the Netherlands – to legalise euthanasia in 2002 when its parliament endorsed a Bill by 86 votes in favour, 51 against, and with 10 abstentions, after two days of heated debate. The euthanasia law enables patients to end their own lives with medical assistance if they are under 'constant and unbearable physical or psychological pain' resulting from an accident or incurable disease. They must be conscious when a demand for euthanasia is made and a second opinion from a doctor unconnected with the patient must be sought before it can go ahead.

Claus's death and the controversy created by the cardinal's comments on euthanasia have also prompted politicians to rethink the scope of the existing law. Bart Tommelein, leader of Belgium's Liberal Party, pledged last week to bring forward new legislation to allow children and teenagers to avail of euthanasia.

Under the current law, minors aged under 18 cannot request euthanasia. But the Liberals, who are members of the coalition, want this to change.

In the Netherlands the minimum age required to request euthanasia is 12 years, and teenagers aged between 12 and 16 must have the consent of their parents.

But amending the law will not be easy, according to Philippe Mahoux, a surgeon and leader of the Socialist Party in the Senate, who drafted Belgium's euthanasia law.

'This is a very difficult legal issue. It comes down to who has the legal right to decide on euthanasia for a minor. Would it be the parents? It is a very difficult problem to solve by law,' said Mahoux, who insists that the 2002 law has gained widespread public support. 'A case-by-case situation for minors may be preferable.'

Tánaiste Brian Cowen delivering the oration beside the grave of former President Dr Patrick Hillery at St Fintan's Cemetery, Sutton, Co. Dublin. Photographer: Dara Mac Dónaill.

Such political controversies do not now concern Claus, whose ashes have been strewn into the North Sea off Belgium's coast. But it is perhaps apt that the *enfant terrible* of Flemish literature went out as he lived, provoking a vibrant debate in his home country.

THURSDAY, 3 APRIL 2008

Bertie Manages Grand Entrance but Final Exit Still Hit him Like a Train

Miriam Lord

Head high, shoulders back and arms swinging, a smiling Bertie Ahern led in his troops. The public gallery was heaving. The press gallery packed.

The Dáil chamber filling up. Everyone waiting for Bertie.

It was a quarter to four in the afternoon. Wednesday, 2 April 2008. It was the end of the Ahern era.

Eleven years as Taoiseach. Fourteen years as Fianna Fáil leader. All over now for Bertie. His backbenchers looked stunned. His Ministers looked pensive.

The Taoiseach's smile remained fixed, his chin set at a confident tilt, as he strode purposefully around the chamber railings towards his seat.

When he reached the top of the steps, his deputies, arrayed in descending rows to his right, rose to their feet and applauded. (They had received a text from the whips office earlier in the afternoon, demanding 'full attendance' for Leaders' Questions.) The Opposition stayed put, and silent.

Still smiling, the Taoiseach bustled to his place. The applause subsided. The deputies subsided. And Bertie – well, Bertie subsided. He had managed the grand entrance. But now, he looked shattered, gazing listlessly across at the Fine Gael leader.

It was a difficult situation for Enda Kenny. Until yesterday morning's shock announcement, he had been preparing a major attack on the Taoiseach's suitability for office and his ability to govern in the teeth of the growing scandal over his finances.

Enda was generous, if somewhat measured, in his tributes to the Taoiseach, who will leave office on 6 May (although in true Bertie fashion, it appears that he won't officially go until 7 May, because the Dáil is closed the day before). 'This day had to come,' said Enda. There was genuine regret in his voice.

It's always the same in Dáil Éireann, when a big star finally falls from the political sky. It may seem strange to hear politicians, who have spent years lacerating somebody from across the floor, suddenly standing up and expressing regret when the outcome they demanded so vociferously, for so long, has finally been realised.

But there is a strange solidarity among the breed. When one of their number is taken down, there is a genuine sense of sadness. There but for the grace of God go us, and all that.

Enda asked about the date for the Lisbon referendum. He could have been reading his favourite passages from *Finnegans Wake* for all the attention people were paying.

Bertie appeared to be listening, but his head was down. He bit his lips, the picture of desolation. Was he that shocked? Had his decision been so sudden? Was it really an overnight thing, as some were saying? What prompted him to make his announcement in such a rushed manner? Is there

Cabinet colleagues applaud Taoiseach Bertie Ahern after his resignation announcement. Photograph: Niall Carson/PA.

THE PASSING OF the MANTLE

PLEASE! PLEASE! NOT the TROUSERS TOO..!

PDs

THE GREENS

OR THE BAGGAGE..

Cartoon by Martyn Turner.

more to come from the tribunal? But yesterday was not the day for such speculation.

The drama began just before half nine yesterday morning, when journalists were told to be at Government Buildings by 10am for an announcement by the Taoiseach. No further details were given.

A large crowd galloped to Merrion Street as rumour spread that Ahern was going to announce he was stepping down as Taoiseach and leader of Fianna Fáil. Journalists, photographers and television camera crews squeezed into the small space at the foot of the main staircase.

A plain wooden lectern was placed on a landing many steps above the journalists. Meanwhile, RTÉ television went live, with newsreader Bryan Dobson plucked from a radio discussion on Irish Protestants to anchor the broadcast, and a dishevelled looking Charlie Bird blinking excitedly into the studio camera.

The Taoiseach had yet to announce his intentions, as former Labour leader Pat Rabbitte was intoning on radio: 'He has done the State some service'. Back at Government Buildings, the media waited. Earlier, in scenes reminiscent of the Oklahoma land grab, they swarmed at great speed from the holding security hut at the gates to the main building. Once inside, their simmering sense of excitement verged on the hysterical as the Taoiseach kept everyone waiting.

Finally, at 10.48, Bertie Ahern appeared at the top of the stairs. He stopped and stared into the distance, above and beyond the crowd and out into the wider world.

Was he a man facing his destiny, or had his eyes been drawn to the large red banner that a number of his constituency workers had unfurled across the road in front of the gate? 'Ballybough Loves Bertie.' Then, having struck a statesmanlike pose, the Taoiseach began to walk down the stairs, a large group of Ministers behind him. It was an impressive show of strength. This was not a man about to hand in his resignation and scuttle away.

He reached the lectern. He looked down, paused, and looked up again. For a second, just a split second, there was total silence. The chatter stopped. The sound of the camera shutters stopped.

Then Bertie spoke.

His hand trembled a little as he held his script. He sounded nervous and his voice wavered a little.

Above his head, his staff looked down from the marble balcony two floors up. From top advisers to the cleaners, they came out to listen to Bertie. Some started to cry.

The Ministers clustered around their leader, Brian Cowen at his shoulder, looking grave. The two Marys – Coughlan and Hanafin – seemed close to tears. This was emotional stuff.

Bertie delivered the most difficult speech of his life with dignity and determination. Once or twice, his voice thickened. Unlike in his interview with Bryan Dobson, there was no doubting the Taoiseach's pain.

His statement can be dissected at another time.

'I know in my heart of hearts that I have done no wrong, and wronged no one,' he said.

But Bertie's problem is that too many people, in their heart of hearts, do not believe him now when he says he has done no wrong.

His fingers played nervously with the end of his jacket as he spoke. Cyprian Brady, his constituency colleague and loyal supporter, stood to one side, like a boxing trainer watching his man going down, in slow motion. Seán Haughey, who witnessed his own father's fall from grace, looked on.

Statement over, Bertie Ahern turned and went back up the stairs, his Ministers applauding and the applause of his staff ringing around the lofty marbled hall.

An hour later, Enda Kenny was on the plinth calling for a general election. (Marvellous move there by the Fine Gael leader, looking to go to the country when the nation is riding a wave of sympathy for poor Bertie.) Various Ministers were talking down their chances of going for the leadership. Brian Lenihan, meanwhile, was ruling himself out. Tánaiste Lenihan? Where did we hear that before? The action moved back to the Dáil in the afternoon, when Bertie took Leaders' Questions.

He looked awful. He looked sad and rather shocked. His backbenchers sat quietly, particularly the new intake, getting their education in the cruel nature of politics very early in their careers.

Labour's Eamon Gilmore welcomed the Taoiseach's decision to resign. He appreciated how difficult this was for him to do. And Eamon said what opposition leaders have been saying ever since the dawn of parliament: he had done his duty as he saw it, but he did it 'on a political basis, not on a personal basis'.

Bertie, head down, slumped sideways in his seat, nodded.

Above anyone else, Bertie, the most successful politician of his generation, should know the score. But yet again, his demeanour showed that no matter how much a politician knows the end is coming, it still hits them like a train when it does.

The atmosphere in the chamber was flat. Perhaps Bertie's news had come as a shock, but not a surprise.

The Taoiseach made a second statement. It echoed the one he made in Government Buildings. His party applauded him again when he finished. So, too, did the Labour benches. But not all on the Fine Gael side afforded the Taoiseach this courtesy, Enda Kenny included.

Then the Ceann Comhairle acknowledged Ahern's enormous contribution to the nation and the 'countless generations of yet unborn Irish men and women'.

We're still scratching our head over that one. One time, when in one of his put-upon modes, Bertie complained that if the cat had kittens, he'd be blamed for it. We fell to wondering if there was another reason for his hasty exit.

He stayed a long time in the chamber. When a vote was called, party members came over to wish him well. Conor Lenihan seemed particularly distraught.

Meanwhile, Brian Cowen and Willie O'Dea shared a joke, laughing uproariously while Brian Lenihan looked on. Biffo took off his glasses and wiped his eyes.

Finally, Bertie's business in the house was finished for the day. But he sat with Minister for Foreign Affairs Dermot Ahern and the rest of his party as he spoke on the Lisbon Treaty Bill. But Bertie didn't seem to be listening. He was gazing into space, a faraway look in his eyes . . .

How could this have happened?

The Secret to Happiness? Splash Your Cash on Others

Under The Microscope, by William Reville

You should pay close attention to my article today, because it tells you how to increase your happiness. In a nutshell, you can become happier by spending more of your money on others.

Like many great truths (e.g. 'Truth emerges more readily from error than from confusion' – Sir Francis Bacon, 1561-1626), this is simple and counter-intuitive. The matter has been carefully researched by EW Dunn, LB Aknin and MI Norton, and is reported in *Science* (21 March 2008), Vol. 319, No. 5870, pp 1,687-1,688.

We all want to be happy and most of us believe that having lots of money will do the trick. Unfortunately, this belief is in error. The correlation between money and happiness has been well researched over the years, and is well understood at

this stage. If you have scarcely enough money to keep body and soul together, you cannot be happy, and acquiring more money will increase your happiness for sure. But once you have enough money to satisfy basic needs, the correlation between acquiring more money and further increasing happiness is surprisingly weak.

Real incomes have dramatically increased in recent times in the developed world but happiness levels have not increased. Obviously, spending more money on consumer goods doesn't increase happiness.

Research, quoted by Dunn and colleagues, has shown that thinking about money in itself promotes behaviour that is inimical to personal happiness, making one less likely to spend time with others or to help charities or acquaintances, the kinds of behaviour known to be positively correlated with happiness. On the other hand, if you have money, investing more of it in helping others should increase your happiness. This was the hypothesis investigated by Dunn and colleagues.

The researchers looked at a nationally representative US sample of 632 people, and asked them to rate their happiness levels, report their annual income, and estimate how much they spend per month on bills and expenses, on gifts for themselves, gifts for others, and donations to charity.

Dunn reports: 'Regardless of how much income each person made, those who spend money on others reported greater happiness, while those who spent more on themselves did not.'

The study also looked at employees in a company before and after they got a profit-sharing bonus of $3,000 to $8,000. Those employees who spent more of their bonus on gifts for others or on charity reported greater happiness than employees who spent the money on themselves.

In another part of the study, 46 people were each given an envelope in the morning containing either $5 or $20 and were asked to spend the money by 5pm that day. Half the participants were instructed to spend the money on themselves and

Fashion designer Katherine Hamnett in Buswell's Hotel in Dublin during Fashion Evolution week. Photograph: Brenda Fitzsimons.

half were asked to spend the money on a gift for somebody else or donate it to a charity.

The happiness of participants was measured in the morning, before spending the money, and in the evening, after spending the money. Participants who spent the money on others were happier at the end of the day than those who spent the money on themselves, regardless of whether it was $5 or $20.

'These findings suggest that very minor alterations in spending allocations – as little as $5 – may be enough to produce real gains in happiness,' says Dunn.

The authors' results harmonise with recent theoretical work on the architecture of achieving sustainable changes in happiness. We readily adapt to stable circumstances in our lives and these circumstances tend to have limited long-term effects on happiness.

Most of the happiness associated with a big house, a big car, a big boat, and so on, comes in the anticipatory period when you are saving up to buy them. You get a boost of happiness when you buy them, but then you quickly get used to them.

On the other hand, deliberately chosen acts of kindness represent a more reliable route to lasting happiness.

So, the way we spend our money is probably more important to our happiness than our total income. Unfortunately, most people focus on total income and on the pleasure that spending money on themselves will bring. The authors surveyed students' opinions as to whether spending money on themselves or on others would make them happier, and the majority plumped for spending money on themselves.

Dunn's research has produced important knowledge and, given the double benefits to both the giver and the receiver, official policies should encourage pro-social spending. And, you don't have to give away all your money to be happy – just be generous. Remember that the oft-quoted Biblical injunction 'Money is the root of all evil,' is incorrectly quoted. The correct quotation is: 'The love of money is the root of all evil.'

Mick! Over here!

Donald Clarke

The *Irish Times* does not do red carpets. Representatives of this newspaper will not be found elbowing aside the mike-handlers from *FabGossip.com* in pursuit of a quote from that idiot out of *Hollyoaks*. If Harrison Ford wants to get into *The Ticket*, then he will just have to invite us to his cabin cruiser.

Yet, here I am in Leicester Square surrounded by dozens of journalists at the premiere of *Shine A Light*, Martin Scorsese's record of a recent Rolling Stones gig. Look, the opportunity to get within spitting distance of a Stone doesn't come along that often.

It is certainly true that the experience is closer to a wildlife shoot – 'The Leather-skinned Jagger Monkey makes his way cautiously to the watering-hole' – than it is to a formal interview, but these are, perhaps, the best circumstances under which to monitor an endangered species.

Even before I get to the barricades, I have gathered some impressions of the dispassion red-carpet journos bring to their work. The Italian hacks ahead of me in the queue at the hotel reception have made a point of decking themselves out in Stones regalia. This one wears a brooch fashioned in the shape of Mick's mouth. Another has the band's name plastered across his T-shirt.

Where is the cynical ennui I have come to expect from my colleagues? ('You interviewing that jerk Brent Sparklestar?' one of us might say.

'Yeah, he's got no more brains than his cretinous, talentless shrew of a wife,' another might reply.)

The wave of enthusiasm is all the more baffling when you consider how red-carpet journalists are handled at such an event. You are asked to arrive at a particular time to be placed into a reserved 'pen'. Yes, you read that right. The gentleman from *The Irish Times* has been placed into the same sort of apparatus they use to restrain pigs and sheep. You never saw Maeve Binchy in a pen.

Anyway, it can't be denied that 20th Century Fox have put on a good show. Spotlights strafe the low clouds, satellite dishes sit waiting to beam the event throughout the world and a massive red carpet works its way along the eastern stretch of Leicester Square. On the other side of the rug, Stones fanatics – many are decked out in stupid hats; one is odd enough to brandish a Jagger solo album – nervously protect the territory they staked out hours earlier.

On this side of the carpet, a wild hubbub persists. The shoulder-shrugging disdain that characterises formal journalism is of no use down here among the pigs and the sheep. The only way to succeed is to bounce wildly from foot to foot and scream the name of the arriving stars like a five-year-old hopped up on Fanta and Skittles.

The lack of dignity is quite startling. Look at them, bellowing at botoxed nonentities and then pretending to be interested in their inane prattle. You'd never catch me doing that. I would rather . . .

Jesus! It's Anita Pallenberg.

'ANITA! ANITA! OVER HERE!' I shout at Mick and Keith's former squeeze.

By the time the words are out of my mouth, Pallenberg, now saddled with the face of an elderly house-cat, has already been swept into the cinema.

Scorsese's film is mostly taken up with footage of a contemporary Stones gig in Manhattan, but the director does also manage to squeeze in some archive material of the band in their chaotic early years. The contrast between the spiralling chaos of their 1960s tours – ambulance men ferrying damply hysterical girls from the auditorium; policemen scowling at the band as they might at escaped gorillas; drunks lurching across the stage – and the military order that characterises the current operation is remarkable.

Back then, more hysterical media commentators suggested that the Stones and their clones might have killed off showbusiness. A brief glance at the spotlights in Leicester Square confirms how misguided those speculations were.

I would like to ask Mick Jagger about that. Hell, I will ask Mick Jagger about that. But not yet.

'Anybody else got a question for Charles Dance?' the PR commandant plaintively asks our pen. Sheep stare at the clouds, pigs suddenly begin fiddling conspicuously with their telephones and the tall actor is led hopefully towards another set of bouncing maniacs.

Then, suddenly, the band is on the carpet. Keith Richards, taciturn in the 1960s and 1970s,

has, it seems, been smiling and cackling for the past 10 years. Wearing a hat at a jaunty angle, he somehow manages to giggle his way past our enclosure and on towards that Scottish woman from the BBC. Charlie Watts, the perennially likeable and taciturn drummer, has, as always, as little to do with the press as he can manage.

Little Mick Jagger, accompanied by his gigantic girlfriend, L'Wren Scott, is slowly making his way towards our corner of the red carpet. His face is heavily creased and his eyes are slightly rheumy, but, at 64, he still seems effortlessly lively and engaged.

'Talk a little bit about the way the business has changed since you first started out,' I intend to say. 'Do you miss the sense of urgency you enjoyed in the early days?' When he eventually stands before us, it quickly becomes clear that I have as much chance of reading out the Gettysburg Address as asking such a complex question.

Aoidin Sammon, winner of the Best Dressed Lady at the Punchestown festival. Photograph: Morgan Treacy/Inpho.

'What's it like working with Christina Aguilera?' somebody shouts.

'What you doing after the film?' another hack blurts.

And then, leaving me opened mouthed and silent, he skips playfully down the red carpet and vanishes from view. It seems as if I do not have the stamina (or the lungs) to attract the attention of the stars that matter.

But, wait a moment. Is that Tom Stoppard? It is Tom Stoppard. The distinguished playwright, author of *Rosencrantz & Guildenstern Are Dead* and *Travesties*, is making his way entirely unmolested towards the entrance.

'TOM! TOM!' I scream.

Stoppard stops, looks over his shoulder to check that Tom Cruise is not behind him and makes his way towards my tape recorder. While the lady from *FabGossip.com* looks on bewildered, we chat about his last play, *Rock'n'Roll*, and about that piece's treatment of the Syd Barrett myth.

Then, after joking that I am, surely, too young to appreciate the Stones, he swivels on his heel. Well, that'll do nicely. I came to the red carpet and interviewed Sir Tom Stoppard. I'm from *The Irish Times*, you know.

SATURDAY, 12 APRIL 2008

Sunderland and Keane Growing into their Skin

A Year on the Wear, by Michael Walker

Someone said 'boll★★★★' to Roy Keane yesterday morning and even though the expletive came from a local reporter in the course of Sunderland's regular pre-match press conference, Keane smiled. It was that sort of day. Those three consecutive victories have rinsed away a lot of tension that would have been present otherwise. Keane may have no desire to get to know anyone in the North-East press pack but he

is rarely worked up in front of the Wearside regulars. When he disappears down the corridor, it could be a different story, of course.

The boll★★★★ came towards the end of another lengthy Q&A. Sunderland have a new kit out and Keane was involved, allegedly, in its design. So it was said by the club, though he laughed off any serious input. 'They showed it to me and I said: "Fine". That would be my contribution.' Yet the kit mattered, Keane said. 'You don't see teams with bad kits win the European Cup, do you? Barcelona, United, beautiful kits. I think it's important to have a nice kit, I really do. I think we need a beautiful kit. I wasn't too happy with it last year, or the training kit. It's part of the package, the pictures, the kit. When was the last time you saw a good team in a bad kit?' The answer came back: 'Man United. Grey.'

That was their fourth-choice kit, not their main kit,' Keane countered. 'They still sold it.' A knowing smile. 'Ask David Gill about that.'

Now, given that Keane had gone down the David Gill route with Tom Humphries in these pages last Saturday, there was little appetite for more Manchester United debate. Anyway, some people are obsessed by jerseys and the like and so the show moved on.

'What was your first replica kit?' Keane was asked. 'Tottenham?' (He was a Spurs fan as a boy.)

'No, you couldn't get that in Ireland because they were made by Le Coq Sportif and you had to send away for that. I wasn't going to do that. I can't remember, not sure.' This felt a bit like a politician's answer, as if Keane knows there is some photo of him locked away in a Cork drawer showing him in Liverpool gear.

Hence: 'Boll★★★★.'

Another smile. 'No, where I lived it was mainly Liverpool, United, Arsenal, Leeds. My younger brother had a United kit. I wasn't a great one for kits. I had vests, for boxing. Jesus, get over it.' And up he got.

It would be stretching interpretation to read too much into the exchange, but what it felt

Israeli ambassador Zion Evrony (left) looks on as the oldest member of Dublin's Jewish community, 101-year-old Louis Wine (seated, centre) prepares to help finish the writing of the new Torah *for the Dublin Hebrew Congregation's synagogue in Terenure, Dublin. The Torah is the first book of the Hebrew Bible. Photograph: Bryan O'Brien.*

indicative of is relaxation at Sunderland. Not complacency; mathematically they remain uncertain, but you could foresee them beating Manchester City today at the Stadium of Light – or at least not losing – and there is then the Tyne-Wear derby at St James' Park tomorrow week. That penultimate game of the season at Bolton does not carry the sense of anxiety it did a month ago.

There is a feeling that even within the Bolton and Fulham dressingrooms there is draining belief they deserve to still belong to the Premier League. At Sunderland it is the opposite: belief is rising. There is always the risk of premature assessment but yesterday Sunderland and Keane seemed to be growing into their skin and into the status that comes with being a Premier League club, Premier League players and a Premier League manager.

There have been times this season, some of them quite recent, when that statement might not have sounded credible.

After losing 7-1 at Everton in November, for example, Sunderland looked Championship-bound.

But Keane was adamant that at no time this season did he lose faith in his players or think that they had lost faith in him.

Even after Everton? Some of his certainty gave way. 'Well, after Everton I had to lift them a small bit. The dressingroom that day was a horrible place to be. I wouldn't expect it any other way. Everton was a big one but in defence of the players that was my fault that day, not theirs. I mean that, my fault, 100 per cent. That was easier to cope with than other games, maybe, because I got that call wrong.

Lucy Carragher, aged 17, from Killaloe in Co. Clare, who won the 54th Texaco Children's Art Competition for **Self Portrait.** *Photograph: Bryan O'Brien.*

'The dressingroom has been the least of my worries this season. I have had other ones but I have never thought: 'We have lost the dressing-room". I have never gone on the training pitch and thought "I need to lift these lads." Trust me, you have setbacks and that's where you need a strong dressingroom. If we didn't have a good dressing-room we'd have been down with Derby, adrift.'

Dwight Yorke was mentioned by Keane as being one of the influential voices in there and his experience has been valuable. For Craig Gordon, Grant Leadbitter and Kenwyne Jones, this has been a first taste of England's top-flight. They should be better for it.

Others such as Nyron Nosworthy and Dean Whitehead had been in the division previously but it was during Sunderland's wretched 15-point season. Individually and collectively that was unpleasant and potentially damaging.

It is easy to forget that was just two years ago. That it feels like ancient history is a mark of Sunderland's progress this season. Few think now they will implode. And they have a shiny new kit, and a manager who can tolerate being informed that he is talking boll★★★★.

MONDAY, 14 APRIL 2008

Throwing Lifeline to Waterford Wedgwood Makes no Sense

Business Opinion, by John McManus

Waterford Wedgwood's attempt to wrap itself in the green flag would be simply laughable, if there was not a prospect, albeit remote, that

A bottle-nosed dolphin following the **Renard** *Ferry to Valentia Island in Co. Kerry. Photograph: Valerie O'Sullivan.*

they may yet succeed in persuading the Government to guarantee some €39 million of new borrowings.

Almost as alarming as hearing the Waterford Crystal CEO John Foley likening the company's place in the Irish business firmament to Bear Stearn's significance to Wall Street, is hearing that some figures in Government are pointing out that if Waterford Crystal was an iconic French brand, then the French Government would not hesitate to prop it up and deal with the legal challenges from Brussels when the time came.

There are so many reasons why this is wrong that it's hard to know where to start.

But one jumping off point is that while Waterford Crystal may well be an iconic Irish brand, the company that is actually looking for a dig out has more operations outside of Ireland than in it.

As Waterford Wedgwood never cease telling us, it is one of the 'world's leading luxury lifestyle groups' with four mail brands – Waterford Crystal, Wedgwood, Rosenthal and Royal Doulton.

According to the most recent set of accounts – for the six months to the end of September 2007, the Waterford Crystal division had sales of €84.9 million; just one quarter of the group's total turnover of €317 million.

The bulk of the balance was made up by the group's ceramics division which incorporates Wedgwood and Royal Doulton, two iconic English brands. This division had a turnover of €214.6 million in the first half of the year.

While all parts of the group are struggling the interim figures would seem to indicate that if anything Waterford Crystal is the best performing part of the business and profitable to boot.

It made an operating profit of €7.1 million against a loss for the group of €29.7 million in the period. Earnings before interest tax depreciation and amortisation (EBITDA) at Waterford Crystal were €12 million, compared to negative EBITDA of €15.3 million.

It is not clear how the Waterford Crystal figures split between the Irish-based manufacturing operation and the outsourced manufacturing operations. And it is obvious the situation has deteriorated since September as the US economy slows and the dollar weakens.

That said it seems pretty clear that the real problem with Waterford Wedgwood lies with the ceramics business and not the crystal business. If the Waterford Wedgwood accounts reveal anything at all it is that the non-Irish brands are dragging down the iconic Irish brand.

It is also clear that the situation at the group has deteriorated to such an extent that the €167 million raised since last April to restructure the group has not been sufficient. And nor will the additional €33 million that Sir Anthony O'Reilly and his brother-in-law Peter Goulandris have committed to investing.

The group needs more cash and the Government is now being asked to guarantee an additional €39 million of debt, in effect making it the lender of last resort for the group.

It's worth noting that all Waterford Wedgwood is saying at the moment is that the State guarantee would 'enable the company to complete the orderly restructuring of Waterford Crystal'.

Even if the Government was to ring some cast-iron commitments from Waterford Wedgwood that every penny it guarantees will be spent on Waterford Crystal, that still has the effect of freeing up some of the group's scarce resources for the restructuring of its other non-performing operations that are the real source of the problems at Waterford Wedgwood.

Rescuing quoted companies, particularly quoted companies that carry out more than three quarters of their operations outside of the State, makes no sense for the Government. Or even to the French government for that matter.

Subsidised Bread Staving off Starvation and Uprisings

Mary Fitzgerald, in Alexandria

For months now, the queue outside Ahmed Shandawili's tiny bakery in Alexandria has formed long before dawn each morning. Men, women and even bleary-eyed children join the often disorderly line to make sure they can buy enough bread before it runs out.

More than 1,200 puffy discs of rough baladi (country) bread tumble out of Ahmed's dusty oven every day but he says he could easily sell five times that amount.

'There is huge pressure these days because other foods have become so expensive,' he explains. 'People are eating more subsidised bread because they can afford little else.'

The global rise in food prices, which has prompted warnings from the World Bank, the IMF and the UN's World Food Programme, is being keenly felt in Egypt, the Arab world's most populous nation and a country where an estimated 40 per cent of people live in poverty.

With almost 20 per cent of Egyptians living on less than $1 a day, even a slight wobble in food prices brings the potential for crisis. But what Egypt has experienced in the last 12 months, say analysts, is not so much a wobble as a devastating lurch. Official figures show the price of food in Egypt has increased by an average of 23.5 per cent in the past year.

The price of both cereals and bread has soared by 48.1 per cent; cooking oil by 45.2 per cent; dairy goods 20 per cent and vegetables 15 per cent.

The price hikes mean rice and pasta – staple foods among the country's poor, particularly when combined with lentils in the popular dish known as 'koshari' – are now out of reach for millions of Egyptians. The government, however, has managed to keep the price of subsidised bread stable at less than one cent per loaf.

It needs to. For decades Egypt, one of the world's largest importers of wheat, has provided subsidised flour to bakers to produce cheap bread for the poor as a costly but essential element of its economic policy.

State-subsidised bread enables millions of Egyptians to survive on meagre salaries and – so official thinking goes – helps stave off political discontent. About 85 percent of Egypt's bread, some 230 million loaves a day, is subsidised.

As a result bread is central to the Egyptian diet – reflected in the fact that Egyptians refer to it using the colloquial word 'aish', which means life, rather than the standard Arabic 'khobz'.

Outside Ahmed's bakery in Ghobrian, a working-class district of Alexandria, Egypt's second largest city, people are getting irritable in the morning heat. Some have been queuing for hours to buy the subsidised bread, which costs less than 20 cent for 20 round, flat loaves, the maximum allowed at one time.

Many will join the queue several times to make sure they have enough for their large, extended families that day. In the jostling for position tempers begin to fray.

'We are close to killing each other for bread,' one woman moans. She is half-joking but others in

Queuing for bread in Alexandria, Egypt. Photograph: Mary Fitzgerald.

the queue talk of what has happened in other parts of Egypt. Since early February at least 11 people have died in bread lines, either from exhaustion, heart attacks or accidents.

Two were stabbed when fights broke out between customers vying for places in the queue. In Alexandria, lurid rumours swirl of the man whose hand was chopped off when he tried to skip a queue, or the angry customer who set fire to a bakery because the owner refused to sell him more loaves.

'All we have left to survive is bread,' says one woman, the mother of five children. Another, Hanan, is six months pregnant and complains of the daily wait. 'Every day I'm standing here for hours just to get enough to feed my family,' she says. 'What did we do to deserve this?' A man behind her interrupts: 'The government is not doing enough. These difficulties will force people to take desperate measures.'

Everyone here remembers the bread riots of 1977, when a government decision to lift subsidies on bread triggered the only mass popular uprising in Egypt in the last 50 years. More than 70 people died before then president Anwar Sadat restored the old policy.

Earlier this month thousands of workers and youths clashed with police in the industrial town of Mahalla el-Kubra in the Nile Delta. Four people, one aged 15, were killed and scores more injured and detained. Many fear wider unrest.

'What we are witnessing now is a very unstable situation,' says Diaa Rashwan, an analyst at Cairo's Al-Ahram Centre for Political and Strategic Studies.

'There is very real suffering and we cannot exclude the possibility of serious violent confrontation. Everyone in government here has such fears.'

In an effort to alleviate the crisis, President Hosni Mubarak recently ordered the army to bake and distribute bread, and drew on currency reserves to import more wheat. An extra $850 million (€540 million) has been spent on wheat

this year and the total bill is expected to be well over $2.5 billion (€1.6 million). Mubarak also ordered a crackdown on unscrupulous bakers who sell their subsidised flour on the black market.

Ahmed El-Naggar, an economist who has advised the government on the crisis, says, 'It's a huge problem. The government should remove all subsidies on flour and put them on bread instead so only the customer benefits,' he said. 'It should also increase the overall subsidy.'

Only months ago some Egyptian officials were proposing a change in the country's food subsidy policy to help reduce a budget deficit estimated at more than 5.3 per cent of gross domestic product in 2006-2007.

No one dares mention such a plan now. Gamal Mubarak, son and heir-apparent of President Mubarak, said recently that the government would not hesitate 'for a minute' to increase subsidies on basic products if necessary.

Meanwhile, back at Ahmed's bakery the grumbling continues. 'Even in Iraq they have enough bread,' says one man bitterly. 'Everything is wrong with our country.'

MONDAY, 26 APRIL 2008

It's Eight in the Morning and There's Nowhere Left To Go

Fiona McCann

'They're infringing on people's rights! The first pub they'd want to close is the bar in Leinster House,' says Noel 'Gura' Murphy as he receives the news that early houses will no longer be able to operate once the new legislation announced this week comes into force. It's 7.30am in the Windjammer pub on Dublin's Townsend Street, on the fringes of the city's docklands, and the atmosphere is calm and convivial as regulars wander in and, with a raised brow or a nod and a wink, order 'the usual' from barman Cathal McFeely.

Early houses – pubs allowed a general exemption licensing them for early morning trade – have been around for more than 80 years. They were given official sanction in a 1927 act that stipulated such establishments were needed to cater for those attending early markets and fairs, or for those whose 'trade or calling' left them in need of refreshment at otherwise unsociable hours.

Murphy, a 70-year-old former docker, has been a regular at the Windjammer for more than four decades, and recalls the days when places such as these flourished as people working on the docks retired to early houses between the arrivals of ships. 'There were no restrictions back then,' he remembers.

But times are changing, and the news that the last few early houses in Ireland will have to cease early trading once the new Intoxicating Liquor/Public Order bill (2008) is enacted casts a sombre pall over the generally upbeat proceedings at the Windjammer. There's a steady trickle of clientele, entirely male and all in their latter years, who take their seats at the bar and take in the news. From the outside, it's hard to even tell the pub is open for business, as the shutters are kept down to discourage passing trade. As I attempt to slip in unnoticed, one of the regulars, on his way out for a cigarette, asks me whether I'm in the right place, such is his sense of ownership and investment in the premises where he spends his early mornings.

The Windjammer is careful about who comes in and out, but, once inside, the mood is cordial, infinitely more so than that in your average late-night boozer. There's a noticeable absence of menace or aggression.

Everybody is on a first-name basis with McFeely; despite his 20 years behind the bar, as a Donegal man, he's still teased for being a blow-in by the punters.

He feels the end of the early licence will have a massive impact on the local community. 'I think it'll be a big loss because it is such a social thing. If people finish shifts, if they find they've nowhere to go in the early morning, we're here,' he says. 'It's a tradition that's always been there and I'd like to see it remain. It's about much more than just getting a drink.'

For those who frequent the Windjammer, mornings at this small, quiet watering hole have become part of the social fabric of the area. It is a place to meet and mix with their peers, and a routine that in some way has become bound with their sense of our national identity.

'It's part of the culture,' says Dubliner Tommy Bisset, who has stopped in for a swift tipple on his way to work. 'I would be extremely disappointed to see it go.'

'It's about the characters that come here in the morning, the *craic*,' Murphy agrees.

John Kirwan, who claims to have been frequenting the Windjammer since 1956, is eager to step in. 'The simple reason [I come here] is that you get better *craic* now, at this hour, than you would in the evening. There's no tension now,' he says.

It's hard to argue as you settle into the kind of easy, low-key conversation that's in short supply in many of Dublin's night-time drinking emporiums. With locals so welcoming they're pressing pints into my hands, and both the barmen on the far side of 50, it's hard to believe that this local boozer is contributing to the kind of social disturbances and binge-drinking tendencies that prompted the new bill.

'There's no element of public disorder about these at all,' admits Dr Gordon Holmes, who chaired the Alcohol Advisory Group whose report fed into the new bill, 'but they are very sordid.' Holmes argues that the original reasoning behind early licences is no longer relevant. 'Historically, it filled the need of people who went to early morning fairs, people who were fishing in open boats at sea ports and came in at seven o'clock in the morning,' he says. 'There is much less early morning activity now.'

Tommy Bissett (left) and fellow drinker Des Phelan in the Windjammer, an early morning pub on Townsend Street in Dublin. Photograph: Matt Kavanagh.

Des Phelan, one of the Windjammer regulars who works nights, argues otherwise. 'The reason why the early houses opened around this area was for the boats coming in,' he acknowledges. 'The boats are gone but there are more people working night shifts now than there were in the sixties and seventies.'

This is what a number of proprietors of early houses argued three years ago when their licences were called into question by the Garda. Since 1962, only early houses with existing licences have been allowed to maintain them, and these were required once a year to apply for a renewal. An objection from a Garda superintendent at the annual hearing in the District Court argued against their reissue. The publicans were represented by Constance Cassidy, a senior counsel and expert on licensing law.

'I argued that it would be unjust, unfair and inequitable to take away a substantial part of their livelihood on a whim when the legislature specifically provided for the granting of a general exemption order in certain circumstances and they complied with the circumstances,' she recalls.

Rory Daly, who owns the Windjammer and was among those involved in that case, says he personally collected signatures from nurses, taxi drivers and all those whose professions require them to work overnight, to show that many of their clientele were those who worked unsociable hours. 'There are far more shift workers nowadays,' he says, a point which he says was conceded by the court.

Daly is angered that, as a proprietor of one of the few early houses that remain in operation, he was neither approached on the matter nor

A hapless motorist abandons his car after getting stranded in flood water on the N1 near Lusk in north Co. Dublin.
Photograph: Crispin Rodwell.

informed that his early licence would be removed. 'I was totally shocked,' he says, of hearing about it from the newspapers. 'It's typical. They're trying to put the boot in on the sly.' He says arguing in court to keep the licence three years ago was a time-consuming and costly process, and he doesn't understand why that decision no longer applies.

'It cost us a small fortune to go to court that time, and what's changed ?' asks Daly. 'What's happened in three years, is what I'd like to know.'

Operating a strict door policy, Daly feels he has done his best to cooperate with both the local Garda and the Government in cracking down on young drinkers. 'We've a great relationship with the Garda,' he says. 'They asked me about four or five years ago to stop opening for the Trinity Balls, so I did. I'm losing business to facilitate the Garda in that respect and I was taken aback that the

Government would shaft me when I'm doing all I can to accommodate them.'

He's not the only one who has been blindsided by the new measure. According to Donal O'Keeffe, Chief Executive of the Licensed Vintners Association which represents Dublin publicans, there was no consultation with the body before the draft bill was published. 'There had been no discussion about it whatsoever,' he says. 'We had no consultations with the Advisory Group or the Department of Justice. We're very disappointed to see that provision [regarding early houses] in the bill.'

O'Keeffe argues that early houses don't contribute to the public order problems the Department was proposing to tackle, and he defends their continued existence. 'We strongly believe that early houses are generally well run.

THE IRISH TIMES BOOK OF THE YEAR

They're traditional businesses. They've been in it a long time,' he says. 'They're a small element of the total pub trade, but we would feel they're part of that trade, part of the fabric of Dublin, and we'd be hoping to see them continue.'

While he accepts that the original reason they were created may be redundant, O'Keeffe feels there are reasons to keep early houses going. 'There is still a very significant night-time economy in Dublin, and, whether people are security guards, or in the hospitality business or working a 24-hour business, if they want a drink or two or coffee after work, the early house is for them.'

Given that the new legislation has yet to be enacted by the Oireachtas, O'Keeffe is hoping there will be a chance to examine its contents before it comes into force in the summer. 'We have to consider the bill in its entirety, but we'll obviously be considering it next week and looking to engage,' he says.

Dr Gordon Holmes is aware that many will be upset about the new restrictions, but defends the decision to call time on early houses. 'I know some people are going to be discommoded by it, and I deeply regret that,' he says. 'On balancing up everything, the view of our group was that they no longer fulfilled the purpose for which they were brought into being, and that on balance there is now more harm than good coming from them.'

For regulars such as Phelan, who is on his way home after work, the real harm is being done elsewhere.

'[Minister for Justice Brian Lenihan] is tackling the wrong end of the industry,' he says as he orders me a drink. 'Nine people out of 10 will have a pint after work.' He shrugs, wondering why he should be the exception. 'You're not coming to get drunk here, you're coming in to relax,' he explains. Murphy agrees. 'The revels at night are one thing, but this man', he nods at McFeely, 'closes the gate. He only lets the working class in.'

There are no binge-drinking youths or drugged-out partygoers on this premises, and you get the feeling that any attempt to order a Bacardi Breezer would send the drinkers dotted around the bar into gales of laughter. 'To be quite honest with you, they should leave the early pubs alone!' says Murphy, with proprietorial pride in his voice. 'It's only the mature people who drink here.'

In June, the Government said it would not now force the early morning pubs to close.

SATURDAY, 26 APRIL 2008

Tibet Protests Fuel Chinese Resentment

World View, by Paul Gillespie

When we were the Sick Man of Asia, we were called the Yellow Peril. When we are billed to be the next superpower, we are called the threat.

When we closed our doors, you smuggled drugs to our open markets.

When we embrace free trade, you blame us for taking away your jobs.

When we were falling apart, you marched in your troops and took what you wanted.

When we tried to put the broken pieces back together again, Free Tibet you screamed, It was an invasion!

So begins a polemical poem posted on several websites to explain why the Chinese bitterly resent the surge of political and media criticism directed against them from the West over Tibet. The country's 200 million internet users have staged a spectacular counter-surge, based on pride in its achievements to be showcased at the Olympic Games 100 days from now.

The poem goes on, in a necessary plea for mutual comprehension: Why do you hate us so much, we asked. No, you answered, we don't hate you.

We don't hate you either, But do you understand us?

Frances Byrne (left) and Kathleen Buckley, of Meath Street Community Service in Dublin, look on as Oleg Ponomarev plays at the **Bealtaine 2008** *launch in the Abbey Theatre.* **Bealtaine** *is the national arts festival celebrating activity in older age. Photograph: Eamonn Farrell/Photocall.*

As seen in counter-demonstrations over Tibet in China itself and abroad in Sydney, London, Dublin and elsewhere, the counter-surge variously combines politically directed and spontaneous elements. Boycotts of the French supermarket chain Carrefour's 119 outlets in China were another popular expression.

Chinese nationalism is an important legitimising glue for its one-party state since the market-based modernisation began in the 1980s. One commentator put it like this: 'Since the Chinese Communist Party is no longer communist, it must become even more Chinese.' But embracing nationalism is a double-edged sword precisely because it is not only a top-down phenomenon but a bottom-up one too. What can be given can be taken away.

The veteran correspondent Philip Bowring writes from Hong Kong in the *International Herald Tribune*: 'On the horizon is the possibility that these [Tibet protests and Olympic threats] will combine with high inflation, stagnating exports and trade tensions with the United States to create a perfect nationalistic storm. The Chinese leadership faces a difficult balancing act.' Endemic social problems, falling stock markets or rising food prices could equally be blamed on party failings in such a storm.

The dilemma can be seen in these comments by the state-run English-language newspaper *China Daily*: 'Patriots are supposed to adopt a tolerant attitude toward others and be broad enough to see what is good and what is bad in them. Over-the-top nationalism is not constructive, but can do harm to the country.' Protest organisers and websites are being curtailed.

There is a worry that protests could backfire during the Olympics, deeply affecting the country's international reputation. But backing off from the official and popular anger is difficult for fear of being seen as weak under foreign pressure. Such 'face nationalism', meaning 'the figurative self shown to others', is an important ingredient of Chinese political culture, according to Peter Hays Gries, author of a study of the subject. Yesterday's news that a Chinese representative will meet the Dalai Lama shows political skills are asserting themselves.

Kenneth Lieberthal of the University of Michigan says the western view of Tibet is shaped by a notion of Shangri-La, while the Chinese assume Tibetans are backward, feudal, superstitious, and badly in need of modernisation. 'So I think they regard it as bizarre that the advanced industrial countries would humiliate them by boycotting the opening ceremonies of the Olympics over the Tibet issue.'

Bowring notes how official Chinese media have portrayed the violence in Tibet as attacks on Han Chinese. 'This predictably arouses the hackles of the Han, who comprise 90 per cent of China's population . . . They see no reason why Tibetans should be unhappy with Han migration and dominance of trade.'

Lieberthal says the Chinese see these anti-Olympic protests as an indication that, regardless of how much China strives to become a constructive player in the world, 'many in the West will never accept that, [and] will seek to humiliate them'.

The protest poem goes on, illustrating this very well:

When we tried communism, you hated us for being communist.

When we embrace capitalism, you ridicule us for being capitalist.

Sharon Sweeney with her son Leon, aged 4, and daughter Anna, aged 10 months, enjoying the Colourscape Maze at the Our House Show at Punchestown. Photograph: Brenda Fitzsimons.

When we have a billion people, you said we were destroying the planet.

When we tried limiting our numbers, you said we abused human rights.

When we were poor, you thought we were dogs.

When we loan you cash, you blame us for your national debt.

When we build our industries, you call us polluters.

When we sell you goods, you blame us for global warming.

When we buy oil, you call it exploitation and genocide.

When you go to war for oil, you call it liberation.

When we were lost in chaos and rampage, you demanded rules of law.

When we uphold law and order against violence, you call it violating human rights.

When we were silent, you said you wanted us to have free speech.

When we are silent no more, you say we are brainwashed-xenophobics.

But it concludes more hopefully:

Enough is enough. Enough hypocrisy for this one world. We want one world, one dream, and peace on Earth.

This big blue Earth is big enough for all of us.

A more critical empathy is needed both ways.

THURSDAY, I MAY 2008

Rush to Fill Seats for Address that Went Beyond Ritual of Thanks

Denis Staunton, in Washington

As the Taoiseach was about to arrive at the House of Representatives yesterday morning, ushers were patrolling the aisles, frantically directing congressional pages and visitors to empty seats in the chamber.

It was a busy working day on Capitol Hill and most members stayed away from the Taoiseach's speech. But what his congressional audience lacked in numbers, it made up for in political firepower.

The most powerful figures in both parties came to hear Mr Ahern, with House speaker Nancy Pelosi and father of the Senate Robert Byrd at the podium and Senate majority leader Harry Reid, Senate minority leader Mitch McConnell, House majority leader Steny Hoyer and House minority leader John Boehner among the Taoiseach's escorts.

Other escorts from the Senate included judicial affairs chairman Patrick Leahy, Edward Kennedy, John Kerry, Bob Casey, Chris Dodd and Susan Collins. Escorts from the House included Friends of Ireland chairman Richard Neal, Jim Walsh, Peter King, James Clyburn and Rahm Emmanuel.

Mr Ahern made a brisk entrance, shaking a few hands and exchanging smiles with congressmen and senators before Ms Pelosi rapped her gavel twice to call the house to order.

'I have the high privilege and distinct honour of presenting to you Bertie Ahern, the Taoiseach and prime minister of Ireland,' she declared.

As he approached the podium to a standing ovation, the Taoiseach looked to his left, where Irish political colleagues and officials were seated in the chamber. Above them, in the gallery, sat his daughter Cecilia and dozens of well-wishers from Dublin.

Yesterday's address was an important personal moment for Mr Ahern but he acknowledged in the first words of his speech that it was a tribute to his country too and to the unique relationship between Ireland and the United States.

The Taoiseach briefly rehearsed the history of Irish migration to America before plunging directly into one of the most fraught policy areas in the US – immigration reform.

Campaigners for undocumented Irish immigrants in the US complained last month that the

Bertie Ahern gestures to US Congressmen and Senators during his address to the Joint Houses of Congress in the House of Representatives in Washington, watched by speaker of the House Nancy Pelosi and president pro tempore *of the Senate Robert Byrd. Photograph: David Sleator.*

Taoiseach had abandoned their cause, demanding to know why he had not asked directly for a deal that could regularise their status.

He not only asked for such a deal yesterday but told his American audience that Ireland's own recent experience of immigration meant that we understood the challenges it presents.

As the EU's ambassador to the US, former taoiseach John Bruton, leaned forward in his seat, Mr Ahern spoke of his belief in the European Union as a force for development, stability and peace in the world and called for a Yes vote in the forthcoming referendum on the Lisbon Treaty.

Few US politicians take an interest in the EU and many are suspicious of multilateralism but the Taoiseach told them that Ireland sees the world differently, calling for 'a true spirit of global citizenship' that complements national pride.

'Ireland believes in multilateral institutions. We believe in the United Nations. We believe in the European Union. And we believe in multilateral action.'

Mr Ahern is viewed in the US primarily as one of the architects of the Belfast Agreement and he received his first standing ovation yesterday when he declared that 'Ireland is at peace'. He went beyond what has become a ritual of thanks to the Americans who helped the peace process, however, urging the US not to retreat into isolationism.

'Do not underestimate the good you have done. Do not forget the legacy you have forged,' he said. 'And if ever you doubt America's place in the world, or hesitate about your power to influence events for the better, look to Ireland.'

Everyone listening to Mr Ahern yesterday knew he was about to leave office and they knew why he was leaving. Many of the distinguished figures before him had faced their own political upheavals and scandals and they listened closely as the Taoiseach spoke about the role of politicians in seeking to improve their societies.

'These are the very essence of politics.

'That is why, for all our faults as human beings, we seek the honour of representing the people,' he said.

Then Mr Ahern anticipated his final hours as Taoiseach, when he would stand 'at the simple graves of the patriot dead' to commemorate those who proclaimed the Republic in 1916.

His final words in the Capitol echoed those of John F. Kennedy on his inauguration as President in 1961. 'In history, as in politics and life, there are no ends, only new beginnings,' Mr Ahern said. 'Let us begin.'

As the audience rose in a lengthy standing ovation, Mr Ahern stood at the podium, neither smiling nor frowning but looking out before him. He turned, shook hands with Ms Pelosi and Senator Byrd, walked smartly into the body of the chamber, shaking hands but exchanging few words.

He stopped to embrace Mr Kennedy, gave a few more brisk handshakes, signed a copy of his speech for a well-wisher, turned back for a moment as he reached the door and was gone.

'Ireland is at peace,' said the Taoiseach. Photograph: Alex Wong/Getty Images.

New manager of the Irish soccer team Giovanni Trapattoni at his first press conference. 'A beautiful game is for 24 hours in the newspapers; a result stands forever,' he said. Photograph: Bryan O'Brien.

FRIDAY, 2 MAY 2008

FAI Introduces Trapattoni! – Our Latest Daredevil on Wall of Death

Tom Humphries

Ta da! And heeeeeere's Giovanni! Into the book-lined RDS Concert Hall, on a bright sunny day, the Football Association of Ireland lowered an oppressively large banner bearing their emblem and, with much ado, introduced Giovanni Trapattoni, the latest daredevil to try his luck on the wall of death, otherwise known as managing the Irish soccer team.

Giovanni came equipped with a translator but she was mute and redundant for most of the afternoon. This was an *uno duce, una voce* type of production and if very little of what was said was audible above the constant whirring of camera shutters, enough was heard to bear out Trapattoni's endearing opening admission that his English was weak.

His English was weak but his charisma was strong and though we only caught one word in three, he made more sense than his predecessor Steve Staunton, and we nodded back enthusiastically and let ourselves be seduced by Don Giovanni.

Memories kept trespassing on previous coronation-style press conferences, which would eventually be counterpointed against the grisly and lonesome end the central participants came to, but this was slightly different.

Trapattoni got through the afternoon without uttering a cringe-worthy phrase like his predecessor's

King Kong-like 'I am the Gaffer' declaration and even his frank declaration of his own footballing pragmatism had a charm to it. 'A beautiful game is for 24 hours in the newspapers; a result stands forever.'

Trapattoni's charm and the steely strength of his character came across through all the proceedings. At 69, the new Irish manager radiates a confidence and energy that few in the room could have matched. And perhaps what impressed the most was his engagement with the job in hand and his polite indifference to whether or not people liked him. Having watched '20 to 30' DVDs of Irish games – he is being well paid but, at 69, isn't life too short for that? – he could rhyme off the names of as many Irish players as anyone present but he never resorted to buttering us up by pretending to like Guinness and the company of leprechauns.

The Irish players, a somewhat sheltered community who in recent years have been finding the rigours of international football to be an unwelcome intrusion into their busy lives, will face a far sterner examination of their commitment than they have so far encountered. Trapattoni merrily announced that Ireland is strong in every position and that he would be taking things from here. He gets his first chance to put pouty faces to lustrous names when he takes charge of a training camp in Portugal later this month.

SATURDAY, 3 MAY 2008

Dark Truths Below the Surface

Derek Scally in Amstetten, Austria

On a chilly Monday morning, a man pulls a huge vacuum cleaner down the spotless Wienerstrasse in Amstetten, hunting for dirt that isn't there. A sticker on the side of the machine boasts: 'Amstetten: Reine Stadt, Feine Stadt' ('a clean town, a fine town'). And indeed it is. The Wienerstrasse's two-storey 19th-century buildings, with their pristine façades in pink, white or yellow, are the epitome of bourgeois respectability.

Across town, however, that respectability is in tatters. On the Ybsstrasse, a satellite transmission van, the tenth, pulls up outside a grey three-storey apartment block, number 40. Nobody is home: the owners, Josef and Rosemarie Fritzl, have quite a few letters in their postbox, but they won't be picking them up.

In just a few hours, their street has become a media Tower of Babel. As a news helicopter swoops overhead, television journalists gabble to cameras in a dozen languages; the only familiar words are 'Elisabeth Fritzl' and 'Natascha Kampusch'.

Kampusch was abducted aged 10 and spent eight years in a cellar before fleeing in August 2006. Elisabeth was 18 in 1984 when she disappeared – for three times as long.

Hours after Elisabeth reappeared a week ago, international television reporters arrived on the scene. With neither the time nor the German to speak to the locals or officials, many quickly delivered a damning verdict: this could only happen in Austria.

It's a leap that defies logic: Austria does not have a monopoly on kidnap, rape or incest. 'I don't even want to know how many people are hidden in cellars around the world, waiting to be found,' says Franz Prucher, a local official.

As the week wears on, though, a very Austrian subplot to this tragedy begins to emerge. This secondary tragedy began hours after Elisabeth Fritzl disappeared, when her tearful father Josef filed a missing persons report. It was the confident opening gambit in a high-stakes poker game that lasted a staggering 8,641 days. Like a seasoned poker pro, the moustachioed engineer with piercing blue eyes distracted local police with a bluff based on the Austrian love of the respectable façade.

'The perpetrator remained undiscovered for so long because he succeeded in presenting the façade

Police photograph of Josef Fritzl.

of normality so esteemed and respected by our society,' says Ernst Trost, columnist with Austria's bestselling *Kronen Zeitung* newspaper.

Josef Fritzl never stopped tending the façade he had worked hard to create, rising from humble beginnings to become first an electrician, then an engineer. A former employer remembers him as a 'near-genius', able to create complex machines, and was sorry when he left to become self-employed in 1969. With his wife, Rosemarie, he bought a lakeside campsite and guest house – and torched it a decade later in the hope of collecting the insurance money. Instead, he picked up an arson conviction, allegedly his second conviction after a rape charge in 1967.

Despite his brushes with the law, Fritzl's self-belief never wavered and he ruled his home like a despot, keeping his wife and children – five sons and two daughters – in a state of fear. 'Elisabeth got rid of us whenever she heard her father was coming back,' recalls a school friend. 'She panicked at the idea of being late home.'

In the late 1970s, Fritzl began investing in property, apparently with loans from bank managers impressed with his expensive suits and handmade shoes. He had plans for his own property, too, applying in 1978 for planning permission to add a cellar and in 1983 for a permit to add facilities to make it habitable: electricity lines, water and sewage pipes.

Today, local officials assume the cellar was intended to serve as a nuclear bunker, unusual but not unheard of at the time in Austria, in the shadow of the Iron Curtain. 'The regulations meant there was no need to inspect the finished cellar,' said Hermann Gruber, spokesman for the municipality.

Sometime around 1984, Fritzl's intellect, engineering skill and what police call his 'high sexual potency' settled on his pretty brunette daughter, Elisabeth.

When her parents found her bed empty on the morning of 29 August 1984, they alerted the police. The police remembered Elisabeth: she had run away twice before. Aged 16, she moved out of home to work and live in a motorway truck-stop but never managed to break free from her father. For nearly a quarter of a century, though, only he knew that. Fritzl told police that his daughter was 'sadly a little unstable' and had probably ended up in the Vienna drug scene or in a cult.

A month later, he 'found' a letter from Elisabeth in the postbox, revealing that she had indeed joined a cult: 'Please don't look for me. I'm well where I am now. I want to begin a new life.' The letter was in Elisabeth's hand, the postmark 'Upper Austria'. The cult story spread and neighbours shook their heads at the no-good Fritzl girl. Josef became distant. He spent hours driving around or in his cellar workshop.

The next contact from Elisabeth came in 1993, when Fritzl 'found' a baby on the doorstep and a note from his daughter: she had two children already and was unable to care for a third.

Two more doorstep babies appeared in 1994 and 1997 and the three children – Lisa, Monika and Alexander – grew up apparently happy and popular at school, as neighbours looked on in admiration and pity. 'She saved her pennies to buy them all musical instruments,' remarked one of Rosemarie.

Then, exactly two weeks ago, Josef 'found' one final body on his doorstep: a pale, unconscious young woman, identified in a letter from Elisabeth

as her eldest, Kerstin (19). She was rushed to hospital where doctors, finding neither cause for the illness nor any medical history, made an appeal for her mother to come forward. Exactly a week later, she did: a bewildered, white-haired woman with rotten teeth and a hunched back.

Sensing something was wrong, hospital staff alerted the police. They picked up Elisabeth as her father hurried her home for a family 'reunion' after her 24 years in the hands of a 'cult'. Only when investigators separated her from her father did Elisabeth open up.

Over two hours, in an unsteady voice, she told for the first time how Fritzl had woken her that night in 1984, whispering to her to come down to the cellar he forbade anyone else from entering. There he grabbed her from behind and knocked her out with ether.

She woke up, handcuffed, in a room she had never seen before, as terrified of seeing her father again as of never being seen again. For four years, he kept her in complete isolation, appearing only to feed her and rape her.

In his spare time, Fritzl used his DIY skills to make the windowless, soundproofed prison more homely for his new partner. 'I took good care of her,' he told police, according to the Austrian magazine *News*. 'I saved her falling into the drug scene.'

The first baby came in 1988; six more followed in a two-year rhythm. When one baby, a twin, died shortly after birth in 1994, Fritzl says he tossed it into a furnace.

With the cellar filling up, Fritzl took three children upstairs to Rosemarie. Three 'downstairs children' – Kerstin, Stephan (18) and Felix (five) – grew up pale and anaemic under naked lightbulbs, stooping under ceilings less than six feet high.

No one but Fritzl knew that, behind a concealed trapdoor in the regular cellar, was a soundproofed corridor and a steel door with an electronic combination lock. Behind that was a tiled kitchen and bathroom, gaily decorated with stickers of a sun the children had never seen. Through a corridor

The search for answers begins: a police officer locks the gate of Josef Fritzl's house in Amstetten, Austria. Photograph: Ronald Zak/AP.

just 60cm wide are two spartan bedrooms. In the gloom, the children grew up speaking their own language, mixing German with feral grunts and coos.

Elisabeth tried to teach them to read and write, to sing songs and rhymes, anything to make their world more normal. She cooked meals with the food – tinned, occasionally fresh – that Josef Fritzl bought in faraway supermarkets. A pantry contained enough provisions to see them through long periods when Fritzl was absent. The painkillers in the bathroom cabinet were enough to see the children through sick spells – until two weeks ago when Kerstin began having painful cramps and fainting fits.

After years of humiliation of the most horrific kind, Elisabeth begged her father to allow Kerstin outside to a hospital. What made him agree? A paternal sense of responsibility, or the arrogance of

a man who has fooled everyone for so long that he had become careless?

'Fritzl is no way crazy or mentally ill; otherwise he would have made mistakes,' said Austrian psychiatrist Reinhard Haller. 'He is a technician who very carefully carried out one step after another. He must have unbelievable self-confidence.'

A week on, the 22,000 residents of Amstetten, on the border of Upper and Lower Austria, are still in shock. Although the locals are friendly to strangers and familiar with each other, that familiarity has its limits.

'It breaks my heart for Frau Fritzl – we've known each other for 30 years,' says one portly woman from the Ybbsstrasse. And what is Frau Fritzl's first name? 'Frau Fritzl,' comes the bewildered reply.

In this part of the world, a respectable façade is everything and what goes on behind closed doors is ignored.

'People are very friendly, but they never tell the truth in public; they're very uptight and very Catholic,' says Lukas, a student born in a town near Amstetten who now lives in Vienna. 'The town is typical for a region that stretches from southern Bavaria across Austria to northern Italy. It's like one of those Hitchcock films set in the American Midwest.'

The local police could also be compared to characters from the film world: the Keystone Cops. Hours after Amstetten hit the headlines, they marched into a hotel room for a makeshift press conference. Waving a photo of Josef Fritzl, police chief Franz Polzer announced that the case was 'by and large, solved'.

'Fritzl deceived everyone for 24 years: his wife, the authorities,' said Polzer, announcing that Fritzl had confessed to 'everything'.

All this before Fritzl had seen a lawyer, before any evidence had been examined and before one witness had been properly interviewed. Journalists asked Polzer why he was so sure that this so-called master of deception was suddenly telling the whole truth. 'There can be no doubt,' was the enigmatic reply.

How was he sure that Rosemarie Fritzl knew nothing, when she had not yet been questioned? 'Let me ask you a question: how can you be sure she knew?' demanded Polzer, apparently prickling with irritation that a lady's honour had been impugned. 'Mrs Fritzl's world has imploded.' It is inconceivable that she could have known, he argued, therefore she didn't know.

There was more to come. Senior official Hans-Heinz Lenze was asked why adoption authorities were not suspicious when Fritzl 'discovered' three babies on his doorstep within five years. And how could they be sure the babies were Elisabeth's and not stolen?

'There was no reason not to believe the story,' said Lenze. A day later he dismissed queries about giving custody of three children to Josef Fritzl considering his criminal record. 'I have inspected the adoption files and see absolutely no reason for an investigation,' said Lenze, puffing out his chest.

Perhaps the oddest twist in a very odd week was the reaction of the Amstetten authorities and the Austrian media to this tragedy.

'I'd like to welcome everyone to Austria,' said security director Franz Prucher in English at the first press conference. His satisfied smile gave the impression that the upcoming Euro 2008 soccer tournament, hosted by Austria and Switzerland, had started early.

The media reaction carried echoes of the Kampusch case. The second or third item on every news broadcast this week began in a similar way: 'The entire world is watching Austria . . .' It all smacked of perverse pride where one would expect squirming or angry denial.

The denial came on Thursday, when Austrian chancellor Alfred Gusenbauer attacked attempts to hold his people collectively responsible for the horrific deeds of one man.

He is completely right. But perhaps there is, nevertheless, a uniquely Austrian element to this tragedy: the quarter-century gap between crime and punishment. Fritzl's real stroke of disturbing genius was not the secret cellar, but his idea to hide in full view, behind Austria's social mores. He created the façade of a self-made man, and used his domineering personality to command unquestioning respect and servility from neighbours and officials.

As one Viennese journalist put it: 'Many Austrians assume that "nice, respectable" people like Fritzl don't do things like this, and that it's impolite to even consider it.'

By the end of the week, some Austrian media outlets began to understand that not all the world's media have it in for them. 'It would make sense to start looking for answers instead of a patriotic knee-jerk reaction,' wrote the daily *Kurier* in a scorching editorial. 'Many of these answers are slumbering deep in ourselves.'

SATURDAY, 10 MAY 2008

Key Question is, Who Killed Meg Walsh?

Ronan McGreevy

Meg Walsh died an horrendous death. The blows that killed her had broken her skull into pieces, and some of those fragments were found in her brain. It had been like 'hitting a boiled egg', State Pathologist Dr Marie Cassidy told the jury. There was evidence of injuries to her head, shoulder and right arm as if she had been involved in a terrible struggle.

Meg Walsh disappeared on Sunday, 1 October 2006. The last independent sighting of her alive was noon that day when a neighbour, Nicky Farrell, observed her in an upstairs bedroom putting clothes away. The last activity from Meg's mobile phone was just before 2 p.m. that day when she accessed her messaging service.

Mr O'Brien said she left home at about 8.30 p.m. on Sunday evening and drove off. She was never seen again. The alarm was raised by Noel Power, Ms Walsh's employer at Meadow Court Homes Ltd, on the following morning when Ms Walsh did not turn up for work.

Despite an extensive Garda investigation and a lengthy trial, what happened to Meg Walsh on that Sunday has never been established. Fundamental questions about how she died, where she died and when her body was dumped in the River Suir remain unanswered.

Instead, the prosecution depended on circumstantial evidence in their attempt to bring a case against her husband.

O'Brien first met Meg Walsh in Crete in 2000 when she was on holiday with her then husband Colman Keating. The couple began an affair and she moved to Waterford in 2001. They married in October 2005. He too had been previously married.

Meg Walsh. Photograph: Courtpix.

There was evidence presented to the trial that their marriage was in trouble. Ten days before she disappeared, Mr O'Brien assaulted his wife following an argument the couple had when they were out with his parents. Mr O'Brien admitted that 'he lost it' with his wife on the night of 20 September.

Two days later Meg Walsh presented herself to her GP, Dr Bernadette O'Leary, with bruises and swelling to the backs of her hands and her right shoulder. She also reported the assault to the gardaí, but declined to press charges. Instead, she contacted her solicitor and bank manager about having the house transferred into her name.

Mr O'Brien told the jury that, following the assault, he had agreed to sign over the house to her 'just to prove it would never happen again' and had agreed to loan her €11,000 to pay off credit card debts.

On the night before she disappeared, the couple spent the night drinking at the Woodlands Hotel near their home in the company of a mutual friend, Owen Walsh.

They invited Mr Walsh back to the house and

she suggested that he stay the night. She showed him to the spare room, while Mr O'Brien went downstairs to turn off the lights. He then flew into a rage when he found the pair kissing in the spare bedroom.

In his first statement made to gardaí on 2 October, he recalled: 'I opened the door and saw Meg and Owen Walsh with their hands around each other, kissing. I said: "What the f★★k is going on?" They stopped and Owen said: "Sorry, sorry".' Mr Walsh later told the jury it was only a goodnight kiss.

Ms Walsh's disappearance prompted one of the biggest searches ever seen in the area. At one stage 2,000 people were involved. Her daughter Sasha Keating and brother James Walsh made a public appeal for information. Her body eventually surfaced at Meagher Quay in Waterford city on 15 October.

John O'Brien was first arrested in December 2006 and was charged with her murder on 22 June 2007. In the court, the prosecution relied on inconsistencies in his evidence and modern technological paraphernalia of CCTV footage, mobile phone movements and an electronic key fob.

He said he had gone to Tramore that Sunday to read the newspapers before returning home at around 5 p.m. However, CCTV footage picked up his car in Waterford city centre that evening and he was spotted by the River Suir at 5.35 p.m.

When it was put to him in evidence, Mr O'Brien said he may have been mistaken about the time. When other allegations were put to him about inconsistencies in his evidence, he said that he had never thought her disappearance would lead to a murder investigation.

Ms Walsh's Mitsubishi Carisma was central to the prosecution case. Prosecution counsel Dominic

John O'Brien leaving the Central Criminal Court with his sister, Sheila, after a jury found that he was not guilty of killing his wife, Meg Walsh, in October 2006. Photograph: Courtpix.

McGinn said the car was 'the real crime scene' as it was covered in her blood. The car was found abandoned in the carpark of the Uluru pub in Waterford city on 4 October.

CCTV footage was shown to the jury which purported to show Mr O'Brien parking the car at 10.03 p.m. on 2 October, walking back to the Tesco carpark where his own car was parked and then driving home, arriving there at 10.11 p.m., when he deactivated the alarm.

The prosecution also sought to argue that whoever killed Meg Walsh must have had a key fob to the Mitsubishi Carisma as it had been closed remotely and the only person who had such a key was Mr O'Brien.

However, the car may also have proved to be crucial in his defence. On the final day of evidence, a witness, Gregory Manberg, told the court that he had seen Ms Walsh's Carisma being driven around at 6.20 p.m. on Tuesday, 2 October, at the time when Mr O'Brien was giving a statement to gardaí about his wife's disappearance.

A unanimous verdict of not guilty was a serious rebuff to investigating gardaí. And still the question remains: who killed Meg Walsh?

SATURDAY, 17 MAY 2008

A Nation's Heart Ripped Apart

Clifford Coonan, in Dujiangyan, China

In the remains of their home, a shattered family is preparing to say goodbye to 16-year-old Zhou Yating, who died in Juyuan Middle School during the earthquake that tore the heart out of Sichuan less than one week ago. To many in the zone, it feels like an eternity.

The quake took place at 2.30 p.m. on Monday and Yating's mother, Wang Kanghua, rushed to the school near Dujiangyan city as soon as the tremors had stopped. The school is just a few hundred metres away from her family's house, and she ran with her relatives to the appalling scene.

'We were already there by the time the rescue team arrived at three. We dug for seven hours with our bare hands to find my daughter's body. She was dead; her hands and feet were all injured,' she says as the final funeral preparations are being made. 'Yating is my only child. She was about to take the high-school entrance exams. Her grades were great and she worked hard.'

The family is gathered around a tarpaulin tent with two large funeral wreaths leaning against it and candles standing on each side of the entrance. Inside the tent is a picture of Yating, a pretty Sichuan girl with a side parting and a resolute expression, with the photograph surrounded by offerings of food for the afterlife. Her grandparents are burning symbolic paper money on a pile in front of the shrine. 'The candles are to light her way to the other side and the money is there to make sure she is looked after when she gets there. She loved sports, was a party member. She was the best student in her school,' says her grandfather, Zhou Shugen.

Yating's father is building a tomb in the family's ancestral home of Wolong Cun, in the countryside one kilometre away, and she will be buried today. 'I want my daughter to go peacefully. This is a disaster; we've no way out,' says her mother.

Just down the street from Yating's house, Xiao Wenyi, 22, is also burying a loved one, his little sister, Dong Yang, who was 17 when she died. The family is currently bivouacked in a tarpaulin-covered tent because their house is too dangerous to enter. 'We found her body the day after. My little sister Yang loved to read books, and loved her music,' he says.

He's minding the house while his mother goes to pick up some supplies. His and Yang's father, a bus driver from Chengdu, is due to arrive later that afternoon.

Juyuan Middle School collapsed quickly, leaving the blackboards exposed on the few supporting

A father carries the body of his son which he recovered from the ruins of a collapsed school complex in Beichuan in Sichuan province, China. Photograph: Qilai Shen Photographs.

walls left standing. Seven hundred of the 900 students inside perished.

As the quake happened in the early afternoon, most of the local children were at school. After lunch, pupils in Chinese schools take a nap, so many were sleeping, while others were doing their afternoon schoolwork. The mud around the school was littered with copybooks and textbooks, and one little boy was found holding a pen.

The stories you hear on the streets of Dujiangyan, which lies about 50km from the epicentre of the quake, are heartbreaking, but they are only some of the thousands of tales of horror that people in Sichuan province have to tell.

It's been a week of unthinkable casualty figures, of relief work hampered by bad weather and by the sheer inaccessibility of some affected areas, of images that are difficult to shake. A man on his motorbike, talking into his mobile phone, with the body of his wife tied with rope to his back. A distraught mother hanging out of a crane's hook, refusing to accept that the machine has not unearthed her child alive. A grandfather sitting beneath a tarpaulin waiting for his real, living, beloved granddaughter to emerge from the wreck of her school, not the dead child over whom the rest of the family is grieving.

Catastrophes on this scale affect all strata of society, but as the news started to emerge from Sichuan it became clear that it was the children who had suffered disproportionately this time. These are the lost *xiao pengyoumen* (little friends) of Sichuan, who died in their thousands.

This was China's worst natural disaster since the Tangshan earthquake in 1976, and it shook buildings right across China, north and south.

Estimates are that 50,000 people have perished, with many towns still buried and the infrastructure still in pieces. It was clear straight away that this was a massive disaster.

The blinds of my office shook in Beijing, hundreds of kilometres away; workers were evacuated elsewhere in the capital and in Shanghai; and the tremors were felt in Pakistan, Thailand and Vietnam. If this was the impact so far away, imagine what it must have done to the towns near the epicentre of the quake. The initial numbers coming out of the Xinhua news agency were four or five dead, which soon became hundreds. Then the figures began to accelerate. President Hu Jintao issued a statement urging everyone to rally behind the relief efforts. Premier Wen Jiabao flew to the scene of the quake and has remained there.

This has been a story of escalation. Each day I have reported the story of the Sichuan earthquake it has seemed impossible to imagine things getting worse. Hanwang, with its bodies lying everywhere, was grotesque. Dujiangyan, where hundreds of teenagers were dragged out dead from the mud, was nightmarish.

But every day is worse than the one before. No one knows what horrors await after Wenchuan, the mountainous county directly above the epicentre, is opened up more fully. At this stage, there can be precious few survivors there. Beichuan is a truly horrendous sight. The prospect of the death toll reaching beyond 50,000 looks increasingly likely.

With 1.3 billion people, everything in China seems to be a question of scale. Sichuan has 85 million people, more than Germany, so the sheer numbers involved are often harrowing. And just as people die on a grand scale, the living need to be accommodated on a grand scale. Refugees have gathered in a sports arena in Mianyang, converted into a shelter for tens of thousands of homeless people, where relatives hold up signs with the names of missing family members.

The grounds around the Second People's Hospital in Deyang City have been transformed into a huge outdoor ward, with thousands of injured lying on makeshift beds in blue tents.

The traditional image of an earthquake, the one I grew up with from Hollywood movies, was of a gaping tear in the road, into which cars fell and from which people ran waving their arms. It was only on the fourth day of reporting from Sichuan that I saw the classic quake image, the fissure made by tectonic plates shifting and ripping the tarmac apart, on the road leading to Beichuan, one of the most hellish places on earth right now.

Many refugees have been airlifted out, and the rescue effort has been going on there since early in the week, but the town is still in bits. It's a real possibility that the government will abandon the old town and rebuild it elsewhere, so great is the devastation.

Dotted along the narrow mountainside road are smashed cars and rocks the size of lorries, which limit traffic to one lane. There are hundreds of military vehicles along the roadside.

Reaching Beichuan is a difficult three-kilometre struggle across landslides and over mountains. When you finally emerge scrabbling through the dirt into the town, what lies before you is a breathtaking vision of horror. It's basically a pile of rubble. Nearly all the buildings are collapsed into a heap at the centre of the valley.

At a kindergarten, a father found his son's body in the pile, wrapped it carefully in a plastic sheet and carried him away. His wife is a migrant worker who lives elsewhere in China, but when he tried to call her on his mobile to tell her their child was dead, there was as yet no signal.

The number of children who have perished also highlights another long-term social problem. The one-child policy, imposed in 1979 to rein in population growth that was already dangerously out of control, limits most families to a single child. What are the grieving parents of Dujiangyan to do, now that they have lost their only offspring?

Even amid the heartbreak of Beichuan there is an occasional story of hope. One of the most affecting sights was, finally, a story of life. 'Don't help me, help the others – they need it more,' one woman said as soldiers ran, carrying her on a stretcher, into a makeshift first-aid centre, seconds after pulling her from the wreckage. She had lived through 72 terrible hours under the rubble.

As the week progressed, initial misery turned to frustration about the inability to do anything about the massive loss of life. When earthquakes, tsunamis, tropical storms and flooding strike down whole communities, there is an awful lot of unfocused anger. There isn't anyone to blame as such.

This anger often turns on the rescuers. In Beichuan, refugees threw water bottles at soldiers, saying they had come too late. There had been hundreds of people crying and shouting in the rubble even on Wednesday, they said, but it was too late now.

The Chinese response to the earthquake was swift and immense, and tens of thousands of troops have been deployed. But there was little evidence of sniffer dogs or high-tech equipment. There weren't many helicopters around either, though you would expect to see choppers ferrying supplies and people.

China has a lot of experience in dealing with natural disasters and claims that this is the reason it did not want to commit itself to letting many foreign aid teams into the country to help. But China is not Burma – it has, cautiously, welcomed some foreign input, including Japanese rescue teams, and has also accepted foreign aid.

When prime minister Wen Jiabao first visited Beichuan he spotted an American doctor, Brian Robinson, of the Heart to Heart International aid organisation, walking with other volunteers along the road. Wen ordered the car to stop, then embraced the doctor, thanked him, and told him to go to Beichuan and help – an unprecedented action.

Overall, the relief effort has been quite primitive: manpower and womanpower. This is largely because the worst-affected places are in inaccessible areas. It's a good time to have the largest standing army in the world of 2.2 million at hand.

The soldiers have been heroic – a propaganda line perhaps, but true. Chi Defa, 29, is an officer in the People's Liberation Army and deputy team leader of a rescue team based in Chengdu but travelling all over the beleaguered province.

'Our first task was to try to get to Beichuan to rescue people there, but because the road had not been cleared, we had to turn back, which was tough,' he says. 'But there is a lot to do, and we went to other damaged areas, where we set up tents for the survivors and for patients and some refugees from other areas.

'My whole team is eager to help people, but everyone is really worried. I come from Chengdu and so do my soldiers. I feel fulfilled by what I've done this week. I really want to help those people affected in the disaster areas. I'm so worried about our people, who have suffered terribly in this tragedy.'

The foreign media have a poor image in China because most people now believe the international community does not want China to host the Olympics and is planning a boycott. This makes reporting the disaster difficult. Before the anti-Chinese riots in Tibet, and the sympathetic portrayal of Tibetan protestors in the western media, foreign journalists were popular. Now we are seen as a threat. But the soldiers are still helpful, even offering to lift us over the worst of the holes in the road.

The Olympics in August are generally far from people's minds. Many are furious about the inferior quality of the buildings constructed in the days when China was a much poorer place, 30 years ago, especially the schools. In Mianzhu, an apartment block collapsed on itself. The flats had been built using contributions from a local work unit, a group of workers organised by the Communist Party at a factory or office.

Residents searching for survivors say it was because corrupt officials had demanded so much in kickbacks that the building fell. The neighbouring buildings had not collapsed, including one that housed cadres from the Communist Party. 'Show me the structural steel in that building,' spits one woman, whose mother is missing in the rubble. 'It all went into some official's pocket.'

But there has also been an incredible sense of community. 'We are all one family and one nation, and when our friend suffers it's our duty to help,' says Lu Fushan, 49, a farmer who is one of a trio of relief workers in a truck, laden with baskets for carrying debris out of the wreckage of Beichuan. Volunteers from nearby Mianyang walk alongside the truck, bringing money, clothes, food and water. Everyone wants to help, be it giving a lift to someone trying to get home or offering food.

By the end of the week, Dujiangyan city is still packed with rescue workers and dozens of army trucks line the streets near the school. Digging for bodies has stopped and soldiers are disinfecting the site – there are fears of disease in the quake zone becoming the next problem.

In the shops and houses, people are trying to gather up what few belongings are left before heading on to refugee camps. After a week in hell, the next challenge is to start putting their lives back together.

SATURDAY, 17 MAY 2008

Realising the True Value of Biodiversity in Ireland

Claire O'Connell

When you hear the word 'biodiversity', what springs to mind? A tropical rainforest? Teeming corals? Quaint hedgerows even? Think again: could it be that biodiversity is just as much about our everyday lives? A new report into the value of ecosystems in Ireland aims to shake up our thinking on the species with whom we share our land and seas.

'Loss of biodiversity is our loss,' states *The Economic and Social Aspects of Biodiversity: Benefits and Costs of Biodiversity in Ireland*, which was released this week. It puts an overall value of more than €2.6 billion on the 'ecological services' of biodiversity, on the ways in which the plants, animals and micro-organisms that surround us contribute to our lives.

'Our angle is to look at the services that biodiversity provides to human beings,' says environmental economist Dr Craig Bullock, one of the report's authors. 'It is becoming a trend in international policy to look at the evaluation of environmental services. Those services can be quantified, with some difficulty, in economic terms.'

By ascribing a practical, monetary value to the activities of species (or by assessing the cost of what we might have to do without them), he hopes that the survey, commissioned by the Department of the Environment, Heritage and Local Government, will make people realise that we rely more heavily on biodiversity than we appreciate.

'We need to demonstrate the value of ecosystem services to us. It's not just a matter of setting aside areas for wildlife, it's about looking after the services that contribute to our own wellbeing,' says Bullock, who prepared the report with Conor Kretch and Enda Candon, with input from experts in Ireland and the UK.

Their results present the current 'marginal' annual values for the goods and services to which plants, animals, fungi and micro-organisms currently contribute. Agriculture was one of the biggest sectors they looked at, with biodiversity clocking up a value of more than €1.2 billion per year.

'Everyone can understand biodiversity in terms of productivity of the soil, pollination, predation of pest species,' says Bullock. 'But because we are not quantifying it so often, we tend to overlook that.'

Wild garlic in Courtown wood, Co. Wexford. Photograph: Frank Miller.

Forestry weighs in at around €55 to €80 million per year, and the marine at €230 million. Fisheries, Bullock notes, have an obvious impact on biodiversity and habitat through practices that have smashed offshore reef systems and depleted fish stocks.

'On the marine side, it is quite shockingly obvious how we have been neglecting the environment,' he says. 'For the last few decades we have been really exploiting marine resources and over-fishing like there is no tomorrow. If you think how much more fish you could have if we managed them properly.'

Meanwhile, the value of ecosystem services in improving water quality is around €260 million, according to the report, while 'human welfare' includes activities such as recreation and tourism to the tune of more than €900 million.

It wasn't an easy task to work out the figures, and the final tally of the value of biodiversity is a 'massive underestimate', according to Bullock, who notes that the researchers left out important contributions, such as the input of micro-organisms into cleaning waste water, or potential sources of medicinal compounds and other benefits to human health. 'We couldn't work it out; it was too complicated,' he says.

Overall, he insists, we shouldn't focus too much on the numbers, but more on the notion of ecosystem services having actual value. 'The €2.6 billion is still quite a small figure in relation to the Irish economy, but it is the tip of the iceberg. It's much more substantial than that,' he says. 'And it's not the figure that's relevant really. It's just a means of getting people to appreciate the value of biodiversity.'

While Bullock hopes the report will help inform future spending on biodiversity protection, he believes we also need to dispense with the notion that biodiversity is something separate from ourselves. Instead, we need to understand that we are an intrinsic part of the ecosystems around us.

'We have to respect the fact that we depend on them,' he says. 'For example, in the fisheries, we don't have to spend huge amounts of money on marine biodiversity, but we do need to stop exploiting by over-fishing. We have to go about things in a better way.'

Bullock is also keenly aware that the current snapshot of ecosystems services in Ireland is set against a backdrop of looming global threats.

'Climate change is also going to have an impact on our biodiversity,' he says. 'Even if we get it right we still have that problem to deal with, unfortunately.'

Welcoming the report, Minister for the Environment John Gormley noted that it made a compelling economic case for strengthening biodiversity policies.

'Our biodiversity now faces increased threats from climate change and other threats, such as the introduction of non-native invasive species,' he said. 'We must develop and implement appropriate policies to meet this challenge.' He added that the Department of the Environment would be preparing a revised biodiversity strategy for Ireland during 2008.

Celine Dion at Croke Park in Dublin. Photograph: Aidan Crawley.

WEDNESDAY, 21 MAY 2008

Truly, Sonny, You're a Snivelling Chip off the Old Blockhead

Emissions, by Kilian Doyle

As you may recall, a year ago I was blessed with a son. You may also recollect that I named him Turbo because he came out like a shot. Well, Turbo is living up to his name. In fact, I do believe I've spawned a monster.

His favourite toy is a push-along car. We bought it in the vain hope he might use it to learn to walk. He has other ideas. The first time he saw it, his eyes lit up bright as a rally car's headlights. Foolishly, I plonked him on to the seat.

As I pushed him across the living-room, he jigged and yapped like a happy gibbon, his eyes madder than an amphetamine-addled stunt motorcyclist's. Whenever I stopped, he made with the waterworks, wailing as if I'd dipped him in a vat of acid. He was hooked.

For what felt like hours, I shunted him around the house on the car, its speed and closeness to disaster correlating exactly with the level of his cackling. Eventually, I collapsed in a heap. Turbo was irate.

'Why don't you get off and push it yourself?' I beseeched him. 'Push it?" he said. "Why should I when all I have to do is burst into tears and you –

Wicklow manager Mick O'Dwyer reacts to the final whistle with selectors Arthur Ffrench (left) and Martin Coleman after his side had pulled off a surprise victory over Kildare in the Leinster Senior Football Championship first-round game at Croke Park. Photograph: Brendan Moran/Sportsfile.

gullible, malleable fool that you are – will put me back on and steer me around for as long as I stay quiet or your back holds out? You think I haven't worked that out? You are evidently stupider than I thought.'

Obviously, being 13 months old, he didn't say that. But he was definitely thinking it. Since then, I've caught him innumerable times climbing aboard, rocking back and forth maniacally and making odd revving noises through what I hope was his nose.

My heart, harder than diamonds at the best of times, melts into goo when I see him grinning cherubically at me from behind the wheel. And, whether my spine be creaking like an oak in a hurricane or not, we're off again.

By the way, the car has a mobile phone. What message does that send out? I must write a firm letter to the manufacturer. I've considered installing a hands-free kit, but what's the point? As far as he's concerned, everything to do with the car is hands-free. I push, he sits, the steering looks after itself.

Turbo is also obsessed with a little trolley that his older sister drags him around in as he sits beaming magnanimously at his peasant parents like the Queen of Sheba (not having ever seen a photo of said regent, I am presuming for the sake of this analogy that she was the living spit of a two-foot long, bald and almost-toothless Irish man-child).

His sister is very careful. She only crashes him into things when she thinks we're not watching. I can only assume it's so as not to upset us. How considerate of her.

Finally, one of the few perks of my job is that I occasionally get to drive other people's fancy cars. I once took one home and decided, for the laugh, to pop Turbo in the driver's seat as it sat parked outside. Bad move. He refused to get out. He threatened to scream until he puked whenever I tried to prise him from the steering wheel.

I was in a quandary. How would I explain to the car's owners why the dashboard was covered in babysick? I would've had to pretend it was mine. I couldn't face living with that shame. I've a reputation to protect, don't you know.

So I called the fire brigade and bribed them to slice the roof off and haul my kicking and screaming son out with grappling hooks. Cost me the guts of €30,000 to fix the car, but I don't mind. I'll just deduct it from his inheritance.

WEDNESDAY, 21 MAY 2008

Irish Caste System Tags Refugees as Lepers

Bryan Mukandi

Someone recently asked my wife if she was Irish. She is a black Zimbabwean who has been living here for the last eight years or so. This was the first time anyone has thought she might belong here.

One of the first questions that I'm asked whenever I meet someone for the first time is where I'm from. Many people who do not ask me that question just assume that I am Nigerian.

In fact, there are quite a few Irish folk who are of the impression that Zimbabwe and Nigeria are the same place, or next door to each other. As a black person, you quickly come to feel that there is one big box in the country's collective psyche called Africa, and that all black people are placed in that box until proven otherwise.

It does not take long for the observant outsider to realise that categories like African, Nigerian, Brazilian, Chinese, Indian, Filipino, Malay, Asian, Polish and east European are all related. Some are subsets of others, many are incorrectly used interchangeably, and all belong to the bigger category known as immigrant.

A lot has been said about the so-called two-tier system of health here. That does not really surprise me because I come from a place that came to terms with the two-tier system a long time ago.

What I found surprising was the subtle caste system.

From my understanding of the Indian caste system, the Brahmins were traditionally the teachers, scholars and priests. The Kshatriyas were the kings and warriors and the Vaishyas traders. Shudras were farmers, service providers and artisans. The Untouchables were considered as a lower section of Shudras or were thought of as being outside the entire caste system.

While political power is said to have been in the hands of the Kshatriyas, the Brahmins were the keepers of religion. Based on that, I do not think it would be too much of a stretch to think of economists, academics and business leaders as our keepers of religion. Although once upon a time the heads of the church may have had that role, I doubt that the same is true today. Were Eddie Hobbs and Archbishop Diarmuid Martin to go out and ask people to do conflicting things, my money would be on Eddie succeeding to sway the majority.

Today's Kshatriyas are led by Taoiseach Brian Cowen, and include his Cabinet, Dáil Éireann, the judiciary and Irish professionals. They are our modern-day kings and warriors, while our Vaishyas are the regular folks who are the heart and soul of this country.

They are Pat the postman in Collooney, the taxi driver who decided he would break down the country for me and orient me around its politics. And the lady from the supermarket on a minimum wage who reminds me of my mum and insists on referring to me affectionately as 'pet'. These people are the Vaishyas as far as I can tell. Then there are the Shudras, those whose role it is to serve but who get to maintain their dignity. From where I stand, that's where that box called immigrant goes. Doctors, accountants, business people, waiters and waitresses, artisans, care givers . . . we all fit into this one group.

The only thing we have in common is that we do not belong. The exclusion many of us feel is such that most immigrants share a connection with others in the same boat even if they are from the other side of the world. My Polish friends and I sometimes play a game where we compete about which of us are most harshly judged based on nationality.

The bottom rung on the social ladder belongs to the Untouchables. These were outcasts, treated almost like biblical lepers. The treatment and attitude towards asylum seekers and refugees in today's Ireland at times is as cold. Lepers had to shout out, 'leper, leper!' when a 'clean' person approached them. Because that requirement no longer exists, there are some in the immigrant community who feel they are treated badly as a result of mistaken identity.

They are professionals who, when at work, are treated respectfully by clients and colleagues. When not in their places of work and with no proof of their social standing, they join the ranks of the Untouchables.

I wonder what it will take for my wife to consider herself, and to have others consider her, Irish. As far as I am concerned, I am a Zimbabwean but she is a Dub. What bar will she need to clear for the guy on the street to consider her one too? And what about her friend who was born in Ghana but has lived here for over 20 years? Then there is the little Nigerian girl from church who has lived in an asylum house for years, speaks a little Irish and was showing off her Irish dancing the other day. Where does she belong?

I am planning on living here for the foreseeable future. This country, all things considered, has been pretty good to me. Because of that, I want to give back to Ireland as I take from it. I want to contribute to this country but I feel as though Ireland does not know what to do with me. Minister of State Conor Lenihan recently reiterated his call for a debate on the integration of immigrants. I sincerely hope his call is taken seriously and some sort of public consensus is reached. If nothing else, we will all know where we stand.

Advice for a Turkey from an Elder Lemon

John Waters

I feel for Dustin. To experience the true nature of dismay is to look in the bathroom mirror the morning after you've been humiliated at the Eurovision Song Contest as you ask yourself: did that really happen? It seems unlikely. Even being there in the first place is so improbable that part of your brain tells you that everything, good and bad, is all part of a dream. But you just can't wake up.

A year ago, I remember sitting on the side of the bed in my hotel room in Helsinki, trying to retrace the steps by which I'd got there. What terrible defects of character, what deep psychological trauma, what profound, unfulfilled need, had led me to pursue this particular adventure?

Why couldn't I have listened to Joe Duffy? Would I ever be able to show my face in public again?

This May, I have to admit to a smidgin of *schadenfreude*. There is something to be said for not making it to the Eurovision. I feel like the elder lemon, offering advice to a new casualty, albeit a turkey, about how to handle failure of this most incomparable kind.

For a start, Dustin, take a boat home. Do not, under any circumstances, subject yourself to that funereal flight back to Dublin.

There is a deep patriotic streak within us all – even, I imagine, turkeys – and, no matter how

Somebody loved Dustin ... but that was before he 'sang': at the welcome party in Belgrade. Photograph: Kyran O'Brien.

incongruously or ironically, Ireland's representatives at the Eurovision do fly the national flag. This will begin to eat at your soul.

To drown their deep tribal shame and embarrassment, those around you will be getting drunk. If you remain sober, you will come to know the true nature of despair. You will gaze out the window as you pass over mountains and wonder why the aircraft cannot crash into them.

Planes crash all the time, you will reason – why not this one?

It won't crash.

When you get back to your turkey coop, lock the door, take to the bed and cover your head. Bring the phone with you, though, as it is important, in this moment of incommunicable horror, to pretend that you are taking the whole thing in your stride.

Those who would like to go to the Eurovision but are too cool or timid to try will be scrutinising your every word for a hint of a whine or an excuse.

Take calls from journalists and the phone-in shows, even Joe Duffy. Engage in deep sociological analyses of the outcome of the Eurovision, as though the whole thing was an experiment.

If anyone tries to argue that you were the victim of an eastern voting pact, be sure to disagree, so that people think you are really taking it well.

Do not read the newspapers. Do not venture outdoors, for at least a week.

There is a particular type of Irish citizen who takes life exceedingly seriously and who is driven by an overwhelming desire to communicate this seriousness at every opportunity, no matter how frivolous the context.

On the Monday morning after Helsinki, I was walking along Merrion Street in Dublin when I noticed a tall male individual lurching in my direction, clearly in the process of dredging from the recesses of his thinking facility something in the way of a witticism. I nodded politely and, taken short, he responded: 'You're an awful f★★kin' eejit, Wathers.'

It was not so much that my inner child was too fragile to deal with this rejoinder, but that, because I still had this sense of being in a dream, I thought for an instant about landing a Zizou-style header.

The worst that could happen, I reasoned, was that it would wake me up. Luckily, just then, I found myself approached by one of those wonderful doormen at the Merrion Hotel, who stretched out his hand and said: 'I bet you had the greatest fun! I hope you try again next year.'

Only then did I become convinced that I was not dreaming.

MONDAY, 26 MAY 2008

Magnificent Munster Simply the Best

Gerry Thornley, in Cardiff

The 2006 day of days was for everybody: for the squad themselves, for those who wore the jersey before them, for every foot soldier in the Red Army, for every member of the Munster nation and for many more drawing succour and relief from it. This was too, but it was also more for the players themselves.

Two years ago the sense of desperation in the build-up to the final and the utter relief made for a more emotional occasion. Mass suicide had been the option in defeat. This was different, all the more so after what Paul O'Connell and others admitted had been a tough two years for most of them, be it the previous Heineken Cup, the World Cup or the Six Nations.

The astonishing resilience in completing this feat underlines the mental strength and sheer desire within the group. They had to swim in shark-infested waters to emerge first from the pool of death, then become the first team to win a quarter-final and semi-final away from home. And then finally they had to beat the best, Toulouse, to become the best.

Such is their total respect for Guy Noves and his European princes, if this had been a 16-13 win, however assured and deserved, over London Irish or anyone else it would not have brought the same sense of completion. As Heineken Cups go, they don't come any more satisfying. This reached every part.

So, while there may have been fewer tears at the final whistle, there was a profound sense of a job well done and a more lasting achievement that establishes Munster as a true European, nay global, superpower.

It's scary to start putting it into context really. Two-time Heineken Cup winners in three years. No team in the world could bring 60,000 or so to a single match abroad, not even an international one, not even the Lions.

They welcome the All Blacks to their 26,000-capacity Thomond Park in November as reigning European champions. In an Irish context, they are quite simply the best rugby team ever. End of the debate. And Declan Kidney to coach Ireland? How was there even a discussion?

An end-of-era feel to it there may have been, but as the retiring Shaun Payne – an integral part of this latest odyssey if not on the day – observed, it also felt like the continuation of something. What an ad for what Munster represent! Were you watching, Jerry Collins?

Once again, their 16th man gave them an almost unfair numerical and spiritual advantage, which Munster readily fed off. Once again, by hook or by crook, they had resourcefully obtained their tickets and by trains, planes or automobiles had invaded Cardiff. Come kick-off there were some 60,000 of them among the 74,417. It was as if the new Thomond Park had been unveiled in Cardiff.

The night before the game Jerry Flannery and Ian Dowling roomed together but kept jumping out of bed and pacing the floor.

'He'd get up,' said Flannery. 'Then I'd get up, and I'd say, "The feeling is awesome, man. I just can't stop thinking about us winning the Cup." Usually when you have these positive feelings it's good but I was afraid that I was focusing on the result rather than the process. But I couldn't see us losing.'

On leaving the hotel on Saturday morning, maintaining one of his mantras to players and media alike, Declan Kidney told his players to enjoy the bus ride.

Paul O'Connell talked afterwards of how he could feel himself building up inside as their coach struggled to make progress through the red-thronged streets around the stadium and how the players so easily recognised friends and familiar faces.

And even the players, not exactly new to these experiences, could scarcely find words to describe the atmosphere that began, as usual, to build from the warm-up, the wall of sound that greeted their arrival and the at-times-deafening din thereafter.

'The more emotion and passion you can bring to the game the better,' said O'Connell, 'and they help us do that every time.'

The closed roof and the darkened stadium may have made for striking television, but the over-the-top choreography and the equally unnatural sight of players slipping on the moist turf with temperatures of 20 degrees outside grated a little. Even so, the players and all in the camp struck the right notes, a case in point being O'Connell's insistence that Ronan O'Gara lift the Cup – no doubt recognition of his own absence in the pool stages when the outhalf led the team so well.

O'Gara explained, 'He said, "I'm not taking no for an answer here." I couldn't believe it. I'll never have a day to surpass this unless I captain Munster but as long as Paul's around I won't captain Munster because he's a better man. But that just sums him up, how touching and considerate he is. So I think we'll see a lot more of him leading teams.'

That the players insisted all their non-playing team-mates and backroom staff clamber onto the podium was also fitting, for this is very much a

The victorious Munster rugby team celebrate their second Heineken Cup victory. Photograph: Dara Mac Dónaill.

squad effort with a bond between all in the camp that is probably peerless in the game. Thus, O'Gara in turn, had to drag a reluctant Kidney to the stage.

'Yes, of course, typical again, isn't it?' O'Gara said of his modest head coach. 'There's going to be a little bit of turmoil with Axel (Anthony Foley) and Shaun, Jim (Williams) and Deccie going. But if ever there was a team to get it right, I hope it's our team because we all care so much about it.'

Though he must have had tinges of regret at not being part of the match-day squad, Anthony Foley joined in the celebrations as if he'd played the full 80, for one of the key ingredients in the Munster desire for success is to savour these moments to their fullest. The more they're enjoyed, the more the desire to replicate them.

Not even a tortuous journey home via a chaotic Cardiff airport – as one female fan succinctly put it, 'You wouldn't treat cattle like this' – could dampen their mood.

A thousand or so awaited their heroes on arrival in Shannon Airport beyond 1.30 a.m., as thousands more were still marooned in Cardiff airport or stayed on at extortionate overnight rates.

Nothing better encapsulates what Munster are about than the way Doug Howlett, the All Blacks' record try scorer, has been consumed by this entire epic. Paul O'Connell railroaded him into leading a version of 'Stand up and Fight', before the Clarion Hotel laid on the first of several parties with customary efficiency at 3 a.m.

Yesterday, an estimated 20,000 lined the streets for the open-top bus ride with the Cup from a reception with the Lord Mayor in Civic Hall to O'Connell Street, Limerick.

The highlight of the day was when RTÉ's Michael Corcoran invited Rua Tipoki, Lifeimi Mafi and Howlett to commemorate the occasion with an impromptu haka on the podium. Eyes and neck veins bulging, their rendition was foot and word perfect. The assembled thousands went ballistic.

The party will go on. Peter Clohessy's Sin Bin awaited them later. The Cup will visit all corners of the province. That way they never stop wanting to repeat the trick. They're some outfit.

Leamy proves that if at first you don't succeed, try and try again.

THURSDAY, 29 MAY 2008

The Smart People of Ireland Have No Excuse, says Libertas

Kathy Sheridan

It bodes ill for the No blitz when a livid fundraiser for the National Council for the Blind demands that the relentlessly perky No activists be moved from her post office pitch. 'It's our one day in the year,' she protests.

Libertas founder Declan Ganley, fresh off the sleek black-and-white liveried No bus (with 'TAX – Don't let Brussels in the back door' on the side), immediately puts his hand in his pocket: 'Here, let me give you something . . .', he says, producing a €20 note with the confidence of a man accustomed to moving things right along. 'That's not the point,' says the woman, only slightly mollified.

Ganley, dapper in his suit, shirt and tie, surrounded by about 10 local volunteers in their blue No caps and T-shirts, moves the troops out. 'Get me caps and as many treaties as you can carry,' he calls to his press officer, John McGuirk, a task which sounds none too onerous, until the 'treaties' turn out to be 384-page tomes produced by the Independence and Democracy Group in the EU Parliament, edited by veteran eurosceptic Danish MEP, Jens-Peter Bonde, and – in theory anyway – Libertas's unique selling point.

'Has anyone on the Yes side sent you a treaty – or even read it themselves?' asks Ganley, early and often.

'Isn't it too complicated to read?' ventures a Danish journalist.

'No,' Ganley replies. 'We're very smart people in Ireland. I have faith in the Irish people and believe they know when the wool is being pulled over their eyes . . . It's the readable version of the treaty,' he explains. 'All the subjects are indexed and what has been added to this treaty is in bold text . . .'

It's true. He and the tome look pretty persuasive, until he tries to give one to James Brady, a bloke in a black vest with a few drinks and a No cap on him. 'I'm a "No" because I'm fed up of this carry-on of people trying to take over the country,' he says with fabulous conviction.

'Do you want to read the treaty?' asks Ganley politely. James looks horrified. 'No, no, no! I don't want a book! Now here's the girlfriend, Jo. We've four kids and what way are we voting, Jo?'

'No,' she says, to no one's surprise. James, a gardener, agrees that it's great weather for gardening. 'But we're just havin' a few drinks today. We'll be back earnin' tomorrow.'

As Ganley stops to politely explain his position – emphatically and at length – to voters and media, the team sweeps on, their local connections cheerfully evident. The connecting thread between most of these local No activists is also strikingly evident.

Olivia Kelly, a 32-year-old former model-turned auctioneer, devotee of the Medjugorje Marian shrine, and a stunningly energetic canvasser, is motivated by her faith. 'I'm here for the Lord,' she says, expressing concerns that the treaty will bring 'abortion, euthanasia, homosexual marriage, that are totally against our Catholic beliefs'. Her sister Edel is also on the team today along with five friends; all are involved in the local youth prayer group.

Tommy Banks, a Fine Gael member since 1973 who works in the stores with the local authority, is also on board, with his wife Magdalen.

Declan Ganley of Libertas talking to James Brady while campaigning for a No vote on the Lisbon Treaty in Sligo. Photograph: James Connolly/PicSell8.

They reckon that the treaty is '<u>bringing us into a dictatorship – Hitler all over again' and that the Sligo business community is run by Masons.</u>

They too are offering gifts, a booklet from the Irish Society for Christian Civilisation, entitled *9 reasons why a conscientious Catholic citizen should reject the Treaty of Lisbon.* Reason number five, for the record, is that 'the amended Treaties, for the first instance in an international juridical document, impose the parity between men and women in all areas'.

Caroline Simons, a non-practising solicitor from Dublin who teaches law part-time, says she got involved with Libertas when she read the treaty: '<u>I looked at the powers being given away . . . and I realised that all the points Libertas was making I agreed with.</u>'

And what motivates Ganley himself? 'Rafaella, Micheal, Clementine and James,' he replies, naming his four children aged 13 down to 6. 'It's about democracy . . . This treaty is not just undemocratic, it's anti-democratic.'

By now we've reached the Wine Street carpark at the rear of Tesco, and to the rich amusement of the Libertas group, we come into contact not only with the Fianna Fáil Yes Bus and its Ógra FF yellow shirts from the east, but a slew of Save Sligo Cancer Services campaigners, using the smoke coming out of their ears to blow furious No signals at the FFers, as well as waving posters featuring the FF logo and the words, 'Final nail – the Privatisation Party'.

Last week's Dáil decision not to retain the local cancer services clearly spells trouble for the treaty in the north-west: 40,000 signatures were delivered to Leinster House, which the group is hoping will translate into a massive No vote.

'It's nice to see a leading politician instead of five children,' says Sligo cancer services activist, Deirdre O'Sullivan tartly, referring to the conspicuous dearth of Fianna Fáil heavyweights among the youthful canvassers, while glaring at her neighbour, Cllr Seamus Kilgannon. A sheepish Cllr Kilgannon, chairman of Sligo County Council, and Cllrs Deirdre Healy McGowan and John Sherlock are indeed the most senior politicians here. 'The big fellas wouldn't come out because they know what they've done. They're afraid,' says O'Sullivan.

Kilgannon points out that there were no TDs out because the Dáil was sitting and the two local Senators also had business. 'We did try to change the bus schedule,' he says miserably, conceding that 'the [cancer services issue] is big and it's taking a while to settle. There's definitely a No vote there.'

Then he rallies: 'But the Yes will carry and carry easily if we can get them out . . .' before trailing off, 'I don't know how we're going to do it.'

Meanwhile, a man from Save Sligo Cancer Services is complaining to Kilgannon that he has been 'threatened' by a Yes youth. Jackie Lally, Fianna Fáil's full-time regional organiser, flounces off when offered a treaty tome by a No canvasser. A few yards away, Ganley is engaging another earnest Yes youth – a law student – who accepts a free treaty tome before walking thoughtfully back to his mates.

Libertas is buoyant. 'The girls today are saying that the No vote is about 80 per cent here,' says Ganley, 'and I was getting that in Grafton Street too. It's not reflected in the polls or in our own internal poll taken about two weeks ago [when the Yes side was 10 points ahead but the undecideds were at 47 per cent] but there has been a palpable tilt since then.'

John McGuirk of Libertas talking to Ursuline College Leaving Cert students in Sligo. Photograph: James Connolly/PicSell8.

THURSDAY, 5 JUNE 2008

Bertie Tries to Clear Tribunal Hurdle with Story of a Horse

Miriam Lord

Quick! Send for the horse. At least it would make better sense than the talking mule in the witness box yesterday.

Just when it seemed impossible that the story of Bertie Ahern's money couldn't get any more ridiculous, he surpassed himself with a series of outlandish explanations about the source of his sterling cash reserves.

By the end of the day even he began to sound slightly embarrassed by the twaddle he was peddling to the Mahon tribunal. The public gallery found it hilarious. And it was.

A thoroughly enjoyable gallop through the fertile fields of thinking, as seen through the fearful eye of a cornered statesman.

At least we now know from what side of the family Bertie's novelist daughter draws her talent.

It took a long time to get to this point, but there was an inevitability to it. When certain people find it difficult to explain to certain authorities how they came by their money – lack of documentary evidence, lack of witnesses, lack of memory, lack of credibility and such-like – there remains an age-old fall-back position.

'Where did you get your loot?'

'Won it on a horse, Guv.'

Yesterday, on Day 868 in Dublin Castle, Bertie finally fell back on De horse, eh, de fence. We saw

Bertie Ahern arriving at Dublin Castle to give evidence to the Mahon tribunal. Photograph: Bryan O'Brien.

it coming and laughed. But in reality it was bloody sad.

The former Taoiseach was finding it difficult to explain amounts of sterling money that found their way into his building society account in 1994, particularly as he was adamant that sterling never went into it. He was adamant right up to the time the building society discovered records it didn't know existed.

Bertie insisted he had not tried to mislead the tribunal. Hadn't he given them full clearance to go through his records?

He had, but he did it after his *amigo* Tim Collins had contacted the building society to ascertain the precise nature of the documentation it had relating to an account he held jointly with Bertie. The institution informed him that their records only went back seven years. Search away, Bertie told the tribunal. They'd find no sterling.

Then a more detailed investigation took place, and they discovered they had documents going back much further. Drat. And after the then taoiseach's secretary, who lodged the sterling sums for him, had been in the witness box swearing that she lodged punts. Just as he had also sworn in evidence.

The secretary, Gráinne Carruth, was then recalled in the light of the new information, where she continued to insist she lodged punts. In the end, she had to concede it was sterling and was reduced to tears.

Bertie was aware, 11 days before her appearance, that it was sterling. He never told her and left her to her fate. Gráinne's ordeal caused public disquiet and anger within Fianna Fáil. It has been said subsequently that her evidence, and her reaction to it, precipitated his resignation. RTÉ's Bryan Dobson asked him in an interview if this was the case, and why he didn't tell Ms Carruth that the money was sterling.

Bertie, ever the victim, went on the attack. It was 'unfair' and 'unnecessary' what happened to Ms Carruth. 'If they'd bothered to ask or tell me

the information, I would have done that, but that's neither here nor there.'

But, of course, it was. Des O'Neill threw his words back at him yesterday. Why did he say what he said to Dobbo when 'it can't be true'? Deathly Des didn't accuse the witness of lying. But the incontrovertible fact is that Bertie told a bare-faced lie to Dobson and the public on the *Six One News*.

'I feel sore about this,' complained Bertie, shamelessly. Not half as sore as Ms Carruth did when he dropped her in it.

No. Bertie couldn't get a message out to Gráinne in 11 days because he was too busy. He added that he didn't have a big staff to do things for him like they do in the tribunal. Who did they think he was? Taoiseach?

He had had a Cabinet meeting and a full week in the Dáil with 'Questions and Answers' to think about. He also had two days at the Council of Europe that week, where he had to 'front for Ireland'. No shortage of front where Bertie is concerned.

And then there was a trip to America, where he made a big speech, and he was expected to think of tribunal matters too?

'I never started this. I didn't put up Mr Robson's (sic) interview.' It's all the tribunal's fault.

Bertie didn't explain the lie but he explained the sterling. You see, in 1993 he was thinking of buying an apartment in Salford for investment purposes. So he went to his multi-millionaire pal in Manchester, Tim Kilroe, on about six occasions and asked him to change small amounts of punts into sterling for him.

Bertie was Ireland's minister for finance at the time. He took the sterling home and put it in his safe, saving for the deposit for the flat. He could, one supposes, have saved his punts at home and converted them when he needed to pay the deposit. But he didn't.

In the end, a familiar story, he abandoned the idea. He lodged the money and blanked it from his memory. Oh, and he also won sterling on the horses. No surprise there from noted student of the turf, Bertie. He kept that talent a secret.

⤳ He also always kept 'a float' in sterling for holidays in England and Scotland. A little-known fact. The former taoiseach had one flash of memory yesterday. He said he won £8,000 on a horse in 1996. That's a new amount of money, and a new excuse.

Sadly, his Manchester foreign exchange man Tim Kilroe is dead. So too, one suspects, is the horse. So it has come to this. Bertie Ahern is reduced to flogging a dead horse.

His evidence is a joke.

What does that make Bertie?

SATURDAY, 7 JUNE 2008

Are We Out of Our Minds?

Editorial

Are we out of our collective minds? We are not going to win our money on 'the horses' if we say No to the Lisbon Treaty. We bought that nag in the last general election and, yet, here we go again. The latest Irish Times/TNS mrbi opinion poll suggests that we are set to reject the treaty in next Thursday's referendum. It is difficult to decipher why we would make such a short-sighted decision.

And yet there is a strange public mood out there that is anti-establishment, anti-authority and anti-politician at this time. There is a breakdown of trust between the political establishment and the electorate. There is a fear that we are being asked to vote for something that we cannot fully understand and they cannot fully explain. There is annoyance that the leadership of all the main parties is telling us what is good for us. There is a realisation that we are the only one of the 27 members to have a referendum because the other states contrived not to put the Lisbon Treaty to their peoples. And we are expected to carry the responsibility for the future of the peoples of all other states who have not been allowed to vote.

There are many reasons to vote No to the Lisbon Treaty. The chairman of the Referendum Commission, Mr Justice Iarfhlaith O'Neill, was embarrassed when he couldn't explain one provision the other day. Some of the main parties, Fianna Fáil, Fine Gael and the Labour Party, appear to be more interested in advancing their own personal images than advocating a Yes vote. The economy is on a downward spiral. Jobs are threatened. And we were never told about the horses last year. These are all serious matters but they don't address the merits of the Lisbon Treaty.

We would be wrong, so wrong, to use these irritating issues as a reason to vote No. In an environment where there is so much spin, counterspin – indeed, downright lies betimes – we must trust our own better instincts to make the right judgment for our country, ourselves and our families in the longer term.

The treaty, for all its detail, is intended to fix and make more efficient the workings of the European Union and we remain, as a people, overwhelmingly committed to our membership. The Lisbon Treaty will give us a better Europe. Do not forget that the formation of the original European Economic Community is the biggest peace project of the 20th century. How many times has John Hume said that it was the template for the Northern Ireland settlement? Remember that our decision to join in 1973 was the most liberating action taken by this independent State setting us on the way to reversing the Act of Union. We moved out from the shadow of Britain for the first time and established our own identity. We took our place among the nations of the world with an influential voice.

At a time when food and fuel prices are increasing and the global economy is in recession, the outcome of this referendum will have a material impact on our individual lives. Now, more than ever, we must take a long-term rational view.

[handwritten margin notes: "no effort on part of politicians", "Wrong reasons to vote no", "intentions of the treaty"]

'It's Like a Death in the Family' as Clinton Bows Out in Washington

Denis Staunton, in Washington

As Hillary Clinton stood before four giant, Corinthian columns at the final rally of her presidential campaign, the mood in the Great Hall of Washington's National Building Museum was one of deepest melancholy.

She arrived on stage to the strains of 'Better Days', a gloomy dirge by the Goo Goo Dolls, and waved to the staff, the fundraisers and the supporters who had seen their dream die with hers last week. 'It's like a death in the family,' said Patricia Lengermann, a supporter from Maryland, as she wiped her eyes.

Built in the late 19th century to receive thousands of wounded Civil War soldiers claiming their pensions, the venue itself seemed to be a metaphor for Saturday's event, as battle-weary campaign workers hugged one another and muttered words of comfort.

After 16 months spent trying to bury Barack Obama, Clinton now came to praise him, offering the Democratic presumptive nominee the unequivocal support she had withheld for almost a week after his victory. 'Today, as I suspend my campaign, I congratulate him on the victory he has won and the extraordinary race he has run. I endorse him, and throw my full support behind him.

'And I ask all of you to join me in working as hard for Barack Obama as you have for me,' she said. 'We may have started on separate journeys – but today, our paths have merged. And we are all heading toward the same destination, united and more ready than ever to win in November and to turn our country around because so much is at stake.'

Before Saturday's speech, some Democrats feared that Clinton would be grudging or ambiguous in her support for Obama, hoping quietly perhaps that he would lose in November so she could run again in 2012.

There was no trace of equivocation, however, as she went through the policies that matter most to Democrats, from economic justice to healthcare reform and withdrawal from Iraq, repeating again and again: 'That's why we have to help elect Barack Obama our president.'

Every time Clinton mentioned Obama, most of her supporters cheered, but many booed, among them Lengermann and her friend Jill Brantley.

'We will not vote for him,' Brantley said.

'He stole the nomination.' Lengermann said they wouldn't vote for Republican John McCain but would write in Clinton's name on the ballot, adding that Obama is 'really, really not qualified to be president'.

During the primary campaign, Clinton won support from 18 million voters, including older people, Catholics and the white working-class, but the core of her support was among women, many of whom saw her candidacy as emblematic of their struggle for equal opportunity.

'As we gather here today in this historic, magnificent building, the 50th woman to leave this earth is orbiting overhead. If we can blast 50 women into space, we will someday launch a woman into the White House,' Clinton said.

'Although we weren't able to shatter that highest, hardest glass ceiling this time, thanks to you it's got about 18 million cracks in it,' she said.

'And the light is shining through like never before, filling us all with the hope and the sure knowledge that the path will be a little easier next time.'

Bruised by defeat and bitter about what they saw as a biased media campaign against their candidate, many Clinton supporters are struggling to move on from the primary campaign. Clinton herself needed a few days to adjust to the reality of losing to a first-term senator who was unknown outside Illinois four years ago, but on Saturday she counselled her supporters against looking back.

'Life is too short, time is too precious, and the stakes are too high to dwell on what might have been.

'We have to work together for what still can be.

'And that is why I will work my heart out to make sure that Senator Obama is our next president and I hope and pray that all of you will join me in that effort,' she said.

Jerry Stein, a campaign volunteer from Virginia, said that Clinton supporters should get behind Obama and accept that they lost the nomination contest fair and square. 'I was a Hillary fan. I think she would have made a better president. But I have no problem supporting Obama,' he said.

'I don't really think there was a conspiracy against her. She went in with a bad attitude, that she was inevitable.'

SATURDAY, 14 JUNE 2008

Member States Have No Appetite for Treaty Renegotiations

Jamie Smyth

Irish voters plunged Europe into political crisis by rejecting the Lisbon Treaty, the blueprint for reforming how the EU takes decisions and tackles global challenges.

Patricia McKenna, an anti-Lisbon Treaty campaigner, and supporters hold cut-outs of EU leaders at a protest outside the EU Parliament offices in Dublin. Photograph: David Sleator.

The No vote means the treaty will not now enter force on 1 January 2009, and raises the possibility of serious tensions emerging between EU states over how to reform the Union. There is also a danger that Ireland could become marginalised in Europe, particularly if big member states attempt to forge ahead and implement the reforms.

'There will be calls in the EU to ensure that a few thousand Irish voters do not hold up half a billion European citizens who want this treaty,' said Antonio Missiroli, director of the Brussels-based think tank the European Policy Centre. 'This creates a political crisis in Europe because it sends a message that Europe cannot agree how to reform itself.'

It took eight years to negotiate the Lisbon Treaty and France, Germany and the European Commission are unlikely to agree to give up the reform package. Even Britain, one of the most Eurosceptic EU states, will continue ratifying the treaty, raising the prospect that Ireland will be the only State opposing.

Sinn Féin and Libertas campaigned for a full renegotiation of the treaty, but almost all other EU states have no appetite for further talks about institutions. Another option is to keep working under the terms of the existing EU treaties, which were reformed via the Nice Treaty. Some say Europe cannot function properly with the current treaties, but sensitive deals agreed on the working-time directive or the unbundling of energy networks show tough decisions can be taken under the current arrangements.

But the real danger for Ireland is if a consensus emerges among other EU states that they cannot give up the Lisbon reforms. French European affairs minister Jean-Pierre Jouyet said ratification should continue and signalled that the reforms could be salvaged. 'We would have to see with the Irish at the end of the ratification process how we could make it work and what legal arrangement we could come to,' he said.

This mirrors comments by senior German

MEPs such as chairman of the European parliament's constitutional affairs committee Jo Leinen and socialist leader Martin Schultz.

Lisbon cannot be legally implemented without the Irish on board, but there are legal mechanisms that could enable the other 26 states to move ahead with the reforms while leaving the Republic as a semi-detached member of the EU. For example, when Denmark rejected the Maastricht Treaty in 1992, EU legal experts devised a method of moving ahead with the reforms in Maastricht themselves. This was never used as Copenhagen subsequently won a second referendum after negotiating opt-outs from many EU policies.

Ireland isolated?

A deliberate strategy to sideline Ireland would be politically difficult and could create huge tensions at EU level. But there certainly could be pressure from some states for the Government to consider holding a second referendum on the treaty – or a version of it with specific opt-outs for Ireland – given the relatively low turnout in yesterday's vote.

For Brian Cowen, yesterday's defeat represents a serious setback for his own standing in Europe. Next Thursday and Friday he will attend his first EU leaders' summit in Brussels as Taoiseach where he will be expected to explain what went wrong and how Ireland intends to fix the political mess Europe is in.

The leaders of the EU's big three – France, Germany and Britain – all have different reasons to be unhappy. French president Nicolas Sarkozy is the first victim of an Irish No vote.

He had grand ambitions for his six-month presidency of the EU, which begins in July. The crisis created by the Irish No will ensnare his presidency in institutional wrangling.

German chancellor Angela Merkel was the architect of the Lisbon Treaty and Germany was the big winner from the shake-up of the voting system at the council of ministers.

British prime minister Gordon Brown, whose steering of Lisbon through the British parliament is

Niamh Uí Bhriain and members of the anti-EU group Cóir celebrate in Dublin Castle after the result of the Lisbon Treaty referendum was announced. Photograph: Matt Kavanagh.

one of his few success stories, now faces a Eurosceptic backlash. He will also face calls in coming days to halt ratification of the treaty.

Cowen will find it difficult to cement personal relationships at the 'EU club of leaders' after a result that causes huge problems for so many of his EU partners.

Ireland could also suffer from a loss of influence. Perhaps the best example of the damage that a No vote can have on a country's position is the French *Non* to the EU constitution in May 2005.

Former French European affairs minister Pierre Moscovici told *The Irish Times* bluntly in an interview last year: 'President Jacques Chirac lost all credibility on the European stage because of the French rejection, which was also addressed to him,'

he said. 'France had disappeared from European radars since the referendum.'

The real fear is that Irish diplomatic initiatives, ideas and arguments will be ignored at the Council of Ministers. Big policy issues, such as reform of the common agricultural policy and the harmonisation of the corporate tax base across the EU, come up for discussion this autumn. There are fears in Brussels among Irish officials that the No to Lisbon will hurt their negotiating position.

'For a country of 4.2 million people, Ireland wields considerable influence in Brussels,' says Hugo Brady at the Centre for European Reform. 'You can't really quantify political goodwill, but there is no doubt that fellow Europeans' image of Ireland as positive Europeans will be reduced . . . it will do us no favours at the negotiating table.' Two No votes in EU referendums in the past seven years (we voted down the Nice Treaty in 2001 before ratifying it 18 months later) will also damage the 'pro-EU' brand that has been nurtured by Ireland over the past 35 years.

New member states that joined the Union in 2004 have looked to Ireland as a role model to follow in their relationship with the EU. Similarly, business will fear that saying No to Lisbon sends a negative message to potential inward investors about Ireland's future in Europe.

There is no doubt the next 12 months will prove crucial to Ireland and the EU.

TUESDAY, 17 JUNE 2008.

Why I'm Thinking of Having an Affair

Give me a Break, by Kate Holmquist

I'm thinking of having an affair. After all I've heard about how marriage-enhancing playing away can be, I reckon it would be positively irresponsible of me not to have an affair. I owe it to my preoccupied spouse, half-asleep thanks to the sofa/TV combo, because he will benefit when I become one happy little nuclear glow-worm spreading love everywhere and returning home with a grin on my face. I will be more loving, patient and kind than ever – if not out of guilt, then merely to create a diversion.

Apparently some woman has written a book about this. I haven't read it. I've heard all I need on the airwaves and in the local café where the MILFs gather. 'Sure, isn't that how the French have always done it? *Cinq à sept* – 5 to 7. If I were French, instead of running home after work to a mountain of laundry and surly faces, I'd be sipping champagne with Pierre.' The woman saying this has amazing perma-tanned legs and she's fiddling with her thinning hair while gazing into the table-

side wall mirror, as though she's considering extensions.

I want to tell her that this is Ireland, so it wouldn't be Pierre, it would be Paddy. And that *cinq à sept* she's collecting the kids and cooking up a man-pleasing meal, à la Delia's *How to Cheat at Cooking*, but why spoil her reverie? What she's saying makes sense, doesn't it? Why fight with an icy spouse when you can ski off-piste. All loved up in the afternoon, it's possible to put up with anything at home – snoring, socks on the floor, boredom.

Niggling marital resentments are hardly relevant once you've left the mummy-track for the affair-track because – and this is the eureka insight – with an affair, you no longer have to work at marriage. No need to strive for intimacy anymore. Just do take-out once a week. The other six nights, relax, put your feet up and savour that bit of naughtiness on the side, like an order of chips feels when you're on a low-carb diet.

So, to make life better for everyone I'm drawing up a shortlist of candidates to have an affair with. It's a very short, shortlist. I think I need to get out more. That's the first step definitely. But where does one go?

A male colleague tells me that there's a particular bar in a particular hotel where married people of like mind meet on a particular night on the mutual understanding that what happens upstairs in the mega-euro per night rooms is nobody's business. Hmm, I don't think I'd have anything to wear. And I don't fancy that meat-rack vibe I put up with as a teenager. I don't want to compete with other women for the *filet de boeuf*.

Do you think that maybe having an affair is awfully expensive, what with the new lingerie, the waxing, the shoes – especially the shoes? As any woman knows, shoes and underwear are the two most essential ingredients to feeling remotely sexy in an undressing situation. Plus, you have to be slightly drunk and in the dark. With a stranger, I mean, as opposed to the husband that has grown to appreciate your abstemious, low personal maintenance lifestyle. Put it this way, marriage has turned you into a cheap date.

So, as I peruse my shortlist, I reckon that my paramour should be rich. Otherwise, I can't afford the taxis, the hotel rooms, the lingerie, the waxing, the meals of truffles and caviar eaten off my baby-flab tummy (note to self: need personal trainer, yet another expense). This narrows the field considerably.

The other requirement is that for a successful affair, the lovers must fancy the pants off one another but not too much. You don't want anybody falling in love and putting marriages at risk. An affair is meant to be a bit of harmless fun, a sort of emotionally lubricating ego-boost – like sexual Botox. You might fantasise about being in a Sarkozy/Bruni situation, when all you want is a good shag and then home to your own bed.

The thing is, how can you have great sex with someone you don't love and can't love because neither of you wants commitment? During a love-less affair, wouldn't you start to identify with being the side-dish? Presumably, your lover doesn't want to go AWOL from marriage either, which leaves you with that strangely detached feeling of sex without intimacy, which is like staring through a shop window at a gorgeous chocolate dessert you can't actually allow yourself to taste.

When the ludicrously lascivious text messages, the discreet emails and the plain-speaking credit card receipts are eventually discovered, you then have the task of convincing your spouse that your affair has been in the best interest of the marriage.

He/she will either call a solicitor, or go have an affair of his/her own, which you certainly will have no right to complain about. And when you're the one left with the sofa/TV combo, you'll remember that when you got married, you were sick to death of having to sexually compete and all you wanted was somebody to cuddle on the sofa with. It'll be too late then.

See also 'Give Him a Break' by Ferdia Mac Anna, 8 July.

Disgrace of Lisbon Vote Built on Fear and Ignorance

John Waters

After my father died, almost 20 years ago, we found among his belongings a faded, decaying draft copy of *Bunreacht na hÉireann*, circulated in advance of the 1937 referendum on 'Dev's Constitution'.

The document was dog-eared and heavily underscored, and had many notes in the margins. Clearly, my father had carried it around with him in his pocket for a very long time, and thought and talked about its contents a great deal.

There has been much said this past week about democracy and the will of the people. The people have spoken and the people cannot be wrong. But, in my father's time, when the people spoke, they did so after informing themselves of the issues and reflecting at length. Tom Waters despised de Valera with every fibre of his being, but voted for his Constitution because he admired it immensely. He was as proud of that document as if he had written it himself. He resisted many subsequent attempts to amend it, but always on the basis of the arguments – never because he did not understand them.

The idea of voting against a proposal because he did not grasp its implications would for him have amounted to sacrilege.

If it could be said that the Irish electorate, after due consideration of the merits of the Lisbon Treaty, had decided to vote No, then this might be cause for all Irish democrats to celebrate. But that is not what happened last week. Judging from the intelligence thus far accumulated about what I will loosely call the logic underlying the vote, the most effective slogan of the campaign appears to have been, 'If you don't know, vote No'. The outcome,

Fianna Fáil TD Ned O'Keeffe canvassing for the Lisbon Treaty in Fermoy mart. Photograph: Michael Mac Sweeney/Provision.

then, was a disgrace, not because of the content of the decision but because of the justifications offered for it.

Now the whole thing is over, there is no sense of exhilaration or achievement, other than among a tiny proportion of activists of the extreme left and right. It is as though we find ourselves in the moment of realisation after a heated but meaningless row, when the parties look into each other's eyes with a feeling of embarrassment and dawning awareness. There is a sense that the frenzy of the moment has taken things too far, and now we must sweep up the broken delph.

The impression to be gained is that we voted No (and, whether we like it or not, we all, as a collective, voted No) because of irrelevancies, or peripheralities, or, in many instances, just plain spite, pique or ignorance. There is even a feeling

that many of us voted No in the belief that enough people would vote Yes to absolve us from responsibility for the consequences of our empty, petulant gestures.

A survey of 2,000 voters conducted by the European Commission immediately after the vote revealed that more than 70 per cent of those who voted No believed the treaty could easily be renegotiated. This poll also found that many people who did not understand the treaty voted No; that the overwhelming majority of women voted No; that young people voted No by a margin of two to one; and that immigration (i.e. xenophobic sentiment) was a significant factor in the No vote.

One of the points consistently made by the No side during the campaign was that Ireland would be the only country in the EU to vote on Lisbon, and this makes it doubly shameful that we threw away

Taoiseach Brian Cowen campaigns for a Yes vote in the Lisbon Treaty referendum in Ballinasloe, Co. Galway.
Photograph: Brenda Fitzsimons.

the opportunity in a jumble of empty gestures. The outcome seems to articulate something much darker than anything remotely to do with the treaty, a kind of fury with no precise centre. It is as though Lisbon acted as a poultice to draw out a whole range of festering resentments, many unspecified and even publicly denied, which have combined to create a single and, for the moment, intractable political conundrum. One ten-thousandth of the EU's population has applied the brakes to the will of the overwhelming majority, and narcissism, rage, envy, neurosis, selfishness, paranoia and various forms of ignorance are the chief identifiable characteristics of this travesty.

We have been assured by the victors that this vote demonstrates the maturity, independent-mindedness and sophistication of the Irish electorate. Clearly, it does nothing of the sort, but was arguably the most disgraceful episode in the history of Irish democratic procedures.

There is a reason why children are prohibited from voting, and this goes also to the heart of why adults are expected to treat the franchise with solemnity. The voter has a duty to try to understand the significance of things, and, if in doubt, to abstain. My father's generation of proud democrats, who witnessed the blood of their contemporaries flow in streams for the right to self-determination, would have despaired at the idea that people could vote on an issue without bothering to find out what was really at stake. It is a comfort that these iron men who built this society were not around to witness this latest exercise in self-regarding ignorance by the most pampered, narcissistic and vacuous generation ever to enter an Irish polling booth.

Any Old Portuguese in a Storm for Limerick

LockerRoom, by Tom Humphries

Scenes from Cristiano Ronaldo's Munster hurling debut for Limerick, Semple Stadium, 22 June 2008.

3 p.m.: Arrives at Semple Stadium by chopper with JP McManus. Repeats 'just good friends' line to waiting media. McManus restates intention to bring the bling to Limerick hurling.

3.15 p.m.: Emerges from physio room after thorough oil and rubdown of hair. Shocks dressing-room by claiming Tipperary have made him a late offer. Boyhood dream to play for the Prem, etc, etc. Long discussions in Portuguese between Gary Kirby and Ronaldo. Furious gesticulating from both men. Ronaldo sulks for a while then Limerick's considered position ('G'wan the feck so') is texted to his agent.

3.25 p.m.: Alarm in Limerick dressing-room. Ronaldo falls to ground, theatrically clutching heart. Appears to be weeping and howling in distress. Refuses to let physio or team doctor touch him.

Stephen Lucey finally steps forward. 'Okay, you have the last blue Powerade then.' Much to relief of all present, Ronaldo recovers.

3:50 p.m.: Parade: Does well. No waving. White suit with black silk shirt is deemed inappropriate but a rookie error. Responds poorly also to encouraging slap on backside from Mark Foley as parade breaks. Falls on ground, clutching ankle. Grimacing. Makes 'substitute me' sign to Richie Bennis, who is daydreaming at time. Several women faint during Ronaldo's lascivious stretching routine. Is it for this good men died? Redser O'Grady spotted heading home busting out some Ronaldo moves, 'for the laydeees'.

4 p.m.: Throw-in and first sign of frustration as lightning touchline run is ignored by Donal O'Grady in midfield. Turns to crowd with hands out beseeching them to urge reason upon O'Grady. Still. Early doors.

4.02 p.m.: Goes down clutching head some distance from action. Looks distressed and shell-shocked. Limerick physio sends for Armani helmet. Limerick fans take it as sign of their new corner forward's passion for the county that Ronaldo is willing to sacrifice his hair for Limerick hurling. Ciarán Carey has often done the same.

Choir of angels and blinding light evident as he affixes the emergency helmet to his world-class barnet. Responds to warm applause by running to Killinan end kissing the Limerick crest on his jersey. Much to irritation of Clare people gathered there *en masse*.

4.13 p.m.: First sign of what just might be as Ronaldo performs three of his patented step-overs through a tangle of bodies in the Clare square. Beautifully judged if irritating for those urging him to pull hard on the breaking ball he has left behind. Still. Boy done well.

4.17 p.m.: Play held up as Ronaldo seeks explanation and then apology from Gary Kirby for the latter's encouraging roar from sideline: 'Pull hard, Ron, he's no relation.'

4.19 p.m.: The player's habit of winking at all around him every time a Clare player gets booked is misunderstood and play is held up while medics attempt to remove rogue item from Ronaldo's eye. No objection from Ronaldo.

4.25 p.m.: Limerick point from Ollie Moran. Philip Brennan in Clare goal is surprised during his puck-out action to see Ronaldo sprint past, arms outstretched like airplane wings and jersey pulled up over his face as he heads to absorb the adulation of the terraces. Play resumes after ugly collision with the stouter of the two umpires.

4.29 p.m.: Ronaldo runs interference for Niall Moran, performing somersault following the latter's fine catch. Moran's quick hand-pass to Ronaldo is somewhat lost in translation but again flashes of potential. Unfortunate interlude as

Ronaldo explores the indiscernible grain of truth behind the cliché that Johnny Clareman doesn't like it up him.

4.35 p.m.: Mistimes catch on water bottle thrown in from sideline. Falls to ground, writhing, gyrating and spasming. Refuses to stop until referee agrees to book water bottle. Gets up and spends interval to half-time winking to team-mates.

4.5 p.m.: Gerry O'Grady, the Clare corner back, is surprised when a courier firm delivers a mahogany sideboard and several hundred scaffolding planks to the right-corner-back spot before second half resumes. Serious misunderstanding of the instruction to give O'Grady timber or sign of things to come. This hurling championship has been crying out for something different.

4.57 p.m.: Clare pulling away. Ronaldo looking conspicuously uninterested. Leaving foot in on challenges made on linesman. Runs into space becoming fewer and fewer.

5.03 p.m.: Ollie Moran goal. Classic route-one, especially from Ronaldo, who sprints from left corner and just as puck-out is being taken leaps and straddles Moran, fondly running hands through the Ahane man's hair and then placing hands on both cheeks before kissing Moran, who maintains statuesque rigidity throughout the entire ordeal.

5.05 p.m.: Moran, still feigning injury, asks to be taken off in case he scores again.

5.16 p.m.: Heroic intervention by Ronaldo. Jonathon Clancy's wristy ground stroke is blocked by the Portuguese corner forward as he does a Jürgen Klinsmann across his own goalmouth while still celebrating Moran's goal. Ball is cleared as Ronaldo lies on back performing a Michael Jackson routine while facing the sky.

5.22 p.m.: Realising that Limerick are losing, Ronaldo literally lets his head drop and gets pulled on several times in waist-high challenges. Asks to be withdrawn after brief sideline consultation with agent.

5.27 p.m.: Summons journalists to media mixed zone under old stand. Waits impatiently for Tipp FM to join small scrum. Announces enigmatically that he has found it difficult to settle in Kilmallock and is looking at houses in Holy Cross. Reading from prompt cards serenely denounces match referee as a melted hoor.

5.30 p.m.: Confusion as Ronaldo sportingly tries to swap jersey with that good-looking interviewer from *The Sunday Game*.

Finally the worst of times turned into the best of times in Portlaoise yesterday. Congratulations to all out around Twelfth Lock on Lucan's brilliant Féile win. For a team who were put through the wringer this week the style and conviction of yesterday's win in Portlaoise was a joy to behold.

Great week's work to pull together mightily and then do the business on the pitch.

Maybe the most extraordinary Féile win of recent years. Well done to Martina McGilloway, Grasshopper and the gang. Great day for Dublin camogie.

WEDNESDAY, 25 JUNE 2008

Vibrant, Beautiful Caribbean Island Bowed down by Poverty

Letter from Haiti, by John McManus

Port Salut, a teeming, dusty town on the south-west tip of Haiti, gives you an inkling of how things could be different for the Caribbean nation which enjoys the status of poorest country in the western hemisphere.

It's a colourful, busy place. Ramshackle huts and gaudily painted corrugated iron kiosks selling lottery tickets jostle with shabby municipal buildings in the sweltering heat.

It is the rainy season, and freshly harvested corn is spread on the pavements, fighting for space with motorcycle repair men, snack sellers, piles of second-hand clothes and impromptu rubbish dumps. School children dressed in immaculate gingham uniforms stand out from the bustling crowd, whose clothes have for the most part seen better days.

There is little to detain the traveller in Port Salut, but drive five minutes up the coast to the serviceable but tired Hotel de Ville and it becomes clear that Haiti has in abundance the assets that characterise the other Caribbean islands, and for most of them form the basis of their economy: beautiful beaches, abundant sunshine and a friendly easy-going people.

In addition, having been founded by French buccaneers in the 1600s and gained independence in a slave revolt in 1804, Haiti has a historical and

cultural depth that few other Caribbean islands bar Cuba can rival.

For now, any traveller taking a dip at Port Salut's palm-fringed beaches will find it hard not to be concerned about what passes for the town drains – and where their contents go.

The decades-long tussle for power between various ruling elites, the army and a populist movement led by charismatic former priest Jean-Bertrand Aristide has meant the economy has been a secondary concern at best for most of the last 20 years.

Depending on your point of view, the United States has either propped the country up for most of the last century or is the prime architect of the chaos, meddling in Haiti's affairs to ensure a

Davina O'Flaherty (8), daughter of the late Capt. Dave O'Flaherty, after she was presented with one of the Distinguished Service Medals that were awarded posthumously to the four crew of Dauphin helicopter 248, which crashed while returning from a rescue mission near Tramore, Co. Waterford, in July 1999. Photograph: Dara Mac Dónaill.

government that suits its regional agenda.

Whatever the reason, the consequences of Haiti's economic failure are plain to see in Port Salut and the surrounding countryside. Foreigners travelling in even this relatively quiet backwater must be conscious of security, which generally means a western bodyguard. Kidnapping for ransom has become a not too pleasant cottage industry.

Once you leave the newish tarmac road from the capital Port au Prince, which is being built by the Taiwanese, a four-wheel drive is deemed necessary to negotiate the degraded secondary roads, although the locals get by on a combination of pick-ups, lorries, motorcycles and bikes.

The red-and-white-painted masts erected by privately owned mobile phone companies – including Denis O'Brien's Digicel – stand out in stark contrast to the tottering electricity poles that represent the best efforts of the state to provide infrastructure. In Port Salut, the local hospital relies on the supply of doctors from neighbouring Cuba to provide a basic level of healthcare which supports the lowest life expectancy and the highest infant mortality rates in the region.

Despite the fertile soil and almost ideal conditions for agriculture, the country's 11 million inhabitants cannot feed themselves. Land redistribution and the free-market-inspired abolition of protective tariffs on local staples such as rice have collapsed commercial agriculture. Small holdings of corn and bananas appear half-heartedly cultivated, while bags of rice stamped with the stars and stripes of the US food aid programme are piled on the roadside.

The country is enjoying a period of relative stability in the wake of the ousting of Aristide in 2004, and aid is flowing once again, but few Haitians believe things will be better this time around. Aid has failed to solve the country's problems, says Jean Maurice Buteau, a businessman and former head of the presidential sub-commission on agriculture under both Aristide and his successor, Rene Preval.

NGOs, of which Haiti has an extraordinary number – many with links to neoconservative American groups – have also failed, according to Buteau, who runs a fruit exporting business in Port au Prince.

Encouraging a latent sense of enterprise among the people of Haiti is the best hope of stimulating the economy, Buteau believes. But it is difficult in a country where farmers leave irrigation systems to rot and depend instead on the rains to grow a single crop of corn on lands that could support two or three harvests a year. Most smallholders cannot invest the five years it takes for a mango tree – the most valuable export crop – to fruit for the first time, says Buteau.

But the opportunities are there. The collapse of the agricultural sector over the past 20 years has meant that farmers can't afford either fertiliser or pesticide, meaning that agriculture is almost entirely organic, and produce – if it can be got to international markets – can demand premium prices.

And there are signs of enterprise amid the prevalent apathy. Haitians are using call credits bought for them by relatives living abroad, and the countryside is now dotted with shacks advertising them for sale.

But in Port Salut they still wait for the tourists to come.

SATURDAY, 28 JUNE 2008

The Geek Still Means Business

Danny O'Brien

Who, exactly, does Bill Gates think he is? Even in 1975, at the beginning of his long career in the computer industry, they were asking that. One of the most infamous, and early, documents in the history of the rise of the richest man in computing first came into being when Bill Gates, aged 20, 'general partner, Micro-Soft', penned an 'Open Letter to Hobbyists'. In it, he lectured his fellow geeks on their tendency to copy programs without paying. 'As the majority of hobbyists must be aware,' he wrote, 'most of you steal your software.'

The rest of the geek community were amazed. Who did this kid think he was, lecturing them on the ethics of their freewheeling, free-sharing tribe? They ask the same thing now, as Gates, aged 52, prepares to retire from his job as chairman of Microsoft Corporation to concentrate on his charitable foundation.

His avowed intent, declared more than 20 years ago, is to spend the rest of his life redistributing his collected billions on good works. As an individual with a net wealth of $58 billion (€36.8 billion), that's not going to be easy. As the head of a charity whose efficient operation impressed the richest man in the world, Warren Buffett, so much that he handed over his charitable billions, Gates has quite the challenge ahead of him.

For some of us, dealing with that much money would be ridiculous; to be that rich is to have money become a kind of game, with few consequences. Who can touch you, who can stop you doing what you want, when you can insulate yourself from the world with bodyguards, exclusive mansions and yes-men?

But Gates always took the games of the world with the utmost seriousness. And when one looks back on 40 years of the game of Gates-versus-the-world, you realise that Bill never believed anyone can be insulated from the consequences of any game. His rise to riches spelled out that unique paranoia. Perhaps his foundation will finally turn that belief into something that benefits us all.

There's a photograph of the Microsoft employees taken some time after the above letter. It regularly makes its rounds as a forwarded file on the internet, usually titled something like: 'Who are these weirdos? And who are they now?'

While the 1970s tended to make everyone look like they were victims of care in the community,

Gates and Co. in this photo look particularly horrific. Standing awkwardly in front of a shopping mall photo-booth backdrop, Bill looks like a teenager surrounded by his boondock hippy family, with the sprawling beards, poor dentition and bad hair of his employees splayed around him.

Back then, Microsoft was run out of New Mexico, funded by investments from friends of the Gates family, dentists, and other part-time investors. There were no smooth-talking Silicon Valley venture capitalists, no Dell, no Compaq. Back then, the idea of IBM making something as dainty and low-volume as a personal computer was laughable. Gates's apparent target customer base, home computer owners, seemed as freakish as trainspotters or real ale enthusiasts. Microsoft's niche would in some ways be comparable to a company pitching miniature model-making kits to Dungeons Dragons enthusiasts.

But even then, Gates knew there was more to it than that. His frustration with his fellow hobbyists that they did not realise or understand the importance of their work emerges in his letter. He, more than anyone, recognised that they were witnesses at the birth of an industry.

Forget the hype about the revolution of the microchip and the death of books and the end of work. Gates's genius lay in realising that the clunky, home-wired, build-it-yourself 'home computer' could be sold as a 'business computer'. His success came from his unstinting dedication to profiting from that transition.

While the Gates story usually starts with him dropping out of Harvard, his 'dropping out' was nothing like those of some of the other members of the computing hall of fame. At the same time, Mitch Kapor, the inventor of the spreadsheet, was investigating transcendental meditation. Steve Jobs had a few years earlier toured India and taken LSD. In Gates's own college, Richard M. Stallman, the pioneer of 'free software' (the political movement of sharing and openness which represented everything that Gates's letter to hobbyists opposed) was 'dropping out' by 'staying in', practically living in Massachusetts Institute of Technology's AI lab and monkishly devoting himself to academic pursuits.

Gates's early leave-taking from college with his friend, Steve Ballmer, was not the result of idealism, disillusion, dissolution or lack of direction in life – it was due to an impatience to make money.

It's not surprising that Gates was in a hurry. He'd been selling software since he was 16 years old. Washington state officials, sold on a proposal to automate the counting of cars in traffic studies, visited the company who had pitched the multi-thousand-dollar deal. They were a little disturbed to find a high-school kid at his family's house; and moreover one that burst into tears when the program (called 'Traf-o-data') failed to work correctly. Gates begged his mother to reassure his potential government client that the software had worked previously.

William Henry Gates III came from a settled upper middle-class family from Seattle. His father, Bill Gates senior, was an attorney. His mother was well known in the charitable social circles of the city. He didn't want for money as a kid, and would have been well-off as a teenager even without his new sources of income.

But big bucks always spelled security to Gates. While his fellow computing fanatics blew off making money as a distraction from the real fun of all-night coding and cool graphics and tricks, Gates realised it was a means to preserve that cocoon of splendid and addictive meddling with computers.

Long after the time when it was a major multinational, Gates argued that Microsoft should have enough cash in hand to pay all its employees for a year even without a single sale being made. Money was safety. Better still, money could be as much fun and as challenging as pinning down an annoying bug or finding a quicker and faster way to draw a bouncing circle on a screen. Indeed, it could be the same kind of game, if you treated it right. If Gates beat down and transcended almost every other figure from his generation of computing

Bill Gates. Photograph: Jewel Samad/AFP.

entrepreneurs, it was because he took the game of business very seriously indeed.

Entrepreneur Jerry Kaplan's fascinating autobiography, *Startup*, describes his experience of having his young company undermined and destroyed by Gates's Microsoft in the 1980s.

Kaplan describes attending Comdex in Vegas, the computer show where Microsoft and its rivals would prepare stalls and pitch new products to businessmen. One day, Kaplan was on his way to the same destination as Gates and his colleague, Steve Ballmer – hardly surprising, as they were both locked in bitter competition for sales to the same companies. More surprising is that Gates and Ballmer offered Kaplan a lift in their cab.

As they were driven down the Vegas strip, with Gates and Ballmer crammed either side of Kaplan, the two heads of Microsoft continued their conversation over him, as though one of their major competitors was not even in the car.

Ballmer had been spying on the booths of other software companies, and proceeded to give

Gates a point-by-point analysis of the other companies' software, its flaws and potential vulnerabilities. The young Gates sat there quietly, appraising the information like a young war general. At the end, Gates turned to Kaplan and noted genially that he'd heard Kaplan's software had a few problems too. The cab arrived at its destination, and Kaplan got out, already feeling like a marked man.

In his business life, Gates never stopped thinking about his rivals; in fact, Microsoft and its products are almost entirely defined by its rivals. Unkind critics have called Microsoft products cheap knock-offs of competing products. But after a few iterations, Microsoft rip-offs have a habit of excelling and outselling their original inspirations.

Microsoft Windows 1.0 was an almost painfully parodic clone of the Macintosh windows interface (to avoid a lawsuit, the first Windows refused to overlap its windows, instead arranging them like a tile puzzle). By Microsoft 3.1, it was arguably on a par with the Mac; by Windows 95, its feature set had outstripped the languishing Apple platform. Gates would learn from the mistakes of others when he copied their work.

He was also dedicated to learning from his own company's mistakes faster than his rivals. As Microsoft's chief executive and chief programmer, he was institutionally paranoid and unforgiving about his employees' weaknesses. Internally, Microsoft coders dreaded the Gates inquisition. No matter how lowly your programming role at Microsoft, you could be called in at any moment by Gates and quizzed on the minutiae of your software.

In the end, smart employees recognised that Gates's interrogation was something of a parlour trick. Before each meeting he'd randomly pick out and research one aspect of the employee's program, ignoring the rest as he focused in on one small coding challenge. Like a spiritualist medium, Gates faked omniscience by careful selection and guiding the topics of conversation. In the game of winning points over his employees and asserting his intellectual superiority, he was not above bending the rules.

The rule of the first hobbyist pioneers was that all information was shared and open. Gates followed that rule when it suited him. The topic of that open letter to hobbyists was Gates's Microsoft Basic; he wanted to prevent hobbyists from stealing his code, but he'd lifted the design of Basic from a University of Dartmouth academic project.

Gates demands honesty from his co-workers in their appraisals, but gambled with the company's future by inventing stories of non-existent software. He told the original purchaser of Microsoft Basic that it was already written and working, then spent two months frantically coding before a planned demonstration (Gates did not even have access to the computer Basic was supposed to run on).

It was bending the rules that finally got Gates into serious trouble. The US Department of Justice had been tracking Microsoft's behaviour for years, and had investigated the company's habit of deliberately blocking competitors' products from running on Microsoft software, and of bundling free Microsoft versions of competitors' software when users bought Windows. When Microsoft included Internet Explorer with Windows, the Clinton presidency's Department of Justice launched a full prosecution.

Nowadays, it's hard to believe that the prosecution was successful and that Gates remains a convicted monopolist. But the Bush administration declined to punish the company, and even under the shadow of this conviction and an EU prosecution, Microsoft continues to grow. But in the last few years, it seems that both Gates and Microsoft have lost their harder edge. The company suffered slipped schedules and seems unsure how to combat new competition such as Google and a revitalised Apple. And since 2000 Gates himself has spent more time on his charitable foundation, which he runs with his wife.

The Gates Foundation is a strange but positive echo of Microsoft values. It demands transparency from those it gives money to. It concentrates on

A new-born female Rothschild giraffe being fed by keeper John O'Connor at Dublin Zoo.
Photograph: Dara Mac Dónaill.

getting results, this time in global health issues. It acts like the big player in the market – which it is, with a budget bigger than the World Health Organisation.

The Gates Foundation has ambitious aims: to eliminate Aids, to green Africa, to deliver the world from poverty. For others, retirement and charitable works are an entertainment, a chance to relax after all the seriousness of a career. For Bill Gates, as ever, nothing is ever just a game – except that he still wants to win.

SATURDAY, 5 JULY 2008

Blazing the Non-PC Trail

Brian Boyd

I t's been a tough few years for people who like to say 'it's political correctness gone mad'. At work, you face a barrage of health and safety regulations; at play, you can't smoke indoors and you're supposed to 'drink responsibly'; foodwise you're up against the disapproving glares of five-a-day, omega-3/probiotic harridans; in society at large you have to grapple with fuzzy notions such as 'inclusivity', not to mention being constantly on guard against gender awareness and ethnic sensitivities transgressions.

If you do something as wantonly reckless as driving a car, you're demonised for destroying the planet. At times it must feel you're being nanny-stated back into a helpless foetal position and you daren't even express an opinion about your predicament lest you cause someone, somewhere, offence.

Turn on your TV and nine times out of 10 someone is telling you why, where and how you're wrong about most everything you think and do – including what you wear and where you live. There is, though, a corner of televisionland that is forever politically incorrect – and gleefully mischievous about it.

BBC's *Top Gear* programme is watched by over 350 million viewers in 100 different countries. It is now, officially, the most illegally pirated TV show on the internet – well ahead of *Desperate Housewives*.

Nominally about cars and motoring, *Top Gear* has now taken on an almost totemic status for viewers – the three fortysomething presenters display a blokeish irreverence towards all manner of contemporary strictures about 'acceptable' behaviour and language.

For the show's star presenter, Jeremy Clarkson, *Top Gear* is 'a relief from the incredibly boring lives we have to lead these days. For the three of us it's like being teenagers again. On the show, smoking is compulsory and high visibility jackets are banned.' If any journalist and broadcaster in the world today doesn't need a high visibility jacket it's Jeremy Clarkson.

Apart from *Top Gear*, there are weekly columns in both the *Sun* and *The Sunday Times* newspapers. He's as ubiquitous as the speed cameras he hates so much, appearing on any amount of TV panel shows, while his books have taken up permanent residence in the bestselling lists.

Hundreds of thousands of people have signed an online petition to make him the next prime minister of Britain.

'Clarkson is as close to a god as any mere mortal can get,' states the petition. 'His straightforward no-nonsense attitude would make our country great once more.'

Jeremy Clarkson as prime minister would be interesting. The job, though, needs to be put on hold as just last week Clarkson announced he was going to become an ambassador. Albeit an ambassador for all that he feels is right and good in this world.

Top Gear makes a small fortune for BBC Worldwide, the commercial wing of the BBC. Up until now, Clarkson and his two co-presenters, Richard Hammond and the one that nobody knows the name of (it's James May) have been paid a standard presenting fee.

For the empire-building Clarkson – who long ago realised his contribution to the show's massive global success – he was basically being paid as a chauffeur. It is believed that he was in talks with ITV (who have deeper, advertising-revenue filled pockets) until the BBC agreed an unusual new contract for the presenter.

Clarkson will now receive a percentage of the profits that *Top Gear* creates, rumoured to be as much as 49 per cent of the overall figures.

The BBC says, 'what percentage he actually gets and how it works needs to remain confidential'. However, it was reported yesterday that negotiations with May and Hammond have stalled as they now seek pay rises in line with Clarkson's.

In his new ambassadorial role, Clarkson will not just continue to present the show but will also travel the world promoting *Top Gear* products such as books and DVDs and hosting *Top Gear* stadium shows. Clarkson's new profit-share contract is believed to be worth more than Jonathan Ross's current £18 million three-year deal with the BBC – and will make him Britain's highest-paid TV presenter.

With his poor man's Leo Sayer haircut, deadpan face and a pot-belly invariably flopping over a pair of ill-advised jeans, Clarkson makes an unlikely celebrity.

Born, 48 years ago, into a comfortably middle-class background, he went to an exclusive fee-paying school where the system of 'fagging' still existed. Ever aware of maintaining his blokey image, he's always quick to point out that he was expelled from the school for 'drinking and smoking'.

After his expulsion, he went into the family business as a travelling salesman selling toy Paddington Bears before becoming an apprentice journalist on a regional English newspaper. He began writing about his great love – cars – and soon he was syndicating his motoring column to various UK publications.

For a while he ran a motoring journalism agency before he found himself sitting beside a BBC producer at a car show. Clarkson kept up a running commentary on proceedings and made the

Jeremy Clarkson as seen by Peter Hanan.

producer laugh so hard that he was instantly offered the presenting job on *Top Gear* in 1988.

At a time when people become famous despite the lack of any discernible talent, his editor at *The Sunday Times*, Nicholas Rufford, says he is a consummate professional: 'He is an old-school journalist who learnt his craft the hard way. He delivers copy on time, word perfect and can produce stories very quickly.'

In a profession where strength of opinion allied with a similar strength of humour is at a premium, Clarkson was effortlessly fluent and entertaining. He adopted the voice of an Everyman, portraying himself as just another regular bloke, with slightly old-fashioned and stereotypical views, who found himself adrift in a politically-correct media environment.

At a motor show a few years ago, he was reported as saying the people who worked on the (Asian) Hyundai stand had 'eaten a spaniel for lunch' and those who worked on the BMW stand were 'Nazis'.

He has gone on to describe how the 'boring' Germans were unhappy with him when he wrote

Actor Peter O'Toole chatting to Raymond Coyne during the actor's visit to Galway's Spanish Parade for the Galway Film Fleadh. Photograph: Joe O'Shaughnessy.

that their cars 'should be built with a sat nav that only goes to Poland'. More recently, he referred to the Daihatsu Copen car as 'a bit gay'. The ensuing complaints that he is merely peddling racist, xenophobic, bigoted and homophobic sentiments are treated as grist to his liberal-baiting mill.

However, you can only repeat tired music hall jokes so many times and, moving with the times, Clarkson has found a new mother lode with concerns about the environment. 'I care more about the colour of the gear knob on my Mercedes SLK than the amount of carbon dioxide it produces . . . I do have a disregard for the environment. I think the world can look after itself and we should enjoy it as best we can,' he wrote recently as he positioned himself as a 'climate change denier'.

In a media world populated by so many liberal hand-wringers, Clarkson is lauded by his many admirers as a 'voice of commonsense'.

While other 'why, oh why' merchants come across as peevish and mean-minded, Clarkson is raffishly sportive and has the almost unique ability of entertaining readers and viewers who would be at the opposite end of the political spectrum to him.

He may, though, be heading for a pitfall that is as old as some of his jokes. As evinced by his new BBC deal he knows his worth, but is he mistaking journalism for showbiz?

Clarkson is always the first to witheringly point out how certain media figures have created a melodramatic, almost pantomime version of themselves in the chase for TV ratings and a place in the celebrity pecking order. But when he begins his worldwide *Top Gear* live tour later this year, he'll soon discover that the audiences are there not for Jeremy Clarkson the journalist, but Jeremy Clarkson the entertainer.

TUESDAY, 8 JULY 2008

Stop Calling Me Mr Holmquist

Give Him a Break, by Ferdia Mac Anna

I used to be a big player in this town. I could usually get a plate of chips at the Del Rio without having to make a reservation. I once had my car parked for me by a concierge who saw my band play the Baggot Inn in '82. The guys behind the counter in Freebird Records knew my name. It doesn't get much better than that.

Now all that has changed. Thanks to my wife. Ever since my wife began writing a column for *The Irish Times*, things have grown weird.

I rarely read my wife's columns. She writes about important issues such as sex, social phenomena, interesting people and trends and Hillary Clinton. My interests are different. I read tabloids for the sports. I read *The Irish Times* for the soccer and *The Ticket*, and sometimes the arts stuff. My wife has her world and I have mine, and that's the way it should be.

I should have heeded the warning signs. Such as the way that work colleagues, friends and acquaintances and sometimes people I scarcely knew, began to adopt a strange, different attitude to me. Once, I looked up from whatever I was doing to find a woman staring at me with big sympathetic eyes, as though studying a dog that had no idea it was about to receive a lethal injection. This came days after my wife's column on being married to a baby boomer who had just reformed his 1970s rock and roll band.

At first the comments were casual, even innocent — the kind of stuff that you could acknowledge with no more concern than an everyday exchange about the weather.

'I see your wife is giving the minister a hard time.' Nod, brief smile. 'That was a really moving piece your missus wrote about that poor family.'

Yes, very moving — it was great all right. 'Very insightful piece by your wife about the children and fatty food issue.' Agree totally. Insightful is the word.

Then the remarks took on a more sinister hue. There was no appropriate response, except deep shock.

'I see your wife wishes she had two husbands.' She what? 'Are you still wearing a see-through bra strap around your head?' A reference to the stage gear I wear on stage when playing in my rock and roll band. The guys in Freebird loved that one. A casual conversation at work was brought to a shuddering halt with: 'Your wife is thinking of having an affair. You must have a great relationship.'

I asked to see that particular column, but she told me it was a long while ago and that it was now 'on the web' — which means, presumably, that millions more have read it.

Last week, though, was the cruncher. I was entering a local second-hand bookshop when a man I didn't know blocked my way to make an announcement to the customers (two) and staff (one). 'Here comes a well-known man, but is he well known for himself, or because he is Mr Holmquist?'

There was a long pause while everyone waited to see my reaction. Perhaps some men would have given in to the second-hand book store equivalent of road rage (paperback rage?), but I am cool under pressure. I gave the man a devil-may-care smile, strolled inside and picked up a slightly bruised paperback. I had read four chapters of *PS, I Love You* before I had recovered my dignity.

Of course, I blame myself. When we got married, 150 years ago, she had wanted to take my surname as is traditional but I, the liberated modern man, said no. I had wanted her to keep her own name on the grounds that it was her identity.

However, I get letters addressed to Mr Holmquist on average twice a week. Doctor's secretaries call me by my wife's surname, as do taxi drivers. My wife has a direct line to the world in which she has casually, but perhaps irreversibly, altered my identity and with it, my place in the world.

Now I know how Guy Ritchie feels. He must get sick of people telling him how much they have enjoyed Madonna's workout videos. No matter how many movies he makes, people will think of him as Mr Madonna. I bet that nobody calls Madonna 'Mrs Ritchie'.

Where I come from, a bloke's identity is important. A man needs to feel free to reinvent himself whenever the urge (or the mid-life crisis) takes him. Having someone else reinvent you without your permission is just not rock and roll.

Somehow, I am managing to cope. I have given up wearing an eyepatch made out of a black bra on stage. I am careful to enter second-hand book stores only when there is nobody about, and I no longer answer the telephone. I refuse to open the door to taxi drivers.

From now on, I have insisted that there should be no further references to me in my wife's columns – not that I expect this to have any effect. She's on a roll, why should she stop now? Besides, the source material is too rich.

Maybe I should have heeded my wife's wishes all those years ago. I am also thinking of arranging a second marriage where my wife can finally adopt my name. But I'm thinking it might have to be a different wife.

THURSDAY, 10 JULY 2008

Little to Separate Deadly Serious from the Bizarre

Kathy Sheridan

For seven weeks, Sharon Collins didn't cast a glance at her co-accused at the other end of the long, wooden bench. Essam Eid rested his head in his hands like a weary country doctor, blearily massaged his eyes, hugged and low-fived his lawyers, chatted happily to the exhibits officers behind him, and occasionally took notes. Collins, by contrast, efficiently chewed gum and drained bottles of water while keeping a junior legal on her toes with post-it notes for her counsel.

A chasm of empty space yawned between the two defendants. On a lively day, Eid might throw a sideways glance at her, mischief playing over his olive, moustachioed features. She pretended that he didn't exist.

Apart from her two sons Gary and David, and her former husband Noel Collins, the boys' father – who arrived each day to collect them – Collins had no personal friends in court, unless you (briefly) counted her partner, PJ Howard.

He was the alleged intended 'hit', who, confusingly, was called by the prosecution, but turned defence witness by indignantly insisting that he didn't believe a word of the case against her – 'It's totally out of character . . . In the eight years I've known Sharon, she has never asked for anything,' – before planting a kiss on her lips and disappearing back to his Spanish penthouse.

Eid, a 53-year-old former poker dealer at the snazzy Bellagio casino in Las Vegas, had no personal supporters at all. Theresa Engle, his wife and accomplice, might have filled the role, until she turned from suspect to star State witness, before hightailing it out of the country immediately after her evidence, armed with Irish immunity in one hand and an American plea bargain in the other.

Engle, the fuzzy-haired brunette in the leather jacket and gloves, was only one of the intriguing characters in the case. She and Eid met while working in a Detroit casino when she was separated from Todd Engle, whom she had married no fewer than three times. She and Eid got married and moved to share the Las Vegas marital home with his first wife, Lisa.

Eid's counsel, David Sutton, was intrigued. 'Is that a rather odd domestic arrangement or would that be considered normal in Las Vegas?' he wanted to know. 'It's quite bizarre,' agreed Ms Engle.

Sharon Collins during her trial. Photograph: Garrett White/Collins.

Equally odd was the soft timbre of her voice, a distinct departure from the 'deep rasping smoker's voice' noted in FBI files. More bizarre was her description of the mini laboratory she claimed to have set up with Eid in their home, after finding an internet recipe (mainly castor beans and acetone) for ricin, the third most deadly toxin known to man, by all accounts.

'You didn't test it on a passing mouse, or a porcupine perhaps?' asked Sutton. No. 'You're an incompetent criminal, aren't you . . . You've been caught every time?' he suggested reasonably, since she was the only convicted criminal in court and Sutton's strategy was to demonstrate that the plot was a thoroughly asinine 'shakedown', a kind of 'Dial M for Money' rather than 'Dial M for Murder'.

Either way, despite her participation in two missions to Ireland and one to Spain, allegedly to carry out the hits on the Howards, she was the only one who escaped unscathed.

Any case that includes charges of conspiracy to kill is serious. In this one, however, farce was ever near. Here was the flirtatious hitman touting his wares on a comical website, featuring a breezy comic book mobster in a trilby hat and trench coat, brandishing a Thompson machine gun of a kind popular with Al Capone, according to Sutton.

There was Lying Eyes, the flirtatious 'devil in the red dress', who haggled him down to a deposit of €15,000 for a hit on her partner and his two sons, and whose choice of the old Eagles song as an alias triggered many a nostalgic sing-along around the court.

Enter the 23-year-old Army private, aka 'Judas69', who marched on to the same site, offered himself as an assassin − 'if you got work, I will do it' − citing expertise in 'handgun, rifle, sub-machine gun, shotgun, sniper, heavy gun, heavy machine gun, grenades, basic booby traps and limited poisons', apparently thinking it all a

Two fans add a splash of colour to the first day of the Oxegen music festival at Punchestown, Co. Kildare. Photograph: Kenneth O'Halloran.

great joke until the arrival of another e-mail requesting some 'strong poison'.

In Las Vegas, there was the FBI special agent who raided the home of Eid and Engle and, confronted with a possible find of ricin, the third deadliest poison, etc, in one of the world's most paranoid nations, she does not evacuate the area, have the coffee grinder analysed or advise the hapless Lisa Eid to get the hell out of there – she hands her camera to Lisa and asks her to take pictures for the Irish media.

A similar imbalance is noted in Limerick Prison, where Army ordnance men get kitted out like spacemen in chemical warfare suits to take apart Eid's cell; they find a contact lens container with suspected ricin (which he'd been contentedly sleeping beside, apparently), and bear it gingerly to their commandant, whose own protection, sensationally, consists of – um – rubber gloves.

In Los Angeles, there is Collins's literary mentor and confidante, the elusive Maria Marconi – 'attractive, taller than me, about five feet seven inches, straight blonde shoulder-length hair, sallow clear skin, brown eyes, little make-up, about 47, well-groomed . . . drove a yellow sports car' – the woman said by the prosecution to be an entirely imaginary friend, never seen or heard of from Clare to California, physically or technologically, despite the best efforts of several more of those laconic special agents, shipped over to give evidence.

Marconi, claimed Collins, was the source of her woes, the woman who blackmailed her or caused her to be blackmailed on foot of an injudicious letter – written while 'pre-menstrual', she claimed

– about PJ Howard and some unorthodox sexual practices. Collins said she only began to confide in Marconi because her 'one good friend' had had a child with Down syndrome, and relationship problems.

She had better luck with the double proxy marriage executed in Mexico, via proxymarriages.com, where love means never having to show up for the wedding. And the 'groom' needn't know a thing about it. Even more remarkable is the fact that Collins applied for and got an authentic Irish passport using the $1,200 Mexican 'marriage' certificate, despite the sceptical response from the Irish embassy in Mexico to an earlier query of hers, saying they had never come across a proxy marriage in Mexico and 'doubted strongly that it would be possible'.

There was the late night identity parade in Ennis involving Eid, an Egyptian whose features include a very large moustache and a sallow complexion, where the other participants sported no moustaches and just one had a sallow skin-tone, and he was in his 30s. Eid was the only one in his 50s.

And there was the Limerick builder, John Keating, summoned for the prosecution, but who – like PJ Howard – ended up proving quite advantageous for the defence. His contribution was to give an alibi for Sharon Collins for a time when crucial e-mail exchanges were being charted between Lying Eyes and the hitman.

After this, Keating found himself ensconced in the bowels of the Four Courts with two detectives for three and a quarter hours, and asked to surrender his diary and phone records for forensic analysis.

Then a Stena Sealink witness was summoned to shatter his credibility by insisting there was no computer record of a UK journey in 2006 which Keating said he took shortly before meeting Collins. The witness roundly dismissed Keating's incentive points as any kind of proof of travel. But the witness turned out to be wrong on every point. The records do exist; Keating did travel; the points are proof of travel. He was the last witness in the case when he showed up for vindication last Friday. No one from Stena was there to say sorry.

And of course, there was Collins herself, the 45-year-old mother of two sons, with a separation behind her before the age of 27, confirmed by a church annulment and divorce. One of three Coote sisters, one a psychologist and one a teacher, whose parents separated when Sharon was in her late teens, she did her Leaving Cert at 17, followed by a computer course in Limerick NIHE which she failed to finish.

In court, she was portrayed as a veritable walking cliché of the sassy, blonde temptress with the knowing smile and get-rich-quick schemes (pyramid-selling, fitted kitchen franchises, aerobics teaching, novels ghosted by internet writers), prone to over-familiarity with detectives, the DPP and strange men on sites like proxymarriage.com, with a devotion to astrology and weight-loss websites, Da Vinci Code-type thrillers and annual pilgrimages to Lough Derg.

She was a martyr to migraine, pre-menstrual tension and asthma, and above all, had an unquenchable yearning to marry her live-in millionaire – 'I wanted to belong' – who had decided not to marry her and had actually signed a letter to that effect.

The €12 million man, of course, was PJ Howard, a property owner from Ennis, Co. Clare, who made his money from rentals, in a business now run by Robert and Niall, his sons by his only marriage. PJ was a man 'with a bit of a temper . . . you wouldn't want to get on the wrong side of him'.

He was separated from his wife and had lived with his partner, Bernie Lyons, until she died of cancer in February 1998. This had left him 'devastated', said Collins.

But while it might have seemed a bit soon to be meeting someone new, he was lonely and needed a woman to look after him, as men do. Plus she had noticed him around Ennis a long time before, when she was nine or 10, and he was a grown man (of 25 or so). So, 'when I saw him coming into my shop, I knew he was coming for me. It was almost like a premonition.'

It culminated in an invitation to her and her sons to stay over Christmas and there they remained, moving out only for a few days around Bernie's first anniversary, when 'he wanted to be alone'.

While living with PJ, her flexi-job as a clerical assistant in the business (for which she was paid €850 a month, in addition to a stipend of €1,000 a month from PJ), enabled her to join PJ on his lengthy sojourns to his Fuengirola apartment – a penthouse over two floors with a plunge pool – plus a boat called *Heartbeat* (named after his quadruple bypass in 2000).

When his wife died of a brain haemorrhage in 2003, Collins thought they could get married, although, as she told the DPP, PJ wasn't keen. In his evidence, however, he said they had wanted to get married very much and he had proposed and surprised her with an engagement ring (to add to the Rolex watch) – an engagement that 'went down like a lead balloon' with his two sons, she informed the DPP.

By one account, the wedding was to be in Dromoland Castle (where she'd had her 40th birthday in the sports complex). After discovering that prenuptial agreements were not legally binding here, he pulled out to protect his sons' interests.

The pair went ahead with the trip to Italy in autumn 2005, and in Sorrento they said 'a few prayers' in church but never got married, he said. She said they got dressed up and pledged themselves to each other and agreed to refer to each other as husband and wife. Although they had drawn up a document for their solicitors, confirming that there would be no 'official marriage, ceremony with a third party', he didn't object when Collins told her friends there had been a marriage, and a couple of months later they held a reception for 40 at Admiralty Lodge in Spanish Point, paid for by him, where they even cut a wedding cake. But even PJ Howard was unaware that around the same time,

Collins was also effecting the Mexican 'double proxy' marriage.

Come April 2006, a partially retrieved e-mail from Collins, which logged an automated response from *The Gerry Ryan Show*, suggested that all was not well in the relationship. She found herself in an 'unbearable' situation, she wrote.

She accused her partner of using prostitutes and transvestites while in his Spanish holiday home, and said she never had a moment's peace; he would constantly pester her to have 'strange sex', to 'pick up a stranger and have sex with him' or 'have a threesome with a male escort and myself . . . He even told me he would love it if I would work as a prostitute and that this would really turn him on.' He would take her to swingers' clubs and even though she had refused to take part, she said she had 'witnessed things that I sincerely wished I never had to see'.

An e-mail from Lying Eyes to Hire_hitman@yahoo.com, recovered from Eid's Las Vegas home by the FBI, was couched in similar language, with the addition that her husband wanted to control every aspect of her life, had a dreadful temper, black moods and tantrums, used 'appalling language' and made sure she had no money. Because of her vulnerable position, 'his boys are going to suffer now . . . I wish so much that it didn't have to be like this, but then again I know that if my husband was dead and they were still here they'd screw me anyway . . . I want to protect myself and my boys.'

From there, depending on where you stood in court, the entire affair teetered further into farce – or into a serious plan to poison two innocent young men and kill their father.

Sharon Collins's next step? There was talk of literary ambitions during the trial, and she mentioned that PJ had been encouraging her to get into magazine writing. 'I'll write a book yet,' she told the DPP in one of her voluminous letters.

There is reason to believe that that particular ambition at least is intact.

Security staff put out small fires on the campsite at Oxegen after thousands of people left their tents and rubbish behind. Photograph: Brenda Fitzsimons.

MONDAY, 14 JULY 2008

Times Are Not Bad Enough for State to Help Out the Banks

Business Opinion, by John McManus

Floating out there somewhere in the ether is a proposal that the Government should give a helping hand to the banks and by inference to some of their more problematic clients: large developers with portfolios of properties aimed at first-time buyers that they cannot shift.

No one is yet prepared to take ownership of the idea, but the bones of it have been well trailed at this stage. It's relatively straightforward. The Government, possibly in the guise of the National Treasury Management Agency or the National Pension Reserve Fund, would start buying packages of mortgages off the banks.

The inability of the banks to package up and pass on mortgages in the current climate is one of the main reasons why they have had to tighten up on lending. The transaction would be done on a commercial basis, but the presumption is that the Government – by lending to the Irish banks – will be going where the wider market fears to tread through ignorance and fear.

The sweetener for the Government is that the new money made available to the banks via the initiative would be lent to first-time buyers, which should, in theory, unlock the property market and get the stamp duty revenues flowing.

The fact that this intervention would also potentially save the necks of some of the more exposed developers – who have hundreds of unsold apartments on their books – is one of the less talked about aspects of this not very talked about scheme.

There is so much wrong with this proposal that it is almost hard to know where to start. But we shall start with the whole moral hazard argument: the concept that if people are protected from the consequences of their decision they will not act responsibly. The Irish banks are not hapless victims of circumstance.

Admittedly, they cannot be blamed for the global credit crisis, but they must take some responsibility for the property bubble which has made its impact here so much more painful. It is easy to say with hindsight – but true none the less – that their lending practices contributed to the boom and also underwrote the crazed speculation by the property developers whose demise now threatens the whole banking system.

It follows from the moral hazard argument that if the banks want money to lend in order to unlock the market and save their developer clients, then they should have the rights issues that they are so desperate to avoid. The pain will then be felt by their shareholders, most of whom happily rode the boom and the associated rise in bank share prices. And if the shareholders feel sore, let them take it up with the banks' management.

It is an appealing, if somewhat extremist argument. And perhaps the more cogent argument against throwing a lifeline to the banks is that it would do more harm than good.

Ulster Bank's economist, Pat McArdle, made a simple point in his economic quarterly update last week. The economy will not return to growth until the painful adjustment needed in the housing market has taken place, he claimed.

Arguably the best thing that the Government could do from this perspective would be to stay out of the market and let prices fall to where they should be. By intervening now with some sort of support for the banks, all they will do is put a false floor in the market, and it is one that will eventually give way.

The only long-term impact of the initiative will be to put money in the pockets of bank shareholders and property developers; not in themselves bad things, but something that is hardly the job of the Government.

The Mayor of Galway, Cllr Pádraig Conneely, and Paul Fahy, artistic director of the Galway Arts Festival, at the unveiling of **The Floating Man***, a lifesize sculpture by Seán Henry, which is on display outside Galway City Hall for the duration of the festival. Photograph: Joe O'Shaughnessy.*

There is of course a time and place for Government intervention. But if the governor of the Central Bank is to be taken at face value, this is not it.

John Hurley was trenchant in his support for the banks last week. Their bad debts have not increased materially; they are not under pressure to raise fresh capital and have a negligible exposure to the subprime market, he told us at the publication of the Central Bank's annual report.

More pertinently, he said, the preliminary results of the bank's latest macro-economic stress test suggest that the banking sector's shock absorption capacity remains strong. One can only presume that this stress test involved assessing the impact on the sector of the collapse of a property developer or two, or else it would be somewhat pointless.

Things are bad, but not so bad that the tax-payer has to bail out the banks or their developer clients.

'Can I Just See my Mam? Please? Judge, Will you Let me See her . . . I Need me Ma. Can you Not Just Sentence me Now, Judge. Please!'

Carl O'Brien, at the Children's Court

The boy's face crumpled and tears began to stream down his face.

'Can you not just sentence me now, judge!' he cried, with imploring eyes.

'Please! . . . I want to see me Ma. Please?

'I'll do anything.'

The small 15-year-old in a white polo shirt had offences stretching back three years to when he

Colm Barrington's yacht, **Flying Glove,** *beating into the wind during racing at the ACC Cork Week. Photograph: Michael Mac Sweeney/Provision.*

was just 12 years of age. Yet none of them had ever been fully heard before the Children's Court.

Earlier, his defence solicitor told the judge that the boy was anxious to have the charges hanging over him finally addressed.

'We have reached a stage where he wants to deal with everything before the court as soon as possible,' his solicitor, Mary O'Sullivan said. 'He has indicated a plea for all the matters, judge.'

It was a frenetic day in court 55 with an impossibly long list of cases to be heard. But Judge Clare Leonard listened patiently and asked to hear the details.

Gardaí said they picked up the boy a few days earlier following two bench-warrants for his arrest for a range of matters. The list ranged from criminal damage to cars, to being drunk in public places.

The boy, who is small for his age, jigged his legs nervously and scanned the judge's face for a reaction.

A probation officer said the boy had not been co-operating with the service since late last year.

'He is at serious risk, with medical and offending needs,' the probation officer said. 'There is no parental control, despite a willingness to engage in services.'

The boy's stepfather, seated at the back of the room, shifted in his seat and rubbed his hand across his chin.

The judge, leafing through the charge sheets, noted the boy had been charged for very serious offences.

'I see there was a threat that he would burn his upstairs bedroom . . . that he was drunk and intoxicated in a public place; I see he had to have his stomach pumped for excessive consumption of alcohol; that he damaged a car door; that he attempted to get into it; criminal damage to another car; bench-warrants on all those charges . . . so, we're not in a happy place, are we?'

Judge Leonard paused.

'I'll have to put all these matters in for one day . . . '

The boy suddenly interrupted. 'Can you not just sentence me now, judge?' he howled. 'Please!'

The boy writhed around on the bench and buried his face under his arm.

'I want to see me Ma! Can I please!'

His defence solicitor pointed out that the boy would be sixteen years old shortly. This meant he could end up in St Patrick's Institution rather than a correctional school which would be in a position to give much more structured support.

'Please, judge! My heart, it's beating, my heart,' the boy cried again. The judge interrupted and said an ambulance should be called.

'I don't need an ambulance!' the boy cried, again.

'Can I just see my Mam? Please? Judge, will you let me see her . . . I need me Ma.'

Judge Leonard adjourned the case, discussing the matters in private with the boy's counsel, gardaí and probation officers. After twenty minutes the case was readjourned.

The boy, who had refused to get into the ambulance, was still upset and wiped his glassy eyes. Judge Leonard told him he would be brought to hospital for a check-up and then on to Trinity House, a detention school, where he would spend two and a half months.

'You've been very upset. I want to make sure you're well . . . A garda will visit your mother and let her know that you're all right. In Trinity House a probation officer will assist you, set things up for you on how to live and look after your health.'

The boy, still crying, said he would do anything if he was allowed to see his mother.

'She can visit you. You have a list of charge sheets – you'll be back before the court in September on them. You'll be put on probation and when you're out . . . things will be set up for you,' she said hopefully.

'Okay, so,' the boy said, sadly, wiping his face with his T-shirt.

'Best of luck now,' the judge said.

Pádraig Harrington celebrates with his caddie, Ronan Flood, on the 18th green after carding a one-under-par 69 to secure a four-stroke victory in the final round of the 137th British Open Championship at Royal Birkdale Golf Club, Southport, England, thus becoming one of very few British Open champions to defend their title successfully. Photograph: Ross Kinnaird/Getty Images.

MONDAY, 21 JULY 2008

Harrington Does it Again

Philip Reid, in Royal Birkdale

O nly those chosen by destiny hear the call. Only the truly great ones hear it twice. Yesterday, Pádraig Harrington, a policeman's son from the foothills of the Dublin mountains, became a legend in his own lifetime by retaining the Claret Jug with an inspired final round in the 137th British Open championship over the sandhills of Royal Birkdale.

Unlike his triumph at Carnoustie, this repeat victory – whereby he emulated Tiger Woods, Tom Watson, Lee Trevino and Arnold Palmer – did not have the heart-stopping moments of that day 12 months ago.

This time, there was no Barrie Burn to suck the ball into its chill waters. This time, there was no need for a sudden-death play-off. This time, Harrington won the oldest major of them all with a commanding performance that smacked of true greatness.

A final-round 69 for 283, three over par, gave Harrington a four-stroke winning margin over

England's Ian Poulter, while Greg Norman – who had started the day with a two-shot lead over Harrington and South Korea's KJ Choi – finished in a tie for third with Sweden's Henrik Stenson.

The win earned Harrington a cheque for €938,565, secured his place on Europe's Ryder Cup team for the match in Valhalla in September and moved him to a career-high position of number three in the official world rankings.

Harrington's win also took him into an elite club of golfing greats who have retained the title.

And, afterwards, as he peered at the names engraved on the base to see the sort of company he had joined as back-to-back champions, Harrington quipped, 'It's a little shinier than I remember . . . they obviously cleaned it up nicely.'

Last Monday, when he returned the trophy to the R&A, Harrington did so unsure if he would be able to play. On the previous Saturday evening, hours after retaining his Irish PGA title, he had sustained a wrist injury while performing an exercise routine in the gym of his house in Rathmichael.

And, in the days leading up to the tournament, he was limited to just nine holes of practice while undergoing intensive treatment from his sports chiropractor, Dale Richardson.

Yesterday, with the famous jug back in his custody for another year, Harrington claimed the disruption had actually worked to his benefit. Because of the fierce winds throughout the four days, the Birkdale course proved to be one of the toughest championship examinations in many years.

Pádraig Harrington makes the V for victory sign with the fingers of his left hand and he holds the famous Claret Jug aloft with his right hand as he celebrates winning and retaining the British Open championship, at the Royal Birkdale golf course in Southport, England. Photograph: Matt Dunham/AP Photo.

'The wrist injury was a great distraction for me,' he said. 'There's no question it pushed everything about coming back to defend (the title) to the side. It took a lot of pressure off me; it took away a lot of stress. It was a good distraction to have.'

Indeed, there was another consequence. Aside from ensuring he did not think too much about the actual defence, the injury also kept him physically and mentally sharp.

'Everybody will tell you this has been the toughest week we could ever have in golf,' he said. 'The fact that I didn't play three practice rounds like normal for a major was a big bonus. I was very fresh going into the weekend. The wrist injury was a saver for me, really.'

He added: 'The injury took all the pressure and stress and expectation away from my game.

'I think my case is slightly different from Tiger's. He was obviously injured throughout the tournament (the US Open at Torrey Pines last month) and it was impairing his ability to perform. My injury didn't impair me at all on the golf course. It kept me away from practice, which as it turned out was a bonus.

'Golfers are very fickle. Little things can change our mindset and our moods, and that can have a huge effect on our golf. Having a little bit of pressure release in terms of having a wrist injury was just what I needed to go out and play my own golf, to do my own thing and not try too hard.'

Although it was Harrington's first win on either the European Tour or the US Tour since his triumph at Carnoustie last year, he reiterated his stance that all of his preparations are geared to the majors.

'My goal is to keep getting into contention in the majors, to keep hanging around. The majors are what it is all about for me. I set my schedule out this year for the four majors and the Ryder Cup and I try to peak for those four weeks . . . if I can get a 50 per cent hit rate and get into contention, then that's two a year (to contend in).

'All you need to do is maybe hit one out of four of those and you're winning one every second year.

That's a pretty high rate for most of us mere mortals.'

Having stalked the leaders for the first three rounds, Harrington pounced in yesterday's final round. Norman, who started with a run of bogey-bogey-bogey to fall back into a share of the lead with Harrington, eventually finished with a 77.

England's Ian Poulter, who finished with a 69 for 287, emerged as the greatest danger to Harrington and had even ventured on to the practice range to hit warm-up shots in case there would be need for a four-hole play-off.

Harrington effectively secured a successful retention of the title with a magnificent eagle on the par-five 17th, where he hit a five-wood approach from 249 yards to three feet. He coolly and calmly rolled in the eagle putt, and – along with caddie Ronan Flood – could enjoy the walk of a champion up the 18th fairway, safe in the knowledge he had a four-shot lead.

He covered the back nine in four under par.

'The way he finished – a true champion finishes that way,' opined Norman.

FRIDAY, 25 JULY 2008

Screen Writer

Peter Crawley

So there I was, sitting in the Peacock Theatre last Friday, immersed in Big Love's playful flutter of action, politics, symbols and set pieces, and busily trying to interpret the fire alarm. What was director Selina Cartmell trying to say by drowning out a quiet dialogue with a piercing siren?

By the time I had a plausible reading – the alarm signified societal impediments to meaningful communication between genders; the instruction to evacuate represented a solipsistic retreat from sexual co-dependency – a stage manager explained that the fire alarm signified a fire alarm and the instruction to evacuate represented an instruction to evacuate. So much for semiotics.

It says a lot about an audience that once we buy into the fictive world of a play in progress, a ringing bell is only ever considered a false alarm. 'Fire!' yells out Rosencrantz, apropos of very little, in Tom Stoppard's *Rosencrantz and Guildenstern are Dead*, before peeking out at the stalls in contempt. 'Not a move,' he says. 'They should burn to death in their shoes.'

At the Abbey, no one seemed unduly worried – the staff responded excellently, and besides, that theatre hasn't burned down for years. But something surreal happened outside when both the audiences and actors of *Big Love* and *Three Sisters* were disgorged into the street. It was like being woken too soon from a dream, dragging shards of broken fantasy into the evening light of the real world.

In fact, Lower Abbey Street wasn't looking very real at all. A valiant troop of 19th-century Russian infantrymen surged through the crowd carrying one of the Prozorov sisters to the safety of the Irish Life Centre. They narrowly avoided a gaggle of women in satin dressing gowns and bridal lingerie seeking refuge near the Salvation Army. Whole centuries and cultures collapsed and folded into one another and the city's credibility seemed to be under strain. Audience members offered words of encouragement: 'It's going very well.'

It really was. A few minutes later, this dream-like piece of impromptu street performance was over and it struck me as a great shame that Hiberno-Russian-miserabilist-period drama is so rarely shuffled into post-modern-American-ancient-Greek-gender-political-theatre.

I don't know if this sort of thing should happen more often, and it must be horrible for actors to be interrupted, but it's nice to see what happens when reality and make-believe are desegregated. When Ciara O'Callaghan and Angus Óg McAnally returned to the stage with apologetic smiles ('wasn't that weird?'), we greeted them with effusive, heart-felt applause ('yes, it was!') as they slipped back into character. From there the company could do no

wrong. The gap between audience and performers disappeared. It was our show now.

A real bond was forged with a false alarm, and it was this, rather than any flames, that finally brought the house down.

FRIDAY, 25 JULY 2008

Grim Tale of Slain Romeo and Juliet

Peter Murtagh, in Sarajevo

Vrbana Bridge in Sarajevo today is a nothing sort of place. It's one of several crossings over the city's Miljacka river and really has no architectural or engineering merits worth mentioning. A thing of beauty it is not.

The bridge leads from the city proper to the more suburban area on the far side of the river. Over there is the Kosevo Stadium and the vast cemetery containing the remains of many of the 12,000 to 15,000 people who died during the city's 1,335-day siege in the 1992 to 1995 war.

Then, Serb snipers installed in the Trebevic hills overlooking the city had a perfect view of the Vrbana Bridge and picked people off at will if they tried to cross.

There's a memorial mounted on the handrail on one side of the bridge to two people, Suada Dilberovic and Olga Sucic, who died there in 1992. Suada was the first person killed in the siege. A medical student, she and Olga took part in a multiethnic peace rally on 5 April 1992. Serbian snipers inside the nearby Holiday Inn hotel opened fire and they died.

But there's no memorial to two other people who also died there, two people whose story in a whole heap of personal tragedies in Bosnia was particularly poignant. They were Admira Ismic and Bosko Brkic and they became known to some as the Romeo and Juliet of Sarajevo.

The bodies of young lovers Admira Ismic and Bosko Brkic on Sarajevo's Vrbana Bridge. Photograph: Mark H. Milstein/Northfoto.

They were both aged 25 when they died and had been going out since they were 16, sweethearts since school when they met at a New Year's Eve party. What seemed unusual to the outside world, but was not, and is not so unusual in Sarajevo, is that Admira came from a Muslim background, while Bosko's family was Serbian orthodox Christian.

Their families approved of their relationship. Nine months before their deaths, they moved in together. As Bosko's mother, Rada Brkic, said later: 'I raised them without thinking about religion or nationality. I never said, "You are Serbs, they are Muslims or Croats." I saw her only as the girlfriend of my son, who loved her, and who I loved, too. I didn't regard her as a Muslim, as different.'

As a report of their deaths noted, 'In a country mad for war, Bosko and Admira were crazy for each other.'

Admira's best friend at school, Tanja Bogdanovic, knew them both well. 'The two of them were very, very different. I loved Admira because she was so different from me. She was very unusual. She was interested in things that were a little bit strange for a girl. She loved to drive motorcycles and she knew how to fix cars very well. She was a little bit of a wild character . . .

'Bosko was different. He was quieter and cooler. He had a smile all the time. He liked to play jokes on people, but in a nice way. He had a real charm that you don't see in people very often.'

But life during the siege was horrific. People couldn't walk the streets freely because of the

The grave of Bosko and Admira in Sarajevo's Lion cemetery. Photograph: Peter Murtagh.

snipers; mortars were dropped onto shopping areas and into markets; artillery shells slammed into apartment blocks.

Through contacts with the Serbian military and the city's defenders, Bosko and Admira negotiated, as they thought, safe passage to a better life elsewhere. The deal was that at 5 p.m. on 19 May 1993, they would walk across the Vrbana Bridge and no one would stop them. They would be safe. But as they crossed, a sniper's shot rang out, the bullet apparently hitting the ground in front of them. The next ones did not miss: Bosko died instantly, Admira fell, fatally wounded.

'They were shot at the same time, but he fell instantly and she was still alive,' according to Dino Kapin, commander of a Croatian unit allied with Bosnian Army forces, quoted in the first report of what happened. 'She crawled over and hugged him and they died like that, in each other's arms.'

That report was written by Kurt Schork, a Reuters correspondent based in the city. He heard of the incident from an American photographer, Mark H Milstein.

'I was not conscious at the time of the importance of the photograph,' Milstein told me. 'Not even half an hour before I took it, seven children playing in a public park were injured by a Serb-fired mortar . . . I went to the hospital with a friend from the *Washington Times* and a gentleman from Japanese TV. The doctors wouldn't let us in . . . I went out again, searching for a photo.'

He described a fire fight between Sarajevo defenders and attackers, presumed to be Serbs. He was in a building with other journalists and was taking photos. One of the others then said, 'Hey, look at that,' pointing to the bridge where two bodies lay.

'I took two frames and then some sort of tank shell fired from the Serbian side hit a building and the whole place shook like hell.'

Back in the Reuters office, Kurt Schork's translator saw the photo and told him about it.

Schork laboured for several days before writing his report. Bosko and Admira's bodies were still on the bridge, unclaimed.

Schork's report and Milstein's photo illustrated something particularly awful about the war and both were published all over the world. The Romeo and Juliet tag was applied almost everywhere. Later, a Canadian film maker, John Zaritsky, made a powerful documentary, *Romeo and Juliet in Sarajevo*, for American TV. The script was subsequently used by an education authority in Scotland as a tool to teach children the consequences of ethnic hatred.

Bosko and Admira's bodies were eventually removed and they were buried in a Serb cemetery outside Sarajevo. In 1995, they were reinterred side-by-side in Sarajevo's huge Lion Cemetery

where they lie today, in a well-kept grave surrounded by marigolds.

Admira's family find the legacy has its own burden. I had hoped to meet them in Sarajevo but, sadly though understandably, another daughter, Amela, declined on their behalf.

'I am afraid that I can not help you,' she wrote to me in an e-mail. 'My parents . . . are 64 and 60 years old, and I want to protect them. It is very hard for them to talk about Admira and Bosko, again and again.

'That is our tragedy and each time when we talk about it, it is like we are going through it again. Believe me, it is very hard.'

Instead, I visit the bridge where they died and their grave. And at the grave, I find a surprise, something I had not noticed in my research of their

Horsing around between showers at Ballybrit, during the Galway races. Photograph: Eric Luke.

story. Kurt Schork died (along with a colleague) in an ambush in Sierra Leone in May 2000, shot dead by a young soldier. Half of Schork's ashes were buried next to his mother's grave in Washington DC. The other half lie in a grave at the feet of Bosko and Admira, his full name, Kurt Erich Schork, inscribed on a simple, low headstone.

It seems appropriate that the reporter whose diligence meant the story of Bosko and Admira's lives did not vanish with them, as did the stories of so many other lives, should also be so close to them in death.

This article was one of a series, Balkan Journey, published during July. They were accompanied by a motorcycle blog, Balkan Bikers, for The Irish Times *website,* www.irish-times.com, *which may be read by following this link:* http://www.irishtimes.com/blogs/balkanbikers/

TUESDAY, 29 JULY 2008

Hands that Shaped Irish History

Elaine Byrne

Things fall apart; the centre cannot hold;
Mere anarchy is loosed upon the world,
The blood-dimmed tide is loosed, and everywhere

The ceremony of innocence is drowned;
The best lack all conviction, while the worst
Are full of passionate intensity.

Surely some revelation is at hand;
Surely the Second Coming is at hand.

So wrote WB Yeats in 1920, when the War of Independence raged and the year Liam Cosgrave was born. Arthur Griffith, leader of the Irish delegation at the Treaty negotiations, sought to ensure the status of the unionist and Protestant minority in a new Irish Free State. The day the Treaty was signed, 6 December 1921, Griffith met with southern unionist representatives and assured them of due representation in the Senate. Griffith did not live to realise his promise and WT Cosgrave, president of the Executive Council, fulfilled Griffith's legacy.

Thirty senators were appointed to the Senate by WT Cosgrave, Liam's father, in December 1922 and a further 30 were elected by the Dáil. The recreations listed by senators were as intriguing as the senators themselves and ranged from pig-sticking to collecting English china. *The New York Times* remarked that the first Senate was 'represen-tative of all classes'.

In all, seven peers, a dowager countess, five baronets and several knights were represented. The Senate consisted of 36 Catholics, 20 Protestants, three Quakers and one Jew. Cosgrave's nominees numbered 16 southern unionists. The first Senate was the most curious political grouping in the history of the Irish state.

Anti-Treaty forces believed, however, that the Senate was 'designed primarily for the purpose of upholding the interests of the pro British element in the Irish Free State'. The execution of Erskine Childers in November 1922 introduced a new dimension to the ongoing Civil War. Anti-Treaty forces gave notice that senators were a legitimate target unless they resigned their office. This request was rejected by the new senators.

By the end of March 1923, 37 senators' homes were burnt to the ground. When asked if he would move to England following the destruction of his home at Palmerstown, senator Lord Mayo replied, 'No! I will not be driven from my own country.' Cosgrave's own home was scorched in early January. Others were intimidated, kidnapped and attempts made on their lives.

These were remarkable times made extra-ordinary by senators who steadfastly observed the principle of sacrifice of private gain for public office. WT Cosgrave commended their 'fine exhibition of citizenship'.

In response to this period of coercion against the Senate, senator Alice Stopford Green commissioned the creation of a casket with a message placed inside: 'Whether we are of an ancient Irish descent, or of later Irish birth, we are united in one people, and we are bound by one lofty obligation to complete the building of our common nation.' This casket was placed on the cathaoirleach's desk in the senate chamber from 1924–1936.

Liam Cosgrave went to see the beautifully ornate casket, made from Norwegian copper and enamel with filigree silver and gold, at the Royal Irish Academy last week. Cosgrave was chief whip and parliamentary secretary in the 1948-1951 inter-party government, minister for external affairs 1954-1957 and taoiseach from 1973-1977.

The casket is accompanied by a vellum manuscript entitled *The First Irish Senate* in elaborate Celtic script. The distinctive fountain pen signatures of the 60 senators are neatly listed underneath, half of whom were appointed by WT Cosgrave.

WT and Liam were the only taoisigh father and son. For this writer, it was humbling and very special to bear witness to Liam Cosgrave's immense pride in his father as he went through the signatures one by one.

'John Counihan, I knew him. I knew [James] Douglas, John Keane, let me see . . . Mrs Costello, she was from Tuam. Oliver St John Gogarty; he suggested Yeats. Knew him well, oh very well. [He removed Cosgrave's tonsils.] I knew [The Earl of] Wicklow's son. Bryan Mahon . . . Peter

Former taoiseach Liam Cosgrave examines the velum manuscript containing the signatures of the State's first senators, which accompanies the contents of the Senate Casket kept in the Royal Irish Academy. Photograph: Bryan O'Brien.

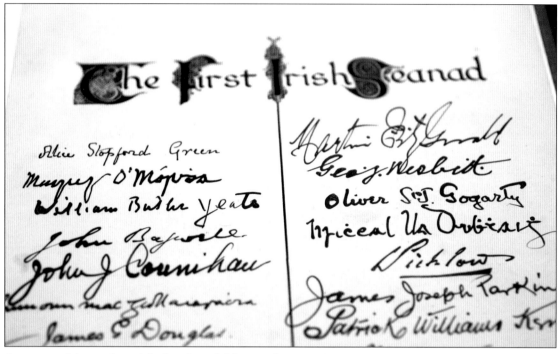

Signatures of the members of the first Seanad. Photograph: Bryan O'Brien.

De Loughry, he was Kilkenny. [WT] Westropp Bennett, I knew him. [Lord Baron] Glenavy. Andrew Jameson.

'I want to see who else I can find out now. Countess of Desart, she was Kilkenny as well; she was married there. [William] Hutcheson Póe. HS Guinness. That's [The Earl of] Granard, see that one, I knew him, and his two sons; one was in the army with me. Where's [Edmund W] Eyre's name? Henry Barniville, he was a surgeon. James Moran, he was Moran's Hotel . . . [Joseph] Clayton Love. [Captain JJ] Henry Greer, he was head of the national stud.

'Martin Fitzgerald, he was the independent; his family had a wine business in D'Olier Street; the name is still over the shop, used to be anyway. Horace Plunkett, his place was burned. George Sigerson. Tom Foran . . . John T O'Farrell, he was Labour. George Nesbitt. James Joe Parkinson, biggest racehorse trainer of his time. I knew him because he was in the Curragh. [The Marquess of] Headfort . . . Some characters.'

And each has their own extraordinary story. Sir Thomas Henry Grattan Esmonde, the great grandson of Henry Grattan MP. Mrs Wyse Power, first president of Cumann na nBan. Colonel Maurice Moore, whose grandfather marched to join General Humbert after the French landing at Killala in September 1798.

Cosgrave explains his father's motivation for appointing a number of senators, such as Senator General Sir Bryan Mahon, from Ahascragh in Co. Galway, and buried in Mulladen, Ballymore Eustace. His military adventures with the 8th Kings Royal Irish Hussars brought him to India, Egypt, Dongola, Khartoum, Kordofan, South Africa, Serbia, Salonika and Sudan. Mahon was commander-in-chief of the British Forces in Ireland from 1917-1919.

After Thomas Ashe, a leading member of the Irish Volunteers and prominent figure in the Easter Rising, died on hunger strike in 1917, WT Cosgrave and Michael Collins travelled by tram to the house of Tim Healy MP at Chapelizod and asked him to represent Ashe's family at the inquest. Healy successfully secured a verdict of negligence against the British government.

Ashe lay in state at Dublin City Hall. Collins, then just 27 years of age, gave the graveside oration flanked by Irish Volunteers. Mahon was given direct orders to prevent this from happening.

WT Cosgrave, chair of the finance committee of Dublin Corporation, recognised the riotous potential of public opinion and feared significant bloodshed so soon after the Rising. Cosgrave directed Edmund W Eyre (also appointed to the Senate), Dublin city treasurer, to persuade Mahon to keep the troops in barracks. Mahon took Cosgrave's advice, disobeyed orders and Ashe's funeral passed off without incident.

At 42, WT Cosgrave was one the oldest members in the Cabinet. The 1922 Government had no practical experience of parliamentary life and were thrust immediately into the responsibilities of office. The young ministers relied enormously on the Senate, the civil service, the Army and the Civic Guard. The Senate enormously influenced the guiding principles and legislative foundations of the State. This was despite great personal risk and at a time when the country seemed on the brink of anarchy.

The weight of the Senate's authority is evident from its legislative record. Of the 1,831 amendments made to primary legislation, the Dáil outrightly rejected only 86 of these. In all, the Dáil accepted 95 per cent of all amendments from the Senate from 1922-1936.

Theses amendments were influential in establishing the Civil Service Commission, the Comptroller and Auditor General, the Gárda Síochána, the judicial system and the organisation

The casket. Photograph: Bryan O'Brien.

and administration of central and local government.

Liam Cosgrave acknowledges that he 'wouldn't be an impartial observer' in any personal assessment of his father. Cosgrave simply believes his father 'did his duty' and that one of his major achievements was 'bringing in the unionists. He wanted to collaborate with the North and, of course, time has proved that policy was the right one. We are still at it'.

The Senate was abolished in 1936 and reconstituted as the Seanad in 1938. Any celebration of the Seanad's 60th birthday this year must confer due recognition to the sacrifice and contribution of Ireland's first senators. One way of doing this is to put the Senate Casket and signatures on permanent public display.

Senator WB Yeats was awarded the Nobel Prize for Literature in December 1923, the first Irish person to receive this honour. Only three years earlier, Yeats had written of anarchy.

For Liam Cosgrave, it is straightforward. 'At times, you have to take the national line as distinct from a party line. I always thought that you must put the state first or the country first, even if it's not sometimes the political thing to do.'

The centre did hold. There was conviction.

SATURDAY, 2 AUGUST 2008

Ratify Lisbon Treaty Regardless of Referendum Result

Inside Politics, by Stephen Collins

The squabble between the Government and Opposition over a proposed Dáil commission to examine the pros and cons of the Lisbon Treaty only goes to prove that a second referendum on the Lisbon Treaty is doomed to almost certain defeat. At this stage it is hard to see how a confused and divided Yes side will be any match for a confident No campaign, awash with money and unhampered by any allegiance to truth.

Attempting to salvage Ireland's place in Europe and protect future generations from the disaster of the Lisbon defeat will be the supreme test of Taoiseach Brian Cowen. If a referendum cannot be won, the only solution is for the Dáil to find a way to ratify the essential nuts and bolts of the treaty, while allowing the electorate to vote again on the issues that caused such anxiety in the campaign.

The Taoiseach will have to summon up the nerve and vision displayed by Seán Lemass when he dragged the country into the modern world in the early 1960s, against some of the most basic instincts of his own party and a large chunk of the electorate. History has vindicated Lemass's decision to abandon protectionism and embrace free trade and the wider world of Europe.

Brian Cowen is now facing a challenge of similar proportions. The referendum defeat has launched Ireland down the slippery slope of a retreat from involvement in Europe and a return to the status of being a client state of Britain. A second rejection of Lisbon would inevitably doom the country to that fate for generations to come.

The Government itself has made the winning of a second referendum almost impossible by compounding its botched referendum campaign with a poor tactical response to the Lisbon defeat. Instead of forcing the electorate to face up to the consequences of a No vote, Irish diplomacy went into overdrive to persuade our EU partners to tone down their response for fear of antagonising the Irish electorate even more.

The result is that the voters have no idea of how much damage has already been done to Ireland's standing and have no comprehension at all of the consequences down the line. All it has done has been to confirm the claims of the No campaigners that a rejection of the treaty would be a consequences-free decision.

The fact that it has been made crystal clear by all other governments that there will be no renegotiation and no reratification of the treaty by other countries has passed most people by. The softly, softly approach has simply made a second No inevitable.

So how can the Government find a way out of holding a second referendum while not ignoring the will of the people as expressed in June? The only way is for the Dáil to ratify the Lisbon Treaty while simultaneously opting out of areas such as the Charter of Fundamental Rights, which probably

Frank Joy and his son Francis on Treangarriv Mountain near Glencar, Co. Kerry, where they captured a wild mountain goat for the annual Puck Fair in Killorglin. Photograph: Eamonn Keogh/MacMonagle.

does require referendum approval, and the new defence arrangements whose misrepresentation prompted so many women to vote No.

Dáil approval, with opt-outs being put to a referendum later, would require the agreement of all 26 of our EU partners, but it could allow all member states to proceed with the new arrangements for the European elections next year as well as adopting technical changes in the way the union makes decisions. A deal to allow all states retain an EU commissioner would be easier to achieve under Lisbon than under the Nice Treaty and could be a selling point of the deal.

With the essential administrative elements of the treaty coming into effect for all 27, and Ireland excluded from the areas that caused the electorate most worry, time could be taken to allow Irish voters to consider some of the issues that generated so much heat during the campaign. Whether or not we finally approve them will not matter to the rest of Europe one way or another, just as the Danish opt-outs after the defeat of the Maastricht referendum there only affects that country.

Such an approach poses huge legal difficulties, never mind political problems of a high order. The Government's expert legal advice is that it cannot be done, as there are legal problems at EU level about opting out of elements of the treaty after the event, never mind potential legal problems at home in the inevitable event of a Supreme Court challenge.

Still, it should not be beyond the wit of constitutional lawyers to devise a solution to the problem. Our EU partners may not like it but for them, as well as for us, it is a far less worse option than the prospect of the treaty collapsing altogether. If the price that Ireland requires to ratify is some fancy legal footwork at European level then it should be possible to come up with a formula, empty or otherwise.

Of course the Government would also have political hell to pay for going the legislative route but it might not be nearly as bad as some Ministers

think. After all the main reason given for voting No was that people didn't understand the treaty.

In that case a good proportion of the electorate might be relieved if the Dáil took on the responsibility of dealing with it, rather than opting for another long drawn out and confused public debate about issues people cannot, or will not, understand.

The Fine Gael leader, Enda Kenny, faces almost as big a test of his political credibility on the issue as the Taoiseach.

There is a great deal of understandable disillusionment in Fine Gael that after acting in the national interest and supporting the Government call for a Yes vote the referendum defeat was followed by a slide in the party's support in the opinion polls.

The reaction of some in Fine Gael has been to suggest total disengagement from the issue and to act as if it is now a Government problem. There is no indication that Enda Kenny is attracted by this short-sighted approach but he needs to get a grip on his party and lead from the front. Fine Gael has everything to gain and nothing to lose by coming forward with its own proposals about how to get the country out of the mess, rather than reacting to whatever Fianna Fáil ultimately decides to do.

During the Dáil debate on the Referendum Bill, back in the spring, Fine Gael Tipperary South TD Tom Hayes asked why it was necessary to amend the Constitution at all in order to ratify the Lisbon Treaty.

Since the referendum defeat many others across the political spectrum have begun to ask the same question and discuss whether there might be a legislative way forward.

There is an opportunity here for Kenny to take the lead and propose the solution. In doing so he would not just show that he is prepared to put the national interest first – he would also demonstrate that he has what it takes to be a genuine alternative taoiseach come the next election campaign.

Passing of a True Gentleman of Politics

Noel Whelan

One of my political heroes died this week. He was 73 and slipped away on Monday after a lengthy struggle with cancer.

It was through him that I became active in politics. My first political memory is asking for votes for him over a car-mounted loudspeaker at the age of nine when he was a candidate for Dáil Éireann in 1977. He was one of three Fianna Fáil candidates, polled 5,200 votes and came close to winning a third seat for the party in what was then a four-seat Wexford constituency. He failed to secure the party nomination for the 1981 Dáil election but did later serve two terms on Wexford County Council.

His own political activity began as a teenager erecting posters with his father for national collections or during election campaigns. In his twenties he became chairman of his local cumann and in the days before constituency offices was the contact point for Dr Jim Ryan, the then local Fianna Fáil TD. In his thirties he was asked to become chair of

A car lies on its side beside the Arra river in Newcastlewest, Co. Limerick, following a flash flood. Photograph: Liam Burke/Press 22.

the party organisation in the New Ross area and, since there were then no term-limits for party offices, served in that position for over three decades. He was later chairman of the party's countywide organisation and director of elections for numerous contests.

In many ways, his politics was merely an extension of his community involvement. In the days before the phrase 'active citizenship' was coined, he engaged in hyperactive citizenship. Long before governments commissioned reports on voluntarism, he had spent a lifetime immersed in and at times leading a spectrum of community activities in his local parish, Ballycullane, in south Wexford.

The fact that neighbouring townlands produced world champion tug-of-war teams and ploughmen was due in part to his role in organising and fundraising for these activities.

There were causes and organisations where his contribution was wider than the parish, sometimes countywide and even national. After politics, ploughing was his passion. As well as chairing the local and county ploughing organisation he had been a director of the National Ploughing Association and, for 35 years, spent five weeks each autumn planning the site for national ploughing championships.

As a community leader and then county councillor he was among the first to whom locals would turn when they wanted help with some bureaucratic process. Those who disparage the localism or clientelism of Irish politics could learn from watching this service close up and seeing the need which it fulfilled. This week at his wake hundreds of people told of how he had helped them at difficult times in their lives.

Time management was another of his skills. He found time for all this political and community activity while working as the local postman, helping to run a local post office and country shop and rearing a family of nine sons and three daughters.

He told me once of his personal memories of meeting de Valera and Jack Lynch a number of times. He was a big fan of Charlie Haughey and, in fact, was one of those party officers whose invitations to functions created the 'chicken supper' circuit which sustained Haughey during his wilderness years. In the 1980s he defended Haughey resolutely against the gripes of opponents but in the late 1990s was one of those devastated by the McCracken tribunal revelations. I, on the other hand, had always been sceptical of the Haughey myth. We differed too in our views of Albert Reynolds, of whom I was, and remain, a big fan. We were *ad idem* in our assessment of Bertie Ahern. We both felt that Cowen was the right choice to be the next leader.

We had many long chats about politics. While we differed on some issues, that was mainly a generational thing. He was, it appears, a fan of this column but apparently, as a friend of his told me on Tuesday, usually felt it wasn't 'Fianna Fáil enough'. In my years working in politics and when I was a candidate, he was my closest political mentor from whom I learnt a few key political lessons.

Among the most important of these was the need for moderation in politics and respect for the views of others. He was committed to his politics but never aggressive about it. He was a gentleman of politics in its truest sense – too gentle for his own good at times. He had the reserve and patience to hold his tongue when others mouthed off – so when he had something to say, it was generally listened to and respected. There was no antagonism in him and there was certainly no antagonism in his politics. Indeed some of his strongest political and indeed personal friendships were from across the political divide.

As well as being a political hero and mentor, he was my dad, and of course also a hero and mentor in so many other ways. Last Wednesday thousands of people from five surrounding parishes and further afield turned out to bid farewell to Seamus Whelan, to comfort us, to recognise his legacy and to acknowledge his contribution.

Following a Trail of Tears left by War's Death and Destruction

Lara Marlowe, in Gori

There was something Biblical about the three old men who hobbled down Georgia's national highway, a few kilometres southeast of the battered town of Gori. Perhaps it was the grey beards, walking stick and leather sandals.

'I have nothing to say. You cannot help us,' said the first man. Houshangi, the second old man, wore a black beret and carried a small cloth bundle. He hoped the fleet of ambulances that had just sped by – to collect the morning harvest of dead and wounded from the daily bombardment of Gori – would pick him up on their way back to Tbilisi.

'We started walking yesterday morning, from Khourtha, in the Liakhvi Valley, near Tshkhinvali [the "capital" of south Ossetia],' Houshangi recounted.

'We walked 50km already. The grads [missiles] drove us out. In the village next to ours, there were 10 dead people, and no one to bury them. There was a whole family of five killed with their animals.' Houshangi pulled a plaid handkerchief from his trousers pocket and wiped tears from his gentle, weather-beaten face.

Despite the 30-degree heat, he wore three shirts under his wool jacket. 'I thought we'd have to sleep outside,' he explained. 'I rested under a tree, but I couldn't sleep. I was the last man to leave my village.'

A farmer, Houshangi already missed what he called his 'good house' and fruit trees.

Russian soldiers on top of an armoured vehicle on the outskirts of Gori, northwest of the Georgian capital, Tbilisi. Photograph: Sergei Grits/AP.

Refugees from Georgian villages on the border with South Ossetia make their way to Tbilisi. Photograph: Lara Marlowe.

Tensions with his Ossetian neighbours started nearly two decades ago, he said, when the Soviet Union began disintegrating.

'Four years ago, Ossetians kidnapped men from my village and cut them into pieces. I left everything, because I am afraid the same thing will happen to me.'

The trail of tears continued. Elen and Shekmadin had walked for two hours. They pointed towards their village of Kheltubani, in a grove of trees east of Gori. 'See The World,' said the cheap carrier bag they set down beside them, over an image of the Brooklyn Bridge and an American eagle.

'We're just afraid of the shelling,' said Elen. She spoke in short sentences, between sobs. 'We had to leave our horse and cow. We'll sleep in the hills tonight, and try to go back tomorrow.'

Gia, a bachelor farmer with a peeling, sun-burned face, walked with Elen and Shekmadin. 'I left my mother and father behind, because she is ill and cannot walk. I didn't want to leave, but she made me go, and I feel guilty,' he said.

'I'll return as soon as I can. The last thing the told me was: "Take care of yourself. Don't worry about us".'

When the war started, Gia was called up by the Georgian army. For three days, he guarded Georgian positions in Ossetian villages. But the Georgians were driven back, and he was demo-bilised. Was he sorry that the army gave up?

'It's better not to have more people killed,' Gia concluded.

In Moscow, President Dmitry Medvedev had just announced the end of Russian operations.

Someone cried out. Three Russian attack helicopters darted up the valley, like dragonflies over water. Blinding flashes shot out of each chopper: rockets apparently aimed at electricity or communications pylons. The freshly cut hay, some of it in bales, caught fire in surrounding fields and burned for hours.

Two men rode by on a tractor. Four others perched atop a lorry carrying bedding, an electrical generator and a television.

'I volunteered for the army, but they didn't want me,' the driver told me.

Around the next corner, I found further evidence of the Georgian army's debacle: armoured personnel carriers by the roadside, hatches open. Abandoned artillery pieces.

Two army lorries straddled the road where they'd collided in panic during a bombardment. More lorries, one with its bed stacked with munition boxes. An abandoned fuel tanker. The charred remains of a tank and civilian car hit by a Russian missile on Monday.

'JStalin's Home Country,' said the sign at the entrance to Gori. Both Ossetians and Georgians claim 'Uncle Joe' as their own. It was he who created the problem, by 'giving' South Ossetia to his native Georgia.

The Stalin museum, birth cottage, private railway car and Saddam-like statue stand untouched.

But the town has nonetheless taken the brunt of Russian bombardment, for three reasons: it sits astride Georgia's main east-west highway, is home to three military bases and is within striking distance of Tskhinvali, the even worse destroyed 'capital' of South Ossetia.

War fell suddenly upon Gori last Friday morning.

'Everything was normal. The cafes and restaurants were open. Nobody imagined these things could happen outside the combat zone,' a university student who fled the town told me.

Yesterday, Gori was a ghost town, save for a horseman galloping down the main street and a crazed old man who warned us, 'The Russians are coming'. Three times, Gori was reported to have 'fallen' to the Russians, who have not in fact entered the town.

Two ageing couples sat beneath a grape arbour, in front of an old house on Gori's main street. 'There's no bakery, nothing to eat, no electricity, no news. When they shell, we go to the cellar,' Levon (77) summarised the situation.

Jagged panes of glass lay in the flowerbeds, among the marigolds. 'There's absolutely no problem whatsoever between Ossetians and Georgians,' Levon said – a dubious assertion I've heard many times here. 'It's the Russians who make trouble between us.'

On the main square, one half expected to see blood or hear screams – some sign of the deaths of five people, including the Dutch cameraman Stan Storimans, in what appears to have been a mortar bombardment two hours earlier.

There was broken glass and rubble at the post office, town hall, university and television station. Two houses burned next to the theatre. In silence.

On the way out of Gori, I saw people siphoning petrol from the reservoir of an abandoned station. A few miles down the road to Tbilisi, I turned down an offer to celebrate Mr Medvedev's ceasefire with farmers, over a bottle of Georgian wine. They may have raised their glasses too soon. The Georgians accused the Russians of shelling four villages yesterday afternoon.

SATURDAY, 16 AUGUST 2008

Foot to the Floor

John Cassidy takes the ferry to Cherbourg, then heads for Murcia, on the southeast coast of Spain, a drive of 1,800km

Captive in a stuffy, 1980s classroom. Exact year and location undisclosed. The words of Robert Louis Stevenson impinge on my consciousness: 'I travel not to go anywhere, but to go. I travel for travel's sake. The great affair is to move.'

John Cassidy and his wife, Helen, having reached La Manga in Spain.

For once I'm paying attention and am in total agreement. Even way back then the phrase made perfect sense, a satori moment.

Now, as myself and my wife, Helen, bowl along an empty stretch of French motorway, roof down, evening sun shining, the still-warm breeze and the happy burble of the engine tickling our ear lobes, those words strike home.

We have decided to take the car to Spain, taking the ferry from Rosslare to Cherbourg. Our final destination is Mazarrón, in Murcia on Spain's southeast coast, a total distance of 1,809km (1,124m) from the ferry port.

We are often asked why we take the car on holiday rather than hop on a flight and hire at the other end. Our response is that driving is still an enjoyable experience on the Continent. There are fewer half-wit drivers.

Another factor in favour of a sea crossing is the increasingly stressful nature of air travel. Baggage charges and limits, time-sapping security checks, lost luggage, increased check-in times, interminable hanging around terminals, lack of leg room, the threat of thrombosis, narrower berths along with wider girths – you name it.

We booked a small villa in Mazarrón online weeks beforehand, through *www.holidaylettings. co.uk*. Thanks to the recent property-buying splurge in Spain there is a wealth of choice. Our two-bedroom villa cost €552 for 19 days and boasted a satellite TV, DVD player, cooker, microwave, washing machine, parking and rooftop sun terrace.

Our crossing from Rosslare to Cherbourg took about 18 hours (including an hour's delay), but once ensconced in our cosy cabin we relaxed and were effectively on holiday. (Our Roscoff-to-Rosslare return was quicker, at about 14 hours.)

We arrived in Cherbourg at 6 p.m., then drove 416km to our stopover, the Campanile hotel in the French town of La Roche sur Yon.

At first the road from Cherbourg is a slow single carriageway. Once on the A84 dual carriageway to Rennes, however, progress is swift, as it is on the N137, its continuation to Nantes. Speed limits are 110km/h, but both roads are toll-free. In fact, the first toll we encounter is on the A83 south of Nantes, which connects to Bordeaux and the south via the A10.

After a good night's rest in the Campanile we set off early the next morning in the direction of Zaragoza, which involves skirting Bayonne-Biarritz and Irun before bearing southeast by San Sebastián, in the Basque Country.

The spectacular roller-coaster roads looping around these conurbations are, unfortunately, punctuated by a cluster of toll stops that spoil the experience somewhat.

Having said that, there were still some stunning views on offer when you get time to look up from your coin tray, as the motorway twists and turns around the shoulders of the Pyrenees.

The AP68 to Zaragoza is a quiet, sweeping motorway that lifts you over the back of Spain's northern interior and sets you down again for the descent to the Mediterranean.

Spectacular mountain views and bridges over deep ravines compete with the road ahead for your attention, and you need to concentrate to take the A2 south towards Madrid, before striking off southeast via the N234 and around Valencia on to the A7.

Finally, and with some stops to restore feeling and circulation to our compressed behinds, we

Splash of summer: Laura Allen and Julie McGreggor in Cabra, Dublin, after flash flooding. Photograph: Alan Betson.

circled Alicante and Murcia, and arrived in Mazarrón that night.

'The Region of Murcia, home of the sun' said our tourist map, but we'd never have guessed it as we arrived at the villa. Unfortunately, this is a recurring theme for us, our last two Spanish trips having been accompanied by downpours that even Shakespeare might have baulked at. On both occasions we were assured that Spain had never seen such inclement weather.

Before emerging from the car we wondered how long it would be before somebody spun the unusually-bad-weather line. It took two minutes for the nice woman with the key to say: 'We've had lovely weather until today . . .'

We nodded ruefully, entered the villa, turned on our satellite TV in the hope of a promising forecast and were treated to images of Spain under a mass of black-cloud symbols while Ireland basked under clear skies.

Weather aside – and it did get a bit better – the beauty of this sort of holiday is that you can make it to measure. You can book two, or even three, villas in different regions if you want.

We chose this spot because we had been here in our younger days, when comfort meant finding a rockless bit of ground to pitch a tent on. That's some 16 years ago, but a cursory look around shows that a lot of development has taken place since then.

All in all, this holiday was a mixed bag. The weather was a let-down, but there were some nice sunny days. The area we stayed in was very heavily developed, but what part of the southern Spanish coast is not?

The better beaches were pleasant and well kept but busy; relatively secluded ones tended to be stony. There were some marked walks and trails but not as many as we've seen in the south of France.

At the end it was time to climb back into the car and get some serious kilometres under us. For the return journey we were taking the ferry from Roscoff to Rosslare. The journey to Roscoff was 33km shorter overall than to Cherbourg, overnighting in Niort, 465km from Roscoff.

Ah, yes. As Robert L pointed out, sometimes to move really is the great affair.

SATURDAY, 16 AUGUST 2008

'I'm Pulling all the Right Faces, Like You Do at School When You're Listening to Some Teacher Banging On and You Haven't a Bog'

Ross O'Carroll-Kelly

This ever happen to you? You meet a bird you like, as in really like, to the point where you go on three dates with her – and yet you haven't the slightest clue what her name is.

I mean, yeah, she might have dropped it when you were introduced – but you were too busy knocking out unbelievable one-liners to hear it and now it's gone, gone like the seven pints of Vitamin H and the kebab you grabbed from Ishmael's while walking Baggot Street looking for an Andy McNab.

See, I blame texting. In the old days, roysh, you met a bird, maybe gave her your number, then three nights – always three, so as never to look John B – she'd ring you and go, hi, this is Jennifer, Suzanne, Danneel, Verruca, whatever.

And you'd either go, 'Yeah, I remember you – do you fancy getting a big of nosebag during the week?' Or you'd go, 'Sorry, Babes – your ticket said One Night Only.'

But texting has, like, ruined the ort of conversation. Now it's all, 'Dinnr thurs peploes@8?' with no actual, like, interaction, which is one of the things I was always amazing at.

Nils Olav, an Edinburgh Zoo penguin and colonel-in-chief of the Norwegian King's Guard, inspects his regiment in Edinburgh, where he was presented with a medal. Photograph: David Cheskinpa.

This bird, I stuck her in the old Wolfe as EP, because she was a ringer for Ellen Pompeo. Still is, I think, looking at her across the table in Bang Café.

She's telling me that the economy was bound to go into recession, propped up, as it was, on the precarious hulk of a property market that had lost all sense of reason, while I'm pulling all the right faces, like you do at school when you're listening to some teacher banging on and you haven't a bog whether you're in chemistry or French.

'Forget all that,' I go. 'Let's talk about the real world. Your name – it's beautiful. Is there, like, a story behind it?' which you have to admit is a clever, I suppose, ruse.

But she looks at me like I'm off my chops. 'A story?' she goes. 'It's hardly unusual.' Must be something plain then. Lucy. Joan. Sandra.

'Although my brother calls me Woo,' she goes. I'm like, 'Woo?'

'Yeah, he couldn't pronounce my name when he was a baby so he called me Woo. It sort of, like, stuck?'

Woo. Koo? Lou? She asks me a question, roysh, about my work as an ortist and I tell her I like to paint what's within, then I order the recession-busting rib of black Angus beef and she asks for the pan roasted scallops, but as, like, a main?

I whip out my phone while she studies the cocktail list and I text JP. He knows her name. He spent two hours chatting her up in Krystle before I breezed over and wiped his eye. I hope he's not bitter.

I'm like, 'Dude im in bang wit dat bird from2 saturdays ago – need2 kno her name!' but he just goes, 'Lol,' which means he is still hurting.

She orders a strawberries and cream martini, roysh, and tells me that I'm not to let her have a second one because she's got Vinyasa in the morning. That could be breakfast, a form of exercise or a child from a previous relationship for all I know – or care.

Vinyasa. Vanessa. Valora. Valgerdr. This thing is actually killing me and I'm about to ask her straight out when she all of a sudden stands up and announces that she's going for a hit and miss.

So off she goes, roysh, and I'm looking down and I notice that she's left her red Lulu Guinness clutch bag on the floor.

It's like, re-sult! Her ID will be in that. A credit cord or something. But I've got to be quick.

I try to, like, hook it with my foot but I'm getting looks from one or two tables, so what I do instead is I get down under the table, on my actual hands and knees, and grab it.

I'm about to, like, open the clasp when I find myself, all of a sudden, staring at a pair of red Miu Mius, which happen to match it quite well. Yeah, she came back for the bag.

'What are you doing?' I hear her go and I end up saying the first thing that comes into my head. 'I, em, dropped a contact lens.'

'Oh my God,' she goes, 'I didn't know you wore contact lenses,' and she suddenly drops to her knees and joins me. 'They're not the disposable ones, I take it.'

I'm there, 'No, er, the other kind. Price of vanity, huh?'

The next thing, roysh, one of the waiters is over. 'Is everything okay?'

'He's lost a contact lens,' she goes. 'Watch where you put your feet.'

So the next thing, he gets down and storts, like, helping us? Pretty much the entire restaurant is looking now.

She's going, 'You know, you really should think seriously about using the disposable ones.'

A second waiter, who brings our Gungas, joins us and suddenly there's, like, four of us down there, combing the floor for a contact lens that doesn't even exist.

I'm about to say fock it, doesn't matter, I'll just keep one eye closed, when all of a sudden I find myself staring at a pair of Dubes. Then a familiar voice goes, 'Hi, Ross – how the hell are you?' It's JP.

I quickly stand up and I'm there, 'I'm Kool and the Gang, my friend,' and, well, you could have knocked me over with a feather when he turned around and went, 'I wasn't talking to you – I was talking to your date.'

Ross. It's her name too. Well, actually, it's Roz, but how could I have forgotten that? 'What are you looking for anyway?' JP goes.

I'm like, 'My, em, contact lens,' and I give him a big wink.

He smiles at me, winks back and, just as I'm thinking what a legend he is for coming through for me like that, he goes, 'But Ross,' meaning me, 'you don't ever wear contact lenses.'

WEDNESDAY, 20 AUGUST 2008

Beach Belles Serve Up a Treat

Tom Humphries

We have seen the future. It wears a bikini. Just about. Everybody say yeah! Says the PA guy whose accent places him as coming from some place mid-Atlantic.

Yeah! we say. Louder! He says. Everyone in that mid-Atlantic spot is hearing impaired.

YEAH! Are you watching? Are you watching, Are you watching Chairman Mao? Revolving quickly in your mausoleum down in Tiananmen Square no doubt. There's cultural revolutions and then there is beach volleyball.

It's just before 9 a.m. in Chaoyang Park in Beijing and 12 women wearing dolls house napkins as swimwear are effectively lapdancing an early morning crowd into wakefulness. It's an easy sell. The gals are dancing on sand specially imported from Canada for it's fine, uhm, sandy qualities. They are striking poses that are still mortal sins in many nations and they are hitting beats with their impressively twitchy asses. Everybody is grooving into the morning except the PA guy who has had too many espressos when kick-starting his own day.

YEAH! YEAH! Enter stage left, surfing into this scene of quintessential California-ness, *The Irish Times*. Less surfing actually than furtively huffing and puffing up to the media tribune. Glancing about terrified of being fingered as a voyeur rather than a serious beach volleyball pundit, *The Irish Times* gazes down at the dancing girls and then holds his little finger aloft against the dazzling morning sun. There is more fat hanging from that chubby little pinkie than from all 12 of the dancing girls put together.

Everybody say, YEAH! *The Irish Times* being as extravagantly overdressed (it could rain) as Nanook of the North in a sauna duly finds a seat for himself. An Olympic volunteer comes running with a bottle of ice-cold water and proffers it as if it was emergency first aid. *The Irish Times* just

Tom Humphries endures another gruelling day at the Olympics forced to observe Misty May-Treanor (right) and Kerri Walsh of the United States celebrating winning a point during their semi-final against Brazil. Photograph: Carlos Barrira/Reuters.

From the horse's mouth: in the stables at the 84th annual Connemara Pony Show in Clifden, Co. Galway.

giggles. This is work? LEMME HEAR YA! YEAH! YEAH! Reading the guilty mind of *The Irish Times* the mid-Atlantic guy makes a pertinent point.

'There are people outside who are dying to get in here,' he roars 'but you are here! Sooooooo CEL – E – BRATE!' And the music goes thump-thump-thump. Twelve asses on the sand go bump-bump-bump and, well, seeing as how it's actually a human rights issue and people are dying and stuff, everybody celebrates. Including *The Irish Times* who mops his brow.

Party style. Totally.

'Welcome the athletes!' says the mid-Atlantic guy as if the athletes had suddenly just turned up at a keg party and needed high-fiving. Mid-Atlantic guy's Chinese counterpart chimes in with some exclamation that has made him so excited he actually sounds like a tape recording being played way too fast.

YEAH! The athletes are beach volleyball royalty. And goddesses of the morning. The Americans and reigning Olympic queens Kerri Walsh and Misty May-Treanor are lightly tanned with lean tummies all brown and hard like skillets and they make the dancing girls seem overdressed and dowdy.

Kerri and Misty are famous for locking themselves around each other and rolling all lithe and sweaty and sensuous in the sand for an unseemly amount of time after winning gold in Athens in 2004. In the media guide, Kerri describes those golden, groundbreaking sporting moments as 'totally spastic'. Which sort of takes the good out of it.

Beach royalty Kerri and Misty may be but even they look like rustic hicks compared to their opponents in this semi-final. Brazilians! Each of them from Rio. Only Rio trumps California in the beach babe stakes. Renata and Taita (for it is they) share many commendable qualities with their city sister, The Girl from Ipanema.

(Cue shocking flash for *The Irish Times* of a desolate and windswept Dublin Olympics. Dollymount strand. Mr Whippy soundtrack and an Irish beach volleyball team both of whom share many qualities with Biddy Mulligan. Vision begone.) Renata Ribeiro lists her hobbies as dancing and watching films. Taita Rocha though says she likes to read. We hope the others don't ostracise her for this. Kerri Walsh, after all, lists 'playing outside' among her hobbies. Bless her.

Anyway, once the athletes have been welcomed, the game which is an Olympic quarter-final and a pretty big deal gets going and sadly for *The Irish Times*, who aloft in his media tribune seat just left of the sun is still snickering in a pool of his own sweaty cynicism, the athleticism and skill takes the breath away. You could actually make an argument for covering this sport without it even being an occasion of sin. No, you could.

The game is a cinch to follow (surprisingly for those of us who thought it would be chess on sand). Each set is up to 21. Best of three sets. And to be sure to be sure the big scoreboard in the corner of the beach area is a neon version of the PA guy.

Kerri hits a spike and the scoreboard says, WOW! Misty makes a save and the scoreboard flashes, NOT IN MY HOUSE! Kerri and Misty overwhelm the Brazilians throughout the first set. They are like, totally, dominant.

Every time there is a break in play a new pulsating dance track breaks out at deafening volume on the PA, drawing the dancing girls onto the sand like moths to a flame. *The Irish Times* tries to take notes on the American pair's solid back court play but a Brazilian girl wearing what could grow up to be a very small skirt keeps jumping up and dancing two rows away.

'This is so, like, you know, covering a league game in Birr,' *The Irish Times* hollers to her. She shoots a look back which says, 'Whatever.' 'Not!' adds *The Irish Times* with perfect timing. Ha.

Minutes later Misty and Kerri are almost done with the Brazilians in straight sets. Little wonder Misty and Kerri aren't so tanned. They don't stay out here long enough.

'Are you kidding me?' roars the PA guy when they get to match point.

'ON YOUR FEET,' he orders the crowd. *The Irish Times,* claiming media exemption from mass callisthenics, keeps scribbling questions for the mixed zone. (First to you Kerri, if I said you had a beautiful body, would you hold it against me?) 'Stand up please,' says the scoreboard a little more politely. Everyone is on their feet now. It is a rally. A festival. An entertainment. An experience.

Misty and Kerri finish the second set and they march off with a flourish but, foolishly we think, forego their lascivious rolling in the sand routine. Everybody goes crazy anyway.

Minutes later all four athletes come to the media mixed zone.

We had expected them to get dressed for this chore but, as the media handout for beach volleyball says, the girls don't wear bikinis because they have to. They wear them because they like to. You go girls! Anyway not since we interviewed Páidí Ó Sé post-match in Mullingar wearing nothing but his football socks (Páidí that is) have we had so much flesh distracting us from our inquiries.

Misty, we notice, has an intriguing roman numeral tattoo just at the top of her ass but she also has a frightening leonine intensity about her which drives us in to the welcoming aura of Kerri.

Kerri describes herself as 'six feet of sunshine' and she has that California way of inserting a question mark after about? Every third word? And today she is like? Psyched? We are just enchanted.

'I wish I could smile? when I am nervous?,' she says thoughtfully to us, as we gaze back at her sympathetically wondering if we could stage a fundraiser to aid research into her awful condition. 'But I can't? But now I am happy? I can smile? We want to go to the final now? And kick butt? We had great energy? Great teamwork?'

Biting our lip, we notice that Kerri has an intriguing and tiny tattoo about six inches below her belly button where her nut brown stomach disappears into her dazzling swimming briefs. We lose track of what Kerri is saying as we try but fail to decipher the tiny letters.

(Later in the media centre in the interests of journalistic rigour we Google the words 'Kerri' 'Walsh' 'tattoo' but are directed to a site which promises to show Kerri in the shower. We sustain an injury to little finger slamming laptop shut in horror.) Anyway Kerri keeps beaming at us. Her right shoulder bears scars from the three operations she has endured for a troublesome rotator cuff and we reflect that she is actually a serious, one million dollar a year athlete with almost balletic skills. And of course she is also six feet of sunshine.

'Kerri,' we say as the novel excitement of the day wells up inside us all at once. Her eyes bestow themselves on *The Irish Times* like morning rays on a lumpen land.

'Kerri? Will you, like, marry me.' 'Yeah. Like, totally? Sweaty dude' she beams. The scoreboard flashes instantly, Way Cool! We have seen the future. It is six feet of sunshine with a tattoo.

SATURDAY, 23 AUGUST 2008

The Great Leap Westward

Mary Fitzgerald

'NI HAO, NI HAO,' yell the Zambian schoolchildren, as they spot a visitor walking past the scrubby patch of earth where they are skipping in a circle. These are the expansive grounds of the Sino-Zam Friendship Hospital in Kitwe, one of the main towns in the dusty copper belt of northern Zambia.

The Mandarin greeting can also be heard echoing through the spotless corridors of the main building where Chinese men, grimy from working in the nearby Chinese-owned mine, queue for treatment alongside local women who chatter loudly as they bounce babies on their laps. A sign directs patients to the acupuncture section. In one room hung with Chinese medical charts, Zhang Shuzeng, a gynaecologist from Hunan province, struggles to piece her sparse English together. She came to Zambia to seek a new life after her son left for university two years ago. 'It's an adventure,' she smiles.

Dr Zhang's personal foray into a continent she admits knowing very little about before leaving Hunan is just one of the thousands of stories that make up what is undoubtedly the most significant and intriguing development in sub-Saharan Africa since the end of the Cold War – the arrival of China as heavyweight investor and political player.

Nowhere in the world is China's rapid rise to power more evident than in Africa, observes Chris Alden, a lecturer at the London School of Economics who has written a book charting the Middle Kingdom's push into a continent many in the West had written off as a hopeless charity case.

One former US assistant secretary of state has called it a 'tsunami'. Others have coined the term 'ChinAfrica' to describe a phenomenon that is redrawing the economic and geopolitical map.

The figures that outline the contours of this relationship make for astounding reading. Between 2000 and 2007, trade between China and Africa shot up from €6.75 billion to more than €47 billion. China has now overtaken Britain and France to become the continent's second-largest trading partner after the US. Beijing hopes that trade will amount to more than €67 billion by 2010, and many analysts believe China will have surpassed US trade with Africa by then. Since 2000, China has cancelled billions in bilateral debt owed by African countries.

China's Export-Import Bank plans to spend some €13.5 billion in Africa in the next three years – an amount roughly on a par with the sum the World Bank expects to spend there in the same time. Last year, the China-Africa Development

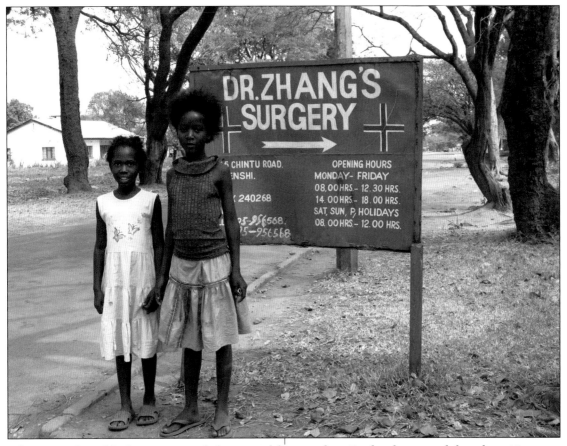

Chinese-run clinics like the one signposted above, in Ndola in northern Zambia, have opened throughout Africa offering traditional Chinese medicine. Photograph: Mary Fitzgerald.

Fund was established, promising to dispense €3.37 billion to support sectors such as agriculture, manufacturing, energy and transportation in Africa in addition to encouraging Chinese entrepreneurs to consider setting up business there.

Travel to any country below – and a handful above – the Sahara and the proof of China's rapid penetration of Africa is everywhere: Chinese construction workers rebuilding post-war Angola, Chinese loggers in the Central African Republic and Mozambique, Chinese farmers in Uganda, Chinese geologists in oil-rich Sudan and Chad, Chinese hoteliers in Sierra Leone, Chinese textile merchants in Kenya and Lesotho, Chinese traders in Malawi and Nigeria.

At present, some 800 Chinese state-owned or state-controlled companies are operating in Africa, with China's Export-Import Bank funding more than 300 projects scattered throughout more than 36 countries. Last year, Xinhua, the state news agency, estimated that more than 750,000 Chinese nationals are working or living for extended periods in Africa, reflecting China's deepening ties with the continent.

In cities across Africa, you will find Chinese restaurants, clinics, massage parlours, casinos and pharmacies selling traditional Chinese remedies. Last year, the Industrial and Commercial Bank of China (ICBC) purchased a 20 per cent stake in South Africa's Standard Bank, the largest in the continent, for $5.5 billion (€3.7 billion).

Pagoda-like structures have popped up in several countries – Zimbabwean president Robert Mugabe's Chinese-built residence in Harare is one particularly ostentatious example. There are Chinese newspapers in South Africa and Chinese channels on African satellite television. On intercontinental plane trips, the in-flight announcements and entertainment are increasingly provided in Mandarin in addition to other languages.

On one level, China's growing engagement with Africa is easily explained. To power its booming economy, Beijing must source more raw materials and explore new markets for its manufactured goods. It's not surprising, then, that it turned to Africa, home to some of the world's richest mineral deposits including 90 per cent of its cobalt and platinum, 98 per cent of its chromium, 64 per cent of its manganese, half of its gold and one-third of its uranium.

But most of all, China is interested in Africa's pockets of oil. Chinese oil consumption is predicted to grow by at least 10 per cent annually for the foreseeable future. A third of the oil fuelling China's economy now comes from the continent. Angola has overtaken Saudi Arabia as China's main supplier of crude and Sudan sells some two-thirds of its oil to Beijing. China has also bought shares in Nigeria's oil stakes. Altogether, it has invested in more than 27 oil and gas projects in some 14 African countries.

In return for mining, logging and oil rights, Beijing has signed off on multi-billion dollar deals in the form of investment, soft loans and development aid. Much of this is funnelled into infrastructure projects.

Over the last decade, China has financed the building of roads, bridges, railways, dams, pipelines, airports, hospitals and parliament buildings across Africa. It has invested €2.2 billion in the construction of 10 hydropower plants which it says will boost power supply by 30 per cent – no mean feat in a region where millions live without electricity and those that do have it are plagued by blackouts.

The Chinese have also built phone networks in more than a dozen African countries and last year they launched a communications satellite into orbit for Nigeria. Of course, proper infrastructure where little or none existed before helps China extract and transport more efficiently the raw materials it craves, but analysts argue it can also provide a crucial stimulus to moribund local economies.

In April, the UN forecast that Africa would experience economic growth of 6.2 per cent this year, up from 5.8 per cent – its highest in three decades – last year in spite of a slowing world economy. Many attribute that growth in part to the shot-in-the-arm effect of Chinese investment and trade.

Last month, a World Bank report praised China's infrastructural investment in Africa, saying it was helping lift the continent out of poverty. No doubt, the report delighted the Chinese, who like to describe their courting of African countries as a 'win-win' situation for both sides.

Interviewing Chinese officials in Angola, Chad and Zambia over the last year, I soon discovered there is something of an official line in describing the relationship. It is always 'win-win', based on 'south-south co-operation', 'equality' and 'mutual interests' but is strictly one of 'non-interference' when it comes to the internal affairs of each country. There are usually references to China's long relationship with Africa to demonstrate that the two are 'all-weather friends'.

During the Ming Dynasty, the first Chinese ships sailed to Africa. According to legend, some traders settled in Kenya and married local women. In 2005, Beijing awarded a Kenyan girl a scholarship to study medicine after announcing it had confirmed her Chinese ancestry using DNA testing. During the Cold War, China sent thousands of doctors, engineers and technicians to the continent to help ground fledgling diplomatic relations. It built prestige projects like sports stadiums and government buildings, and opened its universities to African students. I met one product of that time in Chad – a young man whose Chadian father met his Chinese mother while studying in Beijing.

Zhang Shudong, economic counsellor at the Chinese embassy in Zambia's capital Lusaka, included another commonly held view in his assessment of the relationship. 'Africa and China are the same in that we are both developing countries. That makes it easier for us to understand each other in ways others may not,' he told me. 'We can share our experience of China's economic growth to help African countries develop their economies. We are like brothers and sisters who can grow together.'

In expanding its footprint across Africa, China has ventured where other investors fear to tread because of unrest, corruption, human rights abuses or sanctions. Take the conflict-ridden Democratic Republic of Congo (DRC), a country the World Bank ranks as the world's worst place to do business.

Last year, it signed a €4-billion deal with China in exchange for mining rights to some of the country's rich reserves of copper and cobalt. Beijing has promised €2.19 billion to resurrect DRC's mining sector and another €4 billion to build more than 6,500km of roads and railways. The package also includes the construction of two hydro-electric dams, more than 150 hospitals and health centres, a modernised sewage system for Kinshasa, two universities, a port and 5,000 public housing units.

For all the talk of mutual benefits and co-operation, however, there are many who question China's role in Africa. The issue of whether China is good for Africa in the long term is one that is endlessly debated on the continent.

Veronica Walsh from Navan (2nd place), model Ally Garvey from Bscene agency (winner) and Evelyn Moyles from Kildare (3rd place), winners of the Best-Dressed Lady competition at the RDS Dublin Horse Show. Photograph: Alan Betson.

Some argue that the way China does business – particularly its willingness to pay bribes as detailed by Transparency International, and its 'no strings attached' approach to economic support, which flies in the face of criteria set down by institutions like the World Bank and the International Monetary Fund – erodes efforts to tackle corruption and encourage transparency and good governance.

'China offers opportunities without constraints,' a Chadian journalist told me. 'We have a huge problem with corruption here and the risk with Chinese involvement is that corruption will grow because there are no controls.' In Angola, a portion of investment monies provided by China were found to have been siphoned off to fund political campaigns.

Human rights groups have deplored Beijing's willingness to deal with unsavoury regimes in countries such as Zimbabwe and Sudan. China has given Mugabe civilian and military aircraft and in its arms sales to Khartoum, campaigners charge, Beijing is effectively underwriting the conflict between Sudanese government forces and rebels in Darfur. Mugabe has been particularly effusive in his praise of China. 'We have turned east, where the sun rises, and given our backs to the West, where the sun sets,' he once declared.

Some commentators have noted that despite the rhetoric, there are often strings attached when it comes to doing business with China. One is the Taiwan issue. Severing ties with the island Beijing considers a rebel province is a definite prerequisite. In December, Malawi ceased its 40-year recognition of Taiwanese sovereignty in exchange for a multi-million dollar package from Beijing. Now only four African countries have diplomatic relations with Taiwan – Swaziland, Burkina Faso, Gambia and São Tomé e Príncipe.

Another 'string' is that the major infrastructure agreements often stipulate that Chinese firms, labour and materials are used. The reconstruction deal in Angola, for example, demands that Chinese workers make up 70 per cent of the labour. The practice of hiring Chinese over Africans is not just confined to infrastructure projects. The issue has even arisen in the Sino-Zam Friendship Hospital. Earlier this year, a government minister requested that the hospital recruit Zambian doctors, explaining that the lack of local doctors was causing Zambians to shun the facilities. In a letter to a newspaper, one local wrote: 'It's a pity that we have to beg foreigners to "consider" employing us in our own country.'

African critics also accuse Chinese companies of underbidding local firms and complain about the lax environmental and safety standards of some Chinese companies operating in the continent. Some of the most trenchant criticism can be found in Zambia, where an explosion at a Chinese-owned copper mine in 2005 killed 46 local workers. The resulting outrage was harnessed by a populist opposition leader who ran in the 2006 presidential elections on an explicitly anti-China platform.

Another frequently aired gripe is that Beijing has undermined or destroyed local industries by using the continent as a dumping ground for its manufactured goods. Traders selling African-sourced products and clothing at Zambia's Kamwala market told me they cannot compete with Chinese imports sold for less than cost price. But Beijing's defenders counter that cheap Chinese products have stretched African shoppers' limited budgets and given them access to consumer goods taken for granted in developed countries.

Two years ago, South African president Thabo Mbeki cautioned African countries against falling into a 'colonial relationship' with China. He warned that if Africa simply exported raw materials to China while importing Chinese manufactured goods, the continent could be 'condemned to underdevelopment'. This, he added, would just be a 'replication' of the relationship Africa had in the past with its colonial powers.

Several commentators argue that what Mbeki warned against is already happening. But talk of the Chinese becoming the new colonialists in Africa

The winner of the 2008 Rose of Tralee competition, Aoife Kelly from Tipperary. Photograph: Domnick Walsh/Eye Focus.

rankles with Chinese and African officials alike, particularly when, more often than not, it comes from Western sources. 'We only come here to do business,' China's ambassador to Angola, Zhang Bolun, told me. 'We have never colonised another country, so there is no reason to believe this argument that China is the new coloniser of Africa. I think it is a ridiculous notion.' Zhang Shudong in Lusaka believes the criticism stems largely from other powers' need to safeguard their own interests and influence in Africa.

'They want to reserve for themselves the resources and the market. Their attitude is: this is my field, why are you coming here?' Zambia's information minister Mike Mulongoti says African countries resent being lectured on their dealings with China, insisting there is no danger of a neo-colonial relationship developing. 'The Western world is doing a lot of business with China. What is good for the goose is good for the gander. We are in a hurry to develop, we will accept assistance but we will not accept colonialism from anyone.'

His colleague, Zambia's trade minister, Felix Mutati, puts it another way. 'When we were colonised by the West, what benefits did we get? What, in a physical form, did they leave for us? They extracted the commodities but they did not leave us with any infrastructure.

'If the new wave of colonisation is to build badly-needed infrastructure,' he adds sardonically, 'I think that type of colonisation is beneficial.'

Even someone like the former president of Botswana, Festus Mogae, who has been feted in the West for his country's impressive record on good governance and economic success, welcomes China's embrace of Africa. 'China treats us as equals, while the West treats us as former subjects,' he has said. 'That is the reality. I prefer the attitude of China to that of the West.'

And so the debate over China's engagement with Africa and its consequences for the continent rumbles on. Perhaps the attitude of most Africans can be summed up in the words of Macharia

Gaitho, managing editor of the *Daily Nation* newspaper in Kenya. 'As long as China is so willing to invest in Africa, we must not miss out on the bounty,' he has commented. 'But we must engage with our eyes wide open.'

SATURDAY, 23 AUGUST 2008

The Dubliner We Loved So Well

Culture Shock, by Fintan O'Toole

The last time I spoke to Ronnie Drew, he told me that what bothered him most about his cancer was looking in the mirror first thing in the morning. The hairless face looking back was a real terror. 'Do you know who I see?' And with all the studied nonchalance of that great rumbling Dublin drawl, he drew out the answer: 'Nos . . . fer . . . aaa . . . toooo!'

The vignette contained so much of his unique persona: the erudite reference to FW Murnau's expressionist vampire film; the deadpan Dublin humour that revels in the comic potential of misery; the proud, unrelenting refusal of sentimentality. He really did look like Nosferatu – a shorn, undead version of himself. By saying it himself, he was at once playing up the gruff, hard-chaw persona and displaying underneath it an extraordinary natural courtesy. It was a good-mannered and witty way of sparing everyone else the awkward task of telling him lies about how well he was looking.

By the time he was lying in state in his open coffin in the back room of his house in Greystones on Monday night, a small miracle had occurred. In his last weeks, his hair had returned – luxuriant and almost curly on top; flowing like an Old Testament prophet around his mouth and chin and down in a stately line onto his chest. The beard was back, and with it the Dubliner. It was as if Death himself, a little intimated perhaps, had reckoned against the

Ronnie Drew enjoying his day as parade marshal during the St Patrick's Day Parade in Dublin in 2006 — two years before his death from cancer. Photograph: Julien Behal/PA Wire.

wisdom of messing with Ronnie Drew's afterlife. The last image of him should be the familiar one of the wild balladeer. It wasn't all there was to him, and it was a role he tried hard to shrug off. But his fate was to be the great hairy bowsie of Irish culture, to embody the disrespectable, feckless freedom that was for so long the only kind we had.

He knew this himself. At one stage, late in his life, when he had become a kind of brand, a shortcut to authentic Dublinness, whatever that was supposed to be, he was doing a voiceover for an ad. The producer interrupted at one stage and said 'Ronnie, could you try to sound a bit more like . . . um . . .'

'Like Ronnie Drew, you mean?' said Ronnie. He had the self-awareness to know that sounding like Ronnie Drew was what he did for a living. The amazing thing was that that sound was so utterly distinctive, so much a force of nature, that it didn't really matter how it was sold or packaged. Even when he was being used to supply a sheen of authenticity, he was still ineffably authentic. Even if he was selling you something, the voice, and the attitude within it, told you that he really didn't give a damn whether you bought it or not.

In 'Tower of Song', Leonard Cohen has those wonderfully sardonic, self-deprecating lines: 'I was born like this, I had no choice/ I was born with the gift of a golden voice.' The joke, of course, is that he sings this in his monotonous, mournful drone. Ronnie Drew didn't have a golden voice either, and neither did have a choice. His singing was no thing of beauty. When he was with The Dubliners, his double act with Luke Kelly, whose voice really was golden, could almost have been designed to make listeners wonder whether this Drew fellow was a singer at all. But Drew belonged with Cohen and Bob Dylan and Neil Young in that select company of great singers who don't have great voices. Stuck with that strange, guttural, underground sound, like a fierce beast growling to itself in some distant forest, he had no choice but to be unique. He had to make his own noise and command people to listen to it.

When Ronnie Drew became a national figure with The Dubliners in the mid-1960s, we weren't particularly drawn to unique voices. The hunger was for smoothness, for cosmopolitanism, for a version of America. The Clancy Brothers made a huge breakthrough for Irish folk music, but it was the sweetness, the essential gentility of rural Tipperary and of Tommy Makem's 'Keady' that carried them through. Strange, angular Irish voices frightened us.

When the great Connemara singer Joe Heaney, a consummate artist, was staying with Liam Clancy in Dublin in the mid-1960s and was asked to open a folk concert at the Grafton cinema, he was, as Peggy Seeger recalled, 'booed off by this despicable crowd after the first two lines of his first song'. The hard thing for traditional Irish musicians and singers wasn't just making themselves palatable to an international audience. It was making themselves palatable in Ireland.

Ronnie Drew was an unpalatable singer. He was a hairy creature from the depths of every mother's nightmare. His mother-in-law, whose beautiful and refined daughter he stole away from middle-class respectability, referred to him, not by name, but simply as 'the minstrel'. And she was right. He was nothing but a classless, free-floating troubadour, with a guitar, a beard, a voice from the bowels of the earth and an insolent attitude.

Unlike the Clancys or Tommy Makem or Joe Heaney, he couldn't even claim to be a bearer of tradition who learned old songs at his mother's knee. The only sense in which he wasn't a minstrel was that minstrels were entertainers who set out to please. Ronnie gave the impression that the only person he wanted to please was himself.

Because he became 'Ronnie Drew', a seemingly permanent landmark on the cultural landscape, it is easy to miss the sheer improbability of his achievement, not just of popularity, but of the status of a national treasure. The chemistry of The Dubliners was a huge part of it, of course, but Drew himself was the centre of that great group – he explains them as much as they explain him.

What happened, and what made Ronnie Drew important, was that he found a way to be distinctive and authentic without being sentimental or romantic. He embodied a rootedness that was not at all about the past and all about a presence.

That presence was rough, raw and rebellious. But it was also – and this is what was missed by the dozens of Drew wannabes – immensely sophisticated. In *Ronnie Drew, September Song*, Sinéad O'Brien's superb recent documentary on him, seen on RTÉ's Arts Lives series, Drew said that he thought that he and The Dubliners had not done anything great but that he hoped they had been good. He was sufficiently well-read and intelligent to know that great is a word that belongs to the likes of James Joyce and Patrick Kavanagh. But instead of concluding that everything else could be rubbish, he truly valued the second order of cultural values – the ordinary, the commonplace, the songs and stories that most of us inhabit most of the time. He knew they could be truly good and he made them so.

If you listen to Ronnie Drew sing a song, you will notice that, for all the thick, rumbling echoes of his voice, his diction is crystal-clear. Every word is respected and cherished. He simply loved the language and he used it to tell stories. He knew that, when we hear stories well told, we listen because we want to know what happens next. He also knew that that is what ballads really are – narratives told in song. His gift was, simply and honestly, in the way he told them.

SATURDAY, 23 AUGUST 2008

Another Day, Another Egan Epic in Beijing

Tom Humphries, in Beijing

Kenny Egan climbs to the mountain top. Up there where the air is rare and only the bravest survive he strikes a Rocky pose and lets loose a handsome, high-wattage grin that lights the valleys below. It has been a long haul but tomorrow he fights in an Olympic final with every chance of coming away with the gold medal. Once again boxing salvages the Irish Olympic experience.

Egan, the Ireland team's captain and most gnarled warhorse, was the last into the ring yesterday, charged with the task of ending a series of defeats. He did so in style and with economy and with a touch of respect for the lineage which made him.

'I'm just proud to be an Irish boxer today,' he said afterwards, 'proud of what we have done and hopeful that all this will bring a few young fellas through the doors into boxing clubs to carry it on.'

Indeed there is something sweetly typical of the tight-knit Irish fight community in the fact that Egan's coach here in Beijing, Billy Walsh, is not only a close friend and long time room-mate of Michael Carruth, the last Irishman to win gold in the ring, but that Walsh remembers watching that gold-medal fight from Barcelona in Carruth's sitting-room in Drimnagh.

And standing beside him on that fevered morning was Carruth's uncle, the late Noel Humpson, the man who trained Egan from childhood right into the senior ranks. You pass it on and you pay it forward.

Egan's demolition of the Englishman Tony Jeffries was about the only thing that went precisely as planned on a mixed day for the Irish scrappers in the ring at the Workers' Gymnasium.

Egan, the third and last into the ring, never entertained the notion of settling for a bronze medal to fiddle with on the flight home. He took an early lead and never relinquished that advantage, doing as much damage to his opponent's system as to his morale with a series of well chosen lefts to the body that jarred the big Sunderland fighter.

The fight thereafter was an exercise in economy and wisdom. Egan threw maybe a dozen to 15 punches and landed 10 of them.

He won the second round by three and the third round by four and tapered off as usual, minimising risk to take the last round by two points.

In tomorrow's final he will fight China's Zhang Xiaoping, who scored a slightly surprising victory over the highly rated Kazakh Yerkebulan Shynaliyev in the other semi-final.

The Workers' Gymnasium was once again rattled by the chants of olé and reference to Athenry and environs made in song by a very large Irish contingent, which included many Olympic athletes now finished their events.

If there was pressure to be felt, Egan missed the point entirely.

'It's a sport at the end of the day,' he said when asked about fear. 'You just need to get in the ring when the time comes and enjoy it. That's what it's

all about. Enjoy the training. Enjoying the fighting. I looked up at the crowd when I came out . . . me brother, all the mates that travelled over here, I could see them all. That was great. I don't get to see them too much day by day. I'm here to do business. They are here to go on the p★★★ but I'm looking forward to hearing their war stories.'

Jeffries threw a large number of punches, very few of which landed. He caught Egan with one straight right beneath the eye but though the wound seemed to bleed slightly internally, he failed to open a cut or cause any real concern in the Irish camp, which let the game plan unfold as normal.

'I'm not wasting shots,' said Egan afterwards. 'That's what it is all about here. I throw the right hook sometimes. Sometimes a straight left. They

Ireland boxing team captain, Kenny Egan, celebrates after beating Tony Jeffries of Britain in their light-heavy-weight semi-final at the Beijing Workers' Gymnasium. Egan went on to take the silver medal after being beaten in the final by Zhang Xiaoping of China. Photograph: Lorraine O'Sullivan/Inpho.

get scores. I don't want to throw a dozen shots to score three or four. Throw four and score four.

'I have seven shots conceded in four bouts since I got here. I'm on my feet all the time, slipping and moving. My range is perfect.

'I'm avoiding the shots but inviting them.'

Egan had been content enough to keep matters tight in the first round and restricted himself to exploratory work with a few body shots. In the second, Jeffries opted to step up the aggression and paid the price, suffering a strong volley of counterpunches.

By the end the lead had stretched away remarkably for a man limiting his punches so stringently. Egan has perfected the art of just staying out of reach and Jeffries was frustrated and broken before the end.

Egan celebrated accordingly. He had watched his two compatriots lose their fights earlier in the day. Sutherland, in particular, had mystified him.

'I watched Darren today. He was happy with the bronze. Couldn't understand that but he had his own reasons, I'm sure. Up to himself. He has beaten that guy four times. I won't lecture him. I have a silver but I want more.'

So tomorrow will be another day of work in the epic career of Kenny Egan. He has seen Zhang fight in Chicago last year, where he went out early, and on tape here.

The Chinese is a big man, which Egan likes: 'A big man makes a big target and all the pressure will be on him.'

His routine for fights is settled now. He will weigh in early on the morning. He has kept his diet tight these past weeks and hasn't strayed more

Irish Olympic medal-winning boxers Darren Sutherland (Bronze, left), Kenny Egan (Silver) and Paddy Barnes (Bronze, right) back home in Dublin Airport with other members of the Irish Olympic team. Photograph: Alan Betson.

than a kilogram over. Then back to the team digs and breakfast with the coaches, when they will talk about Zhang for a few minutes.

They have the BBC in the village so as usual he will chill in front of the television accompanied now by the team psychologist.

'I don't talk boxing. Just talk s★★★. Just focus on the telly or whatever we are doing step by step. Might sleep for an hour and then. Onto the bus. More s★★★ talk. Same again. Warm up. Then into focus. I warm up two fights before my own fight with Zuar (Antia, technical coach), we do the pads and I work on all the specifics of the opponent. And that's it down and ready. Bandages and in you go.'

Bandages on and in you go with most of China and all of Ireland watching you. Another day in the life of Kenny Egan.

SATURDAY, 30 AUGUST 2008

Spotlight Turns to Republicans

Denis Staunton, in Denver, Colorado

As democrats left Denver yesterday after their national convention, many were feeling light-headed and a little disorientated – and not just because of the thinness of the air in the Mile High City. Over the previous four days, they had watched the leadership of their party pass from Bill and Hillary Clinton, who had dominated Democratic politics for 16 years, to Barack Obama, a politician who has spent only four years on the national stage.

On Thursday night, Obama accepted his party's presidential nomination before 80,000 people at a stadium event that felt as much like a music festival as a political rally. The supporters who waited for hours in queues stretching more than a mile into downtown Denver were rewarded with a speech that soared with inspiring rhetoric but was packed with policy detail and carried a sharp political punch.

On the 45th anniversary of Martin Luther King's 'I have a dream' speech, the first African-American to lead a major party into a presidential election roused his Democratic audience, moving many to tears.

'I cried my eyelashes off,' Oprah Winfrey said as she left the stadium. 'I think it's the most powerful thing I have ever experienced.'

Obama's *tour de force* reassured Democrats after a convention that had been dominated by the drama surrounding the Clintons and the need to unite the party after a bitter, 18-month primary campaign.

The convention began on Monday with a tribute to the ailing lion of the senate, Edward Kennedy, who was diagnosed with a brain tumour earlier this year, and a speech by Michelle Obama. Caricatured on conservative talk radio and in right-wing blogs as angry and unpatriotic, the candidate's wife sought to present herself and her family as being solidly in the American mainstream.

Most white Americans know so little about their black fellow-citizens that the speech may have been a necessary gesture of reassurance, made more eloquent at the end by the appearance onstage of the Obamas' charming, irrepressible daughters, Sasha and Malia.

Tuesday and Wednesday were dominated by the Clintons, first with Hillary's speech urging her supporters to move behind Obama and then with her husband's resounding endorsement of the candidate he had once dismissed as an inexperienced 'kid'.

The only Democratic president to win two terms in office since Franklin D Roosevelt, Clinton remained the leading figure in his party after the defeats of Al Gore in 2000 and John Kerry in 2004. Before the convention, Hillary said her supporters needed a moment of catharsis that could only be achieved by putting her name into nomination alongside Obama's.

Confetti falls as fireworks are set off following a speech by Senator Barack Obama during which he formally accepted the Democratic Party nomination as its presidential candidate at the party's convention in Denver, Colorado. Photograph: Matthew Staver/Bloomberg.

In the end, Clinton herself provided the catharsis, effecting the emotional turning point of the convention when she called for the roll call of states to be halted and for Obama to be nominated by acclamation.

'With eyes firmly fixed on the future, and in the spirit of unity with the goal of victory, with faith in our party and our country, let's declare together with one voice right here, right now, that Barack Obama is our candidate and he will be our president,' she said.

Everyone agreed that the Clintons played their roles flawlessly, but some Democratic strategists complained that three of the four days of the convention had been wasted because they had not been spent attacking McCain and the Republicans. Others worried that Obama's decision to move his acceptance speech into a football stadium could reinforce Republican claims that he is a narcissistic celebrity too much in love with the roar of an adoring crowd.

Obama's speech had four main objectives: to introduce himself to a broader public as someone who understood them and shared their values; to make his promise of change more specific; to draw a sharp contrast with McCain; and to persuade voters that he is ready to lead.

Standing before a classical backdrop that evoked the West Wing of the White House, Obama set out his vision for the US in concrete terms, defining the change he promises as an end to the policies of the past eight years under President George Bush.

'Tonight, I say to the American people, to Democrats and Republicans and Independents across this great land – enough! This moment – this election – is our chance to keep, in the 21st century, the American promise alive,' he said. 'And we are here because we love this country too much to let the next four years look like the last eight. On 4 November, we must stand up and say: Eight is enough.'

A biographical video before the speech stressed Obama's background as the son of a single mother who struggled financially, and highlighted the role of his white grandparents in raising him. There was no mention of his time at Harvard Law School – too 'elitist' perhaps – and no sign of the Rev. Jeremiah Wright's Trinity United Church of Christ, where Obama worshipped for 20 years.

In his speech, Obama said that when he met people throughout the US who faced economic hardship he was reminded of the challenges faced by his mother and grandparents.

Hillary Clinton and Barack Obama return from a commercial break at the Democratic presidential debate at the National Constitution Center, in Philadelphia, in April. Photograph: Charles Dharapak/AP.

'I don't know what kind of lives John McCain thinks that celebrities lead, but this has been mine,' he said. 'These are my heroes. Theirs are the stories that shaped me. And it is on their behalf that I intend to win this election and keep our promise alive as president of the United States.'

Pushing back against the charge that he has been vague about policy, Obama spelt out what changes his presidency would bring. He promised to end tax breaks for companies that ship jobs overseas, to cut taxes for 95 per cent of families and to end US dependence on oil from the Middle East within 10 years.

'I will tap our natural gas reserves, invest in clean coal technology, and find ways to safely harness nuclear power,' he said.

'I'll help our auto companies retool, so that the fuel-efficient cars of the future are built right here in America. I'll make it easier for the American people to afford these new cars. And I'll invest $150 billion over the next decade in affordable, renewable sources of energy – wind power and solar power and the next generation of biofuels; an investment that will lead to new industries and five million new jobs that pay well and can't ever be outsourced.' He pledged to increase spending on education and to introduce affordable healthcare for everyone, prohibiting insurance companies from discriminating against people with pre-existing conditions.

He would introduce paid sick days and better family leave and guarantee equal pay for women.

Turning to foreign policy, Obama defended his call for a timetable for withdrawing US troops from Iraq, adding that both the Iraqi government and the Bush administration now shared his view. He said he would 'finish the fight against al-Qaeda and the Taliban in Afghanistan' but also promised to rebuild partnerships with the US's allies and to renew 'tough, direct diplomacy' with Iran and Russia.

He insisted that he, rather than McCain, had 'the temperament, and judgment, to serve as the

Barack Obama applauds as he thanks supporters following his victory in the Iowa caucuses January 2008 in Des Moines, Iowa. Photograph: Win McNamee/Getty Images.

next commander-in-chief', accusing the Republican of clinging stubbornly to Bush's failed foreign policy.

'That's not the judgment we need. That won't keep America safe. We need a president who can face the threats of the future, not keep grasping at the ideas of the past,' he said.

'You don't defeat a terrorist network that operates in 80 countries by occupying one country. You don't protect Israel and deter Iran just by talking tough in Washington. You can't truly stand up for Georgia when you've strained our oldest alliances. If John McCain wants to follow George Bush with more tough talk and bad strategy, that is his choice – but it is not the change we need.'

Obama's speech made clear that his strategy depends on branding McCain as Bush's successor and presenting himself as the representative of 'new leadership, a new politics for a new time'. Despite a slide in the polls in recent weeks that has seen Obama's lead over McCain disappear, the Democrat's campaign radiated calm in Denver. Obama won the Democratic nomination in large part because of his superior grassroots organisation, and his campaign. Staff believe that organisation will help him to triumph again in November.

Obama's campaign manager, David Plouffe, has identified 18 battleground states, 14 of which Bush won in 2004, and he believes that increasing voter turnout in those states is the key to victory.

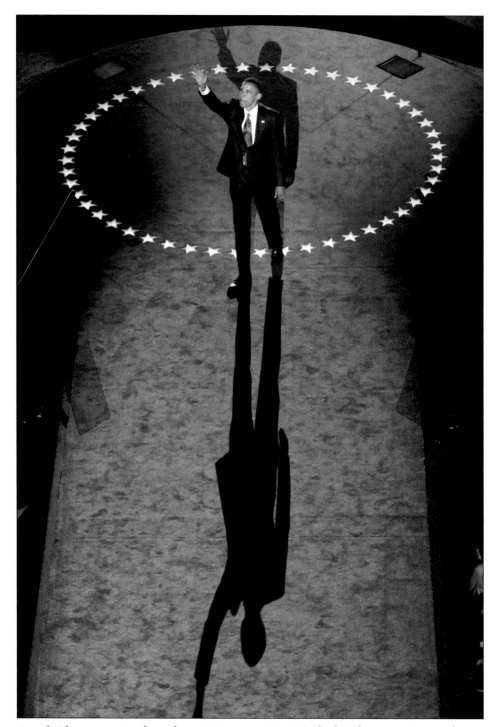

Barack Obama accepting the applause of Democratic Party faithful at their convention on the podium at Invesco Field at Mile High stadium in Denver, Colorado. Photograph: Karl Gehring/ The Denver Post.

In 2004, Bush's field operation increased Republican turnout by 12 million votes over 2000, dwarfing the Democrats' eight million increase.

'I think what the Bush people did in 2004 deserves to be in the political hall of fame,' Plouffe told reporters this week.

'I think that McCain's going to have a difficult time replicating that. And if John McCain doesn't replicate George Bush's turnout, he's obviously going to lose in a very major way. If he replicates it and doesn't grow it, he's going to lose most of these states. He has to replicate it, and increase it.' Plouffe points to Florida, where 600,000 registered African-Americans didn't vote in 2004 and more than 900,000 registered voters under 40 stayed away from the polls. He is confident that a combination of increased voter registration and an aggressive voter turnout operation could swing many of the battleground states to Obama.

'We spend a lot of time on this. And it's not sexy, and it's not something that people are going to spend a lot of time on, but it's how elections are won,' he said.

After the glamour of this week's Democratic convention, which featured performances by everyone from Stevie Wonder and Sheryl Crow to Kanye West, and a Hollywood-style party hosted by *Vanity Fair*, next week's Republican convention in St Paul promises to be a modest affair. Whereas every hotel room within a 20-mile radius of Denver was booked months in advance, rooms within walking distance of the Republican convention centre were still available this weekend.

The editors of many leading British papers were in Denver, but none are going to St Paul, and one European television network that sent 20 reporters to Denver is sending just one to cover the Republicans.

US coverage of next week's convention could be squeezed if Hurricane Gustav, which is heading into the Gulf of Mexico, hits landfall in New Orleans early next week – almost exactly three years after Hurricane Katrina.

The Republicans will have some advantages over the Democrats next week, however, one of which is that they have no equivalent of the Clinton drama to distract from their primary purpose of bashing Obama. It's true that George Bush and Dick Cheney will play the role of the ugly sisters at the Republican ball on Monday evening but, given that it is Labour Day, many voters will be otherwise occupied and might not notice.

The theme of the convention is 'Country First', and each evening will feature a celebration of McCain's life in public service, including his five years in a Vietnamese prisoner-of-war camp. The Republican campaign is based on pointing up the contrast between McCain's political experience and personal heroism and Obama's inexperience and alleged lack of substance.

McCain owes much of his recent rise in the polls to his campaign's success in making Obama the central issue of the election, and next week's convention is likely to feature a relentless bombardment of the Democratic candidate. Republicans are less squeamish than Democrats about what Hillary Clinton calls 'the politics of personal destruction' and they have an impressive record of turning the apparent strengths of Democratic candidates into weaknesses.

McCain has a further advantage next week in that, because he often performs poorly in major speeches, as he struggles with the autocue, expectations are low in advance of his acceptance speech.

Obama and his running mate, Joe Biden, headed directly yesterday for the battleground states of Pennsylvania, Ohio and Michigan in an attempt to drive home their message that the economy is the central issue of the campaign. Bush is so unpopular that, if the Democrats can successfully link McCain with him in the public mind, they believe they will prevail in November. McCain faces a delicate task in seeking to win over Independent voters by stressing his record as a political maverick without alienating conservatives,

Barack Obama on the campaign trail in Iowa with his wife, Michelle, and their daughters Malia Obama, left, and Sasha Obama, second from right. Photograph: Ryan Anson/Bloomberg News.

whose energy and organisation he will need on election day.

McCain's best opportunity to pull ahead of Obama could come in the three presidential debates, a forum in which he has shown himself to be deft, ruthless and persuasive. Obama's hope lies in replicating and maintaining the enthusiasm he generated in Denver on Thursday, persuading young voters to turn out in record numbers while reassuring older Americans that he is ready to lead.

If Obama loses November's election, Thursday night's event at Mile High Stadium will go down as one of the most foolhardy acts of hubris in American political history. If he wins, however, that heady night in Denver might be remembered as the moment when an African-American presidential candidate sealed the deal with a sceptical electorate and helped to realise King's dream.

WEDNESDAY, 3 SEPTEMBER 2008

On the Third Day our Luck Runs Out as the Rear Tyre Rolls Over 20kg of Explosives

A Soldier's Diary, by Lt Paddy Bury

We move into the Green Zone and take over a compound in an area riddled with Taliban. They use this area constantly to launch attacks on the Afghan National Army (ANA) checkpoints on the 611 highway, and we seek to stop them. We have chosen well. The compound we occupy is an improvised explosive device (IED) facilitation point, littered with different pieces of projectiles. At the time we don't realise it, but this is an omen of things to come.

That afternoon, the Taliban launch a brief attack and are repelled by two platoons' worth of firepower. The locals are glad we're here and come to let us know. But in each Shura [council or consultative meeting] held to listen to the locals, there are prying Taliban eyes.

A few days later, I am with a section, clearing a track of IEDs so that our compound – Patrol Base Armagh, as we have named it – can be resupplied. With metal detectors out in front and bayonets drawn to check suspect readings, progress is painfully slow. We cover 100m (328ft) at a snail's pace. As we reach a small bridge, a Ranger behind the lead men inquisitively opens an electrical box at head height on a telegraph pole.

'Boss, I think we've got something.'

We pull back and I go forward to confirm. He's damn right. As I peer at the box cautiously, I see inside a blue plastic bag which reveals a taped-up detonation device and some kind of metal object. That's enough for me. Meanwhile, the Rangers have searched around the device for detonation wires. As they cross a roof, they hear someone scamper off into the distance. Probably the firer.

We've been lucky.

The next day another IED is found right outside our base.

Again we're lucky.

On the third day, however, our luck runs out.

As a Land Rover's rear tyre rolls over some earth, it pushes down on a wooden bar toward

Members of the Garda armed regional support units at the units' launch in Templemore Garda College. Two of the units started operating in Cork and Limerick in September, providing back-up for frontline gardaí in critical incidents. Photograph: Brian Gavin/Press 22.

20kg (45lbs) of packed homemade explosives. The metal on the underside of the bar touches the metal of the battery charge. A spark completes the circuit.

BOOM! The three-tonne vehicle, bristling with weapons and crew, is hurled by an invisible wave up, into and through a three-foot-thick wall, rolling and spinning as it goes. Its occupants, including a colleague, Ranger Delaney from Dublin, are blown 10ft clear of the vehicle and land in an orchard.

Ears ring, silence, then there's shouting: 'Contact! IED. Casualties. Wait out!'

The details of the casualties start to trickle into the operations room in Patrol Base Armagh. Some are serious, some are astonishingly lightly injured. A helicopter is scrambled as a Quick Reaction Force bolts down the 611 to extract the casualties back to the landing site. A multiple casualty scenario is a nightmare scenario, but it's one we are trained for.

The casualties are extracted back to Bastion and our thoughts follow them as we return to our compound. We knew this was coming.

The next day another platoon is ferrying supplies from a vehicle to the base when their commander, Lieut. Franks from Kildare, spots something strange. He concurs with Sgt Maj. O'Connor, another Dubliner, and both decide it's something dubious.

A report is sent up and quickly a US Marine Corps ordnance disposal team is sent to blow the IED. They do, and they have been down to Armagh so often these past few days that we now know them by first name.

'Y'all look after yourselves down here,' they say before leaving.

By now, the Rangers are calling the base questioning the IED detection drill we use. Morale suffers. Hard questions are asked. I learn a lot about leadership.

I tell the Rangers how much they are achieving by being in Armagh. The ANA are overjoyed that they haven't been attacked since we've been

here. The locals have been up to the District Centre saying how good it is we are here.

Already a large irrigation project has been planned. A new vein of intelligence has been opened.

The Rangers, once things are explained to them, quickly come round.

With the IEDs, we are caught in the middle of a technological measure and counter-measure battle where one lapse of concentration can be fatal. Despite all the technology, our eyeballs remain our best defence.

Paddy Bury from Co. Wicklow is a member of the British Army's Royal Irish Regiment. His diary from Helmand province in Afghanistan, published between May and August, provoked a lively debate in the letters page about identity and the appropriateness, or otherwise, of Irishmen serving in the British Army.

SATURDAY, 6 SEPTEMBER 2008

Palin Will Never be Acceptable to the Alleged Liberals

Breda O'Brien

Piper Palin for presidential candidate in 2040! For those of you living under a rock, Piper is the extremely cute seven-year-old daughter of Sarah Palin. Sky News could not resist cutting away from her mother's acceptance speech to show Piper licking her palm and carefully smoothing the hair of her baby brother Trig, who has Down syndrome. Later on, she took the applause of the crowd with aplomb. John McCain bent down to talk to her, and she made him laugh.

Yep, Piper Palin for presidential candidate in 2040.

Hey, by 2040, we may have reached a stage where it is not acceptable to suggest that a woman

Irish swimmer Darragh McDonald, beside his prosthetic legs, during a break in training at the aquatics centre in Beijing. Photograph: Julien Behal/PA Wire.

who has a child with special needs and a teenager who is pregnant should stay home and mind the kids instead of involving herself in politics. Joe Biden was deemed a hero for continuing to work and commute when his wife was tragically killed. No one suggested he stay home and mind his bereaved sons.

By 2040, we may have outgrown the habit of attacking a candidate's family. We might not have commentators like syndicated columnist Froma Harrop, who described Bristol Piper, the pregnant daughter, as looking 'stupid and defiant'. She suggested that anyone who could identify with Sarah Palin's 'dysfunctional family' would have to be 'from Mars, or on welfare'. Froma, why not just come straight out and say that the Palins are white trash?

Then there is the elitism of 1970s feminists. Gloria Steinem, the grand dame of American feminism who is two years older than John McCain, declared acidly: 'Sarah Palin shares nothing but a chromosome with Hillary Clinton.'

Sojourner Truth, a former slave, gave an electrifying speech at a women's rights convention in Akron, Ohio in 1851. Sojourner punctuated her speech with the rhetorical question: 'And ain't I a woman?'

It is a feminist mantra that politics needs the active participation of women. Sarah Palin could echo: 'And ain't I a woman?' However, in the world inhabited by Steinem-style feminists, some women are more equal than others. And women who are anti-abortion scarcely rate as women at all.

On the face of it, Palin should be a feminist's dream. She has made it in politics without having a rich father or an established politician husband. She juggles family life with politics. She is sharp, and tough, and has moved smoothly from state politics to the national stage with style and wit. Instead, she is an old-time feminist's nightmare.

Unlike Hillary Clinton, she can expect no help from the sisters. But I suspect Sarah Palin couldn't care less. She is not there to attract disillusioned Hillary voters who cannot forgive Barack Obama for not putting Mrs Clinton on the ticket. She is there to copper-fasten the conservative vote, and she will do just that. The die-hard Republicans who view McCain with much the same suspicion as Steinem views Palin are back on board. Meanwhile, McCain, with his conciliatory speech, will be the one to target the middle ground.

It is certainly true that there are lots of Americans who will not be able to bring themselves to vote for Barack Obama, simply because he is black. But there are lots of others who will not be able to bring themselves to vote for him, not because he is black, but because he is not one of them. The skinny intellectual with the funny name and the dubious patriotism is just too strange for most of these people. That may be the United States' loss, although it is still too close to call.

On the other hand, Sarah Palin, with her son heading off to Iraq, her pregnant daughter, her high-school sweetheart who is 'still her guy' and her defiant adoration of her baby with special needs, is as familiar as breathing.

Sarah Palin's secret weapon, one that the media and political elite will never fathom, is that she is likeable. Sure, she has absolutely unreconstructed conservative policies. The worst part of Palin's speech was when she started on all the old Republican memes – Fear big government! The Democrats will tax you to death! Drill for oil and to hell with the environment! In spite of, or sadly, perhaps even because of all that, she is a woman that many Americans would be happy to have a beer or even a mooseburger with.

The likeability factor worked for Ronnie Reagan, for Bill Clinton, and for Dubya Bush. For those who are fixated on ideas and policies, it is unfathomable. We Irish should recognise the likeability factor, not to mention that old Teflon thing. Bertie Ahern is writing reflective pieces on retirement for *The Irish Times*, while Brian Cowen is growing ulcers figuring out what to do with an economy in meltdown. Sarah Palin's family difficulties have only made the Republicans, and a lot of middle America, love her more.

In my mythical election of 2040, if drastic action is not taken now, the potential devastation caused by global warming will make being president in 2008 during an economic downturn look like a doddle. Piper may have a hard time in 2040 explaining away Mom's policies. The odd thing is that John McCain, aside from daft ideas like a petrol tax holiday, has taken on board the need for radical action on global warming.

But Sarah Palin's policies on global warming are not the only or even central reason that she is the subject of such dislike for some US citizens. Nor is it the fact that she shoots moose before breakfast and eats them for dinner. (Just not on the same day. Don't you know anything about hunting?) Sarah Palin, with her staunch belief that human life deserves respect and protection from conception onwards, will never be acceptable to alleged liberals.

Perhaps by 2040 we will have left behind that kind of knee-jerk, reactionary attitude to pro-life women. Perhaps Piper Palin will be judged on her ability, not whether she ticks the right boxes. All we would need then is for Sasha, the Obamas' daughter, to decide to run against her. That might be proof that Americans have safely left behind them not only the question of whether they have the heart to elect a black person, but also proof that the shards of the glass ceiling will finally have been recycled into something useful.

This is Greatness. This is Kilkenny Now

Tom Humphries, in Croke Park

Kilkenny 3-30 Waterford 1-13

Won? It was like Bob Beamon's long jump or Usain Bolt's 100 metres. Won is not the word. Winning implies struggle and all the complications offered by another team. This was just an emphatic laying claim to immortality. This was a day when opposition was irrelevant. Waterford, the plucky challengers, hindered Kilkenny about as much as cones in training.

Three-in-a-row. Top of hurling's roll of honour for the first time. The intermediate and minor All-Ireland titles in the bag already. The Under-21 title just lying there waiting to be picked up as part of the clean sweep. Some of these players could go on to win nine or 10 All-Ireland medals. This is greatness. This is Kilkenny now.

They scored 30 points yesterday. And three goals. Could have had a few more of each perhaps, but it was the perfect performance. They conceded not a point from play for the first three-quarters of an hour, and gave away a late, fluky goal having made a sentimental gesture to bring on their beloved sub goalkeeper James McGarry, who was caught cold.

They won every battle, rode every tackle, added value to every ball they hurled. There was a moment in the 24th minute that summed them up. Ken McGrath had the ball on his 45-metre line and he glanced up to see where he might deliver it. He noticed, not for the first time, that there were no options open anywhere. So he opted to swing hard.

He was hooked from behind by Eddie Brennan. Now, Brennan had just sprinted 15

Kilkenny corner forward Eddie Brennan scores his first goal during his team's annihilation of Waterford in the All-Ireland senior hurling final at Croke Park. Brennan finished with a personal tally of 2-4. Photograph: Lorraine O'Sullivan/Inpho.

Waterford's management team, with Davy Fitzgerald on his knees, can't bring themselves to watch as Kilkenny run riot in the first half of the 2008 All-Ireland hurling final. Photograph: James Crombie/Inpho.

metres from the corner forward position in the hope that McGrath might just hesitate. He did and Brennan got in the perfect hook.

Thing about it was, Eddie Brennan, in the 20th and 21st minutes, had just scored the goals which had ended the game as a contest. He had a point in the bag as well. He is a corner forward. If anyone was entitled to cruise for five minutes it was Eddie Brennan. Kilkenny don't do cruise. Brennan doesn't do hyperbole.

'We're just in a privileged position,' he said when asked about Kilkenny's slice of history. 'The display today came from the nights of training we put in. We were back there in the start of December. We are just in a great position at the moment; we have a great team and a great panel. There are lads on the line more entitled to play than some of us.'

Case in point. TJ Reid. Reid was sprung from

the bench in the second half when Martin Comerford came off injured. He scored four points from play and was a sprite-like presence everywhere.

For Waterford it had been a long journey. Davy Fitz, their manager, joined for the last mile. He knew their joy in getting to an All-Ireland final. He felt the pain, too, yesterday.

'I believed coming up here today', he said, 'that we were going to win. If I didn't I would be no good to those boys inside. Ask me to explain what happened? I can't.

'One thing I will say. No matter what the story is, there are probably a few guys out there waiting for this moment to have a go at me. They can have it all. When I came into this job I said if I did everything I knew how to do I would be happy with myself. I did everything I thought was possible. Maybe I will have to look at myself and

Kilkenny captain James Fitzpatrick holds aloft the Liam MacCarthy cup after his team defeated Waterford to win the 2008 All-Ireland senior hurling final. Photograph: Alan Betson.

ask myself questions. I will not blame the boys one bit whatsoever.'

He spoke about half-time, the nightmare scenario of facing the team who have obeyed your rules and followed your plan and find themselves 17 points down.

'It wasn't nice,' he conceded, 'but we didn't drop our heads.'

That, poignantly, was the most that Waterford could take away. They took their drubbing with dignity. They kept working, kept resisting the expanding margin.

It had been 45 years. It will be a few again. We will never see some of these wonderful players again. Their dignity was the least they deserved to bring with them.

Instead of a match we saw an exhibition of power and greatness. And we watched Brian Cody carried around the Croke Park pitch on striped shoulders like a bemused cowboy on a delirious rodeo bull.

It was striking to watch Cody before the game. While Waterford gathered in a great entourage for the anthem, Cody was down the line, a singular, unfussed figure. The game exploded into raw physicality moments later. He stood in the same spot, just as nonplussed.

His place as hurling's greatest manager seems assured. The only questions concern how long his reign will continue.

'Terrific,' he said quietly of the bravura performance he had coaxed from his team on a day when history was on the line. 'Super feeling. That is what this day is all about. The players were outstanding, they were terrific from start to finish and were totally focused, obviously. They hurled at a very serious level.'

On a day of rare sights his quiet smile of satisfaction spoke volumes. This wasn't just about winning or about history. It was about perfection. He had put a team out who had delivered just that at the right time. Perfect. Perfect. Perfect.

Doctors Differ and a Mother Dies

Eithne Donnellan

The revelation that yet another cancer patient in this country was not diagnosed and treated at the earliest possible opportunity is likely to cause further public concern about the state of our health services.

In the latest case Ann Moriarty, a 53-year-old wife and mother, who was in remission from breast cancer, attended Ennis General Hospital on 11 June last year and a chest X-ray on her was wrongly reported as normal.

She had cause to have other visits to the hospital during last summer and at no time was the fact that she was terminally ill picked up on. Even in August 2007, junior doctors told her another chest X-ray looked fine.

And when she attended the hospital's AE unit that same month, having lost a lot of weight, she was discharged home by a junior doctor. This decision even surprised nurses.

A few days later, after a second opinion was sought at a private hospital in Galway, the awful truth was conveyed to her family. She was dying. She died in April this year.

Her devastated husband, Karl Henry, who now wants an independent investigation to ensure no other patients had X-rays at Ennis misread, recalled yesterday how he and his late wife left Ennis hospital in August 2007 relieved she had again been given the all-clear.

'We left the hospital so relieved to have been told that no problem had been found and we walked back to our car like two happy kids.'

Within days though it was discovered errors had been made and she wouldn't be around for much longer; around to see her then 12-year-old son grow up.

Ann Moriarty, her husband Karl Henry and their son Ciarán.

Mr Henry said yesterday: 'The nightmare the family has had to endure over the past year almost defies description . . . the people who fail to read X-rays properly or fail to act on seriously abnormal blood results need to wake up and realise that people can and do die when they don't do their job properly.'

One of the two unpublished internal reviews of the care given to his wife at Ennis carried out by the HSE makes several recommendations and concludes: 'It is difficult to say that if the metastatic lesion had been picked up in June 2007 instead of August 2007, whether the outcome would have been different for Mrs M. It is clear, however, that MWRH (Mid Western Regional Hospital) Ennis did not provide optimal care to Mrs M.'

The report found 'clear evidence that the radiologist who reported on the chest X-ray of 11 June 2007 failed to pick up a 3cm poorly defined opacity just above the aortic knuckle, highly suggestive of a metastatic lesion'. It also refers to 'lack of supervision of junior medical staff'.

Ms Moriarty's family are also upset that a mammogram carried out on Ms Moriarty at St James's Hospital Dublin – one of the State's eight designated cancer centres – in April 2007, when she was also given a clean bill of health, is missing.

She had a breast removed at that hospital two years earlier and the mammogram on her second breast was reported as normal in 2007. However, the family wonder if this could possibly have been a correct report, given that she was found to be terminally ill four months later.

Not surprising, this woman's family, who moved from Dublin to Ennis in 2006, still have many questions. They now want to meet the Minister for Health, Mary Harney, to discuss their concerns.

Over the past year there have been several inquiries into the misdiagnosis of cancer patients across the State. There was the inquiry into the case of Rebecca O'Malley, whose breast cancer diagnosis was delayed by 14 months after an error was made in the laboratory of Cork University Hospital; the inquiry into the delayed diagnosis of a 51-year-old Tipperary woman after her biopsy results were wrongly read at Galway's University College Hospital; an inquiry into care provided to breast cancer patients at Barringtons Hospital in Limerick; an inquiry into the misdiagnosis of nine breast cancer patients at Portlaoise General Hospital; and reviews of the work of locum consultant radiologists in the northeast and in Galway are ongoing.

It is true that mistakes can and will always be made in our health service, but this latest case shows yet again that all the necessary checks and balances are still not in place to ensure errors are picked up quickly. Patient safety, despite all the assurances to the contrary, still does not seem to be the main priority in our healthcare system.

SATURDAY, 13 SEPTEMBER 2008

Palin Brings it All Back Home

Denis Staunton, in Wasilla, Alaska

The snow will begin to fall next month on Fairbanks, Alaska's second city and home to Fort Wainwright, where Sarah Palin stood this week to bid farewell to 4,000 soldiers deploying to Iraq, including her 19-year-old son Track.

But it was almost balmy on Thursday as the 1st Stryker Brigade Combat Team, 25th Infantry Division, known as the Arctic Wolves, marched in formation behind their colours and recited the Wolf Creed.

'Strike fear in the enemy's hearts and minds; I am a lethal and skilled warfighter with unmatched intestinal fortitude,' they said. 'Tough, both physically and mentally, and instilled with the warrior spirit, I can accomplish any mission – anytime, anywhere.'

As Alaska's governor, the Republican vice-presidential nominee is a familiar figure at Fort Wainwright and, as the mother of Pte 1st Class Track Palin, she's a member of the brigade's family readiness group. She agreed to give the keynote address at the deployment ceremony months ago, long before her addition to the Republican ticket had turned the US presidential race on its head.

While the soldiers stood for 90 minutes on a vast airfield, a succession of generals spoke about the importance of their mission in Iraq to America's national security. When Palin's turn came, however, she spoke as a mother, her voice cracking as she addressed the departing warriors.

'As you depart today, don't mind us – your parents, your friends and family – if we allow for a few tears or if we hold you just a little closer once more before you're gone. Because we're going to miss you. We can't help it. We're going to miss you,' she said.

'This is one of the moments when we have to face the fact that you may not need our protection anymore. In fact, you're the ones who will now be protecting us.'

Palin was back in Alaska for the first time since John McCain astonished the political world two weeks ago by choosing the almost unknown 44-year-old as his running mate. Since then, she has become a national sensation, electrifying the Republicans' conservative base and paralysing Barack Obama's usually sure-footed campaign.

Palin continued to dominate the headlines yesterday with her first major interview since she joined the Republican ticket, telling ABC's Charlie Gibson that she didn't hesitate before accepting McCain's invitation to be his running mate.

'I answered him yes because I have the confidence in that readiness and knowing that you can't blink, you have to be wired in a way of being so committed to the mission, the mission that we're on, reform of this country and victory in the war, you can't blink,' she said.

Palin defended remarks she made to a church congregation when she prayed that the Iraq war was 'a task from God', adding that she was not sure if her son was doing God's work in deploying to Iraq.

'I don't know if the task is from God, Charlie. What I know is that my son has made a decision,' she said.

'I am so proud of his independence and the strong decision he has made, what he decided to do and serving for the right reasons and serving some-

Sarah Palin is accompanied by her daughter Piper as she is greeted by a welcome-home rally on her arrival at the airport in Fairbanks, Alaska. Photograph: Robyn Beck/AFP/Getty Images.

thing greater than himself and not choosing a real easy path where he could be more comfortable and certainly safer.'

It's been an unlikely journey for a woman who spent most of her political life in a modest, two-storey building with a clapboard façade, tucked between a couple of strip malls. This is Wasilla City Hall, where Palin was mayor from 1996 to 2002, managing the municipal affairs of about 7,000 people who live in the dormitory town 35 miles north of Anchorage.

Nestling in the Matanuska-Susitna Valley, in the shadow of the Talkeetna Mountains, Wasilla has doubled in size in recent years, attracting families from Anchorage with lower property prices and easy access to lakes and forests for fishing and hunting. The local economy is based on retail stores, with Wal-Mart as the biggest private

sector employer and a local sales tax ensuring a generous revenue stream for the city government.

Despite its endless strip malls, Wasilla retains a small-town atmosphere and when I visited the current mayor, Diane Keller, this week, she sold me a book of raffle tickets for a local youth project and told me how proud everyone is of Palin.

'She's our home town gal,' she said. 'She's the same Sarah that she was before she was mayor, before she was governor. She's been able to keep that same feeling and still be open and accessible to people, no matter what job she's been asked to serve in.'

As reporters swarmed around Wasilla in recent days, locals have been protective of Palin, especially when it comes to questions about her 17-year-old daughter Bristol's pregnancy and Bristol's decision to marry the child's father, a school friend.

Goalkeeper Dean Kiely jokes around during the Republic of Ireland squad training session at Gannon Park, Malahide, ahead of the team's opening World Cup 2010 Group Eight qualifier against Georgia in Mainz, Germany. Photograph: James Crombie/Inpho.

'I've been telling my staff, you know, Sarah puts her pants on the same way today as she did before. She puts her pants on the same way I do, the same way you do. Her family is a normal American family. You know, you have good days and you have bad days,' Keller says. 'All kids make mistakes. It's not the fact that you made the mistake. It's the fact of what you learn from it and what you do with it that counts.'

As close to Beijing as to Washington DC, Alaska calls itself America's Last Frontier, its 600,000 people occupying a state the size of Texas. With some of the most spectacular topography in the world, including America's tallest mountain, Mount McKinley (known to Alaskans as Dinali), and a rich population of bears, moose, caribou, seals and polar bears, Alaska is a nature lover's paradise.

For Alaskans, however, the state's natural resources have been, above all, a source of wealth, starting with the Klondike gold rush in the late 19th century and more recently with the discovery of huge oil deposits in the Arctic Ocean 40 years ago.

Oil is not only at the heart of Alaska's economy but at the centre of its political life and some of the state's leading politicians are currently under investigation for corrupt dealings with big oil companies. Revenue from the North Slope oilfields accounts for more than 80 per cent of Alaska's state budget and finances a $36 billion fund that pays out more than $2,000 each year to every man, woman and child in the state. Palin has topped up this year's cheque, which reaches most Alaskan homes this weekend, with an extra $1,200.

Alaskans pay no state income tax, there is no state-wide sales tax and property taxes, which are levied locally, are low.

'This week, my family of four – my wife, my two children and myself – will get about $13,000 just for breathing here in Alaska,' says Peter Van Tuyn, an environmental lawyer who has fought oil companies over conservation issues. 'So you tell me what you think the general populace is going to think about the oil industry here when it allows us to have a $36 billion bank account, which is more than most countries have in the bank.'

If the oil companies have dominated Alaska's economy, the Republicans have dominated its politics, especially through Ted Stevens, the state's 84-year-old senator. Stevens was indicted last July on charges of falsely reporting $250,000 in gifts from an oilfield service company, including an extensive renovation of his home, a massage chair, a stained glass window and a sled dog.

Stevens's son Ben, a state senator, is under investigation by the FBI and Alaska's sole congressman, Don Young, is also being investigated for taking bribes. When former senator Frank Murkowski was elected governor in 2002, he appointed his daughter Lisa to succeed him in the US senate.

Sarah Palin speaks to the crowd during a rally in O'Fallon, Missouri. Photograph: Whitney Curtis/Getty Images.

'They were so unchallenged, there were so few countervailing powers that they just thought they didn't have to answer to anyone,' says Michael Carey, a columnist for the *Anchorage Daily News*.

'This was essentially one-party rule, where they became so confident of themselves they just did what they wanted.'

Palin challenged Murkowski in the Republican primary in 2006, defeated him and went on to win the gubernatorial election, sweeping into power with a promise to clean up Alaskan politics.

She renegotiated a taxation agreement with the oil companies, sidelined them by contracting a Canadian company to build a new gas pipeline and worked with Democrats to introduce new ethics rules for state politicians.

'People saw her as a modern, suburban woman who was taking on not just the male establishment – but sort of the world,' says Carey. 'She was sort of a cult figure. People really just got turned on for different reasons – new, fresh, tomorrow, sex appeal, all of that.'

Palin has always been upfront about her Christian faith, her opposition to abortion in almost all cases and her support for the teaching of creationism alongside evolution in schools. But as governor of a state with one of the lowest levels of religious observance in the US, she has been careful to avoid pushing a socially conservative legislative agenda.

On environmental issues, Palin has been a fierce advocate of drilling for oil in the Arctic National Wildlife Reserve and has angered conservationists by ignoring scientific reports about threats to Alaskan wildlife. She has authorised private hunters to shoot wolves from the air as part of a predator control programme to protect moose and caribou.

'There's no science base to that programme. It's outrageous,' says Van Tuyn. 'I have a small plane, let's say, and you like to shoot at wolves. So we go up in my plane after the state tells us, this is your area where you get to go kill the predators.

'And you're hanging out the window of the plane as I'm swooping down on them in the spring when the snow makes them easy to track and you're blasting away at the wolves from a plane. What is that? This is ridiculous.'

Lindsay Holmes, a Democratic state legislator, says Palin deserves credit for standing up to the Republican Party establishment but suggests that major reforms were inevitable once the bribery scandals broke. She believes that Palin's remarkable popularity among Alaskans (her approval rating is above 80 per cent) is due partly to her personal qualities but also to profound political cunning.

'She's got a very Alaskan image. She comes off as very personable, friendly and very approachable,' Holmes says.

'She's very, very good at getting out in front of issues. The momentum is already there, they're already heading that way and she kind of is able to step right in front and take ownership of it. She's got very good timing and very good political instincts for identifying an issue that's starting to move and jumping out in front of the bandwagon.'

Palin may be popular among voters but the governor's relationship with legislators has become increasingly strained as politicians in both parties complain that they are left out of big decisions.

'She takes a lot of major initiatives on without any sort of discussion whatsoever with really anybody, which is a little surprising,' Holmes says. 'So I think that's led to some of the rockiness.'

Others in Anchorage mutter that Palin is too quick to bear a grudge, treating policy differences as personal conflicts and depending on a small circle of advisors dominated by friends and family.

Palin's family has been intertwined with her political life since her days as mayor of Wasilla, taking her younger children with her to work and, in recent months, nursing her four-month-old son Trig, who has Down syndrome.

Palin's husband Todd, whom she refers to as Alaska's 'First Dude', sometimes sits in on official meetings, raising questions about his political role.

State legislators are investigating claims that Palin sacked a police chief because he refused to dismiss her former brother-in-law, a trooper in the state police force.

The trooper had been involved in a bitter child custody battle with Palin's sister and the Palin family accused him of everything from 'Tasering' (a taser is an electroshock weapon that causes temporary paralysis) his stepson to shooting a moose without a permit.

This week, it emerged that Palin has been claiming *per diem* expenses for days spent in her own home in Wasilla because her official residence is the governor's mansion in Juneau. She also took her children on official trips to other parts of the US, charging the state for their air fares.

The media have been combing through Palin's past in search of political, financial or personal scandal but Carey says that, so far, nothing has risen above the level of the embarrassing.

'I still think they're not going to find her in some real estate deal like Ted Stevens or some of these other politicians. It's a matter of her age and she's taking care of her family, not trying to make money,' he says.

'I think the problem is going to be the family getting mixed up in policy. Apparently, that's something she just can't stay away from. And she doesn't ask people for advice, that's my impression.'

Having now given her first major interview, she faces an important test early next month when she debates her Democratic counterpart, senate foreign relations committee chairman Joe Biden.

Kate Sheehan and Kate Louise Walsh congratulate each other on their Junior Cert results at St Mary's College, Arklow, Co. Wicklow. Photograph: Michael Kelly.

Carey believes the Democrats would be foolish to underestimate Palin as 'a pretty airhead who's going to self-destruct' but he acknowledges that between now and election day, Alaska's charismatic hockey mom will need all the strength and resolve that have been the hallmarks of her political career to date.

'She's a very determined person but she's on the biggest stage of her life and this is a totally unforgiving environment,' he says. 'You don't get to make one mistake. You get to make no mistakes.'

SATURDAY, 13 SEPTEMBER 2008

Splashing Back

Róisín Ingle

My boyfriend is watching Liverpool while pretending to flick through a stack of interior design magazines. Approximately two centuries after we first applied for planning permission – we did it twice just to be sure to be sure – and decades after everyone else has finished their extensions using SSIA funds which of course we 'forgot' to save, we are, as they say, extending.

I remember the days when we used to have meaningful conversations about art and French cinema. Okay, well, about *Make Me A Supermodel, US* but you know what I mean. Now it's all 'I mean, that's the thing, can you have wooden floors and wooden work surfaces or would that feel like living on a boat or, worse, in a sauna. I hate saunas, anyway. I mean, what is the point of sitting in a steamy wooden room practically naked, etc., etc.' I steer him gently towards work surfaces. We urgently need ideas.

Nobody tells you about work surfaces and the many, many types of surfaces that exist until you suddenly have to decide between melamine and granite and moulded plastic.

Our practical, sensible architect gives us beautiful design books, urges us to decide on carpets,

floors and radiators but we've discovered we are about as good at deciding on these things as Sarah Palin is at keeping her daughter at home on the (shooting) range.

We haven't yet plucked up the courage to tell her we would really much rather she just decided it all herself. Could we pay her slightly more to do that? Something small out of our ever-decreasing budget? I'm sure her choices would be much better than ours.

He doesn't actually have much time for work surfaces, which is infuriating, but my boyfriend is mad for the splashbacks. Every time we have a meeting with the architects, when we are trying to decide between raft foundations and strip foundations, he pipes up about the thing that is number one on his list of priorities. That and shelves. Even I know splashbacks and shelves aren't as important as foundations. Exhausting, it is. In the middle of a chat about stoves versus open fires (eco blah heat loss blah) I toss in a bit of a curve ball.

'So anyway,' I say. 'I'm thinking of going back to writing my column.'

'What?' he says, still flicking through Credit Crunch Interiors. 'But you can't.'

'Why not?' I say as if going back to my column was the most logical thing in the world.

Over the past eight years, I've noticed that when he wants to make a very important point my boyfriend speaks in threes. Suddenly, I sense a classic one, two, three coming on. My intuition is as sharp as ever.

'Number one,' he says, 'you wrote a whole column six months ago saying you were fed up and that you wanted to go "looking out, instead of looking in", whatever that meant.' I say nothing, just surreptitiously flick channels to *Grand Designs*. Kevin McCloud is oddly attractive, especially when talking about delays in the arrival of hand-carved glass from Italy, for some reason.

'Number two,' he says, 'you were supposed to stop writing about yourself so that you could concentrate on more creative writing and getting fit. How are those two life goals going, by the way?' This I don't bother answering. It's rhetorical.

'Number three,' he says. 'Number three, you said you were stopping out of respect for me, that you didn't want to be writing about our lives in a national magazine, you said you loved me too much to do that.'

Yeeessss. I can't quite remember saying that bit. But I'm sure I meant it. It's not as though I like going back on my word, I just seem to have loads left to say and – ah, I know! This is when I try to persuade him the column actually helped our relationship. When I gave it up, one reader sent me an e-mail to the effect that he thought my writing gave us a chance to work out our relationship issues. So I try that. 'Thing is, writing the column, I've realised it gave us a chance to tease out our issues. It was therapeutic and I miss it,' I say.

He narrows his eyes, à la Larry David, and I am forced to concede that it probably wasn't therapeutic for him to go into work aware that his colleagues knew the intimate details of his latest domestic travail. 'But at least I never wrote about your Embarrassing Medical Condition,' I counter. 'That's true,' he sighs. 'I'll give you that.' He is kind and he loves me and so eventually he bestows a qualified blessing. 'Just don't write about my mother as though she is just a bleach-obsessed Protestant, and don't keep going on about me as though I am always cleaning or cooking. We have lots of other interests,' he says.

When he leaves the room to dust shelves and whip up a quick rhubarb crumble, I phone the mother-in-law-in-waiting, Iris, in Portadown where sales of *The Irish Times* have diminished by one since I did my grand departure bit.

'I'm thinking of writing my column again,' I say, testing the waters north of the Border. Iris gives a big Protestant cheer and rushes out to buy a six-pack of celebratory bleach. Which kind of clinches it for me, to be honest.

Saving us from Mother England

Paul Gillespie

Boston, Berlin – or Birmingham? One of the sure consequences of Ireland's No to Lisbon, if it persists, will be to reposition this State back into a closer relationship with the larger island from whose suffocating embrace we have spent the last 35 years of EU membership trying to escape.

That real independence was achieved through a more open-minded official nationalism which expanded Ireland's horizons by pooling sovereignty.

In his revealing letter to this newspaper on 14 August Michael Lillis, an official in the Department of Foreign Affairs from 1966-88, described the impact of those years: 'The change in 1973 was volcanic. Government ministers, TDs of most parties, trade union leaders and members, entrepreneurs, students, journalists, farm leaders and ordinary farmers, as well as officials like myself, were challenged . . . by the complexities and opportunities of the Community.

'We responded with a refreshing enthusiasm which astonished the [European] Commission and the European Community at large and even ourselves. There was no more asking: What did or what would the British do? Rather: Where is our interest here and what is the way to win?'

This has not been better put. Its impact continued through the 1990s, when greater British-Irish equality and mutual respect within a larger setting helped enormously in pursuing and achieving a Northern Ireland settlement. But it began to falter from 2000 or so, as seen in the Nice I referendum; in how the Boston-Berlin question was posed by neo-liberal politicians, journalists and academics as we entered the euro; and intriguingly in the greater normalisation of British-Irish relations that followed the Belfast Agreement.

Leo Enright, chairman, Discover Science and Engineering, speaking at the Science Gallery in Trinity College Dublin, against the backdrop of a live feed from Switzerland, showing the Large Hadron Collider experiment. Photograph: Eric Luke.

Gradually this official Europhile Irish nationalism from the first decades of EU membership, in contrast to the post-imperial British Euroscepticism which provided its continuing Other, lost whatever traction it had with the wider voting public, which in any case remained less enthusiastic and much less well-informed than the political and official elite.

Social and cultural change contributed to this process. Notwithstanding their substantial Irish content, British tabloid and broadsheet titles now occupy some 40 per cent of the print market and maintain the Eurosceptic policy lines decided in London. Television is equally penetrating.

Advertising media are indistinguishable, reflecting the explosion of British retail chains here in the credit boom. British football and celebrity media have huge Irish audiences.

Trade and investment both ways are central, especially in the Irish-owned sector of the economy – but at a quarter or a third of the economy, compared to the two thirds-plus in the post-independence decades. Euro membership strains that as sterling's value declines. And the flow of people between the two islands continues strongly.

Another former senior Foreign Affairs official wonders whether the centrifugal forces which propelled Ireland away from British rule and influence during the last century are being replaced in this by the pull of the larger island on the smaller one now that the imperial and post-imperial phases have passed. The Northern settlement contributes to that. So does economic policy and structural convergence, shared credit and property booms, and our mutual membership of the Anglosphere.

But it is ironic that this should be happening just as a more stable Ireland contrasts with a less stable Britain grappling with the possibility of Scottish independence and facing an increasingly inevitable Conservative election victory that could encourage that to happen. Such traumatic changes in their cultural moorings would prompt a profound unionist rethink of where their best interests lie – perhaps in Irish reunification.

Lillis sets out a convincing scenario of how the geopolitical shift between Ireland and Britain could happen. As Ireland decides how to handle the Lisbon No the Conservatives commit themselves to a referendum which would copperfasten the end of the treaty and then to a renegotiation of their relationship with the EU. This would leave the French and Germans determined to go ahead with it in some other way. Inevitably Ireland would be reclassified into the British camp. This would have many unforeseen political and economic consequences, amounting to a loss of Irish independence, since the negotiating terms would be set in London.

Official Europhile nationalism came under parallel pressure North and South. John Hume's influential belief that Europe contained a model for a settlement was displaced by Sinn Féin's insistence on sovereignty and by a similar resurgence of such feeling in the Republic's successive referendum encounters with European integration. Despite Sinn Féin's Anglophobia its attitude to sovereignty and neutrality shares traditional British mindsets.

This week's publication of research on the Lisbon result nevertheless shows Irish opinion far more Europhile than Britain's. More people consider themselves Irish and European than Irish only.

There is a willingness to examine a revised treaty, but a marked resistance on the No side to accept that the result has such costs and consequences.

It also reveals a collapse of political authority, with 50 per cent of voters not feeling close to any party and a clear loss of trust in political representation. That probably explains why official Europhile nationalism no longer has a convincing traction with the public. It needs to be reinvented and communicated far more effectively to citizens and voters, if we are not to sleepwalk back into the arms of mother England.

TUESDAY, 16 SEPTEMBER 2008

A Wrenching Shake-Up on an Unparalleled Scale is Under Way

Arthur Beesley

After a weekend of frenzied brinkmanship on Wall Street culminated in the abrupt demise of 158-year-old investment bank Lehman Brothers and the sale of rival firm Merrill Lynch, stock markets responded with severity yesterday to extract punishing losses from the value of bank shares around the world.

With a wrenching shake-up of unparalleled scale under way in the very foundations of the international financial system, all the signs are that this period of exceptional volatility will continue for some considerable time as the banking crisis deepens. The crisis 'is probably a once-in-a-century event' that will lead to the failure of more firms, said Alan Greenspan, former head of the US Federal Reserve. 'There's no question that this is in the process of outstripping anything I've seen, and it is still not resolved.'

More than a year since the seismic outbreak of disruption in international credit markets, the affair took a decisive new turn on Sunday when US

Despairing traders in the pit at the New York Mercantile Exchange in New York. Photograph: Seth Wenig/AP Photo.

treasury secretary Hank Paulson baulked at the provision of any government guarantee to Lehman to facilitate a rescue sale to Barclays Bank.

Paulson had already let it be known that he would not follow the federal rescue of wholesale mortgage giants Fannie Mae and Freddie Mac last week and assistance for the bailout of Bear Stearns with any public underwriting of Lehman's liabilities.

He held firm on the *ne plus ultra* for government intervention over a weekend in which Wall Street's most eminent bankers shuttled in and out of a hectic series of meetings at the New York Federal Reserve, where he held court. Three hours after Barclays pulled away from Lehman, Bank of America walked out of its own talks with the bank.

Lehman then put plans in motion for a bankruptcy petition, starting an ignominious winding up of a storied institution which survived railway

bankruptcies in the 1800s, the ravages of the Great Depression and two World Wars. Brought to heel by the subprime mortgage debacle it helped create, Lehman's bankruptcy is the world's largest. With some $613 billion in debt, Lehman has $80 billion in 'bad assets'.

There was more to the drama. Having opted against a deal with Lehman, Bank of America moved with great speed into the final stages of takeover talks with Merrill Lynch, a Wall Street luminary whose own business might have been at risk as a result of Lehman's collapse.

The transaction, hammered out in a 48-hour negotiation, values Merrill at $50 billion.

Meanwhile, it emerged that insurance giant AIG was working on a plan to raise capital as a result of huge losses it incurred from guaranteeing bad mortgage investments. AIG may need to raise as much as $20 billion in capital and sell $20 billion of assets to ease its financial crunch.

No surprise, then, that stock markets around the world had a hard time of it yesterday. Financial stocks took a drubbing in Dublin, where the Iseq index dropped more than 3 per cent, losing €1.2 billion of their value.

The decline was in keeping with a downturn already well entrenched, as such stocks have lost €42.29 billion since the market peaked in February 2007.

If those losses underline the vulnerability of Irish institutions to external shocks in markets in which their profits and bad debt levels are under pressure due to the property downturn, there is no sense that recent events will expedite a return to stability.

'I'd agree with Alan Greenspan's interpretation today that what we're going through is unprecedented and a one-in-100-year event. There's probably still more correction to go before the market reaches that tipping point that means the market is back to equilibrium,' said Mark Duffy, chief of Bank of Scotland (Ireland).

'I didn't think anybody could reliably guess when that tipping point is. It could be today or over the next few months; it's just too difficult to predict.'

Similarly, Merrion Capital chief John Conroy said it would be 'dangerous' to assume that the lowest point of the international crisis had now been reached.

'The fact that the authorities have demonstrated that they will allow a major bank to collapse will have to be digested by investors worldwide and naturally investors will seek out weaknesses in other big names,' he said.

'Given the interconnections in the global banking system, what's happening in the US cannot be divorced from the European banking system, in which case the lending environment is going to remain very constrained for a significant period and that is going to impact on economic performance in the world's major economies.

Stock markets will generally recover ahead of the economies, and indeed valuations in some markets are now looking attractive, but it's still too soon to call any sustainable upturn.'

Conroy acknowledged that Irish banks had 'considerable domestic issues to worry about, primarily on the property side'. But he pointed out, nevertheless, that leading Irish banks 'haven't had exposures to some of the major international issues like subprime losses'.

Inasmuch as a constant feature of the current crisis has been the tendency of the market to move its attention from company to company once their vulnerabilities spill into the open, there is every possibility of further volatility in the short term.

Paulson's decision to allow Lehman's collapse is important in that respect, as it is likely to hasten scrutiny of weaker banks, in the US system at least.

'Various banks, within a sector that is basically well capitalised overall, will be in difficulty,' said Italian central bank governor Mario Draghi this weekend, before Lehman's insolvency.

European banks seemed to be far better protected from the crisis than US or emerging market counterparts, he said. 'The conclusion is that there will be a series of consolidations in the world banking system. We've seen some already but we are a long way from seeing the end of this.'

Sobering thoughts indeed.

WEDNESDAY, 17 SEPTEMBER 2008

Bertie Convinced by One Thing – A Lot of People Had It In for Him

Miriam Lord

Hands in his pockets, looking heavy of heart, Bertie Ahern left the Mahon tribunal for the last time. He isn't taoiseach any more, so there was no need to put on his happy face for the cameras. But,

Former taoiseach Bertie Ahern leaving Dublin Castle after his last day at the Mahon tribunal. Photograph: David Sleator.

courteous as ever, he stopped for the microphones.

'Hiya folks, howya doin'?' It was hard to hear him as the competing roars from supporters and detractors grew louder in the background. He waited for the questions.

So Bertie, any final thoughts after another day repeating you never took a penny from anybody? 'And I didn't. I made that [clear] from start to finish and, you know, the reality is, I didn't and I had to be brought to the end, you know.'

A lot of people had it in for him – of that, he is convinced. Information was used against him in 'a selective' manner. Right to the end, Bertie insists he is a victim of individuals who were out to get him. Clearly, he believes they got what they wanted – but he won't name names.

'Start at the start and work it all out,' was all he would say. The former taoiseach couldn't disguise his bitterness at the way things have turned out for him. Bitterness is a most un-Bertie-like trait, but you could hear it in his voice and see it in his eyes.

He was years trying to defend himself 'on the one issue', he shrugged. The tribunal exacted a toll on his family and on his friends, he sighed. 'And it did politically. Of course it did.'

His voice trailed off. He got into his car. It wasn't as clean and polished as the one he used to arrive in and it had a scratch along the side. The reporters turned away quietly. The one sentence Bertie didn't say was hanging in the air, because we read it in his expression: 'I hope yis are happy now.'

Despite the evidence of earlier hearings, when Dublin Castle listened to his financial explanations with open-mouthed incredulity, the Bertie factor was still working its cloudy magic. At the finish, he had some of us doubting ourselves and feeling sorry for him.

One long-time tribunal observer struggled to remain strong after witnessing Bertie's downcast exit. 'You'd have to feel for him, but with the best will in the world, no sane person could believe his stories,' he murmured.

Bertie's final day in the witness box was fascinating. There came more memory lapses and more strange coincidences. Deathly Des O'Neill continued to grind his way through the near impermeable mass that is Ahern's Wall of Sound, unstoppable as a glacier. In his wake, he leaves behind mounting shards of circumstantial evidence.

The implacable lawyer exposed meetings with businesspeople followed by mysterious lodgements, followed by more meetings and further lodgements, turning up dates that corresponded with money and correspondence that contradicted evidence.

What the former leader brought to the table instead was his impeccable record of public service and his unswerving belief that Irish government ministers have never done anything as grubby as accept money in return for favours.

Never, ever, stressed Bertie to O'Neill's upturned eyebrows.

'That's my evidence,' said the witness. 'I never saw it linked up and other people have been in trouble over other things, but it has never been linked back.'

Bertie had news for sceptical Des: 'That is not the way democratic politics has worked in my long experience, and I have been in 10 Dáils, at cabinet tables for over 25 years.'

That was his evidence yesterday. Unfortunately for Bertie, there's his other evidence to digest. It suggests he got shedloads of money when minister for finance and cannot credibly explain its source.

Could it be that Eamon Dunphy was right when he told the tribunal how he was told by developer Owen O'Callaghan that the trouble with Bertie Ahern was that you give him money, but he does nothing in return? Hence, working by Bertie's compass, there is no link. He got money, but did nothing for it. Where's the problem if it didn't interfere with the proper execution of office?

So, it may be possible to believe that Bertie Ahern really believes he did nothing wrong, that he somehow believes he worked on the right side of an invisible moral line between private donations and public duty.

He has already thrilled the tribunal with his take on the subject of donations for political/ private use.

During his days of giving direct evidence, when he came out with truly risible excuses to explain how large amounts of money, much of it in foreign currency, came to rest in his many accounts, did Bertie honestly expect sensible people to take him seriously? Maybe he did, for he insists he adhered to the rules of good government.

Owen O'Callaghan was told a rival firm would not be getting tax designation. Good news for Owen. Yesterday, Bertie said that was because it was policy. (Whether or not he told Owen this we don't know.)

And sure if a few rich businesspeople thought they were on to a good thing because he gave them his ear – but nothing much else, it transpires – then nobody was hurt. Bertie did nothing wrong and he was in a financially strapped position at the time.

Sure wasn't everyone at it? It remains to be seen whether the tribunal judges adopt a similarly morally ambivalent approach when it comes to writing their report. In the meantime, Bertie will nurse his hurt and hope the public comes around to his way of thinking come the next presidential election.

Failure of PDs to be Radical Enough Sealed Party's Fate

Stephen Collins

The near-certain winding up of the Progressive Democrats next month has been inevitable since last year's general election disaster. Reduced to two Dáil seats, the party was no longer viable, as the leadership has now acknowledged. The harsh reality was cloaked for a while by the fact that Mary Harney continued to serve as a senior Minister but the speculation of recent weeks over Noel Grealish's departure plans presaged the end.

The party didn't help itself earlier this year by picking the worthy but totally inexperienced Senator Ciarán Cannon as leader instead of Fiona O'Malley, who had the advantage of five years in the Dáil, a bubbly, likeable personality with a relatively high public profile.

Still, it probably didn't matter who took over as leader. The party's death warrant was signed on the night of the election.

Looking back over 23 years, the remarkable thing is that the PDs survived for so long. Apart from its first general election breakthrough in 1987 it has always skated on the brink of electoral disaster. It only needed one run of bad luck to push it over the edge.

That bad luck struck with a vengeance almost immediately after Michael McDowell took over as leader from Harney in the autumn of 2006.

There had been a tussle between the two a few months earlier when McDowell claimed Harney had not honoured a commitment to step down. In the event she gave way and he took over for the run up to the general election.

Disaster struck immediately with the disclosure in *The Irish Times* of the Mahon tribunal investigation into Bertie Ahern's personal finances. The new PD leader at first supported Ahern, then challenged his initial account and finally backed him. From that point on the PDs were fighting for survival.

It can be argued that the party was on the slippery slope from the moment it agreed to go into a second government with Fianna Fáil in 2002, when they were not needed to make up the numbers.

That meant the party lost the leverage it had between 1997 and 2002. McDowell's challenge to Ahern on the payments issue was undermined by the fact that Ahern could have continued in office without his junior coalition partner.

When McDowell repeated the mistake of flip-flopping on the payments issue at the start of the general election campaign, the party's fate and his own was sealed. If he had withdrawn from government, as he threatened during the first weekend of the campaign, the PDs might have had a chance of salvaging something. As it was events took their course.

Finally, McDowell's decision to throw in the towel on the night of the election undermined any remote prospect the PDs might have had of recovery.

It was also a sad end to his own political career during which he had a number of significant achievements to his credit, whatever his legions of detractors might say.

Now that the party has come to an end, its influence on the course of Irish political, social and economic affairs can be assessed with some degree of objectivity.

On the economic front, it undoubtedly played a role in the transformation of Ireland from an economic basket case in the 1980s to one of the most prosperous countries in the world. The extent of that role is a subject for debate but things would hardly have turned out the same if the party had never existed. From the very first, the PDs set out with a liberal economic agenda and a heavy stress on tax cutting. This agenda was reviled by all

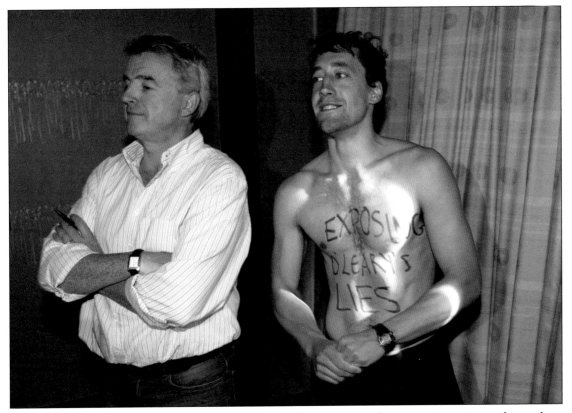

Ryanair chief executive Michael O'Leary maintains his usual composure at the company's 2008 annual general meeting in Dublin on being interrupted by an environmental protester from an organisation called Plane Mad. Photograph: Frank Miller.

of its opponents 20 years ago, yet in the intervening period most of it was implemented.

As well as implementing its policies in government, the PDs managed to shift the political centre of gravity.

It has often been remarked that Margaret Thatcher's greatest achievement in Britain was not that she changed the policies of the Conservative Party, it was that she changed the policies of the Labour Party.

In Ireland the policies of all the other mainstream parties have shifted decisively in the direction of the PDs.

The presence of the PDs in government allowed Fianna Fáil to agree to policies it would have been slow to implement on its own. To be

fair to Fianna Fáil, Fine Gael and Labour, all of those parties wrestled with the economic problems of the 1980s and came to accept the need for stringent control of public expenditure to get borrowing down.

What was unique to the PDs was that the party laid such emphasis on the need to cut taxes on work to stimulate economic growth, job creation and prosperity.

The PDs were in the right place at the right time, but it took some courage to propose and develop its agenda in the face of deep hostility from its political opponents, almost all of the media and the social partners.

In political terms, the main achievement of the PDs was, paradoxically, to make Fianna Fáil the

Leas-Cheann Comhairle of the Dáil Brendan Howlin with Selma Brandao (left) and Vanessa Coelho outside Leinster House in Dublin for a brief preview of Culture Night. Photograph: Bryan O'Brien.

semi-permanent party of government. By forcing Charles Haughey to abandon the Fianna Fáil core value of not participating in coalition governments in 1989, the PDs set Fianna Fáil on a path that has allowed it to enter government with anyone.

Once Fianna Fáil discovered the advantages of coalition they did a deal with Labour in 1992, went back to the PDs in 1997 and then on to the Greens. The corrosive effect of Fianna Fáil's near permanent grip on power for parliamentary democracy has become obvious in recent years, and there is no sign of it coming to an end.

It is ironic that the party, which was established to oppose the abuse of power by elements of Fianna Fáil, ended up by tightening that party's grip on power and patronage for almost 20 years.

As Fianna Fáil went from strength to strength the PDs struggled to find even a small niche for themselves on the political spectrum.

It should have been able to broaden its base and establish deeper roots in the community, particularly in urban Ireland, where its tax-cutting philosophy directly benefited a swathe of ordinary middle-class voters.

Instead, the party always lived on the edge and never even had one safe seat in Dublin. That was the problem well before the last election.

A year before the last election opinion polls showed that there was not a single safe PD seat in the country. The party had always lived on the boundary of success or extinction on a share of the vote that ranged between 3 and 5 per cent, and the writing was effectively on the wall before McDowell ever took over.

He coined the phrase that the PDs had to be radical or redundant. In the event, it was the failure to be radical enough during the 2002 to 2007 period, and particularly its failure to risk all by pulling out of government with an increasingly discredited taoiseach, that sealed the party's fate.

Few in the media or political world have been willing to give the PDs any credit for the economic and social changes of the past two decades. That media hostility, particularly to McDowell, also played a part in ensuring the party was never given the credit for its achievements but was instead subject to a constant diet of abuse.

One of Ireland's most distinguished economists, Prof. Dermot McAleese, commented some years ago on the general reluctance to acknowledge the role the PDs had played in promoting the economic changes of the past two decades.

The former member of the Central Bank board remarked that the emergence of the PDs in 1985 had a more positive influence on the economy than many were prepared to recognise.

He expressed the firm opinion that the low-tax, pro-business economy that developed in the 1990s was based in large part on PD policies.

'They proved that there was a constituency for this and they gave the intellectual power to it,' he said.

Now that that economy is facing a crisis in the autumn of 2008 it will be interesting to see which, if any, of the political parties has the courage and vision to challenge the current sacred cows and develop a workable vision of the way forward as the PDs did 23 years ago.

SUNDAY, 21 SEPTEMBER 2008

Tyrone Leave Kingdom Desolate Again

Seán Moran

Tyrone 1-15 Kerry 0-14

One of the few things accurately foreseen by the prevailing consensus was that yesterday's GAA All-Ireland football final would be a tight affair, in all likelihood still open up to the 70th minute.

That's how it turned out, but in an emphatic conclusion to a fascinating contest it was champions Kerry who, once more in the face of Ulster opposition, faltered in a delirious finish. Afloat on their trademark swirling energies, Tyrone brought home the Sam Maguire for the third time in a memorable decade that began with the county still to make its mark on the roll of honour.

Maybe the match swung on a sequence in the 66th minute when in a trademark move, Declan O'Sullivan surged on to the ball and created the space for a shot at goal. Trailing 0-14 to 1-12, Kerry would have moved two clear if he had scored. Instead Pascal McConnell, a late call-up to the Tyrone goal after John Devine's bereavement on Saturday, managed to block the ball away for a 45.

In the process of being replaced, Bryan Sheehan stayed on long enough to send the kick wide and puncture Kerry's confidence in a likely recovery. The reason the match only 'maybe' swung on this is that Tyrone could hardly be written off on the basis of a two-point deficit with five minutes left, but Kerry's opportunity to govern the momentum for the remainder of the match was lost.

The consequences of this were brought home in the space of a brutal minute when Tyrone stunningly found that extra gear and rattled off three points, from Enda McGinley, Kevin Hughes (finally, after three howling wides) and Colm Cavanagh, to kill Kerry's ambitions of three-in-a-row in the dying moments of the 2008 championship.

That's an indication of how close Kerry came but there was no doubting the merits of Tyrone's victory. Once again they imposed their game on Kerry and countered the champions' strongest points to the extent that the game was played on their terms.

Aside from the enforced switch in goal, manager Mickey Harte made two changes before the throw-in, replacing Ciarán Gourley with Ryan Mellon and sending Joe McMahon back to mark Tommy Walsh. Martin Penrose came in for Brian McGuigan.

Tyrone's Joseph McMahon moves in to challenge Kerry's Tommy Walsh in the 2008 GAA senior football championship final at Croke Park in Dublin. Photograph: Eric Luke.

For most people, Kerry were an improved team compared to 2005 because Kieran Donaghy had transformed their ball-winning capacity in the full-forward line. This season that improvement had been accelerated by the arrival of Walsh but Tyrone coped in textbook fashion by making a serviceable supply as difficult as possible.

Kerry didn't help themselves in this process by displaying so little variety in the building of attacks but McMahon, especially, his brother Justin and Conor Gormley did everything to disrupt possession of what did come through.

Ironically, if the full forwards disappointed the high expectations, the Kerry full backs improved considerably on recent matches.

On a downbeat note it's worth remarking the final marked a fitting end to what has been a disciplinary shambles of a season. Repeated fouling by

Tyrone went inadequately punished yesterday, as referee Maurice Deegan opted to save his cards for more vivid transgressions of which Kerry provided plenty.

But that's the way the game has developed and until indiscipline becomes an impediment to winning, things will hardly change.

Yet this was an undeniably enthralling match – during which the sides were level on 10 occasions – with a number of wonderful individual performances.

Leading the way for Tyrone was Seán Cavanagh with five points from play capping a masterful display. He started at full forward but, as has been the team's constant conundrum, when the supply dried up had to move out the field. He remained centrally involved in the team's effort and kicked a critical point to equalise just after

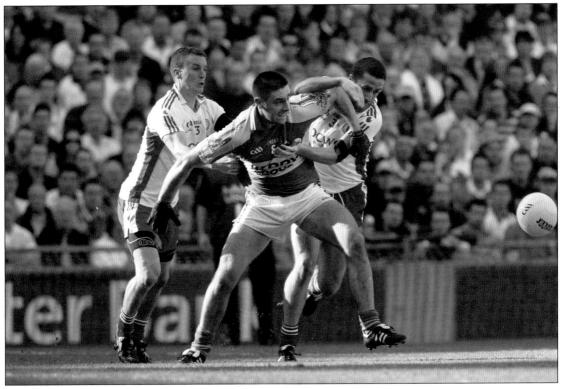

Tommy McGuigan (left) and Kerry's Stephen O'Neill during the 2008 All-Ireland senior football championship final at Croke Park, Dublin. Photograph: Dara Mac Dónaill.

Kerry had regained the lead in the 57th minute.

At centrefield, McGinley maintained his consistent excellence, moving tirelessly around the middle and kicking the point that pushed his team two ahead after Kerry had pressed hard for an equaliser for five minutes.

It was the ultimate superiority of Tyrone around the middle that decided the match. Darragh Ó Sé played exceptionally well in the first half, mocking apprehensions that he might struggle to win high ball against opposition spoiling.

In the 55th minute he kicked Kerry level for the first time since conceding a goal just after half-time – a fine finish after some virtuoso probing by Colm Cooper.

In the first half Declan O'Sullivan put in a terrific performance, thrusting forward and kicking two points and also covering back to assist the defence, at one stage bringing off a fabulous block on Cavanagh and recovering in time to win possession and launch a solo run back up the field.

But Kerry couldn't get sustained traction around the middle and appeared to lose significantly the breaking ball count. Davy Harte, Philip Jordan and Ryan McMenamin got forward as expected and if they didn't get on the scoreboard as much as previously, the ball-carrying kept Kerry under pressure.

Captain Brian Dooher also maintained his driven form of this season, covering oceans of ground and kicking one of the great points of the afternoon in the 24th minute, bouncing off three intended tackles before kicking over from the right wing to tie up the match at 0-6 each, seconds after McConnell had saved smartly from a great goal opportunity from Walsh.

Tommy McGuigan of Tyrone celebrates his goal against Kerry during the 2008 All-Ireland senior football championship final in Croke Park, Dublin. Photograph: Dara Mac Dónaill.

This maintained the incremental scoring pattern of the first half, which saw Kerry pull ahead, 0-8 to 0-7, through a Cooper free before going in at half-time. Tyrone must nonetheless have been happy with the way in which their opponents were struggling to mobilise the threat of Donaghy and Walsh.

The second half had only started when Tommy McGuigan followed the ball into the net after replacement Kevin Hughes had been sent in by Stephen O'Neill – introduced to great excitement in the 25th minute but unsurprisingly after a year out of the inter-county game, he struggled to make an impact – but seen his shot blocked.

Kerry spent most of the second half chasing down the deficit of that goal but three times Tyrone replied with points of their own within a minute of conceding a score. Darren O'Sullivan came on and made an impact for Kerry, his pace opening up avenues to goal, but team captain Paul Galvin, back after suspension to a hair-raisingly thunderous reception, was unable to impact on the match.

As the deposed champions ponder this latest crushing disappointment at the hands of Tyrone they can at least reflect on still having won more All-Irelands this decade than anyone else.

Dejection after stacking up four All-Irelands in eight years is a crisis of self-esteem 31 other counties can only dream of addressing.

Index